I Have Arrived, I Am Home

Happy Mothers' Day! (note)

May 2005

love, Lynne

Other Books by Thich Nhat Hanh

Anger: Wisdom for Cooling the Flames

Be Free Where You Are

Be Still and Know: Reflections from Living Buddha, Living Christ

Being Peace

The Blooming of a Lotus: Guided Meditation Exercises for Healing and Transformation

Breathe! You Are Alive: Sutra on the Full Awareness of Breathing

Call Me by My True Names: The Collected Poems of Thich Nhat Hanh

Cultivating the Mind of Love: The Practice of Looking Deeply in the Mahayana Buddhist Tradition

The Diamond That Cuts through Illusion: Commentaries on the Prajñaparamita Diamond Sutra

Each Breath a Smile

For a Future to Be Possible: Commentaries on the Five Mindfulness Trainings

Fragrant Palm Leaves: Journals 1962–1966

The Heart of the Buddha's Teaching: Transforming Suffering into Peace, Joy, and Liberation

The Four Noble Truths, the Noble Eightfold Path, and Other Basic Buddhist Teachings

The Heart of Understanding: Commentaries on the Prajñaparamita Heart Sutra

Hermitage among the Clouds: A Historical Novel of Fourteenth Century Vietnam

Interbeing: Fourteen Guidelines for Engaged Buddhism

A Joyful Path: Community, Transformation, and Peace

Living Buddha, Living Christ

The Long Road Turns to Joy: A Guide to Walking Meditation

Love in Action: Writings on Nonviolent Social Change

Master Tang Hoi

The Miracle of Mindfulness: A Manual on Meditation

My Master's Robe

No Death, No Fear

Old Path White Clouds: Walking in the Footsteps of the Buddha

Our Appointment with Life: Discourse on Living Happily in the Present Moment

The Path of Emancipation

Peace Is Every Step: The Path of Mindfulness in Everyday Life

A Pebble for Your Pocket

Plum Village Chanting and Recitation Book

Present Moment Wonderful Moment: Mindfulness Verses for Daily Living

The Raft is Not the Shore (with Daniel Berrigan)

A Rose for Your Pocket

Stepping into Freedom: An Introduction to Buddhist Monastic Training

The Stone Boy and Other Stories

The Sun My Heart: From Mindfulness to Insight Contemplation

Sutra on the Eight Realizations of the Great Beings

A Taste of Earth and Other Legends of Vietnam

Teachings on Love

Thundering Silence: Sutra on Knowing the Better Way to Catch a Snake

Touching Peace: Practicing the Art of Mindful Living

Transformation and Healing: Sutra on the Four Establishments of Mindfulness

Transformation at the Base: Fifty Verses on the Nature of Consciousness

Under the Rose Apple Tree

Zen Keys: A Guide to Zen Practice

I Have Arrived, I Am Home

Celebrating Twenty Years of Plum Village Life

by Thich Nhat Hanh
and the Global Plum Village Family

Parallax Press
Berkeley, California

Parallax Press ✦ P.O. Box 7355 ✦ Berkeley, California 94707 ✦ www.parallax.org
Parallax Press is the publishing division of Unified Buddhist Church, Inc.

Printed in the United States of America.
Cover and text design by Gopa & Ted2
Cover painting by Thi Hop Nguyen

Photographs courtesy of:
Sister Chau Nghiem; Eveline Beumkes; Marjolijn Van Leuwen; Plum Village Archive; Deer Park Archive; Parallax Press Archive; Mindfulness Bell Archive; Gaetano Maida; Wietske; Patrick Thornton; Karen Hagen Liste; Simon Chaput; Shantum Seth; Sister Tue Nghiem; Minna Roisko; Leonie W. Hansen, Inklings Photography; Sister Jina; Robert Harrison; Theodore Sexauer; Gert Ulrich Rump; Svein Myreng; Sarah Ciborski; Al Lingo; Jessica Tampas; Chan Khiem Cung; Lorena Monda; Cat Tuong; Eliane Chappuis; Hung Nguyen; Lorrie Harrison; Anneke Brinkerink; Kare Landfald; Jack Lawlor; Karl Schmied; Chris Dawkins; Sister Tin Nghiem; Kate Atchley; Dat Nguyen; Christopher Ayers; Sandra Alderden; Kristen Hachenberg; Sister Thieu Nghiem; Sister Khe Nghiem; Sister Thuan Khanh; Brother Phap Hoi

We wish to thank and acknowledge all who offered us their photos. We have given credit when we knew the photographer's name and apologize to friends whose photos came to us without attribution.

Calligraphy by Thich Nhat Hanh

Library of Congress Cataloging-in-Publication Data

I have arrived, I am home: celebrating twenty years of Plum Village life
/ by Thich Nhat Hanh.
p. cm.
ISBN 1-888375-25-6 (hard cover : alk. paper)
1. Spiritual life—Buddhism. 2. Village des pruniers (Buddhist Community)—History. 3. Nhât Hanh, Thich.
BQ5660 .I2 2003
294.3'927'094472—dc21
2002153422

1 2 3 4 5 6 7 8 9 10 / 10 09 08 07 06 05 04 03

Contents

Preface

Dear ancestors, dear Father, dear Mother, dear Buddha, dear Patriarchs, dear Teacher, dear Friends, I have arrived. I am home. While I am still making steps, I have already arrived, I am already home. I have stopped wandering. This is the teaching and the practice of Plum Village, the Dharma Seal of Plum Village.[1]

I have arrived in the Pure Land, a real home where I can get in touch with both my ancestors and my descendants. I can touch the paradise of my childhood and all the wonders of life. I am no longer concerned with being and nonbeing, coming and going, being born or dying. In my true home I have no fear, no anxiety. I have peace and liberation. My true home is in the here and the now. I have found true happiness.

During so many lifetimes I have been a wanderer, searching for peace and happiness. On my path of seeking I have fallen into the abyss of mistakes, bitterness, and despair. There were so many times that I thought I would die before I would find what I was seeking. Dear Buddha, you have helped me, you have saved me. You have shown me that what I was looking for is within myself and can be found in the present moment.

The project of building is the project of ten thousand lifetimes.
But looking deeply, we see it has already been realized.
The wonderful wheel of transformation is always leading us ahead.
Take my hand and you will see that we have been present together for a long time in this wonderful existence.

Our wonderful existence includes both happiness and suffering. How can happiness be possible without suffering? When we are able to see that suffering is the element that can be used to make happiness, we suddenly stop suffering. With this understanding, my happiness becomes immense and is able to embrace all the suffering. I no longer need to search or run after anything. I have stopped.

I am no longer a wanderer because I have a path and I don't have to worry anymore. My path is the path of stopping, the path of enjoying the present moment. It is a path where every step brings me back to my true home. It is a path that leads nowhere. I am on my way home. I arrive at every step. I am taking my steps with leisure because I don't have to hurry. That is my life; that is my practice.

The wind is still circulating. Don't you know that my child?
While the faraway rain is approaching the nearby cloud,
drops of sunshine from above are falling down,
helping Earth to see the blue sky.

I am still moving around with ease, freely,
not bound by the idea of being and nonbeing.
Therefore my child, on your way home,
make peaceful and leisurely steps,
because there is only one moon,
there is no waxing, there is no waning.

The Dharma Seal of Plum Village is "I have arrived, I am home." It means happiness is possible. Freedom is possible. Right now. Right here.

— Thich Nhat Hanh

Acknowledgments

We want to thank all who, coming together across thousands of miles, offered their stories, their guidance, their assistance, and their support for the book you hold in your hands. We appreciate everyone who shared poems, stories, Dharma talks, songs, drawings, and pictures. Your generosity, courage, humor, and wisdom helped make this book a true celebration. Though every offering we received is precious and meaningful, we could not include all of them here. To enjoy the contributions that are not in this book, please visit the Website: <www.ihavearrived.org> and look for them in future issues of the *Mindfulness Bell.*[2]

Editing as a team, we learned to trust the process of letting go and to allow the collective insight to manifest. Many times we delighted in the wisdom of the Sangha's eyes, ears, heart, and mind. We also learned to lean on each other for support. When one of us felt stuck or overwhelmed, another member of the team would be there with just the right words of insight or encouragement. We offer a deep bow of gratitude to our teacher, Thây (Thich Nhat Hanh), who offered us this opportunity, and to the Buddha's teachings that help us learn to live and work in harmony and openness.

With deep gratitude, we thank all those who helped us in the beginning stages to brainstorm and look deeply into what we wanted this book to be, especially Shantum Seth and Lorrie Harrison. We thank all our contributors. We thank everyone who helped to send out requests for submissions and those who translated from Vietnamese, German, and French into English. We thank those who transcribed interviews and Dharma talks, those who typed handwritten submissions, those who read through previous issues of the *Mindfulness Bell,* and those who helped gather biographies of contributors. We also thank the many bodhisattvas who helped with editing and read through the manuscript in the final stages, especially Carl Stahmer and Matt Bortolin. We thank Sister Thuong Nghiem who contributed much-needed insight and support throughout the project. Without all of you this book would not be possible. Let us enjoy it together!

From the Editors: Sister Chau Nghiem, Brother Phap Ngo,
Barbara Casey, and Lorena Monda
September 2002

Introduction

This book is a delicious buffet of stories, teachings, poems, and images that offers a taste of the harmonious life possible through practicing mindfully as a Sangha. Each of the contributors has been part of the Plum Village family in some way during the past twenty years, touching the practice of understanding and love in their own lives.

There are those who have been present since the beginning of Plum Village, those who have come and gone, and those who are newcomers. Coming from all over the Earth, speaking many different languages, they offer personal experiences of nourishing joy and transforming suffering.

In preparing this meal we received files and files of ingredients, each with its own distinct flavor and aroma. Some arrived ready to serve, others needed a little chopping and cooking. Many good dishes had to be left out because of space considerations. When editing has been necessary, we have tried our best to look deeply to find the heart of each delicious morsel and retain the flavor intended by the contributor.

Part One, *Taking Root,* begins with Thich Nhat Hanh's personal journey founding and guiding the Plum Village community and includes stories of Plum Village in the early days and reflections on the student-teacher relationship. Part Two, *Blossoming of Community,* includes the personal story of Sister Chân Không, Thich Nhat Hanh's student and companion for over thirty years, and sharings of family practice and community life. Sister Annabel Laity, one of Thây's first monastic students, tells how she came to the practice in Part Three, *Stories of Transformation.* Other practitioners relate how they practice to heal self-criticism, grief, and the wounds of war. Part Four, *Seeds of the Future,* includes inspiration from Sangha members in Maple Forest Monastery and Green Mountain Dharma Center in Vermont, and Deer Park Monastery in California. To close, Thây shares his vision of the future of Plum Village.

Finally, we offer this book with gratitude in our hearts, honored to celebrate our precious teacher and Sangha family. We hope you will be nourished and inspired by this feast — a celebration of Plum Village and the deep and life-transforming sustenance available through daily practice. Please enjoy and share with friends — there is enough for everyone!

— The Editors

taking root

Reflections on Twenty Years of Plum Village Life

A Dharma Talk by Thich Nhat Hanh

Dear Sangha,

Today is the thirteenth of December, 2001. We are in the Dharma Nectar Hall, at the Lower Hamlet, during the Winter Retreat. The committee working on the book for the twentieth anniversary of Plum Village has asked me to talk about the history of Plum Village. There are so many stories that I don't know where to start!

The Six Umbrella Pines

We held our very first Summer Retreat in the Sweet Potato Hermitage in the north of France. However, it was such a small center that we could not receive many students. So we came to the south to look for land and establish a practice center that could hold more people.

When we first saw the Upper Hamlet, I liked it immediately because it was beautiful. I saw the path that we could use for our walking meditation, and I fell in love with it at first sight. However, Mr. Dezon, the landowner, did not want to sell the property. He loved that piece of land very much since he had been a farmer there for a long time.

We continued looking for land, and a few days later, on September 28, 1982, we found the Lower Hamlet and purchased it. But we still wanted the Upper Hamlet, so we continued to pay attention to what was going on up there. That year, there was a hailstorm that destroyed all the vineyards on Mr. Dezon's property. He got angry and put the land on the market for a very high price, not really intending to sell it. In spite of the increased price, we bought it because we liked the land so much.

Anh Thieu came from Vietnam by boat with his wife and two children. They were the first people to help us start Plum Village. From the winter of 1982 to the summer of 1983, we had to work a lot. In early 1983, we began to plant some trees in the Upper Hamlet. The first trees were six umbrella pine trees. The land in the Upper Hamlet was full of rocks, so we needed the help of a local farmer and his machine to dig holes for the trees. We put a little cow manure in

Above: The walking meditation path in Upper Hamlet

the bottom of each hole. It was raining that day, and everybody was soaked. Afterwards, I got sick and stayed in bed for three weeks. Everybody was worried. Fortunately, after a while, I could get up and eat some rice soup.

In those days, we called our new home Persimmon Village, the name of a practice center that the School of Youth for Social Service and the Order of Interbeing had planned on building in Vietnam.[1] In the 1950s, we had the Fragrant Palm Leaves center in the highlands of Vietnam. However, the School of Youth for Social Service wanted to have a center closer to the city. When I wrote *The Miracle of Mindfulness,* I mentioned the idea of founding a practice center called Persimmon Village. Eight years later, our vision came true. We thought of planting persimmons, but we realized it was not practical, so we planted plum trees instead. We were naive, thinking that, if we planted many plum trees, we could make enough income to support ourselves. We were not horticulturists, so we did not do very well. We have enjoyed more plum blossoms than plums. The name Plum Village is beautiful, so we changed from Persimmon Village to Plum Village.

Many of those first plum trees were bought with the pocket money given to us by children who came to Plum Village. The children were told that in seven years the plum trees would bear fruit, which would then be dried and sold. That money would be used to help hungry children in Vietnam and other poor countries. Many children saved their pocket money in order to buy plum trees. Sometimes the children would combine their money and the tree we planted with their money would have the names of the child sponsors. It cost thirty-five French francs to plant a baby plum tree. We planted 1,250 trees because that was the number of the original monastic Sangha at the Buddha's time.

First Summer Opening in Plum Village

In 1983, we held our first Summer Opening with 117 practitioners. We had not yet developed the practice of Touching the Earth[2] or the daily practice with gathas (meditation poems). However, we already had sitting meditation, walking meditation, Tea Meditation, and consultations. There were no monks and nuns yet, so I led all the practices from the beginning to the end, from A to Z. I had to walk around and correct people's sitting posture, straightening each person's back and neck. During our first Summer Retreat, there were a few Westerners among the many Vietnamese people.

In the second Summer Opening, there were 232 people. In the third, 305, the seventh, 483, and in the ninth, there were 1,030. In 1996, 1,200 people came for the Summer Retreat, and in 1998, there were 1,450 practitioners. In the year 2000, the number increased to 1,800. Of course, not all 1,800 came at the same time. Some came for one, two, or three weeks, and some came for the entire four weeks of the retreat. There were also those who liked it so much, that after four weeks, they asked to stay on longer. People also came throughout the year to practice with us. In the first few years, Western practitioners stayed in the Upper Hamlet while Vietnamese and Asian practitioners stayed in the Lower Hamlet so they could enjoy traditional dishes of their homeland.

The Atlantic cedars, which you see in the Upper Hamlet, were planted during the first year. They were just four feet tall and took a long time to grow, but the more they grew, the more beautiful they became. They will be very beautiful in three hundred years. There are two different varieties of Atlantic cedars; one is a smoky gray color and the other is a silvery-blue. When we do walking meditation in the Upper Hamlet, we start at the linden tree. As we pass the Transformation Meditation Hall, we see the Atlantic cedars on the right. They are already so beautiful. I often look at a tree and see it as a monk or a nun who is growing strong in Plum Village. I stop to offer praise, "This young novice is doing quite well!" because that cedar has grown healthily and beautifully. Twenty years have passed, and they are now grown — no longer four-foot high baby cedar trees. In Plum Village, many other things have grown up as well. Not only the monks and nuns and lay practitioners have grown up, but also our methods of practice, our experiences, and the lessons from our own practices have matured like the cedars.

The Signless Nature of Plum Village

In 1983, standing on the hill, I could already envision the plum trees in flower, whitening the whole land. That was the sight in the ultimate dimension. Within four years, when the spring arrived, the plum trees really did blossom so beautifully.

Many are surprised when they come and see that Plum Village is not what they imagined. For example, we had forewarned a delegation from the Buddhist Association of China before their arrival to Plum Village that we had only trees and cow barns converted into meditation halls and living quarters. We told them this many times, but when they arrived, they were still surprised. They had not expected Plum Village to be so poor, simple, and rustic. Each one of us has a different understanding of Plum Village.

Brother Phap Can grew up and studied in Germany and came to Plum Village to be ordained. Last year, he went back to Germany with a delegation from Plum Village, and he discovered a new Germany. When he had lived in Germany, he had never been in touch with the Plum Village Sangha there. But returning, he encountered a large number of Vietnamese and German people following the

ree thou-
ere walk-
n people
any. Plum
the seven
th the eye
ey exist in

necessarily

Otherwise, ... Plum Village, we only have a superficial and vague notion about Plum Village. If we look deeply, we see that Plum Village is also unborn and undying.

A few years ago, we went to visit the Jeta Grove in India, one of the places where the Buddha lived. We saw that the Jeta Grove Monastery was no longer there. Japanese archeologists came to excavate the area, and discovered remnants of many large monasteries adjacent to one another, buried under the Earth. They could identify the places the monks slept, the Buddha hall, the teaching hall, and so on. Yet, we know that the Jeta Grove has never died, because when we go to other countries like Japan, China, Korea, and Tibet we see the Jeta Grove is still there in its new forms. Thus, the true nature of the Jeta Grove is that of no-birth and no-death. Plum Village is the same. For example, if tomorrow Plum Village is closed down, and people build large shopping malls in the Lower Hamlet and the Upper Hamlet, Plum Village will still exist, in its new manifestations everywhere, especially in our hearts. When we come to Plum Village, we must look deeply to see its nature of no-birth and no-death; we must see the reality of Plum Village beyond all forms.

Writing *Old Path White Clouds*

During the Summer Opening in the first years, I stayed in the room above the bookshop in Upper Hamlet. We had very few rooms then, and I had to share the room with four or five children. They stayed in the room with me and at night they sprawled out on the floor.

Thich Nhat Hanh, or "Thây" (meaning "teacher" in Vietnamese), and a young practitioner enjoy each other's company in Plum Village

I thought that children needed to sing; that chanting alone was not enough. I intended to write the song, *"I take refuge in the Buddha, the one who shows me the way in this life . . ."* for the children. One afternoon we did sitting meditation in the Bamboo Hall. The walls are made of stone. Facing a big block of stone, the tune for the song came to me. *"I take refuge in the Buddha, the one who shows me the way in this life,* Namo Buddhaya*."* I thought to myself, "I am here to do sitting meditation and not to make up songs. Let's continue it after the sitting meditation." However, after a few minutes, the music returned to me. I thought, "If it's going to be like this, I might as well compose the song now." So I continued writing that song and, after the meditation, I recorded it in order not to forget it.

At that time I was also writing the book *Old Path White Clouds.* We did not have central heating yet, only a wood stove in the little room above the bookshop, and the weather was very cold. I wrote with my right hand, and I put my left hand out over the stove. I was very happy writing. From time to time, I would stand up and make myself a cup of tea. Every day, the few hours I spent writing was like sitting with the Buddha for a cup of tea. I knew that the readers would have much happiness while reading the book because I had so much happiness while writing it.

Writing *Old Path White Clouds* was not hard work; rather, it was an immense joy. It was also a time of discovery. Some sections were more difficult to write than others. One difficult section was when the Buddha first gave teachings to the three Kashyapa brothers and received them as disciples. There are documents that say the Buddha had to use miracles to do it, but I wanted to show that he did it with his compassion and understanding. The Buddha has a great capacity of understanding and compassion, so why would he have to use miraculous powers? I had a strong faith that I would be able to write the chapter in that light. That was the most difficult chapter for me, but I eventually succeeded. The second most difficult chapter was when the Buddha went back to visit his family after becoming enlightened. He was still the son of his parents and a brother to his siblings. I wished to write in a way that would retain his human qualities. The way he took the hand of his father upon their meeting, the way he related with his younger sister, with Yasodhara and Rahula, was very natural. I could only write in that way because I felt the ancestral teachers supporting me. In reading *Old Path White Clouds,* we find that Buddha is a human being and not a god. That is precisely the aim, to help readers rediscover the Buddha as a human being. I tried to take away the mystic halos people ascribe to the Buddha. Not being able to see the Buddha as a human being makes it difficult for us to approach the Buddha.

The First Blossoms of Awakening

I became a monk in Vietnam. I grew up in Vietnam. I learned and practiced Buddhism in Vietnam. Before coming to the West, I taught several generations of Buddhist students in Vietnam. But I can say that I realized the path in the West. In 1962, at Princeton University, where I was invited to teach, I began to have many deep insights, flowers and fruits of the practice. If you have read my journal, *Fragrant Palm Leaves,* you will see that, for me, going to Princeton was like going into a monastery. It was far from the pressing demands of the current situation in Vietnam. I had much time to do walking meditation, assisting the maturation of insights that had not yet ripened.

I wrote *A Rose for Your Pocket* in the summer of 1962 at Princeton. It is a simple little book, but it is, in fact, the fruit of my awakening. In it, the practice of "dwelling happily in the present moment" is first described. We need to live in a way that does not allow the wonderful things in life to slip through our fingers. We need to live deeply, present for each moment. This is what is contained in *A Rose for Your Pocket.* It can be considered the first blossom of my awakening. Since then, that insight has continued on its path of deepening.

The shortest and most profound Dharma talk I can give is, "I have arrived. I am home." Only six words, "I have arrived. I am home," can be considered the Dharma Seal of Plum Village. Any Dharma talk, any teaching that goes against the spirit of "I have arrived, I am home" is not truly a teaching or method of practice of Plum Village. This Dharma Seal was first expressed in *A Rose for Your Pocket.*

In 1974, while I was working for peace in Paris, I wrote *The Miracle of Mindfulness.* I wrote it out of love for my monastic and lay students, young social workers working in Vietnam in the dangerous circumstances of wartime. After it was written, I sent it to Vietnam to be published, and it was translated into English. This book teaches us how to dwell in the present moment and to live mindfully with awareness of what is happening within us and around us. Between writing *A Rose for Your Pocket* in 1962 and *The Miracle of Mindfulness* in 1974, there were twelve years during which I wrote and published many titles. In those twelve years, you can recognize the progressive change in my way of looking at things. That was the process of the blooming of a lotus.

In my life of practice, I have had the opportunity to bring Buddhism back to the original teachings of the Buddha. Before this, I had the insight about dwelling happily in the present moment. Once back in the stream of the original teachings, that insight was experienced fully and with more clarity.

The Miracle of Mindfulness was published by Beacon Press, and now, more than two decades later, it continues to sell very well. *The Miracle of Mindfulness* is a meditation guide to use if you want to share the Plum Village style of practice with people. It has been translated into at least thirty languages.

Mindfulness is the basic meditation practice in Plum Village. Mindfulness means dwelling in the present moment to become aware of the positive and negative elements that are there. We learn to nourish the positive and to transform the negative. Twenty years of Plum Village life has helped me to learn so much and has helped the Sangha of Plum Village to grow up so much.

Sangha Building in the West

In May 1966, when I left Vietnam, I did not think I would be gone long. But I was stuck over here. I felt like a cell precariously separated from its body, like a bee separated from its hive. If a bee is separated from its hive, it knows that it cannot survive. A cell that is separated from its body will dry up and die. But I did not die because I had come to the West not as an individual but with the support of a Sangha and for the sake of the Sangha's visions. I came to call for peace. Our work in Vietnam at that time had strong momentum in the areas of cultural development, education, and social development. We had established the Van Hanh University, a university for higher Buddhist studies, the School of Youth for Social Service, the La Boi Printing Press, and the weekly newspaper *Hai Trieu Am (The Sound of the Rising Tide).* We also had a campaign calling for peace within Vietnam. I came to the West with all these things in my heart, so I was not in danger of drying up. If I had come as an individual, looking for a position, for a bit of fame, then I surely would have dried up. The life-and-death issue was Sangha. That is why I began building a Sangha with the people who were helping me to call for peace. The people who came and helped me were pastors, priests, professors, schoolchildren, and university students. I met with them, befriended them, and invited them to join the path of service for peace.

From 1968 until 1975, I established and led a delegation in Paris of the Vietnamese Buddhists for Peace. Many young people volunteered to help us. They would work, and at lunch-time we offered them a simple meal. After dinner, they stayed on to practice sitting meditation. We shared how to practice walking meditation, Deep Relaxation, and singing. When we were working for the Delegation of the Unified Buddhist Church of Vietnam in Paris, we organized sitting meditation sessions for Western practitioners in Paris once a week at the Quaker Center on Vaugirard Boulevard. By offering the practice to the young people who came to help, many seeds were sown. This may be one reason why many young people came when we organized the first Summer Opening in Plum Village.

When I was in touch with individuals and communities doing peace and social work, I saw they had difficulties. After a period of time, they became divided; they grew tired and abandoned the cause. To prevent this, when meeting with any organization or individual, I shared my practice. Before we had the Sangha gathered together in one place, we already had the Sangha as individual elements in many places.

Pastor Kloppenburg, a Lutheran pastor from Bremen, Germany, was someone who loved me very much. He organized occasions for me to give talks in Germany calling for peace and helped me translate and publish *Vietnam: Lotus in a Sea of Fire* in German. He also raised money for me to send to Vietnam so the School of Youth for Social Service could continue its work. He helped me organize the peace talks in Paris. In Holland, Minister Hannes de Graff, of the Dutch Reformed Church, supported me immensely. In my journeys to call for peace in Vietnam, I made many friends in the religious circle, in the human rights circle, and among the younger generation.

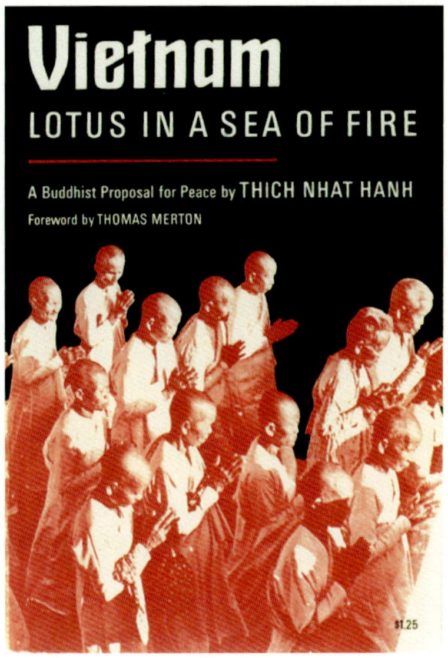

Published in 1967 by Hill and Wang publishers, New York City.

Living Simply and Happily

When we first established the Vietnamese Buddhist Peace Delegation in Paris, we faced many difficulties, like getting residential permits and finding enough food to eat and clothing to wear. Our headquarters was small but housed many people. There were nights when Sister Chân Không, who had been a professor at a university in Saigon, had to ask to sleep overnight at a restaurant because we ran out of space. Instead of buying regular rice at a supermarket, we bought the cheaper broken rice, usually sold as bird feed, from the pet store. One day the man who was selling the broken rice asked us, "Why do you come and buy so much rice? You must have a lot of birds in your house." We said, "Yes, many, nine in all, and each one is very big!" We showed with our hands how big those birds were. But our life was full of happiness. I found a place to teach, and I received one thousand French francs as salary every month. Other people in the delegation also had to find work. Sister Chân Không used to teach mathematics and tutor young students to add to our income.

I took a course on printing as a trade. I am still a good printer and can bind books quite well. We had a printing machine and produced books for refugees to help them suffer less and to help them learn a foreign language so that they could settle in other countries. I always printed and bound books in mindfulness, breathing and smiling as I printed. I never let the machine run at full speed, always slowly and always a smile every time I changed pages. I have printed several dozen books and I have bound thousands of books.

I have never wanted to build a luxurious, beautiful monastery here. When I am able to sell my books, that money has been used to bring relief to the hungry and to victims of the floods in Vietnam. There are still many people in our Sangha who sleep in sleeping bags. Sister Chân Không still sleeps in a sleeping bag. In Plum Village, I used to sleep on a very thin mattress on a plank of wood on top of four bricks. That did not prevent me from being happy.

In all the years of exile from Vietnam, I have never felt cut off from my Sangha in Vietnam. Every year, I compose and send manuscripts to Vietnam, and our friends in Vietnam always find ways to publish our books there. When they were banned, the books were

Harvest time at the Sweet Potato community in Fontvannes

hand copied, published underground, or published under different pen names.

From being like a cell separated from my Sangha body in Vietnam, I was able to practice cloning; and, not only did I not die, from a cell I have become a body. That body has become the Sangha body we see today. If, wherever we go, we go with our heart full of our Sangha, then we will not dry up and die. If you come to Plum Village, you have to take home with you no less than Plum Village in its entirety. Bringing Plum Village home, you will be able to survive longer. The teaching and practice of "I have arrived, I am home" always complements the teaching of "going as a river and not as a drop of water." If you are a drop of water, then you will evaporate halfway; but if you go as a river, you will surely reach the ocean. I have never gone as a drop of water. I have always gone as a river.

Vietnamese people on boats hired by Thây and Sister Chân Không in Thailand

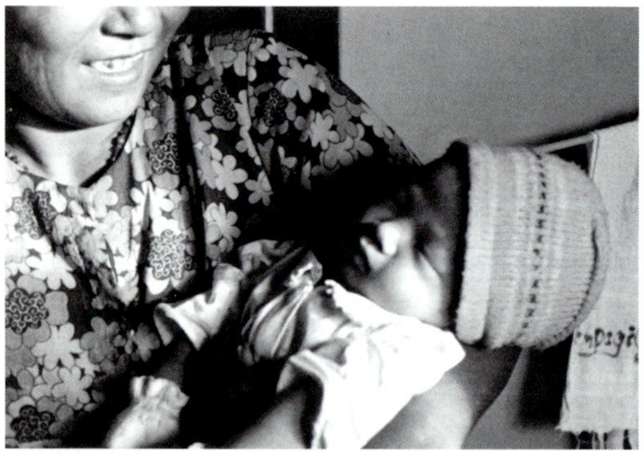

Responding to Suffering

Working in Paris, the Vietnamese Buddhist Delegation was able to sponsor more than nine thousand children who were orphaned because of the Vietnam War. We didn't support the building of orphanages, but we tried to find relatives of the orphans to take care of them. At that time, I was very busy, but every day I spent time translating twenty files on the orphans. The files were sent to us by social workers in Vietnam. There was a photograph of each orphan, the name of the father and the mother, and information about how the father and mother died. We had to translate these files into English, Dutch, French, and German to find sponsors for each child. The sponsor would donate twenty-five francs for each child. I used to hold up the file with the photograph of the child. Looking at the face of the child, I would smile and breathe. The energy of compassion would come up in me, and my heart was full of love. Then I would be able to translate easily. The translation was very poignant because there was a lot of love and compassion flowing out of my pen. There was a Danish lady living in Holland who was so inspired to help us with the program for orphans that she took a course to learn Vietnamese. Her Vietnamese became good enough to help translate the files.

In 1975, when the Americans left Vietnam and the North took over the whole of Vietnam, our Sangha in Paris retreated to a hermitage in the countryside outside of Paris, Sweet Potato Hermitage, where we had gone every weekend to rest and renew ourselves. At Sweet Potato Hermitage, I wrote *The Moon Bamboo*, *The Sun My Heart,* and the second and the third volumes of *The History of Vietnamese Buddhism*. Sweet Potato Hermitage is still there, near the forest of Othe. We should organize a pilgrimage there one day as a fun outing. It is very beautiful, and the climate is colder than Plum Village.

During this time at Sweet Potato Hermitage, from 1975 until 1982, Sister Chân Không and a number of others in the Sangha organized relief work for the refugees, the boat people, escaping Vietnam at that time. We rented three boats, *The Leopold, The Roland,* and *The Saigon 200.* Our aim was to pick refugees up on the ocean and secretly take them to countries like Australia.

Once, we rescued five hundred and fifty people on our boat, but our underground work was exposed. Both Sister Chân Không and I were driven out of Thailand and our secret headquarters there. Our work was exposed by journalists scouting for news. If this had not happened, the refugees would have been taken to Australia. But instead, we had to turn them over to UNESCO of the United Nations, and those boat people had to stay in refugee camps for three, four, or five years before their cases were finally reviewed and processed for immigration. So unfortunate!

Before Sister Chân Không left Vietnam to come help me, she worked in high spirits with the School of Youth for Social Service. She has been with me from the beginning of 1968 until now, supporting all the work for peace. Since

1968, she has worked constantly, never once having the idea of giving up. Of course, I have had many other friends and many other disciples, and some have given up because there are many dangers, difficulties, and obstacles on the path of calling for peace, human rights, and building up Sanghas. Others have abandoned the cause because of a variety of difficulties. But Sister Chân Không always accompanied me with great dedication.

Creating a Teacher-Disciple Relationship

Early on I trained several generations of monks and nuns in Vietnam. I looked after them with all my heart, and I thought taking care of them was enough, that I didn't need disciples of my own. When I came to the West, I still had that idea. Then, one day, I saw clearly that if I didn't have a direct teacher-disciple relationship, the practice of the disciple would not deepen. When I taught students in meditation centers in North America and in Europe there was a link, a relationship between teacher and disciple. But after I left, the relationship weakened, and students never really matured in the practices I offered. Because of the lack of the teacher-disciple connection, the students did not practice continually and ceaselessly. I saw that the relationship between teacher and disciple is very important, not only for the disciple but for the teacher as well. After that, I decided I would have monastic and lay disciples. I have learned a lot having disciples living and practicing with me. I have grown up a lot in my way of teaching and caring for my disciples. In the beginning, I did not have as much courage or patience as I do now. Traveling and offering teachings have also helped me grow a lot.

The relationship with my students has helped me see ways of teaching that can most likely ensure success. It brought together the teachings, the practice of Mindfulness Trainings, and fine manners, so they are not separated from each other. We have been able to discover wonderful Dharma doors, or practice methods, which many people can use. For instance, the idea of the Sangha body, using the Sangha eyes, Shining Light, Touching the Earth, and the Second Body system are the fruits and flowers of our practice here in Plum Village.[3] They are not only used by monks and nuns, but also by laypeople. The presence of monks and nuns in Plum Village has brought me much happiness, because of their commitment to the practice and their determination to follow our ideal together. In Plum Village, monks and nuns vow to live together as a family for the rest of their lives.

In the past I taught several generations of monastic disciples, but I was never as happy as I am now, with teacher and disciple living together and practicing together. Every day I find ways to transmit all that I have realized for myself to my disciples, like the first banana leaf transmitting to the second and the third. The happiness that monks and nuns give me is very great. Monks and nuns in Plum Village all have beauty, sweetness, bright smiles, and twinkling eyes. I don't know if they were so beautiful before they became monks and nuns or whether they became beautiful afterwards. Or is it just because, like any other father and mother, I see my own children as more beautiful than other people's children? I do see them as beautiful, whether they are from North America, Europe, or Asia. I think some of you must agree with me. Just a few hours after the ceremony transmitting the Novice Precepts, their faces are so much more radiant, their eyes more bright, and their smiles fresher. That has to do with their determination, their commitment, and with the precepts' body. Sitting with the monks and nuns to drink tea or to have Dharma discussion, to talk about happiness in the present and the future, is one of the things I like doing best of all. I spend a lot of time with the monks and nuns and that brings me great happiness.

Thây and Sister Chân Không

Renewing Buddhism in Asia

Our practice at Plum Village has contributed a great deal not only to Buddhism in Europe and the United States, but also to Buddhism in Vietnam and other areas of Asia. Without monastic disciples, I would not have been able to write *Stepping into Freedom,* our handbook sharing practical guidance and requirements for novices. The book that is currently used by novices in Buddhist countries was written over four hundred years ago. I felt it was outdated and no longer appropriate. I sat with my disciples to compose thirty-nine chapters on mindful manners, instead of the original twenty-four.

The Sugar Palm Tree family on ordination day

This new handbook includes such areas of practice as how to use a computer in mindfulness and how to facilitate discussions about the Dharma. The Ten Mindfulness Trainings are also presented here in a complete, practical, and beautiful way.

Without the monastic Sangha, we would not have been able to offer to Vietnam the daily chanting book, written in modern Vietnamese, which many temples are now using. (Most traditional chanting books in Vietnam are written in Sino-Vietnamese, which many people do not understand.) We have been able to write and publish many reference books that temples, meditation centers, and Buddhist universities in Vietnam and other countries in Asia find beneficial. For example, *The Heart of the Buddha's Teachings,* a book on basic Buddhism as taught to monks and nuns, is now used as course material in Buddhist institutes in Vietnam.

We created a four-year training program for monks and nuns, helping monastics become capable of organizing retreats and leading days of mindfulness. After five years, monastics can be considered to receive the transmission of the Dharma Lamp to become a Dharma teacher. In Plum Village we have three kinds of Dharma teachers: monastic, lay, and honorary monastic Dharma teachers. About eighty monastics and fifty laypeople have received the Dharma Lamp and led retreats all over the world. There are also numerous honorary monastic Dharma teachers who are teaching in Vietnam.

A Meeting of East and West

The difficulties we encountered in establishing Plum Village were the problems the Buddha also had, but there were new difficulties, too. One difficulty the Buddha had a little of (and we have had a lot of) is differences between cultures. Our Sangha is made of twenty or more nations and cultures. This is not a Vietnamese temple set up in Europe. It has roots in Vietnam, but it has to grow and be appropriate for the environment where it is growing. When we bring plants from Vietnam and plant them in the West, they do not grow the way they would in Vietnam. When we grow mustard greens in France, they grow thorns. That would never happen in Vietnam. We have to know how to adapt to our surroundings, and we have to know how to absorb the beautiful things from the culture. Sometimes, people from both the East and West come to Plum Village and find forms of practice that are not suitable for them, because they carry expectations that it will be like their respective cultures. But Plum Village is a combination of East and West. When a person from Asia hangs clothes out to dry, they hang the trousers lower than the shirts, and the two legs have to be hung close together. It would be strange for an Asian person to see them hung any other way. An Eastern person can never accept feeding a cat out of a person's bowl. The bowl the cat eats out of should be different from what humans eat out of. When a Western nun cooks, putting all her heart into cooking, a Vietnamese nun may look at the food and go somewhere else to eat instant noodles. This makes the Western nun very unhappy. This happens every day in Plum Village. So the cultural gap brings difficulties. It is not anyone's fault. It is just our differences.

In the Buddhist religion of Vietnam there are many jewels. But if we want to offer them, we have to have them within ourselves first. We have to put our roots down in our own tradition very deeply — our educational, ethical, cultural, and our spiritual traditions — to be able to share them. We have to keep the most beautiful things in our culture to be able to offer them to others.

Sharing the practice, we have to learn to understand the culture and the environment of the West. We have to present our own jewels in the way that is appropriate to the Western way of thinking. If we don't understand anything about the language or the behavior of the Western people, how can we offer anything? There are teachers from the East who have jewels from their own cultures, but they have not understood Western culture; so there is no way they can transmit these jewels to Western people. You have to understand Western culture before you can share the jewels of your own tradition. In these last thirty-five years, I have learned so much about this.

I have also learned from the East. In the light of Western culture, I have seen the beauties of the East in a way I had not recognized before. Before, I was only able to see 70 percent of the beauty of Vietnamese culture. But now, under the light of Western culture, I can see 100 percent of its beauty. When Western friends come to Plum Village, they also must have their roots in their own culture and spirituality. Then they have something to share with us. It is not that they are hungry ghosts, wandering around with nothing to offer. If they have put down their roots in the Western culture, they will have something to offer us. Because we are open, we can receive from them and both sides will profit. The basic condition to have a successful exchange between different cultures is for each person to have his or her roots firmly established. This process takes place year to year, and Plum Village is still learning these things.

Sangha as a Family

There has to be a residential Sangha that practices all year round, twenty-four hours a day. Building a permanent Sangha is the basis of all our teachings of the Dharma. That Sangha has to live together as a family. They have to be committed to staying together their whole lives. They don't just stay together a few years. Although there are people who leave from time to time, the number of people who leave Plum Village is small, less than 10 percent. Over the past twenty years, many have committed to join the Sangha for their whole life.

If we talk about the success of Plum Village, we have to talk about the commitment to stay even though you have difficulties. That kind of commitment helps us to go through transformation. If we leave the community because of our suffering, we cannot transform. An authentic Sangha can only be created when people live together twenty-four hours a day and share the same roof and the same economic resources. They practice Days of Mindfulness together and make decisions by consensus. Building a Sangha is not something we do by organizing meetings, or by transmitting the Mindfulness Trainings. If people do not live together and decide together, they are still operating as individuals. They have a retreat for seven days, but then everyone goes home. That is a floating Sangha. The essence of Sangha is to live together and decide together.

If laypeople want to benefit from the practice, they need to build residential Sanghas, like Intersein in Germany and Clear View in Santa Barbara, California. We have to create many Sanghas where we live according to the six harmonies,[4] recite the Mindfulness Trainings together, eat together in mindfulness, walk together, and work together.

Everyone Transforms

The difficulties in the monastic world are the difficulties of any community. From time to time, there is someone who is angry with her brothers or sisters and leaves. That happened in the Buddha's Sangha, and it has happened at Plum Village. In the Sangha of the Buddha, there were monks who were angry with the Buddha and they left. They came back after a while, because they saw they had been happiest when living with the Sangha. Here also, there have been monks and nuns who have gotten angry with the Sangha and left for one or two years, then they remembered how happy they had been and came back again. Everybody values the Sangha when they come back. But they may get caught in the outside world and not come back. There are people who have a wandering soul and do not feel at ease staying in one place. They may have that seed from their ancestors; we all have that in us. If the seed is watered, we may get up and go. If our practice is not successful, we leave for awhile and soon see how much we suffer outside of the monastery as well. We miss Plum Village, and we want to come back. Some people see that

A formal lunch in Summer Retreat

to stay in Plum Village is the most solid, stable thing they can do.

There are a few people who we decide cannot stay in the Sangha, and we have to send home. It is not that we are angry with them or want to punish them; but they have too much sexual energy, and it is very difficult for them to be monks and nuns. We look with the eyes of compassion at these people. We see that we have done everything we can to plant wholesome seeds in them. Although they are not practicing as a monk or a nun anymore, they have good seeds in them, and when they encounter suffering they will know how to withstand difficulties. All the people who have left are still in our hearts. We are not angry with them. We do not blame them. They went with us a short distance as a monk or a nun, and they will go the rest of their path as a layperson. When we look at things this way, we feel peaceful, pure, and happy. There is nothing that has been lost. There is nothing we need to regain.

There are a few people who have a lot of difficulties in their practice, in their relationships with brothers and sisters in the Sangha. But when we have difficulties, we get to hear very helpful Dharma talks about our situation. It is because there are people with difficulties that the Sangha has a chance to practice. If everyone is very good and kind, why would we need the practice? We wouldn't have to practice to love him or her. The presence of people who have difficulties is very beneficial to the Sangha. People who come to Plum Village transform. Some people transform very quickly, and some people less quickly; but everyone transforms, even if it is slow as a tortoise.

Love and Trust between Teacher and Disciple

When monastic and lay disciples do something wrong, clumsy, or unskillful, the Sangha should help them. I have learned over the past thirty years not to use my authority as a teacher to resolve conflicts. We have to use awakened understanding and love. This has to be applied both in the East and in the West. If we do not use this in Asia, we will not be successful as a teacher. Often, disciples cannot see the mind and heart of their teacher. We have to be patient. They think that their teacher's heart is as small as a peanut. They think I do not allow them to receive the precepts because I am punishing them, because I do not love them.

When a student looks at us like that we smile. We understand that our student does not know his teacher's heart. After he is angry with me, six months later, he will see that I love him, and he will love me even more. But he needs time to grow up and to see more clearly. Everyone is like that; they need space, time, and the opportunity to grow up. They learn that my deepest desire is to see my disciples grow and to become big sisters and brothers for all our little sisters and brothers, to take my place. The more they do that, the happier I am.

The teacher is someone who has the capacity to allow his students to make mistakes. But we have to learn from our mistakes. If we fall down, we have to stand up and begin anew. We cannot make the same mistakes again. Our teacher has the capacity to help us do this. This is something very precious. Our teacher is ready to trust us. But we have to help our teacher, so his trust in us can grow every day. If my students do not help me, then no matter how I try, my trust

Thây and an attendant in Upper Hamlet after a ceremony

will grow smaller. Teacher and disciple have to help each other. I am doing my best, so my students can continue to trust my wisdom, virtue, and love. And my disciples do the same. They do their best to help my trust in them grow stronger every day. The trust between teacher and disciple brings a lot of happiness. Trust is not an idea. Trust is something living that is expressed in our daily life. Our teacher has to live in such a way that we continue to trust him. And we have to live in such a way that our teacher continues to trust us. Then we both continue to be happy. If we doubt our teacher, if we doubt how our teacher treats us and feel that our teacher wants to limit our freedom, we cannot be happy.

When we are a teacher, we have the capacity to see all our disciples as our continuation. We help everyone grow. We don't just want to support one or two of our disciples. We want everyone to grow, just as mothers and fathers want all their children to grow up. If we are an older brother or sister in the Sangha, we have to look after every younger brother and sister equally. If we do that, we already have begun to be a teacher. If we know how to love all our disciples with equanimity, then, when we officially become teachers, there is no reason why we should not be successful.

Developing a Fourfold Sangha

Some difficulties in Plum Village happen because we come from different cultures. In Vietnam monks and nuns have different activities than laypeople. The monks and nuns are in the central circle, and the laypeople are in the outer circle of the community. In the time of the Buddha, monks and nuns lived with the Buddha in the monastery, and laypeople came to hear the Dharma talks and to give offerings. In the beginning, in Plum Village, there were only laypeople, so they were my principal disciples. When I ordained monks and nuns, the monastics became the primary focus of attention.

When monks and nuns begin their practice, they are often very weak. But because they are determined and committed to practice, because they have invested their whole life into the community, they have a very high degree of practice. If they were not monastics, they could always leave, they would have money in the bank and a home to go back to. But as a monastic, they have given up everything, they shave their heads and have nowhere to go. That is why they are 100 percent committed. They put all their time and energy into the practice; they do not think about their position, power, or things like that. So they progress quickly. After five years, they are ready to become a *Dharmacarya* (Dharma teacher). But laypeople cannot be trained twenty-four hours a day, 365 days a year. They cannot become Dharmacaryas in five years only. They need a longer time. But we don't have enough monastic Dharmacaryas to go around, and lay Dharmacaryas also have a high degree of understanding of laypeople's situation and needs.

~

I want all our monasteries to have a fourfold Sangha composed of monks, nuns, laymen, and laywomen, and for the laypeople living there to be a bridge between the monastic community and the laypeople in society. We can call these laypeople *upasika* (lay disciples who have received the Five Mindfulness Trainings) because they are close to the monks and nuns. As their understanding deepens, they will have the capacity to hand the insights and the happiness of the monastic Sangha to larger society. There are many laypeople who have helped develop the Order of Interbeing. They have received the Fourteen Mindfulness Trainings, a bridge that connects the monastic community to the lay community.

The Order of Interbeing began in 1966, with six people. Today there are more than seven hundred members all over the world. Now we want to establish lay communities led by laypeople, like Intersein in Germany (led by three lay Dharma teachers) and Clear View in Santa Barbara, California (led by two lay Dharma teachers). We hope there will be many lay centers led by members of the Order of Interbeing in the twenty-first century. We also hope there will be many Mindfulness Practice Centers[5] to offer a secular practice of mindfulness without religious overtones. In these centers, people from any belief can comfortably practice without feeling they need to become Buddhists.

Buddhism Beyond Religion

When I was last in China, I met with the vice-minister of religious affairs, and we offered calligraphy saying "The Spiritual Dimension." Although China is developing and strengthening their economy, education, arts, and politics, many people still suffer because they lack the dimension of spirituality in their lives and activities. Giving support to Buddhism, so that Buddhism can contribute to that spiritual dimension, will help people in China suffer less.

A few weeks ago, the School of Medicine of a university in Geneva asked me to teach about the human brain. They organized a week-long symposium on the brain, gathering neuroscientists and brain specialists to offer illumination on this topic. I am not a brain specialist, but they invited me because they want the spiritual dimension represented. I was also invited to the international conference of politicians and business leaders held at Davos, Switzerland. Neither am I a businessman, so why do they invite me? Because they see that business people and those in politics have suffering, worries, and fears, and they feel the need for the spiritual dimension. The Harvard medical school invited me to give a Day of Mindfulness for doctors and medical researchers. The spiritual dimension brings relief to people's suffering, anxieties, and fears in all fields.

Thây giving a public talk at Berkeley Community Theatre, 1991

Monks, nuns, and lay practitioners have to bring Buddhism out of its religious context, to be able to share it with, and serve, the world. We have to bring Buddhism into prisons, schools, hospitals, and police headquarters so that people can live and work with more ease and less suffering. We need methods of mindfulness practice that can be used in all aspects of society, not limited by the form of religion.

Looking at the Plum Village Sangha's activities, we see that the practice of mindfulness has been able to reach many sectors of society. We host retreats not only in Plum Village, but also in other countries of Europe, America, and Asia. We have had many retreats where parents, children, and teenagers practice together. We have hosted retreats just for young people in the United States, Australia, and Europe. We have had retreats for psychotherapists in America and Europe. We have had retreats for war veterans, environmentalists, doctors, nurses, psychotherapists, teachers, peace activists, and business people. We have brought the practice into prisons. This year the School of Medicine at Harvard University wants me to come and receive an award. They say our retreats have helped heal many people, greatly relieving their suffering. They want to affirm that fact with an award. This is an indication that we have been able to surpass the limits of religion and enter the mainstream of society. We are not doctors, nor are we psychotherapists, but our retreats have brought rejuvenation, joy, and hope to thousands of people.

The Seed has Traveled Far

Whenever we have a retreat, people from different religions practice together without any discrimination. Our teachings have been received easily, enthusiastically, and happily. Our methods of practice seem to be applicable for many schools of Buddhism as well. Whether practitioners come from Japanese Zen meditation, Korean meditation, *vipassana* meditation, or Tibetan Buddhism, they all practice together and feel at ease in our retreats.

Business people who participated in a retreat held in Plum Village reported that, a few months after the retreat, they continue to have more insight into what they learned. The seeds that were planted in the retreat continue to sprout bit by bit, offering deeper understanding. We have been able to present the teachings in such a way that young people and Westerners can understand them, accept them, and apply them. That is a big success of Plum Village, but it is not the work of one person alone or just the work of a few years. It is the work of thirty-five years that includes twenty years of Plum Village and the work of the entire Sangha.

We have been able to present the Five Mindfulness Trainings in non-Buddhist terminology. The Five Mindfulness Trainings are very true and very deep expressions of the practice of Buddhism. They are a concrete way of practicing mindfulness — not restrictive commandments. We have also presented the Fourteen Mindfulness Trainings as the essence of the practice of Buddhism. Many people who do not call themselves Buddhist like to recite the Fourteen Mindfulness Trainings. We have established more than eight hundred local Sanghas all over the world. In large cities like London, there are over ten Sanghas. Small towns also have their Sanghas. In Israel, there are Sanghas. In Australia and in Germany, there are many Sanghas. In Vietnam, there are numerous temples and Sanghas following the mindfulness practice of Plum Village. If you do not see these eight hundred manifestations all over the world, you have not seen Plum Village.

One day while sitting in London during a retreat, I was very moved to receive letters from practitioners in Edinburgh, Scotland, who wrote thoughtful letters about their practice and about their Sangha and shared their happiness. I have never been to Edinburgh, but the seed of Plum Village has traveled to Edinburgh and it has grown in the soil there. That is something that surprised me and made me very happy. This is just an example of one of the many places I have never been, but where the seeds of our practice have flown. Here in France, there is a plant called *pissenlit*, the dandelion. When the dandelion plant ripens, it produces seeds, which the wind carries very far. In the same way, the seeds sown by Sanghas of Plum Village have spread very far. They have traveled into prisons, into Catholic cloisters, into schools, families, hospitals, and communities around the world, and they will continue to go far in the future.

Harvesting Every Moment

Yesterday, Fei-fei, a lay practitioner living in Plum Village, asked me, "Thây, you work so hard, have you harvested the fruit that you want yet?" I responded, "My dear, what else do you want Thây to harvest? Every moment of my daily life is a moment of happiness, is a harvest. As I sit with you now and teacher and disciple drink tea together, it is not to achieve anything. When we drink tea together, we are already happy. To give a Dharma talk is already happiness. To do walking meditation with my disciples is happiness. To organize a retreat is happiness. To help practitioners be able to smile is happiness. What more do you want me to harvest?" Our work should be happiness. Our practice is "dwelling happily in this moment." Every Dharma talk I give has to reflect the Dharma Seal of Plum Village: "I have arrived. I am home."

Drawing of Lower Hamlet by Wietske

Please Call Me By My True Names

Please Call Me by My True Names

Based on a poem by Thich Nhat Hanh

My joy is like spring, so warm
It makes flowers bloom all over the Earth.
My pain is like a river of tears,
So vast it fills the four oceans.

Please call my by my true names,
So I can hear all my cries and laughter
at once,
So I can hear that my joy and pain are one.

Please call me by my true names,
So I can wake up
And the door of my heart
Could be left open.

Stories of Plum Village in the Early Days

My Love Story with Plum Village

Pierre Marchand, True Great Togetherness, is French and lives in Paris with his wife and four children. He is founder of Partage, a humanitarian organization.

I met Sister Chân Không one evening in Paris, in September 1972, at a meeting of a nonviolent activist group led by César Chavez. She came to share her commitment to reduce the suffering in Vietnam. It was a time of war. She was a laywoman, and it was so easy for me to see that she was moved by love. This love touched me deeply, and has completely changed my life. At the end of the meeting, I was eager to support her that I asked her if it was possible to meet her again. She agreed, and I was happy because my wish was not, in fact, to meet her again. It was to meet her again and again! And I have had the chance to do it.

The next day, I went to Sceaux, in the south of Paris, where she was working with the official Delegation of the Unified Buddhist Church of Vietnam. She was teaching me as we sat on the floor, when someone came into the room with such silence that I barely noticed him. He sat down and smiled at me. Sister Chân Không introduced me and said his name was Thich Nhat Hanh. I have never forgotten that moment. It was like a light that changes all that we see by its bright appearance. Nothing was the same as a result of his simple presence. But I am still ashamed to remember that I took out a cigarette and started to smoke while Thây was speaking to us! I was seventeen, young and foolish. Thây didn't embarrass me or ask me to stop. He just accepted me the way I was. This was a very, very special experience that still nurtures me. I have forgotten his words, but not the effect of his presence and his behavior. Slowly, I became aware that I was in front of a holy human being, a real spiritual master.

Sister Chân Không had given me some material to read. In it, there were some private letters. In the evening, I started to read them. Then I fell into tears. I spent the whole night reading those letters and crying. The author of the letters was Nhat Chi Mai. They were the letters she left just before her immolation. Through the media, I had heard about the people who immolated themselves in Vietnam, but I was unable to understand it as anything other than suicide out of desperation. Reading Chi Mai, I realized fully her sincere wish to become a light to help all of us to see what was real. She became the light she had wished to be. Mai has become my beloved light since that night, and she is still here for us in Plum Village, even if we do not notice her.[6]

This was how Plum Village was born in my heart. A gift from sisters and brothers living in heaven and hell at the same time, but firmly refusing to leave hell with so many people still in it. They were trying to bring everyone to heaven, while living simply with a spiritual practice given thousands of years ago. They have broken my heart by their way of life, and this is how Plum Village started to grow deeply in me. The Tiep Hien Order has nurtured the seed planted this that night, day by day.

At this time, there was no such place called "Plum Village." The name was yet to come, but the heart of Plum Village, the Tiep Hien Community, had been already established by Thây in a remote place in Vietnam. Nhat Chi Mai and Sister Chân Không were among the first laypersons of that community. Each member was sustained by the commitment and the practice of the others. Thây was the example for each of us to follow, our guide, our spiritual father. His teaching wasn't only his writing, but his own practice in each moment. A kind of polestar for people like me, lost in the ocean. He was showing us the way then, as he is today. Aware of the need for a retreat center to feed our happiness and deepen our practice, Thây first started a little retreat center in Fontvannes, not far from Paris. It was very helpful for all of us. But, at this time, at this place, the "all" was only five to ten persons!

The end of the "official war" came in Vietnam. A few months later, the flow of refugees on the dangerous sea started. "Plum Village" became a ship on the ocean to rescue them, with Thây and Sister Chân Không aboard. The refugees reached Europe. The government and people were giving relief and help, but there was such pain in each heart. How to bring peace to those broken hearts? How to offer spiritual support to each one, especially the children? I remember the feelings of Thây and Sister Chân Không for all the children.

To me those children were the real founders of the Plum Village. It was so difficult to be a refugee after such a hard life in Vietnam. I think that Thây heard the call of a refuge — a real spiritual refuge, a community of practice. From this need, Plum Village was born. A real refuge for the Tiep Hien Order, to welcome those who suffer. Plum Village has never been a concept; just an appropriate answer to real need, and it came from the love and the open hearts of Thây and Sister Chân Không.

Thirty Years Later

Recently, I visited Plum Village. I was moved by the stones that are still the same. Their transformation is slow. I bowed to them, as I know how slow I am in my own transformation. I was moved also by the plum trees. I remember them as being so small. I spent time looking at each of them, one by one. Each one reminds me of the wisdom of Thây. He loves children so much, and his love is profoundly creative. He had the idea to offer a small tree to each Vietnamese child refugee and invited each one to care and nurture the tree and then to offer the fruits of the tree to a child in Vietnam. Each tree in Plum Village has helped two children. One was a refugee, and one was in Vietnam. The plums were fruits to nurture the spirituality of each child by sharing the process. The wisdom and creative love of Thây seems to have no limit. Many people have come and gone, but the trees remain.

Plum Village is one of the homes of the Tiep Hien Order — the Order of Interbeing. It is not always easy to inter-be mindfully, but those who came there were not looking for an easy way. Just committed to try, again and again, to follow the way of mindfulness. The first people to live in the hamlets were from Vietnam and refugees from various places. Plum Village was born from them and for them. Later, the Americans came, but very few French. Then, step by step, people from all over the world visited, most recently from China. Then the French at last! Each person brings her own culture, and Plum Village seems to be able to welcome and integrate it without any discrimination. Plum Village is alive. It is never the same but always surprisingly new at each moment, as a love story with no end — a story of inclusiveness.

One day some years ago, I saw a monk working our Mother Earth. I thought it was Thich Nhat Hanh, as I have seen him doing many times. Happy to see him, I called out "Thây." When the monk turned his face to me and smiled, I realized he was not Thich Nhat Hanh. At the same moment, I concluded that he was Thich Nhat Hanh too. I became suddenly delighted. Thich Nhat Hanh, my father, was here in many bodies!

When I sat with Thây and Sister Chân Không before leaving Plum Village recently, I deeply realized that I was in front of my father and my mother. I enjoyed their presence a great deal, just like the first time I saw them. We were together again, the three of us, in a small, simple room. I realized that we have never been separate since the first time we met thirty years ago. This time, he was dangling quietly in a hammock, and the quality of the light shining from him was still the same. At the end, I told Thây that I was happy to have such a father. He smiled at me gently, like the sweetest kiss. Plum Village is also many smiles and kisses from many eyes!

Plum Village is a gift from the children of Vietnam to all the children of the world. May we bless them by our practice. Thirty years ago, Plum Village was only two loving faces, Thây and Sister Chân Không. I am thankful that they have given me many sisters and brothers. I feel that Plum Village was born from love — to celebrate and practice love. ✻

The Eldest Brother: An Interview with Anh Thieu, the First Resident of Plum Village

by Shantum Seth, Brother Phap Ngo, Sister Chau Nghiem, and Brother Phap Lu

Le Nguyen Thieu, called Anh Thieu in Plum Village, is from Vietnam. He was Thây's student in the 1950s and then a social worker in the School of Youth for Social Service from 1965–1975. He now lives in Blaye, near Plum Village, France. He visits the community regularly.

How did you first meet Thây? You've known Thây since you were young in Vietnam, right?

Thây had a big impact on me because he and his brother were the first two young monks to study outside the monastery and attend university. At that time, I saw that the educational programs in the Nam Viet Buddhist Center, where I studied in Saigon, could not fulfill our needs. We all felt a need to learn more from the outside world. I also felt we had to attend college in order to learn and understand Buddhism.

From time to time, the dean of our center invited Thây to teach Vietnamese Literature and Language to young monks and novice students. From 1950 to 1954, Thây often came to stay at the Nam Viet Buddhist Center.

When the Geneva Peace Treaty was signed in 1954, and the French lost, all the students at the center were shaken up. We felt things had to change. We felt that the education program at the Center could not meet the demands of the current state of affairs. I thought Nam Viet Buddhist Center would be shut down, but the dean asked Thây to talk to the students. Thây calmed everyone down. After Thây's lectures, the dean of the Center gave all the teaching responsibilities to Thây. Thây thoroughly planned out the education courses at the Center, and everyone, including the monastic students, were very jubilant.

When did you come to France, and how did you connect with Thây in France?
From 1965 to 1975, I was working under Thây's guidance at the School of Youth for Social Service in Saigon. When I escaped from Vietnam in 1981 and arrived at the refugee camp in Palawan, Philippines, I requested to go to France to see Thây. My wife, two sons, and I arrived in France in 1982. In September of that year, Thây asked us to go to Bordeaux to look at the property of Lower Hamlet. At that time, my wife was pregnant, and the due date was near. On October 5, my third son was born, and soon after our whole family traveled to Ste. Foy La Grande. I think that was the beginning of Plum Village.

What was Thây's purpose for asking you and your family to come here?
Thây did not tell me. But before we came, Thây asked me, "How do you want to live? Do you want to open a restaurant or have a farm?" Even though many Vietnamese people liked to open restaurants, I wanted to farm. So when I saw this big property, I thought Thây wanted this place for me to farm.

What did you do after you arrived?
In 1983, Thây wished to organize a gathering, the first Summer Retreat. So, in the beginning of the year, we cleaned up the cow stable, now the Red Candle Hall, to serve as a meditation hall. We built a wall to make an office and library.

The first Summer Retreat at Plum Village started on July 15, 1983, and it ended on August 15. The retreatants stayed in the Plum Hill building. At that time, it was used for drying tobacco leaves. Throughout the year, we planted some Vietnamese vegetables and later grew soybeans.

Did you practice meditation in addition to farming?
Thây started to teach a simple meditation practice for everyone.

What was the Summer Retreat like?
There were roughly one hundred retreatants. There was a Dharma talk everyday and private consultation with Thây in the afternoon. At that time, the activities of the Vietnamese people were fun because it was just like a village. Summer Retreat was like being on holiday. There were two daily meditation sessions of thirty minutes each. One session was in the early morning, and the other was at night. Besides that, there were Tea Meditations and ceremonies, like the Rose Festival or Ancestor Remembrance Festival.

Several women taught the children how to speak and write Vietnamese. Many children who came here could not speak Vietnamese. But they learned to speak and read it in just a few weeks.

How many years did you live in Plum Village?
I lived here from October 1982 until July 1987.

What were the major events you remember from that time?
There were many. For instance, in the winter of 1982, I planted pine trees in Upper Hamlet and Lower Hamlet. At that time, there was no car. We only had a small motorcycle. My younger brother drove me to Upper Hamlet to plant pine trees. In Upper Hamlet, at that time, there was only one building to protect us from the rain and sun. The rest of the other buildings were stables with a lot of old things lying all over the place. While planting the trees, it started to snow. I continued to plant, but my younger brother pulled me inside the shelter. I did not understand the reason, but I let him pull me into the shelter. He said, "If you continue to stay outside, the snow will completely bury you." It was the first time he had ever seen snow. After entering the room, we built a small fire and ate a bag of instant noodles.

Why did Thây call you "eldest brother"?
In a Vietnamese village, the most respected and highest-ranking person in the village is called *Ong Ca* (meaning "eldest sir/mister"). So, Thây replaced the word Ong with *Anh* (meaning "brother"). Using the phrase "eldest brother" expressed Thây's wish that we build a Vietnamese village, and his trust in me to be the founder.

Did Thây give you any instructions or teachings about how to live here?
Thây gave progressive teachings. I felt Thây wanted my family to be a family role model for a new village.

Upper Hamlet
Buddha Hall
in the early days

What do you mean by that?
I mean our family lifestyle. For instance, how did we treat each other? How did we walk? How did we talk with each other? How did we organize a Sunday meal in mindfulness as a family unit?

How did Thây teach you? Did Thây have tea with you or work with you?
His teaching was very informal. He just did things and we followed him. Thây talked to my children and played with them. He didn't teach them through lectures. There were no special teachings for my wife and children.

Thây gave me paper or wood, and I made calligraphies for decoration. I did the ones in the Lower Hamlet.

How did you balance your life between taking care of your family and taking care of the village?
To take care of the family, I farmed. We had to pay taxes on the land, so I planted vegetables and sold them at the Bordeaux market. At that time, Thây gave me a small car.

How did our neighbor, Mr. Mounet, help you during that time?
Mr. Mounet was a very kind and helpful neighbor. He showed us in detail how to prepare the land in order to plant vegetables. I was not used to the land, so whenever I had a question, I went to him. I asked him about everything because Mr. Mounet knew everything. He was the original owner of some of the Lower Hamlet land.

Do you see any changes in Thây or is Thây the same as many years ago?
I don't see any changes in Thây. He is the same as in the old days.

Why did you leave in 1987?
Near the end of 1986, I was involved in a major accident while driving on the Bernac road. After having four surgeries, by the middle

of 1987, I was so weak I could not walk by myself. I had to use a walker. Thây allowed me to rest because of my poor health, and I thought I should be in a private place to recover my strength. So I moved to a small farm nearby. Since then, I come often to visit Plum Village.

What do you think when you come to visit Plum Village now, having seen it develop from the very beginning?
There are many changes in Plum Village. I'm very happy because Thây has created a peaceful place. It is like a Pure Land for young people to come and practice. That makes me very happy.

I Am Not Different from You
A Portrait of Sister Chân Không

Eveline Beumkes, True Harmony/Peace, lived in Plum Village for three years from 1988 *to* 1991. *She has helped to organize the practice in Amsterdam, Holland and helps translate Thây's books into Dutch. She was ordained as a Dharma teacher in* 1994.

Her original name is Phuong; her monastic name is Chân Không (True Emptiness). Thich Nhat Hanh and Sister Chân Không started Plum Village together in 1982. That Plum Village has become what it is today and that people all over the world have been inspired by Thây's teachings is, to a great extent, a result of Sister Chân Không's enduring support and untiring initiative. Feeling grateful for having come in contact with Thây's teachings is feeling grateful to Sister Chân Không in the very same breath.

I first met Thây and Sister Phuong in 1984, during a meditation weekend in Amsterdam. In the evening, there was a special program with Vietnamese music. At one point, the music stopped abruptly, and Sister Phuong began to sing. I was deeply touched by her voice. Never had I heard someone sing like that. She sang my heart open, and I cried and cried, not understanding what was happening to me.

During the first summer I spent in Plum Village, Sister Phuong wasn't yet a nun. She had lovely long black hair that, when in her way, she would casually put up in a bun by sticking a pen through it. She warmly welcomed the few Westerners that visited Plum Village in those days, and she did what she could to make us feel at home. At that time, she was the only person able to translate from Vietnamese into English or French. When Thây gave a Dharma talk, or when there was an event in Vietnamese, she would sit next to us and translate for hours on end without ever appearing to get tired. Sister Phuong's way of translating was so expressive that, even after having translated for hours, her voice sounded as colorful as it did when she began.

Three years later, when I moved to Plum Village, I was often the only one during the winter season who didn't understand Vietnamese. There were about ten of us by then, and after dinner, as we were enjoying countless cups of tea, there was usually a lot of conversation, all in Vietnamese. During those moments, I felt so left out, but when Sister Phuong was around she would always come sit next to me and, while participating wholeheartedly in the conversation, she would translate for me at the same time. I savored those moments in her presence.

She strengthened my confidence that there is always a solution to any problem. One winter, I had promised to make a flower arrangement for a Tea Meditation in the Lower Hamlet. I looked all over and could not find a single flower. When everyone was seated in the zendo and Sister Phuong was about to enter, I ran to her with an empty bowl in my hands, telling her, quite unhappily, that I had not succeeded in making the flower arrangement. Even before I had finished speaking, she picked up some tufts of grass that were growing along the path, added a few handfuls of pebbles from the path we were standing on, picked up a stick lying nearby, planted it in the middle, and . . . voila! Her creation was complete, and the Tea Meditation could begin. While we entered, she gave me a mischievous wink and whispered, "Pure nature."

As the years passed, more and more people came to Plum Village, and new sleeping quarters needed to be created. One of the places chosen for a future dormitory was the attic of the house where my room was. Cleaning it was a gigantic job, with spider webs from floor to ceiling and the dust of ages everywhere. After cleaning for just a few minutes, I looked like a mineworker. Many hours of scrubbing and sweeping later, I seemed to have made no progress at all. One afternoon, after a few days of lonesome work in that cheerless place, Sister Phuong suddenly appeared, joining me in my work with great swiftness. Her help and enthusiasm were most welcome, but at the same time I felt embarrassed that she was there mopping the floor with me while she had countless other things to do. No matter what I said, she was not at all receptive to my urging that she spend her time in a different way; she continued until the job was done. She never felt that any job was beneath her.

I was often amazed by her inexhaustible energy. If something needed to be finished, she simply continued until it was done, if necessary beyond midnight, without eating and often all by herself. When packages of medicine needed to be sent to Vietnam, she sat for hours on the stone floor, addressing labels and writing uplifting words to each family. Others came and joined her in her work, but when they left she continued. And never have I detected a glimpse of self-pity in her. Despite all she has to do, I never heard her complain that she was too busy. I also never heard her complain of feeling cold, although in the wintertime in the drafty rooms of Plum Village there is certainly reason enough to do so. In early autumn, when I was already wearing two pair of socks, I saw her walking without any. She never gave the slightest attention to her own discomfort.

Sister Phuong as a layperson in Plum Village, back row on the right

During a Tea Meditation, many years ago, I remember her telling us that she had just received a message from Vietnam that a number of artists had been imprisoned. She cried openly as she spoke. I felt so touched. While I suffer from my own pain, I saw her suffer from the pain of others. Far more often though, I saw her laughing, because she is very open to the comical aspects of a situation. Once a small group of very important Vietnamese monks from America paid a short visit to Plum Village. On the morning of their departure, we were all, about twelve people, called to the zendo. We sat in a circle while Thây spoke for a while in Vietnamese. We had just adopted a new routine in Plum Village; when someone was leaving, in order to say good-bye to him or her on behalf of the whole Sangha, one of the permanent residents would practice "hugging meditation" with the parting friend during a communal meeting. Hugging meditation is done in the following way: you first bow to each other, aware of your breath and forming a lotus bud with your hands to offer to the other person. Then you embrace the other person, holding him or her during three in- and out-breaths, fully aware of the fact that (1) you yourself are still alive, (2) the friend in your arms is still alive, and (3) you are lucky to be able to hold each other. Well, that morning Thây asked one of the nuns to come up to say good-bye to one of the visiting monks. In the meantime, he explained to the monk how hugging meditation was done. Only those who know the tradition well can gather how revolutionary Thây was at that moment. It was obvious to us that the monk in question was clearly not accustomed to this form of meditation. And certainly not with a nun! They both stood in front of each other. After exchanging a short, uneasy glance, they started bowing very deeply, and the inevitable happened: their heads collided. It took all of us great pains to refrain from laughing out loud; and, like us, Sister Phuong sat for a long time with a twisted face that she just couldn't manage to get back into the right expression, however hard she tried.

Though countless practical things continuously demanded her attention, Sister Phuong also kept an eye on how we were doing. And if she suspected that something was wrong with one of us, she asked straightaway about it. Whatever it was she wanted to discuss, she always came immediately to the heart of the matter. When I wanted to tell her something, she usually got the point long before I had finished. Her way of listening was very attentive and without judging. When I spoke with her, I always felt a lot of space. Yet I also know from experience that her way of communicating has its own rules, and at times that has been quite difficult for me. The hardest to digest was her sudden way of stopping a conversation — completely unexpectedly, in the middle of a story, in the middle of a sentence. Since I learned that this moment could arrive at any time, I brought up what I wanted to talk about right away, or else she'd be gone long before I'd touched the topic I'd wanted to discuss. And that would be really bad luck. Because she was so busy, you'd never know when your next chance would be.

She could abruptly cut off a conversation on the telephone as well. Just like that. It has happened to me more then once. In the middle of a sentence, I would suddenly hear "beep, beep, beep" in my ear, the connection having been broken. At first I felt really hurt, but as time passed I learned to see that as her "suchness" and to simply accept it as just one of her many sides.

As far as I could see, the contact between Thây and Sister Phuong was very harmonious and without tension. Once, however, at the end of dinner, Thây spoke to her in an unusually stern voice: "Finish your meal!" Because it was so different from how Thây normally spoke to her or to any of us, I never forgot it. There were a few grains of rice (maybe eight or twelve) left on her plate, and Thây further said something like, "Many people are hungry at this moment." To my surprise, Sister Phuong, with a look of remorse,

Eveline Buemkes

proceeded to eat the remaining grains of rice on her plate, without any protest at having been addressed that way.

The first year I lived in Plum Village, Thây was the only monastic. But after their trip to India in 1988, Sister Chân Không, Sister Annabel, and Sister Chân Vi returned with shaved heads — they had become nuns. This unexpected change was a great shock to me. Thây must have noticed, because soon after their return, when I happened to be alone in a room with him and Sister Chân Không, he invited me to touch Sister Chân Không's head and to feel for myself how it felt without hair. While I was very carefully touching her head, she laughed at me in a playful way and then took me warmly into her arms and said, "I am not at all different from you, even if I am wearing other clothes and have a shaved head. There is no difference at all between us."

I felt that something had changed in Sister Chân Không. I felt the practice had really become number one in her life and that she had made a vow to try with all her heart to live as mindfully as possible. I noticed, for example, that in the middle of a conversation that was getting too noisy, she would become quieter, or while doing something very quickly, she would suddenly slow down. Because I so clearly felt the change that took place in her, it was quite natural for me to start calling her "Sister" instead of just "Phuong." Speaking about her new position as a nun, she once told me that she wanted to be careful that she didn't become proud. She explained to me that in the Vietnamese community this could easily happen because, as a monastic, Vietnamese people have the tendency to look up to you very much.

I have always known Sister Chân Không as a jack-of-all-trades. According to her, she has much less energy than ten years ago, but when I see how much she takes on, seemingly without any effort, I am truly amazed. During a retreat some years ago in a Tibetan monastery in France, Thây fell ill. From that moment on, Sister Phuong took care of every aspect of the program, including the Dharma talk. On top of that, she cooked twice a day for Thây and the three Plum Village residents who had come to take care of the children's program. In her remaining time, she was available for retreatants who wanted to discuss their problems with her. And when the children's program didn't run so smoothly, she took care of that as well. She was the last one to go to bed and the first one to get up, and she continued to be in good spirits.

I have often wondered where her endless supply of energy comes from. I partly attribute it to the fact that she truly lives in the present; from moment to moment she deals with what is coming up, and she doesn't lose energy in worrying about what may come next, which to me is a reflection of a deeply rooted faith. Even more important though, I think, is her compassion. When she became a nun, she received from Thây the name "Chân Không," "True Emptiness." "My happiness is your happiness" and "your pain is my pain" is something that she truly lives. Seeing the self in the nonself is not a theory for her but the very ground of her being.

Receiving the Heritage

Sister Chân Vi, True Taste, is from Vietnam and was one of the first three monastics Thây ordained. She lives and practices in Tu Hanh Temple in Hawai'i.

From a Philippine refugee camp, I came to France in 1987. Sister Chân Không's brother brought me to Plum Village, and I met Sister Chân Duc (Sister Annabel Laity). It was May, but the weather was still quite cold, so cold that I shivered wherever I sat. All the walls had openings where cold drafts continuously came through. The houses were all old, made of stone in a rustic style. The building that is now called Purple Cloud was a storage place for cow manure. Sister Chân Duc and I used the manure as fertilizer to grow vegetables. Working mindfully every day, Sister Chân Duc would tear the manure into small pieces with her bare hands to make compost. I admired her way of working, and this image of her is still with me today. I felt she did not discriminate between pure and impure. For myself, I don't have that insight.

Sister Chân Vi before she was ordained and a young friend in Plum Village

Sister Chân Duc was very happy to have my company because there was no one else there besides myself. Her Vietnamese was not as good as it is today. I remembered whenever we talked in Vietnamese, she kept asking, "Young sister, could you repeat what you just said?" So I kept repeating until she got it. As time went by, she learned a lot from us, but we did not learn much English from her. It was really unfair!

In the beginning, all our activities were held in the very small kitchen. This was where we ate, studied, and practiced because there was a decent working heater that helped keep us warm. Then, in the evening, we had to retire back to our sleeping quarters where we used our blankets to cover ourselves from head to toe — this was the only time we dared to stay in our rooms because they were very cold all the time!

In June, Sister Chân Không came back. She stayed in the same bedroom with me. She always went to bed late and woke up early. Sometimes I woke up at two in the morning, and I saw she was still there working. I asked her, "Why do you have to work so hard, Sister?" She said, "I need to read letters and answer them, to say thank you to everyone who has given us money to support hungry children in Vietnam." I was very touched. She has a lot of compassion and love in her heart, always thinking about the well-being of those who suffer and forgetting herself. I admire her bodhisattva nature.

Every day we ate silently. The silent meals helped me a lot. I felt very lucky to have a full bowl of rice with many kinds of food in front of me. I also saw clearly that, in that moment, many people were hungry and had no food. Our life in Plum Village was very simple. In each room, we had four bricks and a long piece of wood to use for a bed. Nothing else. Little by little, we made shelves and tables to meet our needs.

In July, Thây came back from America. He began to teach us mindfulness in walking, working, and in every daily activity. I remember one day, Chi Doan, a young woman from Switzerland, worked with Thây. They were counting the pages of the Plum Village newsletter. Chi Doan shared later, "Thây is very mindful while counting, but he does it twice as fast as me. He finished two piles of newsletters while I just finished one." Thây works fast, but he is always at ease.

His image of walking, working, and standing mindfully is the living Dharma. To me, Thây is a teacher worthy of respect and love. He raised me, embraced me, and helped me develop my mind of love and understanding. I feel I am very lucky to receive the heritage that Thây has transmitted to me.

The Good Life

Sister Chân Anh Nghiem, True Adornment with Quintessence, is Vietnamese and grew up in England. She was ordained in 1998.

In the summer of 1984, I went to Plum Village for the first time. I was nine years old and my parents took me, my younger brother, and my sister to this unusual place for a two week holiday. They never told us where we were going. It was all a surprise, from the journey to the destination.

I remember a cloudy, wet day, and there were various people gathered in an old, bare, and run-down hall in a run-down farm building. Everything seemed dark. The walls were gray stones and the floor gray concrete. It felt like a way of living that existed before the modern world. But the people's faces were happy, faces of young children and their parents, some old people, and some teenagers. We were all Vietnamese, and this interested me most. I felt immersed in my mother culture, which was new for me, growing up in an English society. There was a monk amongst us, though my memory of him is vague. I was a little girl who was more interested in meeting kids her own age than anything else. Most of us were dressed in traditional Vietnamese *Ao Dai* and waited our turn, in twos, to touch the Earth before an altar. (I later learned that it was paying reverence to our ancestors in the Ancestors Ceremony.)

Later that first evening people dispersed and seemed to have disappeared. I felt lonely and sad, not having yet made any friends, and wondered where they had all gone. But then a girl a few years older than me invited me to her room. She kept talking about us being Vietnamese and saying that we should speak Vietnamese. Since she lived in France and I in England, Vietnamese was the only language we could communicate in. Being with her that evening, I felt clearly that by coming to Plum Village I had returned to my roots.

In its simplicity, Plum Village brought the good life to us and brought out the good life from within us. We returned to nature and to the very basic enjoyment of life. Once or twice a week, we had entertainment evenings where hidden talents were revealed and shared with the community. My little sister was a child star. This small, chubby, and cute four-year-old was often invited to sing. Always smiling, and not the slightest bit shy, she would go onto the simple stage made of wooden boards before an audience seated all around on wooden benches and sing her Vietnamese ABC song. I completely forgot about the existence of television, as my days were filled. My friends and I would draw hopscotch on the dusty ground and play for hours, or we'd play Vietnamese skipping using an elastic rope. There was a pair of wooden stilts, and the kids would take turns. In time, I learned how to walk several meters without falling off these stilts. In the afternoons, under the two oak trees in the

Lower Hamlet, we would gather to sing songs and eat desserts. There was a dessert stall made of a wooden frame and a straw thatched roof. Mothers would gather in the kitchen to prepare the desserts, sitting together talking and laughing. Each small bowl of dessert cost between two and five francs, and the money went to the Hungry Children Fund. We'd buy for friends and return for seconds. The children would either run around playing or sit with their parents in groups. Sometimes, Thây would join us in the oak grove, sharing the desserts happily like one of the villagers.

There were about forty or fifty of us, and the memories add beauty to what was, for me, a golden childhood. The next summer, when my parents could not go to Plum Village, I cried and cried. It was too terrible for my young heart to not be able to return. Plum Village had become my homeland.

Since then, Plum Village has changed dramatically. The population has increased from one small residential family to an ever-increasing community of monks, nuns, and laypeople. Two simple hamlets have multiplied to five. In the summer, there might be over five hundred retreatants a week, ten times more than there once was. It was once a place that united Vietnamese people to their cultural roots, and now it unites a whole world of different nationalities. The monastics alone consist of over twenty nationalities. One summer, during the mid-1990s, I remember a group of Vietnamese youths went to have tea with Thây in his Sitting Still hut in the Upper Hamlet. These young friends were saddened by what they thought was a diminishing of the Vietnamese culture in Plum Village. Even when Plum Village had become more international, there was still a time when the Vietnamese alone occupied the whole Lower Hamlet. Gradually, as more Americans, English, Dutch, and French people came, the Vietnamese were settled in the smaller Middle Hamlet. These young people, who had been visiting Plum Village since the early 1990s, felt that their root culture was being lost.

Thây told them Plum Village was not the cause of their loss. It was up to the Vietnamese people to retain Vietnamese culture. He told us about the early days when there were very few French people, and they had to find their own corner during activities for translations. But as the years went by, more and more French-speaking people came to Plum Village, so that now a whole New Hamlet catered to the French. Plum Village is a practice center, and Thây is available to anyone who comes for the teachings whether they are English, American, Dutch, or Vietnamese. I will never forget Thây's explanation. I felt deeply moved by his wide embrace and deep vision. Plum Village belongs not to one people, but to one common aspiration: the aspiration to practice, regardless of nationality and culture.

Perhaps that is why Plum Village, under Thây's guidance, will always grow and expand. It will never remain the same. One time, I said to Thây that in the future I would like to lead hiking retreats and retreats on boats out at sea. Thây replied, "It is up to you." So just as it is up to the Vietnamese to revive our culture within the culture of Plum Village, it is up to all of us to help shape our future. I look back with joy at the memories of Plum Village, but without yearning for its past. I know Plum Village will never remain static. It will forever change, and perhaps that is its characteristic: that change is Plum Village.

Celebrating at Plum Village in the Early Days

Sister Chân Tu Nghiem, True Adornment with Loving Kindness, is from the United States and grew up in New York City. She was ordained a Dharma teacher in 1996.

Near the end of the Winter Retreat in 1993, Thây announced that we would have a Dharma Festival. What he meant was that each practitioner would give a Dharma talk. He wrote topics on the board, such as the Four Noble Truths, the Noble Eightfold Path, the Three Dharma Seals, and the Five Powers; all the central teachings of basic Buddhism. Then each topic was written on a small piece of paper. On the designated day, the whole community present for the three-month retreat gathered in the Dharma hall in Lower Hamlet. The small pieces of paper were put into the large bell on Thây's table at the front of the room. Then Thây called us up one at a time, and we had to come up, breathe three times, and pick a piece of paper out of the bell. We would read the topic out loud and had to give a Dharma talk on that topic for at least five minutes. I think we all felt a lot of fear and nervousness. This might have been Thây's way of seeing how well we received and remembered his teaching!

I enjoyed so much living in a Vietnamese Sangha. My parents were children of immigrants who had come to the United States from another country, so dual cultures were part of their growing up experience. I remember as a child hearing different languages in the home, and I felt comfortable with that. My parents didn't strongly identify as Americans, so I didn't either. Living in Lower Hamlet in the early days gave me the experience of living in an Asian culture, and I liked that very much. I appreciated so much the politeness and gentleness of everyone.

I loved all the singing we did in the early days. After a meal, Thây would come with Sister Chân Không, and we would pass out the Vietnamese songbooks and sing together. There was always singing on Thursday and Sunday lazy evenings. We were watering the seeds of happiness together, being in touch with the music of the Vietnamese culture.

The annual observance of the Vietnamese Lunar New Year, *Tet,* the welcoming of spring, was a happy celebration lasting for days and days. I remember we would wrap the Earth cakes and Sky cakes and then Sister Bao Nghiem and other sisters and brothers would stay up all night tending the fire as the Earth cakes cooked outside in Lower Hamlet. There was a lot of singing during Tet, and Brother Nguyen Hai and Sister Chân Vi sang traditional Vietnamese opera in an energetic and beautiful way, always creating much joy and laughter in the whole Sangha. I remember the weather just before Tet was usually still dark, rainy, and cold; yet Thây would arrive in Lower Hamlet by surprise, carrying in his arms bundles of branches blooming with delicate pink blossoms, a sign of spring! We were able to enjoy the spring branches during the whole celebration of Tet, watching the flowers unfold each day. It was such a happy time, with many Vietnamese friends visiting from Europe and the United States.

Bac Tu sings for the Sangha

Sometimes, Thây would ask everyone in the Sangha to write a song. One time, Thây gave us the assignment of writing a song about anger, and then a few weeks later, Thây called on a brother or a sister to sing their song in front of everyone! In the early days, there was a lot of song writing and singing, under the blossoming plum trees in spring, and especially during the Plum Blossom Festival in April. We sat on white plastic chairs, in a circle under the Plum Trees, and sang about how to practice when our anger manifested.

Every year we had two flower festivals: the Daffodil Festival and the Plum Blossom festival. When the daffodils began to show signs of opening on the slopes of the forests in Upper Hamlet, the Daffodil Festival was organized, usually by the first or second week of March. We gathered in Upper Hamlet and did walking meditation to the daffodil fields, bright with yellow flowers. We sat among the daffodils and sang songs in Vietnamese, English, and French. Later, we had a picnic brunch outside. Long tables were placed on the grass, and we ate *soi*, sticky rice, and there was *che*, sweet soup, and hot tea, as well as muesli and bread. A talented young violinist named Truc played the violin each year, beautiful selections from classical music. Sister Chân Không always sang a particular Vietnamese song about the daffodils as little fairies that were bodhisattvas. Later in the morning, Thây gave a Dharma talk in the Upper Hamlet meditation hall. I remember it as a day of celebration and joy.

The Plum Blossom Festival, usually in early April, was celebrated in Lower Hamlet. Thây led us in walking meditation through the acres of blossoming plum trees. We would stop in front of a plum tree, chant the name of Avalokiteshvara in Vietnamese, and then continue walking until Thây stopped at another tree. We did this around the plum orchard. The trees probably felt so nourished by the Sangha visiting them and chanting for them! The beautiful lotus ponds in Lower and Upper Hamlet were started in 1995, after Thây's first trip to mainland China, where we saw temples with big lotus ponds. Thây's Root Temple, Tu Hieu Monastery, has a beautiful ancient lotus pond just inside the entrance.

I noticed when monks and nuns from Vietnam came to Plum

Truc, or Little Bamboo, playing violin among the daffodils

Village they brought with them the traditional ways of practicing as monks and nuns in Vietnam. We began to learn so much from them about how to practice. Slowly, there have been more practitioners of Western origin coming to ordain, from Europe as well as North America. This has broadened our Sangha so that we are now an international Sangha representing twenty-four countries. We are learning ways of being brothers and sisters together in the same spiritual family.

Thây with Arnie Kotler, founder of Parallax Press, and Therese Fitzgerald, retreat coordinator for Plum Village Summer Retreats and Thây's United States tours

Becoming Whole in Plum Village

Svein Myreng, True Door, lives in Oslo, Norway, with his wife Eevi Beck, True Compassionate Action, and their son, Kyrre. Svein was ordained a Dharma teacher in 1994 and practices with the Sangha of Floating Clouds in Oslo. He has written two books: Plum Poems *and* A Handbook of Meditation, *and translated two of Thây's books into Norwegian.*

In 1987, when I was still a young, eager student of Japanese Rinzai Zen, Thich Nhat Hanh visited Norway. Though it is hard to believe now, the five-day retreat had to be canceled because too few people signed up for it. Instead, the Vietnamese Buddhists in Norway stepped in and organized a Rose Festival, a public talk, and a day of mindfulness. Thây was accompanied by Sister Phuong, who still had her long, flowing hair.

Thây's public events in Norway were successful. After the Day of Mindfulness, a friend said, "It is amazing how the Vietnamese, who have suffered so much, can teach us so much about happiness."

I was a firm believer in "struggling for enlightenment" at the time and was rather shocked by Thây's teaching, "Do you have to make an effort to enjoy the blue sky? No, you just enjoy it." Still, his words, and even more his being, sowed some seeds in me, and in the summer of 1989, a friend and I set course for Plum Village.

In Ste. Foy, we were picked up by two smiling Vietnamese gentlemen in an old, battered car and were placed among gas flasks and lettuce boxes for the final part of the journey. The weather was hot — one of the worst heat waves in decades struck southern France that summer. The stone houses were low and irregular, with fascinating beams and rocks to rest your gaze upon. Flowers and bamboo rested peacefully next to grass and weeds. A few people worked cheerfully emptying a ditch where the sewage had been clogged. The relaxed beauty and friendliness of Plum Village was different from anything I had met before.

We got rooms in Lower Hamlet, with many Vietnamese families, a few Westerners, and a young man from India, Shantum Seth. Compared with today, we were few, maybe fifty people. Sister Chân Không and Sister Annabel were there, and two other nuns. The rest were laypeople, permanent residents or visitors for the summer. In the Upper Hamlet, Arnie Kotler and Therese Fitzgerald led the practice of a group of Westerners. Apart from Thây, the only resident monk was Thây Giac Thanh.

In the Lower Hamlet, we enjoyed the atmosphere, a mixture of family gathering and summer camp. We spoke half in awe and half jokingly about the "serious practice" that we believed was going on in Upper Hamlet. Yet, it was actually the relaxed family atmosphere that was healing for me. The kindness of the elderly Vietnamese ladies was great. After I was briefly hospitalized during the retreat, they supported me in gentle, unassuming ways, bringing bowls of delicious desserts.

In 1989, Plum Village was just at the beginning of the expansion that would continue to this today. At that time, the big meditation halls had not yet been built. Thây gave his Dharma talks outdoors, under the linden tree in the Upper Hamlet. I felt I had been transported to the time of the Buddha, as Thây talked about the Four Noble Truths and the Four Establishments of Mindfulness. The Plum Village mixture of mindfulness and a loving atmosphere made possible a deep healing. Returning to Plum Village again and again in the following years, I knew I had found a new home.

During the autumn of 1991, I spent two months in Plum Village, living in the Upper Hamlet with four monks, five laymen, and Sister Annabel, who was then head of practice. A beautiful autumn with ripe figs and plums changed into a cold, wet period. Icy winds crept through the cracks and holes in the walls of the meditation hall; the kitchen was the only warm place. Thây was absent much of the time due to illness and travel, but just practicing with the Sangha was nourishing — and challenging — enough.

Almost every day, the residents played volleyball. At first, I stayed away, feeling sad. Growing up with a congenital heart disease, I had sad memories from sports activities at school. Either I could not take part, or my lack of aptitude and strength made me feel a failure. The

Plum Village jogging meditation also reinforced this feeling. Then, one day during walking meditation, I suddenly remembered a dream from the night before. In the dream, a young Sangha friend asked me, half incredulously, "You mean you can't even run?" In the next moment, a different image flashed into my mind. A little boy — me — was out of breath and felt helpless and full of sorrow. Immediately I saw how I had tried to restrain my breath, not wanting ever to appear out of breath — pushing away my heart disease and myself. Seeing this little boy with a lot of compassion, something shifted in me. A new freedom appeared. That day, I started playing volleyball and enjoyed fumbling around.

A few days later, Thây — who had been away traveling — came back to Plum Village. I had written a letter to him, telling him about my life and practice. During the evening meal I heard him ask one of the monks, "So now Svein is playing volleyball?" Cutting through the other things I had written, Thây focused on the most important part — and let me know that he had truly seen me.

As the years have passed, the feeling that Plum Village is my home has deepened. We have both changed, the Village and I, but we belong to each other. In Plum Village, I received the Five and the Fourteen Mindfulness Trainings and was ordained as a Dharma teacher. In Plum Village, my beloved Eevi and I were married by Thây and the whole Sangha in a beautiful ceremony. When Eevi was pregnant, we spent Christmas vacation among caring friends in Plum Village; and, as soon as our dear son Kyrre was two, we brought him to the place we hope will be a beloved part of his childhood.

My life has been deeply touched by Thây, the Sangha, and Plum Village, not because it has been perfect — rather because it has been imperfect, and in this imperfection there is room for great love and wisdom. Through Plum Village, we have made so many good friends from various parts of the world. In Plum Village, we continue to learn and gather new insight into the endless, joyful path.

Celebration

(For the ten-year anniversary of Plum Village, 1992)

I want to celebrate chaos.
I want to celebrate old worn-out cars,
Broken tiles, ever-shifting
Schedules, misplaced letters,
And nettles next to flower-beds;
To celebrate toilets out of order,
As well as friends who will remind me
That mistakes are good, failures a success,
And that a pure heart *may* prevail
In the non-end.
I want to celebrate being left alone,
Or assailed by talkers
(Or, disturbing others' quiet).
I want to celebrate gentle smiles,
Good intentions, and, *especially,*
One step after the other.
"If arrow number 100 hits the target,
How can you say the first 99 were failures?"

—From *Plum Poems,* Parallax Press, 1999

Coming Home

Sister Trung Chinh, Correct Faithfulness, is from Vietnam and lived in Australia before moving to Plum Village in 1994. She was installed as Abbess of the New Hamlet in 1997. She is currently Abbess of Clarity Hamlet in Deer Park.

The things I remember most about my first contact with Plum Village are the method of practice and the way the brothers and sisters practiced mindfulness in every aspect of their lives. Although new to it, I felt immediately at ease. I had lived in other temples, but in Plum Village the Sangha was so harmonious that I felt already part of it even though I had only just arrived.

During the Dharma discussions, I was so moved by the participation of the non-Vietnamese practitioners that tears kept flowing down my cheeks. The whole environment was, to me, a dream come true, a place where I could take refuge, an opportunity that I had longed for all my life.

Much has changed since I first arrived. The Sangha is growing and now we have three separate hamlets. But I miss the simple things of the early years. I remember we used wood-burning stoves for heating in the winter. I liked it very much and still do. When the wood burned, it emanated a fragrant smell and radiated a warmth that I cannot find in a gas or electric heater. The secret of keeping continuous warmth in the stove is to maintain a good supply of wood in it, so before going to bed, a large log was placed in the stove, then in

I Have Arrived, I am Home

I have arrived. I am home,
In the here and in the now.
I have arrived. I am home,
In the here and in the now.
I am solid. I am free.
I am solid. I am free.
In the ultimate I dwell.
In the ultimate I dwell.

I Have Arrived, I Am Home

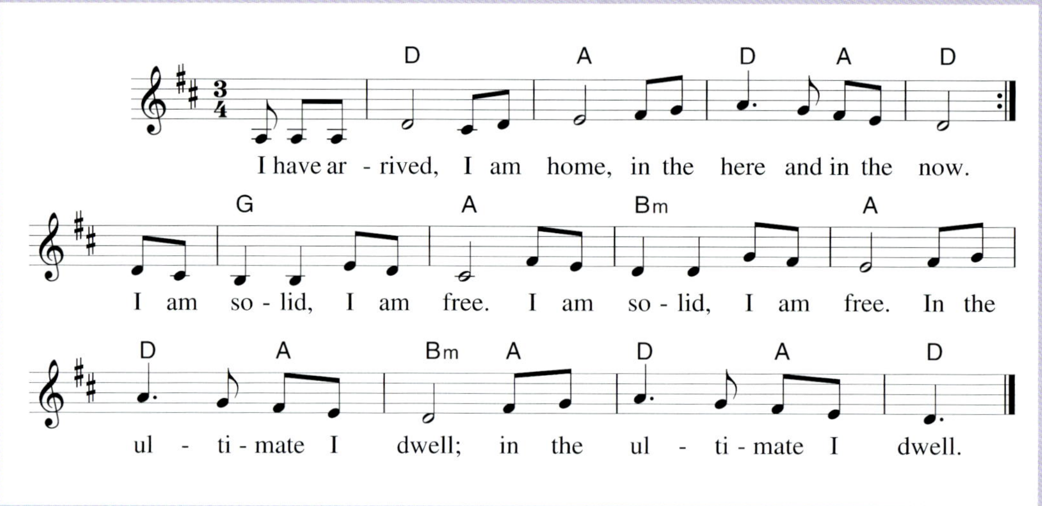

Je Suis Chez Moi, Je Suis Arrivé

the early morning, before sitting meditation, some more wood was added to keep the fire alive. Now, all the wood-burning stoves have been replaced with gas ones — another footprint of impermanence.

I remember the festival days. Each of them had its own unique character, helping participants touch their spiritual tradition. The Christmas ceremony was a surprise for me. Coming from a Buddhist tradition, I was somewhat reserved about celebrating it. However, Thây had a way of bringing out the best of the true spirit of Christmas. He has shown us that Buddha and Christ are really two brothers. The participants were so grateful for his insights. Then came the Vietnamese Tet celebration. Living abroad, we missed our traditional family celebration atmosphere. The brothers and sisters of Plum Village helped us relive the Tet we used to know. The days I have spent at Plum Village have nurtured my mind and body by allowing me to take refuge in the Sangha. They have also helped me to see the path clearly on my journey of emancipation and of helping others on their way.

The lyrics of the song, "I have arrived. I am home. I am solid. I am free," seem like they are a part of me that I had forgotten. The day before my first Summer Opening, Thây came to the Lower Hamlet for a tea ceremony. After everyone shared their stories, Thây turned to me and asked, "You have known Plum Village for over ten years, why has it taken you so long to come home?"

Shantum Seth

Pilgrimage to India: In the Footsteps of the Buddha

Shantum Seth, Satya Marg (True Path), is Indian and has been leading pilgrimages to sites of the Buddha's life since 1988. He spent one year in the Upper Hamlet with his wife, Gitanjali, and their daughter, Nandini, much to the delight of the Plum Village community. He was ordained a Dharma teacher in 2001.

A Path of Peace

I met Thich Nhat Hanh for the first time at a retreat in California at the Ojai Foundation in 1987. Being active in the peace movement, I used to get angry and frustrated and found I was fighting for peace, not being peace, not creating peace. I was searching for a teacher and a path of peace and had been looking in India, England, and was now in the United States. Thây reminded me of Mahatma Gandhi, of someone who practiced what he preached. And he helped me feel compassion even for those who I felt were the perpetrators of injustice, terror, and violence.

I resonated on a philosophical and practical level with what he was teaching. I was born as a Hindu, and on a philosophical level I had always had difficulties with the stratification of castes and the concept of soul. On a practical level, I liked being slow, touching, seeing, feeling, and living in the present moment. Thây helped me touch the magic of the present moment and shared a path that I could understand and practice — a practice that has brought me happiness in my everyday life. As Thây left Ojai, he said, "Help bring Buddhism back to India." I went back to India feeling I had met someone who could guide me.

Arriving at the Bodhi Tree

Thây had finished writing *Old Path White Clouds* (a biography of the Buddha) and wanted to come to India. Sister Phuong, a longtime student of Thây, telephoned me and said they were planning to come to India with about thirty people from nine different countries. She asked if I would help organize their pilgrimage, and I readily agreed. Thây had been to India before, so he knew all the places he wanted to go and also suggested the number of days he would like to spend at each place. He was keen to start at the Deer Park in Sarnath, where the Buddha had given his first teachings. It was a journey of nearly forty days.

It was fourteen years ago that we undertook this pilgrimage, yet some of the aspects of the journey are vivid in my mind's eye. The day after Thây and the group arrived in India, we went to my parents' house in Delhi, where we had a reception for them. My sister, Aradhana, joined us for the pilgrimage and helped in co-organizing it, while my brother, Vikram, decided to join us for the first part. The next day, we took a train to Varanasi and proceeded to Sarnath, ten kilometers away. At Deer Park, as we became more mindful of our steps, we realized that we were, literally, walking in the footsteps of the Buddha. It was wonderful. Thây gave teachings on the Four Noble Truths, the Eightfold Path, and the Middle Way, as the Buddha had done 2,600 years before.

Visiting a school in Uruvela village

After a few days, we took a coach ride to Bodhgaya, where we stayed at a newly built Vietnamese temple. Every day we would go and sit in meditation under the large, ancient Bodhi tree and walk mindfully around the Mahabodhi Temple adjoining it. Thây would tell us stories of the Buddha's life. The knowledge that this tree, more than a century old, was the descendant of the tree under which the Buddha had sat on the night of his enlightenment gave us a deeper sense of arrival and the realization that the Bodhi tree is our spiritual ancestor too. We saw that pilgrims from various countries all blended together, expressing their gratitude and devotion in their own unique forms of practice. Some doing thousands of prostrations, some repetitive chanting, some silently meditating, some lighting oil lamps and candles, some circumambulating around the temple, some reading texts, and some offering money, flowers, incense, fruit, grains, and cloth.

Tea Meditation in Uruvela

A Tea Meditation with the Uruvela Children

One day, Thây suggested that we organize a Tea Meditation for the children in the village of Uruvela (now known as Bakrour) which is across the river from Bodhgaya. This is where Sujata and Svasti, two children who helped the Buddha, used to live. I met two young people, Munni, a girl of about thirteen, and Rajesh, a boy of about eleven, the present-day Sujata and Svasti, and asked them to get all the children of the village together. Aradhana and I spent a lot of the day with them organizing the gathering. Many of the local people thought that getting all these children together was a bad idea because when foreigners come they usually begin begging and misbehaving.

By evening we were all gathered together, about seventy children and thirty of us, interspersed in a big circle. Thây told them the story of Sujata, the girl who gave the Buddha rice pudding and saved him from dying of starvation, and of Svasti, the "untouchable" buffalo boy who gave the Buddha *kusa* grass to make a cushion to sit on. The young people listened attentively to the story of their ancestors, and later, when we had mango juice meditation, they were all playful yet caring of each other. The spell of mindfulness had fallen over the whole circle.

The Story of Sujata

When Sujata brought Siddhartha's food that noon, she found him sitting beneath the pippala tree as beautiful as a young morning. His face and body radiated peace, joy, and equanimity. She had seen him sitting solemnly and majestically beneath the pippala tree over a hundred times, and yet today there was something different about him. Looking at Siddhartha, Sujata felt all her sorrows and worries vanish. Happiness as fresh as a spring breeze filled her heart. She felt there was nothing else she needed or wanted on this Earth and that no one needed to worry or despair anymore. Sujata took a few steps forward and placed the food before Siddhartha. She bowed before him. She felt the peace and joy within Siddhartha enter herself.

When he finished eating, Siddhartha asked Sujata to return home. He wanted to meet with the village children that afternoon.

Many children came, including Svasti's brothers and sisters. The boys had all bathed and put on clean clothes. The girls wore their loveliest saris. Sujata's sari was ivory colored, Nandabala wore a sari the color of banana shoots, and Bhima's sari was pink. The children, looking as fresh and colorful as flowers, sat around Siddhartha beneath the pippala tree.

Siddhartha said, "Children, living in awareness means to live in the present moment. One is aware of what is taking place within one's self and in one's surroundings. One is in direct contact with life. If one continues to live in such a way, one will be able to deeply understand one's self and one's surroundings. Understanding leads to tolerance and love. When all beings understand one another, they will accept and love one another. Then there will not be much suffering in the world.

Love is possible only when there is understanding. And only with love can there be acceptance. Practice living in awareness, children, and you will deepen your understanding. You will be able to understand yourselves, other people, and all things. And you will have hearts of love. That is the wonderful path I have discovered.

— adapted from *Old Path White Clouds*

Many of the children didn't know the story of Sujata and Svasti, though they lived in the same village. They really liked it.

Munni got married the next year and moved to another village, and we still meet occasionally. Rajesh is still there and has become a close friend. He lives with his mother, wife, and three children in half a small hut he has built. The other half is the shelter for the cow. Ever since then, each time I organize a pilgrimage on the Buddha's path, we visit Rajesh and his family. We have tea and cookies at his mud hut. It's a nice continuation from the time of our visit with Thầy.

A few days later, we waded across the Neranjara River to Dungasiri Mountain and the cave where the Buddha practiced harsh austerities before coming down to the Bodhi tree. Sitting quietly in the warm cave, we could visualize the strong intention and concentration of the Buddha-to-be. As we walked back across the river, facing the setting sun, our feet glided gently under the water. It was wonderful walking lightly, walking as a Sangha.

On Vulture Peak

Following our visit to Dungasiri Mountain, we took the road to Rajgir, which used to be the capital of the powerful Magadha kingdom at the time of the Buddha. We drove past the Gaya Shisha, Elephant Head Mountain, where the Buddha had given his famous fire sermon to a thousand recently ordained monks who had been cult worshipers of fire. As we drove into the area enclosed by the five hills that provided a natural fortification for Rajgir, we could see the path leading up to the Buddha's favorite meditation place, Gridhakuta — Vulture Peak.

Thầy watching the sunrise on Vulture Peak

Shantum and his wife, Gitanjali, planting cypress trees in China

Thây loves Vulture Peak, and so we visited it every day for the five days that we were there. Sometimes we would spend the whole day there, sitting around the peak with Thây and the Sangha, watching the sun rise and set the same way the Buddha did. This allowed us to see through our Buddha eyes. When we walked in mindfulness up the slopes of Vulture Peak, on the very road that King Bimbisara had built at the time of the Buddha, we realized that we were walking on exactly the same path that the Buddha used to walk every day, and that his feet were our feet.

The hills are forested, and there are families of rather well-behaved, black-faced langur monkeys who swing from tree to tree with their long tails following them. As we sat picnicking on the side of the mountain, they would watch us from a safe distance, enjoying the spectacle. It was fun just being there, sitting in caves where the Venerable Ananda and Shariputra used to take shelter, watching the birds and our breath, and reciting the *Heart Sutra* on the spot where this sutra was supposedly first delivered.

One morning we were told that there was to be an ordination ceremony the next day, so we all dressed up in our best clothes to go up the mountain. We reached Vulture Peak before sunrise, and in the first light of dawn the *bhikshuni*[7] ordination ceremony of Sisters Phuong and Annabel started. It was a very moving ceremony. As their heads were shaved, they were given the names Sister Chân Không, True Emptiness, and Sister Chân Duc, True Virtue. Nine years later, when Thây visited Vulture Peak again, all the monastics wanted to get their heads shaved there as a way of continuing this sacred act and starting a Plum Village tradition.

It was a beautiful morning; and, after the bhikshuni ceremonies, Thanh Minh was initiated as a novice and given the name Sister Chân Vi, True Taste. Five people received the Fourteen Mindfulness Trainings, including Arnie and Therese, from the United States, and Khanh and Mai, from Australia. And five pilgrims (including me) received the Five Mindfulness Trainings.

From Kushinagar to Lumbini

We took a long bus journey to Kushinagar, where the Buddha passed away. On the day of the full moon, Thây gave a talk on birth and death. We sat by the six-meter statue of the Buddha reclining in the same position as the Buddha had been, between twin Saal trees, watching the sunset when he left his bodily form. His last words resonated in us: "All conditioned reality is subject to decay. Strive on diligently."

The *stupa* built on the site where the Buddha was cremated sits in a peaceful park a couple of kilometers from where the Buddha lay down. Circumambulating the stupa, I felt I touched the truth that there is no beginning and no end, no birth and no death.

We proceeded across the border of Nepal to Lumbini, the birthplace of the Buddha. Thây told us the story of the birth of the Buddha, how his mother, Maha Maya, was traveling to her parental home and, en route, delivered the baby boy in a pleasure garden full of Sita Ashok trees. The way Thây told the story it was possible to see the whole event unfolding before our eyes. Thây also emphasized how important the birth of every child is and that, if the conditions are right, a Buddha will manifest.

We met a number of Shakyans, who are from the same tribe as the Buddha, and when Thây suggested to one of them that the Buddha may have looked like him, he recoiled in shock saying that the Buddha was a God and he was only a human being! As we visited the temple nearby, we met the only monk who lived in Lumbini at the time, Bhikshu Vimalananda, and he happened to be a Sakyan too. He presented Thây a robe and a bowl. Thây gave me the robe. I understood the message, but gave it back to him about eight years ago, at which time I knew that I didn't want to be a monk. I felt that much of the suffering people face is due to relationships and livelihood, and so, to really understand the difficulties, pain, and attachments of most people, I should share their experience as a layperson. If I can overcome the difficulties myself and am able to lead a contented life and taste the nectar of liberation, then I shall truly be able to help others. That same night we headed towards Sravasti.

The Jeta Grove

The Buddha spent twenty-four of his rain retreats in Sravasti, mainly in the beautiful Jeta Grove that had been given to him by the merchant Anathapindika and Prince Jeta. So many of the teachings of the Buddha were given here, including the *Anapanasati Sutra* on the full awareness of breathing. We also visited the Angulimala Stupa, in remembrance of the highway killer from the Buddha's time who became an example of nonviolence after becoming a monk. As the pilgrimage was ending, we sat on the spot where the Buddha's hut, Gandhakuti, was in the Jeta Grove and had a closing ceremony. Each one of us shared some of the deeper realizations we had gleaned on the pilgrimage in the form of an insight poem.

Finally, after a visit to the Ajanta caves, Thây led a retreat near Pune for social workers who were working with Dalits, people who have converted to Buddhism due to the stigma of untouchability. Thây felt it was a good way to give back something to India, as he and the Sangha had gained so much from the pilgrimage.

Seeing the Buddha in the Here and Now

I learned a great deal from traveling with Thây. By the end of the trip, I realized that Thây was my teacher. I had found someone who could help me, who could be my guide. Thây really enjoys himself. He is very free. He absolutely loves the Buddha. He knows him very well, like a friend. I saw that, in making many of his decisions, he refers back to what the Buddha would have done.

With Thay it is not only the historical Buddha that comes alive, but the Buddha in the present time. We meet the people the Buddha met, like the young buffalo boy, Svasti, and the young girl, Sujata. Suddenly, we start to see the Buddha in India now. We realize that he crossed this river. It's still here. Thây helps us see the Buddha not just as a historical character. We see him here, now. The most important thing Thây transmitted is that the Buddha is not someone outside of us. He is part of us. All of us have Buddha nature. Once we've sat under the Bodhi tree, every tree becomes the Bodhi tree. Thây really looks with Buddha eyes.

I also learned from Thây's non-discriminating nature. He does not seem to have a bit of a bias. Although he prefers a simpler life, he's very compassionate to everyone he meets, rich or poor. He's also very politically suave. Whether he meets a high official or a street sweeper, he knows how to deal with them in the right way, a very nice way. Whether he meets the president, or a mother, or a boatman, Thây offers dignity to everyone.

At the end of the trip, Thây suggested that I organize and offer this trip every year. Thây saw that this was work that suited me, and it would combine both service and practice. Since that time, I have enjoyed taking pilgrims each year on a traveling retreat in the pleasant winter months of the Buddha land.

People are More Peaceful Now: Interview with Jean-Pierre D'allanesse

by Sister Chau Nghiem and Sister Bi Nghiem

Jean-Pierre D'allanesse is a Plum Village neighbor. He was born and raised in Loubes-Bernac, one kilometer from the Lower Hamlet. After a career as a musician, he became a sculptor and returned to Loubes-Bernac in 1992. He lives with his partner, Clodie.

How did you feel when you heard about Plum Village?
I've been interested in Buddhism since the age of twenty. I was surprised to find out a Buddhist monastery was established here in Loubes-Bernac. It is really unexpected. Nobody could have imagined that this farm would one day become a Buddhist monastery.

I visited Plum Village for the first time two or three years ago. It was during the Open House Day, when neighbors are invited to spend the day. Since then I have come a couple of times — when we were invited or when I went for a walk. When I walk near the monastery, I go to see the lotuses. Sometimes I talk to someone I know. We have been to two Dharma talks. I am very interested in the wisdom of the master. The Dharma talks were a very deep experience, so deep that I'm planning to follow more diligently the master's teachings and go more often to listen.

Who lived on that land before it became the Lower Hamlet of Plum Village?
It was the farm of the Mesclauts family. I still meet Mr. Mesclauts from time to time. I remember I once had a meal in that farm, and I used to visit them often. We were very close. We would buy products from their farm. When Mrs. Mesclauts passed away, Mr. Mesclauts sold his land.

It is a wonderful story of how this farm became a monastery. It's very rare and a great opportunity for this area. Since the monastery was established, I have the feeling that there is a kind of aura on the whole area, an aura that did not exist before. I was born and raised here; and, since Plum Village is here, I feel something has changed, something you can only feel. I can feel it very clearly. I have the feeling people are more peaceful. Something has happened in the direction of good, something for the better.

What is the response to Plum Village in Loubes-Bernac?
Some people are suspicious and will suspect all that is different. This is where intolerance comes from. Some people say, "Plum Village is a cult. They take drugs." I've faced that intolerance too. When you're an artist, instead of a farmer or a mason, you become a little suspect. People wonder, "How does he earn his living?" It's inevitable in the countryside. It is true that in France, with all the problems linked to cults, people have the tendency to be defensive. Most of the time, they don't even try to understand, they just judge. It's a pity. It is important to help other people understand, as you have done at Plum Village, inviting people to come and visit for Open House Day. This is the most beautiful thing you can do. It clears up wrong perceptions about the community. People come see for themselves that this is no more a sect than Christians, Protestants, Jains, or Sufis. I know some people who were gossiping, making mean comments, and who little by little participated in the Open House Days. It made me happy. I said to myself, "At least they understand they haven't understood." For my part, whenever people would ask me anything about it, I have always said that it can only be for the good of everybody.

Why?
Because it promotes the spirit of tolerance. In the end, people become more tolerant, or at least less intolerant. I think that you share your practice with a lot of intelligence and discretion. Opening your doors shows that you have nothing to hide.

What was your reaction when you first came to the Lower Hamlet?
There was no problem. I've seen some documentaries about this kind of environment, a Buddhist environment with bells, so I wasn't disconcerted. On the contrary, I was comforted by the simplicity. In some places, there are so many idols and things like that — it looks like Disneyland or a marketplace. Here was a kind of integration between the community and the place, between the farm and what it is now. There is a continuation. Everything is harmonious. Even with the small lodges on the hill in Thénac (Upper Hamlet), they preserved the harmony. As an artist, I look at things with a critical eye of course. Everything is in harmony with nature and very simple. It reflects perfectly Buddhist thought.

Did you ever meet any Buddhist teachers before?
Only through books, but I've never been able to relate to a master the way I do with Thich Nhat Hanh. I will always remember the day I was there for a talk, and he made fun of Descartes. I really enjoyed when he said, "I think. Therefore I am not." It was so clear and disconcerting. As Westerners, we are used to speculating, but to speak that way was very powerful. And there was a general reaction from the audience. I thought to myself that someone who can say things like that is not just anyone, but a very rare person.

The way Zen Buddhism is explained in Thich Nhat Hanh's book is something very strong and very clear. Everyone can understand this teaching. This is what I like about the master, his logic, like the philosophers of ancient times. It's comforting. They do not try to throw you into sophisticated reflections. Everything is very clear and simple. This gave me a strong faith in his teachings.

In one question and answer session I attended, I remember a young man who cried because he wanted to help homeless people, but he didn't know what to do. The answer was so intelligent. Thây said that he could give a shelter to someone only if he had a house himself. Without a house, he could not offer shelter to anyone. It was so clear that this young man had to build his own house, and only then could he offer shelter to others. And Thây helped him to understand that his house wasn't built yet. It was a great moment.

Drawings of the countryside around Plum Village by Sister Tue Nghiem

Bouquet of Memories
Lawrence Ballon

Predawn shadows walk to Transformation Hall
To dip life giving waters from the well of emptiness.

Sisters arrive for the daffodil festival.
Faces radiant like candles floating on the empty river.
Eyes smile and joy dances between sister and brother.

Thây sitting amidst the daffodils,
Surrounded by sisters and brothers
With children at his side.
Songs serenade the delicate yellow flowers
Which have greeted hundreds of springs.
Now offering hope and a home
To a people far from their native land.

Encountering Thây Nhat Hanh's spirit seems like
Walking into a vast mountain range
With high peaks and deep broad valleys.
Fruit trees spread across the foothills,
Flowers teach joy in nature's garden.

Coming down from the mountain
Dances a beautiful gentle stream called Thây Giac Thanh.
Turning into Quan Yin's waterfall, smiling as he
Travels down the mountain offering nourishment
To those living on the slopes and in the valleys,
Filling hearts with peace and joy.

Bells sound,
Returning the Sangha to their breath,
Awakening lotus blossoms in their hearts
As spring sun awakens
Daffodils on the hillside.

I celebrate the tree
To which the bud of my life is attached.
I feel like a blossom on a spring branch,
As the radiance of the Dharma
And the warmth of the Sangha unfold my petals.

Empty Sky
Rolf Hoffmeister

A full moon is cruising across an empty sky.
Seeing full is also empty and moon also sky
Our mind is free and our ignorance dies.

Voices of Vietnam

Verses from *Enjoying the Dharma while Living in the World of Dust* by Bamboo Forest Master

After the 10,000 actions have calmed down, our nature will be peace and relaxation.
You only need to practice half a day in order to be free in body and mind.

When the source of craving and attachment has dried up, you do not have any longing for jewels, money, and valuable things.
When speculation about right and wrong is silenced, you have ample opportunity to listen to the birds' singing.

Drawing by Nguyen Thi Hop from *Hermitage Among the Clouds*, by Thich Nhat Hanh

Lessons from the Patriarchs: Master Tang Hôi and Bamboo Forest Master

Sister Annabel Laity, or Chân Duc, True Virtue, was ordained in 1988 and became a Dharma teacher in 1990. She is Abbess of the Green Mountain Dharma Center in Vermont.

Master Tang Hôi is revered by Vietnamese Buddhists as the first patriarch of the Vietnamese Meditation school. He was born around the first decade of the third century C.E., and his practice and teachings were based on both the Mahayana and Theravada traditions. He went to southern China in 247 C.E. and established a practice center known as the First Temple. He endured a great deal of persecution from the king and his son there, but because of his strong practice he was able to persevere. His teachings had a far-reaching effect, and they are still applicable to practitioners today. To learn more about him, see *Master Tang Hôi* by Thich Nhat Hanh.

When I think about Master Tang Hôi's interaction with kings and ministers, I remember when Thây and a delegation from Plum Village went to India. Thây had a private meeting with the leader of the Parliament; and, as a result, a Committee for Ethics in the Parliament was set up. During two visits to China, Thây talked to the minister of religious and cultural affairs, and that minister spent time in Plum Village. After Thây's latest visit to Beijing, in October 2001, the minister exclaimed, "How clever Thây is!" This is true, but there is much more than cleverness in what Thây says. When Thây praises Buddhism and the role of Chinese Buddhism in the world, you can feel compassion. It is diplomacy, but a diplomacy that is full of compassion. During the previous visit, in May 1999, our delegation arrived in China at a difficult time. There were several North American monks and nuns in that delegation, and many North American laypeople. As we walked into the minister's reception room, we could feel tension in the air. The minister began his address by saying that the day before he had gone to the airport in Beijing to receive the corpses of the embassy officials who had been killed when the Chinese embassy in Belgrade was bombed by United States bombers. He apologized that, as a result, he was not at his best to welcome us. Thây began speaking by saying, "I know exactly how you feel. I too have experienced times when my friends have been killed." At once the atmosphere in the room calmed down.

Drawing of meditation master Tang Hôi, the First Patriarch of Vietnamese Buddhism

In the Ly dynasty in Vietnam, high monks would represent the king and the ministers receiving ambassadors, and I see how Thây continues that work. Of course, skilled diplomacy is part of what is needed; but, when a monk talks with an ambassador, it is not just to negotiate for his own country. A monk cares for everyone and every country and speaks out of compassion for everyone, so it is a special kind of diplomacy.

I have always felt very close to Master Tang Hôi, because he practiced in such a simple way the sixteen breathing exercises of the *Anapanasati Sutta.* Conscious breathing was the basis for the concentration and insight he acquired. His bodhisattva ideal enabled him to give up all worldly comforts, and his motherland, in order to go to a place where Buddhism was unknown.

Although Plum Village has not needed to undergo the tremendous difficulties that Master Tang Hôi underwent in setting up his meditation center in Namjing, it has been a pioneer Buddhist center in France. What enabled Master Tang Hôi to bring the practice to the kingdom of Wu was that he spoke Chinese and was accomplished in his understanding of the Confucian and Taoist scriptures. At Christmas and Easter, in Plum Village, Thây always teaches practices that are derived from both Christian and Buddhist concepts. Plum Village has also had the occasion to celebrate Jewish festivals, such as Shabbat and Yom Kippur, when practitioners of Jewish roots have been present. In China, Master Tang Hôi transmitted the Five Mindfulness Trainings to King Ngo Ton Quyen, a rather cruel and violent ruler. After the king received the trainings, no doubt many of his ministers in the Wu Kingdom must have followed him, and his subjects enjoyed a more compassionate rule. In the same way, we strongly emphasize the practice of the Mindfulness Trainings in Plum Village.

In Plum Village, we have a portrait of Master Tang Hôi displayed for all to see. Actually, that portrait is not based on the physical body of Master Tang Hôi, since it was made by a painter in our own time. Whenever I see it, it reminds me of the qualities of Master Tang Hôi and inspires me in my practice, helping me to keep my *bodhicitta* alive. Master Tang Hôi must have undergone so many hardships with joy and equanimity; he was even threatened with the death penalty at one time. He gave teachings to kings and ministers who were not Buddhist and managed to influence them. In order to do this, he could not have been caught in Buddhist doctrine and must have practiced, as we do, with the first of the Fourteen Mindfulness Trainings.[8]

In a gatha praising his virtues, he was said to have been silent and alone. I understand this to mean that, when he was not speaking the Dharma, he did not speak, and he knew the better way to live alone — how to take refuge in himself — which we are taught in Plum Village.

The first patriarch of the Bamboo Forest School was King Nhan Tong. Known as Bamboo Forest Master, he was born in 1258 in Dai Viet, which is early Vietnam. When I first read his poem "Climbing Mount Bao Dai," I was moved to tears.

The scenery is so deeply silent it makes the moss seem very old.
Spring has come but the colors are not yet too bright.
In the distance and nearby clouds gather around the mountain.
The flowering trees give shade to the path.
Everything is like water pouring into water
For our whole lifetime mind makes known the mind
Leaning on the veranda rail, raising the flute to my lips
My heart's universe is brimming with the bright moon.

Bamboo Forest Master was a king until he was forty-one years old and then trained himself to become a monk. He was a monk for eight years before his death, touring amongst the laypeople and transmitting the Five Mindfulness Trainings and the Ten Wholesome Trainings that resemble the Fourteen Mindfulness Trainings.[9]

He lived very simply and wore an old, faded brown robe. Like the Buddha before him, he traveled everywhere on foot, doing walking meditation. Bamboo Forest Buddhism is engaged Buddhism, being in the world and helping others. This practice is continued today by Bamboo Forest Master's spiritual descendants around the world.

Following are the first four lines of his practice poem, "Enjoying the practice as we are engaged in the world":

To enjoy the practice when engaged in the world
You need to adapt to circumstances
When you are hungry you eat, when sleepy you sleep.
If your home is full of precious jewels, do not run
after them somewhere else.

If you keep your mind free when the object presents itself
Then you do not have to search for meditation.

Plum Village practice is not caught in the outer form of appearances and is always adaptable. Thầy warns us that concerning ourselves only with the outer form of the practice is a trap, and we can deceive ourselves. When we are in Plum Village, the practice has to be interesting, enjoyable, and nourishing. If it is not, we are not practicing correctly. In Plum Village, we are always practicing to experience the precious jewels we already have rather than to run after something that is not yet available. The Pure Land is full of

Ceremony to install the Ancestor Tablet for Master Tang Hôi in Upper Hamlet's new Ancestor's Hall, Summer 2002[10]

Top: Formal procession to the Ancestor's hall
Center: Brother Phap Nhuan holds the ancestor's lamp and candles
Bottom: Brother Trung Hai plays the drum

precious jewels. There, the trees are jewels, the paths are jewels, and the surrounding walls are jewels. When I wrote the song "Breathe and You Know That You Are Alive," I used the teaching of Bamboo Forest Master, "Breathe and all you touch is new and real." Bamboo Forest Master had said to his disciples that whenever he picked something up it was new.

In the same poem, Bamboo Forest Master teaches:

As long as the mind is not busy,
You do not need any other practice.

Bamboo Forest Master means that our own mind has a tendency to be busy organizing, administering. In Plum Village, we do our best not to be busy and to release our mind so that it can be in touch with all the wonderful things around us. Plum Village is a Pure Land that should not be polluted by preoccupation with worldly activities. When we are walking, our mind is not busy with some project we wish to realize, because we are walking as a free person. Walking meditation does not become an outer form repeated day in and day out. It is a time of newness, where insight can truly be possible. Just because I practiced walking meditation yesterday, does not mean that it is the same today. It is the same in the sense that I am making steps and breathing, and I am truly present in that moment, but the insight I have, the beauty I experience, the joy I feel is like fresh water from the spring. You may say that the spring is the same but the water is always different.

The Pure Land is the Pure Heart,
Do not keep asking to go to the western direction
Amitabha is the shining silence,
Do you have to struggle to find Sukhavati?[11]

With Bamboo Forest Master's words in my heart, I go out into the garden. Some people say that the New Hamlet lacks space, but space is within yourself and not just outside of you. When I walked out, my mind was free. It is now near the solstice, and at five p.m. the sun is on the horizon; the sky is a tender rose color. There is a light breeze; the slender branches tremble against the blue of the high vault. With that sense of freedom, happiness is possible and the question of birth and death does not make sense anymore. Life is fully present, and nothing else matters. The New Hamlet is the platform of enlightenment.

Breathe and Know that You Are Alive
A Song by Sister Annabel

Breathe and you know that you are alive.
Breathe and you know that all is helping you.
Breathe and you know that you are the world.
Breathe and you know that the flower
is breathing too.
Breathe for yourself and you breathe for the world.
Breathe in compassion and breathe out joy.

Breathe and be one with the air that you breathe.
Breathe and be one with the river that flows.
Breathe and be one with the Earth that you tread.
Breathe and be one with the fire that glows.
Breathe and you break the thought of birth
and death.
Breathe and you see impermanence is life.

Breathe for your joy to be steady and calm.
Breathe for your sorrow to flow away.
Breathe to renew every cell in your blood.
Breathe to renew the depths of consciousness.
Breathe and you dwell in the here and now.
Breathe and all you touch is new and real.

Breathe and Know That You are Alive

Mindful Walking in the Streets of Hue

Thây Thanh Tam, Devoted/Sincere Mind, is from Vietnam. He is a monk and a poet, author of a recently published collection of poems called Blossoming Plums, Ginger Fragrance. *He is presently one of the Directors of Aspirant Training at Tu Hieu Pagoda, in Hue, Vietnam.*

On March 12, 2001, a delegation of monks and aspirants from the Tu Hieu Temple in Hue (the root temple of Plum Village), along with the monks and nuns of Plum Village, organized an excursion around Dong Ba market and the adjacent streets. We were American, Canadian, Spanish, and Vietnamese monastics.

At breakfast, one of the Dharma teachers said, "Our purpose is to touch the hearts of the people of Hue, to introduce everyone to the image of a true monastic, and to give them faith in monks and nuns." We gathered in a circle next to the persimmon tree in the front yard of the temple to share the purpose of this trip. Thây Phap Hien reminded us that, "Our walking is a live Dharma talk. We are "walking just to walk, not to arrive anywhere."

We took a taxi to the National School and started from there. It rained lightly — so beautiful. As we walked along Le Loi Street, everyone scrutinized us, whether Westerners or local Vietnamese, and there were looks of surprise in all their faces. There were two shoeshine boys who followed us for quite a long way. Two students saw the Western monks and said, "Fake Westerners." There were also two laywomen who saw us walking mindfully and followed us, taking pictures continuously until we reached Trang Tien Bridge. Then they left, beaming and very joyful. As we arrived at the foot of the Trang Tien Bridge, we took pictures at the monument of martyrs, beside the radio station of Hue.

We walked in the spirit of a community. We walked focusing only on our mindful breathing and our steps. We took care and protected each other through the "second body" system. This means we cared for the safety, fine manners, and happiness of one person we were assigned to take care of. It also means we protected the well-being and happiness of the whole group.

We crossed the bridge and turned into the Dong Ba market. Buddha's children walked lightly, freely, taking each step slowly in the rhythm of our breathing, not rushing, or hurried — a rare sight in the busy city. The peaceful, comfortable manner of Buddhist monks and nuns surprised Hue's inhabitants, making them joyful and happy. They were very fond of us. One man said to his friend, "Seeing such a sight once, I can now die in peace."

We walked in one line through the narrow street. We moved silently. As we passed by, the business of selling and buying came to a halt. People stopped to look at us. "Where is this beautiful group of monks and nuns from?" they murmured. We just walked and walked, not discussing anything. Sometimes we smiled in friendliness or joined our palms and bowed to lay practitioners who stood with heads bowed and palms joined to greet us.

When they saw the Western monks and nuns, some were surprised and wondered, "Westerners can become monastics?" "Who says Westerners can't become monks and nuns?" "They are so handsome." "Oh, Western nuns are so beautiful." There was ceaseless talking — compliments from all sides. One lay friend said, "Wherever the Buddha is, there are monastics; it is not a matter of East or West."

We turned into Phan Dang Lun Street and came back to Tran Hung Dao Street. Everybody looked at us because this was quite a new image for the year 2001, for the new millennium. In the old time, whenever the king went on an excursion to the countryside, the people were informed in order to welcome the king with parasols, flags, drums, and trumpets to make the occasion very festive. Now, without informing anyone, without lanterns or parasols, we walked lightly and serenely. I thought some people would wake up upon seeing us and question themselves, "How can I walk naturally and lightly like the monks and nuns?" Or, "We bustle here and there, going round and round like a spinning top, from nowhere to nowhere. What is true happiness? Can I really find it in fine food, clothes, and jewelry?" I visualized people gathering around their dining tables for dinner that evening, remembering together what they saw.

At this time of year, Hue is getting cold. Perhaps the images of the brown-robed monastics walking serenely like bodhisattvas through the busyness and noise of daily life would warm up the people's hearts, dissipate the coldness, and help them touch the coming of springtime.

Stopping at Tu Hieu

Heidi Gans and Marc Rothmeyer live in Seattle, Washington. They were on staff during the 2001 Summer Retreat in the Lower Hamlet, where they were married. This article was written in Spring 2001.

In 1999, at a retreat in New York, Thich Nhat Hanh spoke about two elements necessary for meditation. The first element was "stopping," and the second was "deep looking and listening." He taught that we first must stop and calm our bodies and minds. Only then can we nurture the concentration we need for mindful awareness.

For the last three months, we have been traveling in Indonesia and Southeast Asia. We have been moving almost continually. The moment we arrived at Tu Hieu Pagoda, one month ago, we were mesmerized by the calm waters of Half Moon Pond, the trees and gardens shining their glorious light, and the Pagoda tended with care and love. We both knew we had arrived someplace special and knew it was time to stop.

The Sangha was on vacation during our first visit to Tu Hieu, but Thich Tu Hoa welcomed us warmly, introduced us to Master Thich Chi Mau, invited us to share a mindful meal, and encouraged us to enjoy sitting meditation in the Meditation Hall. We asked if foreigners were ever permitted to practice mindfulness at Tu Hieu, and were invited to return at the full moon when the Sangha reconvened.

For the past two weeks, we have bicycled to Tu Hieu each day. We join the Sangha for meditation and chanting each morning, study Buddhism from books the monks have lent to us, eat lunch in mindfulness with the novice monks, practice walking meditation, watch the graceful art of kung fu, and join the Sangha for evening sitting meditation.

The entrance gate and pond of Tu Hieu Temple

Today, every day, the monks dressed in saffron robes eat separately, in silence, in the main dining room. We eat in silence in the kitchen, beside the giggling "baby monks" with their shaved heads and three tufts of hair, symbolizing their novice status. Mountains of white rice serve as the staple (pebbles included), along with sweet tofu, salty greens, delicious giant olives, and sumptuous but homely jackfruit. The monks always insist we eat until we are full, and never forget to offer tea and a "toothstick." Dinner is leftovers from lunch, simple and delicious. We will not forget the women who cooked all day over a wood fire.

The community of monks has been so kind, patient, and gentle with us. They have generously and lovingly shared the Dharma, their presence, and their smiles. Their care and acceptance have been a precious gift. Each monk has been our role model and teacher in mindfulness. Not only the monks at Tu Hieu have been our teachers. Each morning, practitioners from the surrounding area also come to meditate and have shown us deep respect and kindness. This is a true Sangha.

During our stay, we had the honor of speaking with the Venerable Thich Thai Hoa. We asked him for guidance in ways to bring peace and mindfulness into the world of distractions, toxic stimuli, pollution, and busyness. He advised us to look deeply and find the calmness within the bustle of daily life: "Within busyness, there is calmness." He asked us to be aware of calming elements, to embody peace, and to serve as a balance for chaos. In this way, our energy will not be depleted.

This teaching is invaluable to us. In America, speed and busyness are rampant, and it seems calm and peace are increasingly difficult to touch. We hope that our practice can serve as a source of peace in our own country and in the world. The Sangha at Tu Hieu gives us the tools we need and an ideal to strive for.

When we leave Tu Hieu, we will be a Sangha of two, but we will carry the serenity we feel here with us as we travel. When we return to America, we hope to continue our practice and build a Sangha of mindfulness in our own community. In this way, the wisdom and skills that we have learned at Tu Hieu will continue to grow in us and in the world.

Turning into a Buddha

Do Thi Phu, Dharma name Dieu Phuc, is fifty-four years old and lives in Hanoi.

Hanoi, November 11, 2001

Turning into a Buddha
Every morning my heart calms when I go to the temple
The wind blows away my ego-self
What's left is my true self
And the lotus smiles at me.

Dear Thây,
I am a Buddhist practitioner in Hanoi. I first met Thây[12] through *The Miracle of Mindfulness* that I copied with my own hand twenty years ago. I never forgot Thây's teaching on enjoying the tangerine and washing dishes in mindfulness; and, since then, I do not mind washing the dishes.

I attended the retreat at Dinh Quan and Van Tri Temples led by the abbesses Dam Nguyen and Hanh Chau. Their teachings were close to Thây's methods and were very effective for the practitioners. I feel like I have already met Thây through their teaching. I was able to listen to Dharma talks given by the abbesses who studied in Plum Village. I felt like I was going back in time; the two abbesses were the Buddha, and I his disciple. Thây has transmitted wonderful teachings to them, and now they are transmitting them to us.

I understand more deeply my happiness and suffering. I see the causes of my suffering more clearly and am better able to handle it.

Before, every time the phone rang, I used to be upset. But now I really enjoy going back to my breath and feel very lucky that I am alive. I have learned more about my weakness and negative habit energy. It's not easy to see other people's negative habit energy. It is even more difficult to see our own. But, thanks to the Dharma, I vow to understand and transform the causes of my suffering.

I also realized my father really loves me, even though sometimes he does not show it. More and more I live humbly. I smile at my weakness and forgive people for their mistakes. Thây's presence in books and videotapes has helped me transform.

I still have many things to learn, but I feel much happier now. I know there are many brothers and sisters in the Sangha to help me when my problems arise. I am grateful to Thây, to the Dharma, and the Sangha.

Sunlight Sprinkles Gold

Venerable Thây Phuoc Tinh, Pure Merit, is a Dharma teacher at the Quan Am Temple in Dalat, Vietnam. He visited Plum Village in 2001 and 2002, and he has recently joined the Plum Village community. This is a letter to his disciples in Vietnam.

Plum Village, July 28, 2001

Dear brothers and sisters, monastic and lay,
Today is the last day of the Summer Retreat, and I will use this "lazy day" to share with you a few things about *Su Ong*[13] (Venerable Thich Nhat Hanh), and the power of his Dharma talks in watering true happiness in everyone. I hope that my words bring you the warm and sweet energy of Plum Village, so that you will make the vow to take refuge and practice in order to elevate the quality of your life.

I arrived at the Upper Hamlet on the second of July. On the airplane, I could not imagine what Plum Village would be like. I thought I would open my eyes wide to see the road leading to Plum Village and satisfy them with the view, making up for all those years of yearning. What a shame that I fell asleep the moment I got on the van and didn't wake until we arrived!

Even though I have not lived with the Sangha for long, I already feel that the monastic brothers and sisters are lovely. Happy, fresh, and sincere, they are building a powerful community. Even the very young monastics' aspirations are solidly nourished, and their practice of meditation is quite deep. They live, work, and care for one another with the energy of understanding and compassion. If our brothers and sisters in the monasteries in Vietnam can practice deeply to have concern, love, and respect for one another like this, we will form lovely communities of practice. If our lay practitioners do the same, they will empower faith in practitioners from other centers.

On Thây's last teaching tour in Germany, there were seven thousand people attending one public talk. A majority of them came from the Christian tradition. What is important is not the number of people, but their sincere practice and their powerful energy of transformation. With his mindful steps, Su Ong guided a seemingly endless succession of people on a walking meditation. There were silent meals outdoors and Dharma talks in a quiet and peaceful atmosphere. Whether in France, Germany, United States, or England, the same wonderful energy is present.

Dear brothers and sisters, on the afternoon of July fourteenth, I attended the Rose Ceremony held in Vietnamese, organized by the Middle Hamlet. (The other hamlets organized the Rose Ceremony for the Western practitioners.) Everyone seemed to be touched by the calm and solemn atmosphere of the ceremony. After the ceremony, there was Touching the Earth, so that we could reconnect with our cultural traditions and with our blood and spiritual families. I returned to the Upper Hamlet late and watched as the Western practitioners practiced Touching the Earth. They were so solemn and sincere. I was moved looking at them. There were people crying while Touching the Earth. There were people telephoning home to mend the difficulties with their loved ones after this practice of gratitude.

~

Su Ong started writing books when he was very young. His ability to create language is miraculous. He molds it. Then he breathes into it, so it marches to the beat of the present culture. There are words that have become frequently used in Buddhist circles, such as the "Sangha body." To me, these words carry great sounds, because when read out loud, they increase the energy of stability, peace, and freedom in the brothers and sisters who surround and embrace us. What I am most astounded by is the *Plum Village Chanting and Recitation Book*. Su Ong has spent forty years in the West, and through his practice and service, he has received and blended the most beautiful aspects from the Western and Eastern cultures, joining them into one flowing stream. When I witness the Western practitioners participating in activities and chanting in their own language and cultural style, I am both astounded and joyous.

Having sat in the meditation hall to listen to the Dharma talks, I have realized that Su Ong speaks and writes the way he breathes. His writing is light, quiet, deep, and joyful. It is also fluid, natural, and real. Writing is a wonderful reality that Su Ong exhales and allows to manifest on paper. People from everywhere feel this energy from his books and are inspired to practice in order to bring peace to themselves.

Venerable Thây Nhat Tam on the lotus pond in New Hamlet

As Su Ong grows older, his language becomes simpler, gentler, and less academic. The Buddha did not use the language of abstract knowledge, even though he was versed in the *Vedas.* He let his compassion guide his wisdom, in whatever way others could receive and understand most easily, so they could practice it. The great compassion and true wisdom of the enlightened master are present behind the words. You will ask me how enlightened I think Su Ong is. It is a question I will never answer. Instead, I will send you as gifts more books and cassettes of Su Ong's Dharma talks, so that you can feel his capacity to express the wonderful energy of compassion and profound wisdom.

You need to come to Plum Village and have contact with the Sangha in order to witness her powerful energy. You need to be here at the Dharma talks to realize Su Ong's energy of understanding and compassion, and you must meet the Western practitioners to appreciate the joy and happiness truly present in them. The depth of my sharing is too modest.

This afternoon, the sunlight sprinkles gold onto the Upper Hamlet. The young oaks stretch their arms, waving and calling people to Plum Village. Gazing at the sunlight dancing in the oak forest calls up the wonders in my heart. I hope that all of my brothers and sisters practice deeply with your breaths and your steps, so that your own wonders may immediately blossom.

To Be a Monk: A Western Monk Visits Vietnam

Brother Chân Phap Hien, True Dharma Goodness, is from the United States and grew up in New York State. He was ordained a Dharma teacher in 2001. Every year, Thây sends a delegation of monks and nuns to Vietnam to visit the Root Temple and share the practice of Plum Village throughout the country. Brother Phap Hien and nine other monastics traveled to Vietnam in February 2001. Following are excerpts from his journals.

I am floating over the clouds once again, on our way to the "root land," to be in touch with the spiritual energy of the ancestors. I am so happy to be given as a gift like this. There are nine other brothers and sisters traveling with me. I hope they feel the same space and freedom. It is truly wonderful.

~

Tomorrow we are supposed to go to Hue, to the Root Temple. But the brothers from Deer Park haven't arrived yet, so we will wait another day here with Sister Thang Nghiem's family. I really like living in a compound like this, with so many people. Four families share four small buildings and a small courtyard. There are only two toilets, and one of them has been designated for the visiting monks and nuns. Things are so simple. Yet there is color and life and bright eyes and children's laughter. To the Western eye, it seems impoverished, yet everything works well enough and everything has its place. It's a lot like the Upper Hamlet used to be, before we became "modern." I really feel we do not need anything more than this.

~

I closed my eyes and breathed in. I breathed out. Clad in my *sanghati* robe, palms joined, I knelt on the cool tile floor in front of the Patriarch's altar. Nine of my brothers and sisters were behind me, entrusting their hearts to the words I was about to speak. This was part of the tradition, a formal request to pay gratitude and offer respect, but there was nothing at all formal about this moment. It felt so natural. My heart was so open and full of reverence that if I were to do anything it would be exactly this "formality." The tradition was beginning to live in me.

I was deeply aware of the presence of the Buddha and the Patriarchs all around us. Directly in front of me stood a picture of Grandfather Teacher Thien Hanh, his hands folded together and his small delicate body held perfectly still. With gaze turned down, content and concentrated, I knew he was listening deeply. To the left stood Venerable Abbot Chi Mau and to the right Venerable Dharma teacher Thai Hoa, all silent, patient, open, and accepting. I breathed in one more time.

"Homage to Shakyamuni Buddha. Venerable Grandfather Teacher, Venerable Abbot, Venerable Dharma teacher, I am Bhikshu Chân Phap Hien, and I wish to represent this delegation of ten brothers and sisters to speak words of greeting and gratitude." I paused to allow Sister Giai Nghiem time to translate.

"Venerable Grandfather Teacher, Venerable Abbot, Venerable Dharma teacher, we come from Plum Village, Maple Forest Monastery, Green Mountain Dharma Center, and Deer Park Monastery, in Europe and America. Our teacher has given us this chance to travel to Vietnam, our spiritual and cultural homeland, to pay respect to the Patriarchs, and to be in touch with the Root Temple, Tu Hieu, and the Sangha of the Root Temple. Yesterday afternoon, we arrived here, and we were welcomed with more love and care than we could possibly ask for. The embrace of the Root Temple Sangha makes us feel very much as if we are coming home. We are grateful for this embrace. Now we have had the chance to pay respect to the Buddha and the Patriarchs. Please allow us to touch the Earth to you, Venerable Grandfather Teacher, Venerable Abbot, and Venerable Dharma teacher, for it is through your living presence that we can be directly in touch with our spiritual ancestors."

As I spoke, my eyes and hands were flushed with love. I was completely honest with every word, and tears of deep happiness welled up inside. I raised my joined palms to my forehead. The brothers and sisters behind me did the same. The warm resonance of the bell filled the air and we laid our bodies on the Earth.

~

Venerable Abbot Chi Mau is so kind, generous, and powerful! He seems to be everywhere in the temple at any time. Whenever a guest arrives, whether it's a pre-arranged visit or simply tourists wandering through, he is there to make sure they see what they want to see or receive the care they need. He was there to welcome us as we stepped out of the van, with his bold features and immense loving kindness. Venerable Abbot is like a real father. Every morning, without fail, he joins us for tea in our room; and, when we hear the clacking of the wood block, he escorts us to breakfast. Throughout each day, his eyes and hands care for us as a provider and a friend. Many times when I happen to walk in the same direction as he, his strong warm hands take hold of mine, and we share peaceful steps on the ancient paths. These are treasured moments. He seems to instantly release the thousands of things I imagine he must have to do and is totally there as we walk together. I feel as though I am walking with Thây.

I have often seen him walking through the monk's quarters, gently observing the activity. Sometimes he uses the showers and washing area that the young monks frequent, or just passes through to share some of the joyful interaction that always bubbles up there. If you wish to wash your clothes, to shave your head, or even to shower at the Root Temple, rarely can you accomplish the task without the smiling and laughing assistance of one or two other brothers. Pouring a bucket of cold rinse over your *su anh,* or big brother's head, scrubbing each other's back and shoulders, and wringing out your *su em,* or younger brother's clothes, are simply the daily practice of being present for one another. Experiencing these moments with the brothers of the Root Temple, I know what it means to be cared for and what it means to be there for the ones I love.

~

Brother Phap Hien in Upper Hamlet

Monastic culture has offered me a new kind of medicine for the individuality of my American upbringing. I was born into the monastic life in Plum Village with four others. We were named the "Coconut Trees." Every time a group of monks and nuns ordain, our teacher names them after a fruit tree, a flower, or an animal. We Coconuts had elder brothers and sisters like the "Orange Trees," "Birds," "Fish," and "Oak Trees." Now we have many younger brothers and sisters like the "Magnolias," "Mangoes," "Cherries," etc. There is a huge garden of trees and fruits and flowers in our Sangha. Our teacher is cultivating us, and we are being transformed by each other on the path of learning and growing, on the path of the Dharma.

This way of living places one actively into the heart of a lineage. To have a very clear and definite place between elder and younger brothers and sisters has brought the treasure of humility and responsibility into my life. It gives rise to a sense of responsibility that is different from the one I knew before. No longer can I act because it is my duty, or to accomplish something, or to succeed. I am not interested in acquiring recognition or fame. My sense of responsibility is now founded on respect and genuine care. Love becomes action, and every peaceful breath, every stable step, has meaning. Gratitude and an attitude of obedience live in me for my ancestors and elders. I cultivate peace and stability to hand on to younger siblings and descendants. It is a responsibility that I want with all my being, not one that is forced upon me by circumstance.

~

On any given morning, the brothers of the temple sweep the entire grounds with brooms made of thin branches. Fallen leaves and twigs are gathered into piles to be collected and offered as compost in the forest. To a passerby, it may seem like simple manual work, but to a community of monks, it becomes a practice of awareness, grace, balance, and silent communication. It was Venerable Dharma teacher Thai Hoa who gave me initiation into this art. He deftly guided my hands and the direction of my effort into the act of sweeping in such a way that stability was both the ground and the fruit yielded.

In the past I would have had a difficult time accepting instructions on how to sweep up a pile of leaves. My pride would have jumped up and made a mess. I would have felt that I was being talked down to, that I looked like a fool because I didn't know how to do it properly, or that I had failed and was not good enough. But in these past years as a monk, I have discovered the way of humbleness — not shame and guilt, but humbleness. As a monk, I am a student of a teacher who in turn is a student of a teacher who in turn. . . . In order to learn from a teacher, one must adopt an attitude of reverence and humility, or one does not learn very much.

The monastic tradition is full of these kinds of tools for practice, only they are not tools you pick up and use every once in a while, they are your life, they are you, and you are them. Step by step, they strip away your pride and remove the notion of self, of right and wrong, freeing the mind to live and to enjoy living. Then you are not always caught in gratifying a self-centered desire or need. In the monastic tradition, our elders are elders in spiritual life and experience, not only elders in age. Yet they are also human beings; and sometimes they do not meet our expectations, and we are disappointed. But they are nevertheless our elders, and as our purpose is spiritual practice, we must go in the direction of understanding and compassion and remain humble and respectful of our elders. This practice challenges everything self-centered in us, everything self-righteous in us, and propels us forward on the path.

~

Yesterday we paid respect to the Patriarchs, offering incense at each altar, even though, as Thầy Thai Hoa said, "Just to walk peaceful steps through the Temple Gate and up to the Main Hall is already to succeed in coming home and paying respect."

When we arrived at Grandfather Teacher Thanh Quy's stupa, I followed elder brother Tu Dao, leading the delegation to the altar. It is in a beautiful place under tall trees and built from stones that look solid, simple, and elegant at the same time. The closer we came, the stronger the energy of gratitude and reverence grew in our hearts, so that it was impossible not to touch the cool Earth and breathe deeply in the presence of the Patriarch. Many of us cried. We stood up and practiced walking meditation around the stupa. We had come as grandchildren to receive the love and energy of our Grandfather Teacher. We also came as children of Thây, and our steps were his steps. We had brought him home to offer his respect and gratitude to his Teacher as well. Those steps were very powerful. Then, standing together in a moment of reverence, we offered Grandfather Teacher the chant "We Are Truly Present" in English. It was not difficult to enjoy the rest of the day.

~

To become a monk is to become part of a family, a family that dwells and thrives across space and time. Little did I realize that when I left behind my dreams of marriage, a home, and children in order to become a monk, I would be entering such an immense family and that I would suddenly have real brothers and sisters, real parents and children, all over the planet.

One evening, sitting on straw mats by the Half Moon Pond, eighty men, women, boys and girls, all shaven and dressed in brown and gray, enjoy che (sweet soup) as the clouds reflect the silver sheen of the Buddha soaring across the sky. The songs and laughter that echo into the night are of brotherhood, of sisterhood, of family.

Yet there is more than that in these songs and in this laughter. If you listen carefully, you will hear not only the joy and comfort of being together, but you will hear the deep appreciation for life and for this precious moment that reveals Truth and Beauty. If you look deeply into these smiling faces, you can see calm and clarity. You can see the carefulness and attentiveness that grows insight like fresh budding leaves, and you can see faith, stable as the mountain. You can see ease, and you can see an expression of love that is freedom, inner freedom.

Sangha celebration
in Vietnam, Spring 2002

A Silent Promise

Sister Chân Ha Nghiem, True Adornment with Lotus, is from the United States and grew up in New York State. She became a Dharma teacher in 2001 and was one of the monastics who traveled to Vietnam in 2001.

I feel very blessed to have the Vietnamese culture within me. My trip to Vietnam was one of the deepest experiences of my life. I have hardly dared to write about it because it was such a profound experience for me. Although when I was with people in Vietnam we could not always speak the same language, I discovered that on a deep level we have the same heart because we are all turning towards the Buddha. We know how to sit silently, and in that silence our hearts become one — looking with the Buddha's eyes at the children playing in the street, and at the undercover government official in the corner photographing us. Following our breath together, we see the pain; we feel compassion; we see that there is a way out. We feel the beauty of the breeze moving the trees, the miracle that we are alive and the miracle of the Buddha's teaching, which has the capacity to relieve suffering and restore happiness. All this flows in our hearts as we sit silently next to each other.

One afternoon, we came to a beautiful temple near the sea. The monk who met with us remembered Thây, our teacher. He was very old, and his presence carried both sorrow and joy. I was looking into his eyes when I began to see his teacher. This monk had come to the temple as a child, and his teacher had shown him how to look at the world. All the wisdom and sentiments of his teacher had been transmitted to him. His eyes were so deep, so full of wisdom and compassion. I knew then that I was not looking in one person's eyes, I was looking into the eyes of many great monks. I felt such love and gratitude for all of our spiritual ancestors.

A young novice, only eight years old, slips his hand into mine, as soft and light as a flower petal. We are walking down a busy street in Hue. He doesn't need to look up at my face to ask if it is OK to hold my hand, it is so natural to him that I am his elder sister. He is practicing walking meditation, and so am I; and now we are walking together. His presence is so calm and gentle. As we walk together, we smile because we are aware of each other and of the Sangha all around us, walking with ease and freedom. His innocent eyes shine so brightly, yet very peacefully.

I discovered a tremendous amount of courage in the hearts of our Dharma brothers and sisters in Vietnam. In temples all over Vietnam, we were discretely told stories of our brothers and sisters who had been killed. How, in the face of cruelty and death, they offered their lives in hopes of keeping alive what is beautiful. These people were sometimes great old monks and sometimes only teenagers.

Near the end of the trip, we went to Saigon. I was sitting in the meditation hall in what used to be the School of Youth for Social Service, staring at a picture of one of the young women students who was killed during the war. She was so young and fresh. As I stood up and walked in the garden, I felt I was walking with her feet. I knelt and offered incense at their memorial stone. I know I must practice to be their continuation. I felt their presence near me; and, in my heart, I listened to them. I shared about my life in the West and received their guidance. Then I continued to walk in the garden, where I met several brothers from the Root Temple. We sat together. I told the brothers that we are the continuation of those who were killed, and we have to continue their work to bring relief to those who suffer. One of the brothers said, "But *Su Chi* (elder sister), the people now are so greedy and corrupt, they only want more money and things for themselves." I said, "We have to show them. They will not be really happy if they just keep trying to get more for themselves. We have to show them the joy of working together to help each other. We are part of each other — we can never be happy if our neighbor is starving. The real joy in life is to help each other as brothers, as friends of the same human family." He said, "Sister, I still suffer, how can I help?" "You can. We all still suffer sometimes; but, if we keep practicing, we will find ways. We have to." We sat quietly.

An aspirant novice at Tu Hieu Temple, Hue, Vietnam

From the temple, we could see out onto the dusty street where children in their tattered clothes played and fought, their legs and arms thin as young bamboo. The noises of the city were not pleasant. In them, you could hear the people's suffering. Here in the temple, at least, it was a little fresh and peaceful, with its garden and the sound of the chanting echoing from the meditation hall. Many young students and children come here for refuge. "Promise me," I said, "let us promise each other, right now, that we will never forget our path, that we will find a way to help our people to suffer less." We all looked at each other. We were all deeply moved by what we heard in that moment of silence — the suffering of our people, the call of the Buddha, the deepest aspiration lying in each of our hearts. Silently promised.

Some days before, I had asked this same brother when he was born. He said 1972. "Same as me," I said. I asked him where he was born. "Quang Tri. They bombed my house that year, and I almost died. That is the year the Americans killed many, many people in Quang Tri." He looked at me seriously; he did not smile; he just looked at me. In his eyes, I could see his pain. Everyone in the room was still; it seemed as if everything stopped. He could not be angry at me. But, at the same time, he could not hide the horror that his people had experienced, and that it was my country that had dropped the bombs. "I am so sorry," I said, and a moment later I jokingly said, "But I was only this big then," and I held out my hands to mark about a foot high, and we all laughed. We all felt the incredible suffering of our ancestors; and, at the same time, the love and energy of the Buddha between us that day as brothers and sisters was very real and was somehow embracing the past. I had many spontaneous Dharma discussions like this with the monks and nuns there.

When I was in the airplane flying back to the U.S., I closed my eyes and looked inside. All I could see was Vietnam — the dusty roads and shacks, the mountains with their villages and majestic temples, all the people, old and young, the great virtue and purity in their eyes, and the great suffering they still endure. When I arrived in Vietnam, they took me in their arms like their long lost child come home, and my heart opened. My heart and eyes stayed wide open the whole time I was there, and it felt like all of Vietnam had entered. Now, in the plane, that was all I could see. I had no desire to come back to the West, where everything seemed so cool in all its modern prosperity.

While I was in Vietnam, I reflected on the virtue I saw in so many of the people. I realized that our spiritual ancestors must have been very talented and virtuous; and, due to their guidance, the people still maintain many of these beautiful qualities today. Vietnam is a precious treasure.

Returning to the Village

Tran Van Huyen is from Vietnam and West Virginia.

Ever since leaving our homeland in search of a different way of life, we, the Vietnamese abroad, rarely talk about "returning to the village." Because everywhere we go we find estranged people, living in foreign lands without a place to return to. Now, when I think about returning to the village, I suddenly remember my childhood. Though it was not a happy time, it did have many memorable moments.

My country was in the midst of war. My parents had to evacuate, moving to a safer place where we would not be captured. Houses were burned; rice fields were abandoned. When it was deemed safe enough, mothers would bring their children, wives would follow their husbands, people would return to their villages, rebuilding their straw huts to shelter them from the rain or the heat of the sun. They cleared front yards to grow vegetables and hoed backyards to cultivate potatoes, hoping to secure food and clothes for their families. Though faced with many difficulties, my parents were happy to be able to return to their home, their garden. Returning to the village in those days was like looking for memories — breathing, once again, the familiar air and reliving times that were overflowing with love. That was enough to give them peace and calmness, moments filled with bittersweet tears.

Though our village was poor and life was simple, there was harmony and goodwill among the villagers. There was also love and respect for our ancestors. The village seemed to be sustained by their spirits. It felt as though there was an invisible bond that connected our hearts to the land. We did not want to leave it behind, though we knew that by remaining there we would not have a future.

Quang Tri, my hometown, has soil that is full of rocks, and the weather is unbearable. There are two seasons, wet and dry. When it is hot and dry, it can burn your skin. But when it rains, it can rot the soil. Life is hard, and often there is not enough food to eat. On the other hand, the fragrance of our homeland is ever present. Life in the countryside — what is happier and warmer than that? On moonlit nights, family members would gather outside, on the front yard, listening to grandparents telling folktales. On cold winter nights, they would sit around the fire stove. Such a simple way of life helped lessen desire and the struggle for fame in us; and, most importantly, it helped weaken the roots of war.

After returning to our village, life slowly returned to normal. Houses were rebuilt, though the walls were still made of Earth and the roofs of straw. The familiar sites re-energized the villagers. Abandoned gardens were re-cultivated; the scenery, once empty, was now much livelier. For the villagers, this was enough to be happy. We accepted our humble situation just so we could be able to live on our own land, in our own villages. We only wanted to be near our ancestors' graves, to pay gratitude to our rivers and mountains, to live in harmony with our neighbors. That was all that we wanted.

But society did not leave us poor people alone. We were not able to survive under the new government. With the effect of the war not yet forgotten, we once again had to leave our land in tears. Living so far away from our homeland was difficult. Whenever we encountered a new environment or people we did not understand, we felt sad and lost. However dark it was, we were unable to leave the memory of our homeland behind. We felt unsafe and dispirited.

Then we had a great opportunity: we were allowed to return to the village, Plum Village. We felt very fortunate. Being in Plum Village was a great source of relief. There, we had a chance to learn methods to transform suffering and lead a happy, peaceful life. Now, "returning to the village" carries a special meaning: a chance to relearn how to be a person and to relive what we once felt so close to.

When I came to Plum Village, I found a village-style environment, with banana plants and gardens of green vegetables, with onion and pepper plants, and with trellises of gourds and squashes. When I saw the vegetable gardens behind the meditation hall, I wondered how long it took for the garden to become so green, the color of our homeland. But how could I tell if that was really the color of our homeland? Was this garden not being cultivated on foreign soil? Suddenly, I understood that I had been carrying this precious green inside my veins, inside my heart and mind. Since the conditions had not yet come together, the color of our homeland had not manifested. The closed doors of fear and isolation had kept the image of our homeland from us. Those doors had now swung open. What I saw here lessened the nostalgia in me. I no longer felt apprehensive about this new land. Here, there was a great lotus pond, a beautiful grove of bamboo swinging in the breeze. The scenery of the heart connected this reality with the land I once knew as my home.

A Fresh Flower

Sister Tinh Luu, Calm Clear Stream, is a novice at the Dinh Quan Temple in Hanoi, Vietnam.

October 15, 2001

Respected Su Ong, Sister Chân Không,
I have the great opportunity to be your student. I have never set foot in Plum Village, but, within me, Plum Village is always present because here I am able to do Plum Village practices, like listening to the bell and enjoying silent meals. These practices have nourished my love and bodhicitta. Respected Su Ong, when I was an aspirant, I wasn't like the other aspirants. My bodhicitta was very small; and, if there was anyone who accidentally made me feel uncomfortable, I would think to myself, "Why is that person so difficult?" Because of this, I have suffered, and many times I have drowned in the ocean of suffering. There are times I imagine that I cannot cross over it and will never become a nun.

Friends enjoy the bamboo grove in Upper Hamlet

But how wonderful the practice has become for me since I have learned the Dharma doors you have transmitted. I have learned to stop when my mind manifests the seeds of jealousy and hatred. I have been able to take each step and coordinate it with my breathing, to embrace my mind so it will settle down, and to practice Touching the Earth so I can send good energy to the person who has made me suffer. Practicing like that every day has made me realize those habit energies aren't anyone else's but my own. I see I am very fortunate to receive the merit and the virtues of both spiritual and blood ancestors so I can receive true happiness in the present moment. I am not waiting or wishing for anything anymore. Everything lies within and around me; I just need to open my eyes and enjoy immeasurable happiness. My body is open every time I want to chant, practice sitting meditation, walking meditation, or enjoy the flowers and the grass, and I can do it right away. Su Ong, can you see that I am happy? I am able to meet the wonderful teachings and walk on the bright path because there is a teacher and there are older and younger sisters walking together. If there is any obstacle on my path, Thây is always there to support me and show me a Dharma door that I can practice to overcome it.

My older sister, Tinh Kien, has praised me, "Tinh Luu, you have changed, and you have improved a lot already." I am very happy about the path that I have chosen to take. I don't know how to repay a teacher who has transmitted to my sisters and me a teaching that makes each of us more fresh.

Dear Su Ong, Sister Chân Không, and Sangha, I know what I have practiced is very little, but I would like to offer it as a fresh flower to celebrate the day Plum Village becomes twenty years old.

Drawing by Svein Myreng

The Student-Teacher Relationship

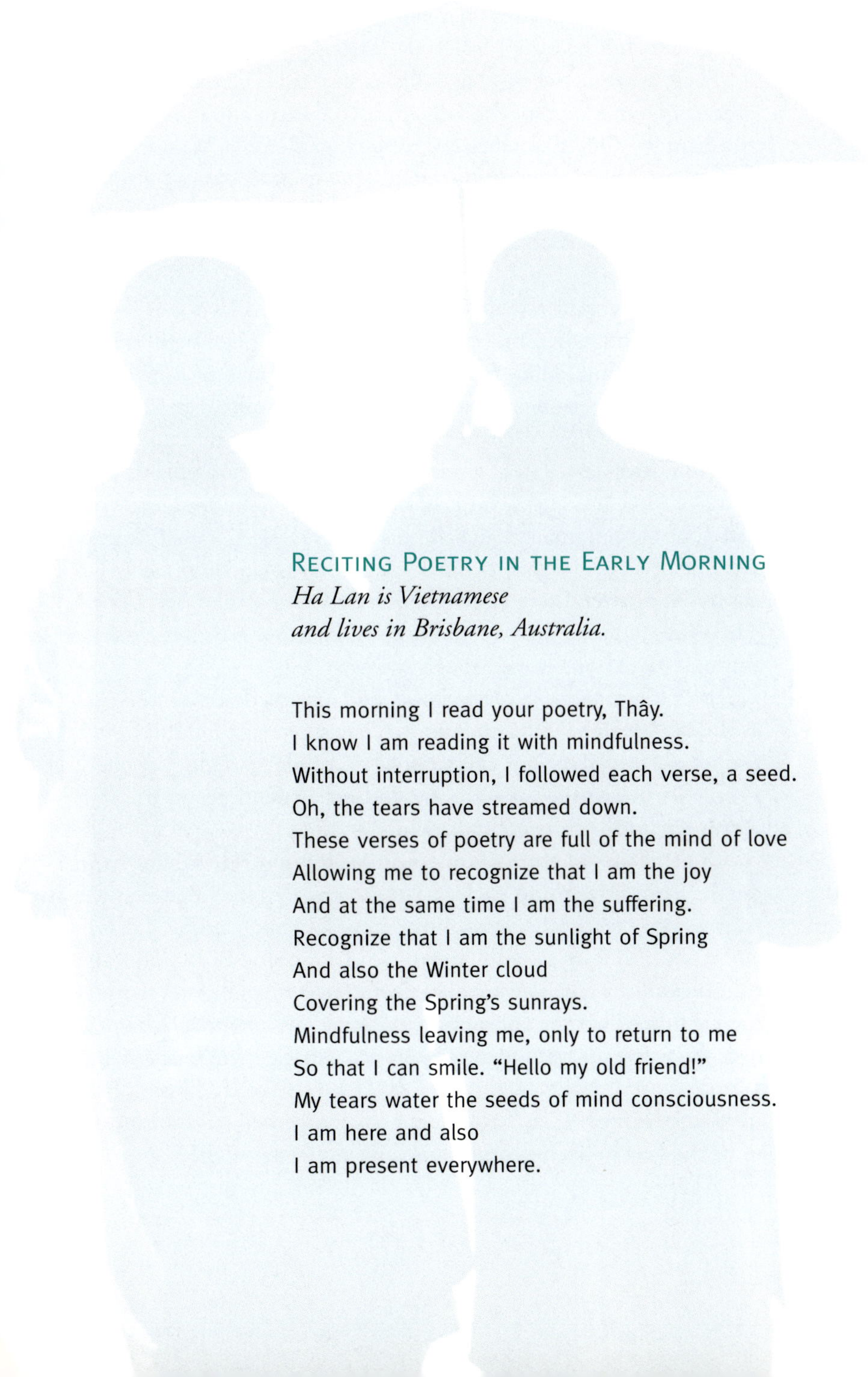

The Old Teacher

Julia, from St. Petersburg, Russia

The students came.
They're beautiful.
But for the old Teacher,
It is difficult to reach the suffering Russia.
At last he arrived.
I couldn't recognize him.
He's younger than the boy Oleg
Sitting in front of him.

Reciting Poetry in the Early Morning

Ha Lan is Vietnamese
and lives in Brisbane, Australia.

This morning I read your poetry, Thây.
I know I am reading it with mindfulness.
Without interruption, I followed each verse, a seed.
Oh, the tears have streamed down.
These verses of poetry are full of the mind of love
Allowing me to recognize that I am the joy
And at the same time I am the suffering.
Recognize that I am the sunlight of Spring
And also the Winter cloud
Covering the Spring's sunrays.
Mindfulness leaving me, only to return to me
So that I can smile. "Hello my old friend!"
My tears water the seeds of mind consciousness.
I am here and also
I am present everywhere.

Thây and Brother Phap Niem in India

Thây is in Me

Sister Chân Hoa Nghiem, True Adornment with Flowers, is from Vietnam and London. She ordained as a Dharma teacher in 1999.

I sat for a long while on the top of the hill, silently looking at the colorful beauty of the mountains and forest. Autumn had returned. The evening sun gradually set, leaving a soft shade of purple at the foot of the sky. A crescent moon appeared, hanging over the peak of Ascutney Mountain. The crescent moon made me suddenly remember Thây.

After a month and a half of guiding retreats, Thây and the Sangha settled at Green Mountain Dharma Center to rest for ten days before returning to France. It was a great happiness for the Sanghas of Green Mountain and Maple Forest Monastery. I had the opportunity to cook for and attend Thây one day. I had learned how to make Banh Tro Cau, a kind of savory cake from Hue that Thây likes very much. When I was learning to wrap these cakes in banana leaves from Sister Nhu Huy, Thây passed by and stopped to watch, his eyes shining with interest. When it was my day to cook, I made them for Thây. When Thây saw Banh Tro Cau on his tray, he beamed a joyful smile and asked, "You made the Banh Tro Cau?" Then he ate one and praised them, "Very tasty, you make it like Sister Nhu Huy." I smiled with delight, happy not because Thây had praised me, but because I had given Thây some joy.

There are times when Thây is like a protective, gentle mother, his eyes tender and loving as he asks, "Are you warm enough?" or, "Are you happy?" One day, when we were all gathered at a meal, Sister Chân Duc was sitting beside Thây. Thây picked a piece of green vegetable and placed it into Sister Chân Duc's bowl, and then added a piece of tofu. This small action revealed the limitless love of a father for his children.

One day, while I was attending Thây, I entered his room to find him sitting in meditation. I silently tiptoed to a place behind him. After a long while, Thây turned and signaled for me to come closer, "Sit here. It is very beautiful, my child." He pointed to the view through the window. A crescent moon was hanging in space with a few twinkling stars. The sky was still dark. Thây stood up and went to make some tea, and I clumsily stood up after him; but Thây signaled for me to remain seated. In his hands were two small cups of tea, one of which he gave to me. I silently reprimanded myself, "I'm supposed to attend, yet Thây had to make tea for me." Yet, I knew Thây likes to take care of his children. Thây's love is expressed more through his actions than through words.

For a longtime both teacher and student quietly drank their tea as the sky became lighter. Suddenly, Thây spoke just loudly enough for me to hear. "Try your best to practice wholeheartedly, my child. People in the world are suffering and are depending on us." His words return to me again and again.

Once, Thây taught us how to do calligraphy. He taught us in detail, from how to do each stroke, to the distance between the words. Thây teaches us everything: how to walk, stand, lie down, and sit in mindfulness, and how to close doors and open doors and eat mindfully. Thây is aware of each student's mental state, in order to give him or her the appropriate teaching. We are people from all over the world — Europe, Asia, America, Africa — and we differ in culture, in nationality, and in age. We are also like wild horses who need to be tamed. Thây has brought us all together, has transmitted to us the way to live in compassion and understanding.

One time, we wanted to offer Thây a gift for Thanksgiving. My job was to find out what Thây really wanted. I asked, "Dear Thây, what is it that you like the best?" Thây looked at me and smiled, "What do I like? Thây doesn't like anything the best." I asked again, "But dear Thây, there must be something that you like most?" He looked straight at me. "There is. Thây wants all his students to love each other; to love Thây means to love one another."

After Thây and the Plum Village nuns had returned to France, the rest of us sat together one evening sipping tea and enjoying incense and candlelight. None of us said anything, but looking into the eyes of each person, I knew that we missed Thây and our sisters of Plum Village. I remembered something Thây often says: "Thây is there in every cell of his students."

Dear beloved Thây, in the historical dimension, you are thousands of miles away from us; but, in the ultimate dimension, you have never been far away for even a day. Thây is present every morning, before dawn, in the meditation hall, when Thây's students are sitting beside one another following each breath. Thây is present in our every step, as we walk up and down the stairs. Thây is present when we practice Beginning Anew. We see that what Thây has taught us has been absorbed into our blood and our hearts.

Dear Beloved Teacher, you often remind us that we must travel together like a river and not as a separate drop of water, which would quickly evaporate on its journey. The passing months and years have given me faith in the strength of the Sangha. I know that we are not a Sangha full of saints. We make mistakes and create suffering for one another. But we have never deserted one another. If we are angry with one another, there is a practice to resolve the conflict. If, within the Sangha, one person is suffering, everyone else tries to find means to bring joy to that person. The Sangha is truly practicing the teachings of the Buddha, keeping the trainings and mindfulness manners, bringing love and understanding into our lives.

I know that my practice is not yet strong and often times there are "storms in a teacup" in my life. I vow to flow with the Sangha, like a river heading towards the ocean. And one day, when Thây must leave, I know Thây will always be in me. Although his children are living in different monasteries all over the world, we are still connected and will continue to meet each other on the same path that the Buddhas, the patriarchs, our grandfather teacher, and Thây have also traveled on.

Embracing Doubt

Brother Chân Phap Ngo, True Dharma Awakening, is from the United States. He grew up in Texas and was ordained in 1998.

After practicing as a novice for two years, I crossed a threshold in my practice and in my relationship with Thây and the Sangha. At that time, I felt a desire to leave Plum Village. I wanted to visit Mother Meera, a spiritual teacher in Germany, and sit a ten-day vipassana course. I had had a very deep and transformative experience in Mother Meera's presence some years before this and had always wanted to go back and see her. My twin brother practices vipassana meditation with Goenka; and, after talking with him about it, I wanted to attend a ten-day retreat. I was entering a deeper level in my practice and beginning to feel resistance in the form of insecurity and doubt. I wasn't sure that my path was to stay with Thây and the Sangha. I thought I needed a more formal and intensive practice environment, and regular contact with Mother Meera.

I met with Thây to tell him I wanted to leave the community. He told me to ask the Sangha for permission. He did not want me to

Sister Hoa Nghiem sitting between her two Dharma and biological sisters. On the left is Sister Tri Giac, and on the right is Sister Doan Nghiem.

leave. He said, "Don't run around in circles. You have to stick to Thây and the Sangha to make a break through. The Bodhi tree is inside of you. You have to be strong and not moved by anything." I had to meet with him several times because I was very stubborn. I felt like I had a stone wall around my heart that Thây was trying to chisel through with his words. I would question him and say things in a very critical and unkind way. I kept pushing, because I didn't want to stop and look back into myself. Finally, my heart opened, and I was able to let go. I felt sincere humility and asked for help. Thây responded with a lot of patience and compassion. The seed of understanding was sown.

Soon after that, I traveled with Thây Doji to give retreats in France and Switzerland. There was a lot of harmony and deep connection between everyone at the first retreat in Lyon. Towards the end of it, I had trouble breathing. For most of the last night, I couldn't lie down because the muscles in my diaphragm would lock up and I would stop breathing all together. The next day, a Sangha member who is a healer helped me with a combination of massage and psychotherapy. During that session, memories of my birth came up.

Right after I was born I was taken from my mom and twin brother and put into a bassinet in the nursery. Being separated from them was very painful. The harsh lighting and lack of physical contact in the nursery made me feel very isolated and cut off. I felt a lot of aversion towards being alive in that way. Then I felt my body deaden and my spirit go out the top of my head.

That was all I could remember at the time. I don't think I was actually in the process of dying after I was born. I think I was just disassociating from my body in response to the trauma. After that experience, I could see more clearly what the true source of my insecurity and doubt was and why I wanted to leave Thây and the Sangha. During those two years as a novice, my brother chose to live as a layperson and practice in a different tradition, so our life paths were separating. My commitment to life as a monk meant that I couldn't go home anytime I wanted, or visit Mother Meera, so I was feeling another separation. I was also growing up and becoming stronger as a person, so I was experiencing a kind of rebirth. The combination of all these things caused the trauma around my birth to come up. With the help of Thây and the Sangha, the strength of my ancestors, and my own practice, I was able to break through and overcome this suffering.

Now, my body and the Sangha body have become more unified. I feel closer and more trusting. I practice to water the seeds of gratitude and inclusiveness in me so that I can feel my connection with everyone, both in and outside of Plum Village. I practice to let go of acting as a separate self. The more I can recognize and embrace my doubt, the happier and more stable I become.

Nothing is Lost

Sister Chân Uy Nghiem, True Adornment with Mindful Manners, is from Vietnam and California. She was ordained in 1998.

July 21, 1998

In the twenty-one day retreat at St. Michael's College in Burlington, Vermont, I had the good fortune to be Thây's attendant. Besides learning from Thây's Dharma talks, I also learned directly from his way of being. After serving as Thây's attendant, I found I was able to look with more love and compassion at life, to walk and stand more serenely, and to speak and laugh with more lightness. All this was the fruit of practicing mindfulness while I was alongside Thây.

One day after lunch, Thây jokingly said to me, "My child, write a letter on my behalf to people who are angry with me." I just smiled. What did I know? What could I say, except to ask them not to be angry with someone as lovable as Thây. Thây is like the rainfall watering the seeds of the mind of love in all his students. Thây was speaking of the small number of the families or beloved ones of the monks and nuns who feel that they have lost their beloved one to the practice. But, if the monks and nuns had not inherited the seeds of the mind of love from their parents and their loved ones, however much the Dharma rain fell on their hearts, it would not make any difference. I know that these people who are angry with Thây are only angry for a short time. In the beginning, they feel that their loved one, who had been so close to them, has suddenly been taken away by a stranger. In fact, the monastic is giving his or her life to an ideal of love and awakening, and that is something that their loved ones can feel proud about. Do they know that the Bodhi tree in the hearts of the monks and nuns wants to grow in order to be a shady place for many people and other species? The more space that tree has, the bigger it will grow. The more freedom the monastic has, the more benefit he or she will bring to people. So many young people of our time are being carried away by the emotions of the majority. They cannot find happiness in the present moment; rather, they look for refuge in short-term happiness. When you see that your child has become a monastic, knowing how to live a life of peace and joy, ease and happiness, and encouraging so many others to live the same way, then how can you not feel proud?

This morning I was jogging down the driveway to the practice center. Returning, I saw a pink balloon that had fallen down in the rain, clinging to a tree in the forest. I reached up, took hold of it carefully, and carried it home; but, on the way, I opened my hand a little and the balloon flew away. From my old habit energy, I cried out, "Oh no!" But when I looked up at the balloon floating high and far away, and I saw its lightness, it made me feel light as well. I smiled, waved good-bye to the balloon, and said, "Oh yes!" It made me feel happy the whole way home. ▣

Opposite: Sister Uy Nghiem on the far left with Sister Hoa Nghiem and aspirants on an outing near Plum Village

Path

Sister Chân Dao Nghiem,
True Adornment with the Path,

I have gone looking for liberty
I have gone looking to love
I have gone looking for beauty

I have walked down busy streets
Hoping to find reality
I left alone, dressed in my pride
Hoping to be able to abandon myself
I lost myself in enamored eyes
Hoping to forget myself

I tired myself out
I became sad
I stopped

It is in me that liberty is inscribed
Authenticity is the only beauty
It is equanimity that teaches me to love

Little by little I discover my true magnitude
As my heart stretches with understanding
And opens to me the doors of emancipation

I have found
What is
For all eternity

Larry Ward, True Great Voice, receiving the Dharma Lamp, Winter 2001

A Lamp Transmission

Every year or two, in Plum Village, Thầy transmits the Dharma Lamp, ordaining senior lay and monastic disciples as Dharma teachers. In this ceremony, candidates present Thầy with an insight poem, or gatha, the fruit of their practice. In return, Thầy presents each candidate with a poem, a teaching to help him or her on the path. Then Thầy speaks words of encouragement as he offers each a Dharma Lamp. The candidate then gives a short Dharma talk.

Chân My

Tuyet Mai Thi Nguyen, Dharma name Chân My, or True Beauty, is a Vietnamese lay practitioner. She lives in London, England, where she practices with both English and Vietnamese Sanghas. She was ordained a Dharma teacher in 2001.

Insight Gatha from Chân My to Thầy:

In forgetfulness, I invite the bell.
Thầy taps my head, I wake up.
Suddenly, mindfulness is there.
I return to my ancestral land.

Thầy's Gatha in Response:

Suchness smiles in the sunny sky.
Beautifully, the moon embraces the whole autumn ocean.
The ultimate dimension (Old Path, White Clouds) is always manifesting.
On the path of return to the ancestral land,
Everything is as beautiful as poetry.

Thầy's Explanation of His Gatha:

"The moon embraces the whole autumn ocean" is an image often used in Zen poetry. We think we can see the moon only when standing at this one spot. Yet, strangely, we can still see the moon when standing somewhere else. Does the moon move or not move? Is it we who move or do not move?

"Old Path, White Clouds" is the ultimate dimension — the Buddha of the ultimate dimension. Thanks to mindfulness, when you walk the old paths the Buddha walked, you become the Buddha. The old paths are not just in India, they are also here. Any path we walk is the old path, the path the Buddha walked on. Any patch of white cloud you see is the same patch that the Buddha saw. And the Buddha asked, "Dear child, do you see what I am seeing? Everything you see is what I am seeing." All paths lead back to the ancestral land, and every land is your homeland; and it is always as beautiful as poetry.

Thầy's Words of Encouragement:

Our happiness is generated entirely from our heart. Happiness is made of two factors. The first is freedom — the freedom of non-attachment. This means being free from chains that bind us, such as desire, fame, power, or fear.

The second factor of happiness is loving kindness. Loving kindness helps us to be in touch with all beings, especially human beings. When we are in touch, we can communicate easily and help many people. As a result, our happiness will increase. Our practice is to expand our freedom and increase our loving kindness every day. Chân My, you have understood these teachings. Today is an opportunity to remember and entrust yourself to this insight.

Our happiness is very important because without it we cannot share happiness with others. Therefore, the lamp that our spiritual ancestors transmit to you today is to remind you that you are a light. You need to look after this light and keep it alive. It is the light of Sangha. The Sangha has supported us and helped us achieve our aspirations; therefore, we wholeheartedly resolve to build the Sangha. The work of Sangha building will make the ancestral lamp grow brighter every day.

We are fortunate to reside and practice in the West. We have the duty to shine the light of our ancestral lamps where we live. That is how we pay tribute to the spiritual ancestors, and how we show gratitude to our blood ancestors. We are ambassadors of a cultural and a spiritual tradition. When we succeed as ambassadors, our happiness will increase greatly, and we will be able to share it with many people. Dear child, do remember this.

Chân Huy

Chân Huy is a lay Dharma teacher from Montréal, Québec, Canada. This poem is the insight gatha that he presented to Thây when he was ordained a Dharma teacher in 1994. "Nang Mai" (morning sun) and "Mac Hanh" (secret action) are the names that Thây gave to Chân Huy's daughters. "Tam Luong" (immeasurable mind) is Chân Huy's Five Mindfulness Trainings Dharma name, and "Luu Ly" (lapis lazuli gem) is his wife's "true name."

Chân Huy's Insight Gatha

Practicing secretly the wondrous teaching
 of the immeasurable mind,
Breathing and smiling mindfully with every step,
The morning sun bursts out,
Shining after the long dark night.
The pebble glows like a lapis lazuli gem.

Awakening My Mind of Love: Becoming a Monastic

Brother Chân Phap Can, True Dharma Diligence, is from Vietnam and Germany. He was ordained in 2001.

I first came to Temple Vien Giac in Germany on Vesak Day, the Buddha's Birthday. Crowds of people were busy setting up small shops around the temple or gathering to buy. The atmosphere was festive. While I was immersed in this happy energy with other Buddhist practitioners, I suddenly heard the chanting from the temple. The *Prajnaparamita Sutra,* in Chinese, resounded powerfully. Although I did not understand a word of it, it moved me deeply. I had not visited a temple since leaving Vietnam, years before.

I returned to this temple seven months later. The falling snow whitened the world outside. At the gate, I bowed down to touch the Earth deeply three times, to express my gratitude to the Buddha, the Dharma, and the Sangha. I took each step carefully as I crossed the threshold. When I reached the statue of Avalokiteshvara, I knelt down completely. The snow was cold beneath my knees. However, my mind filled with a strong energy — perhaps inspiration from the marvelous bodhisattva. Then I went to the main hall to touch the Earth in front of every statue, in the most solemn manner. I was also permitted to go into the temple tower, where several Buddha statues were kept. The tower was seven stories high, and I knelt down to prostrate on each step of the stairway. I felt a deep desire to come back to take refuge in the Three Jewels.

I asked permission to stay at the temple for two weeks to familiarize myself with the life of practice. I happened to see the book *Old Path White Clouds,* by Zen Master Thich Nhat Hanh, in the library. I read this book avidly during the time I was there. Thây described clearly practices such as sitting meditation and walking meditation. Following these guides, I began practicing right away. The book awakened deep aspirations in me. The more I read it, the more interested and happy I became. The Buddha came alive on each page. I felt as if he were still here, very close to all of us. I wanted to find my way to Plum Village.

When I came to Plum Village, I looked carefully at each well-walked path, each copper bell hanging on a tree branch, each flower. I observed the daily activities. I listened to Thây's Dharma talks. When I returned to Germany, I was determined to apply the things I had learned from Plum Village to my life. I had concrete practices. I had happiness in order to transform pain and sadness. I decided to throw away all my videos and music that nourished yearning and craving. I did not want to listen to them anymore. I reorganized my way of living. I decorated all the rooms with gathas and Zen phrases. I found a path for walking meditation, where there were trees offering shade, a small running stream, and bird songs. I set times for sitting meditation and chanting at home. On the weekends, I practiced offering food to the hungry ghosts and prayed for their liberation. I imagined that the energy from the sutras and chants was spreading in all directions of the world, helping to relieve the suffering of all species. Before I began to eat, I thought of the hungry children in Africa, India, and Vietnam.

I also went back to Vietnam to help rebuild the spiritual practice in my family. Their faith in the Three Jewels was rejuvenated. My younger brother decided to become a monk. My family learned to share their income with children in the orphanages and with poor people. During my stay in Vietnam, I often spent time with the children and old people who were begging on the streets of Nha Trang, Da Lat, and Saigon. I talked to them and began to better understand their situation. I felt deep compassion for my people and my country. I also went to see my maternal grandfather, who was in the hospital for eye surgery. I saw many blind people, and those who were old, sick, and dying. I asked myself, "Why is there so much suffering?" My eyes, too, would become weakened. My body, too, would age and die. My tears rolled down onto the cement floor.

My practice at home did not yield absolute happiness. I wanted to do something that could help relieve the suffering in the world. Compassion began to grow in me. The aspirations — to join the monastic life, to transform, to live with true happiness, to attain freedom within birth and death, and to benefit others — grew in me. At the same time, there were many issues that were difficult to resolve with my partner. I decided to remain a layperson practicing the bodhisattva path with her. However, when I was out on the streets, witnessing the suffering of others, my determination to become a monastic returned stronger than ever.

Reborn As a Monk

On the morning of May 18, 2000, I woke up while it was still dark outside. The bamboo groves whispered in the wind. Hundreds of birds sang to greet the coming of the twelve newborns. My ordination family was named the "Plumeria Trees." When Thây cut my hair, I had the feeling I had become free from all afflictions. I received the Dharma body from Thây, which untied my knots of attachment and opened wide the path before me. I was reborn in the Buddha's Land. I have brought with me the seeds of bodhicitta, happiness, compassion, and understanding. I have also brought with me unskillful habit energies and many difficulties. Thây and the Sangha are helping me embrace and transform my difficulties. I am learning to listen to the pain in me and around me. I feel more love for my body and mind and now choose healthier foods for them.

I remember, one day, I was in the kitchen in the Upper Hamlet when Thây walked up to me and asked, "My child, what are you doing?" I answered quietly, "Respected Thây, I am cutting vegetables." "I think you are breathing, my child," Thây said softly. His voice was full of compassion. I stopped suddenly. "Perhaps you have forgotten," Thây said and walked away, with such ease and freedom. Thây's words have remained indelible in my mind. When I am sitting alone, I often think of Thây's question, "What are you doing?" I come back to my breathing and return to the present moment.

During a trip to Germany with Thây and the delegation, I

Walking meditation in Oldenburg, Germany, 1993

discovered a new Germany through her people. I lived in Germany over ten years, but I never knew there were so many Sanghas there practicing in the Plum Village tradition. In Oldenburg, six hundred people came for the retreat, and the quality of transformation was as profound as that in Plum Village. After the retreat, everyone's face beamed with freshness and peace. At a public talk, seven thousand Protestants attended. I discovered a new country and a new people, who, like myself, were gentle, practicing to breathe, to do walking meditation, and to transform suffering into peace. I am moved again and again by the attentive listening and the sincere practice of the people, whether the retreat is in Germany, France, or other countries. Sometimes, when we monastics are on the stage to evoke the names of the Buddhas and bodhisattvas, I look out at the audience. Many are crying. In this atmosphere of solemnity and serenity, my consciousness, too, is awakened.

Since the day of my ordination, I have not once wished to leave the monastery. I desire to follow this path my whole life. I know that only the path of practice brings true happiness. Of course, I have also had difficulties. There are times when I am unskillful in my speech and actions. I do my best to understand my unskillfulness so I can learn from it. The more suffering I encounter, the more determined I am to practice and the deeper my happiness becomes.

Jewel

Lorena Monda

Because of you
When we walk
Our feet lay trails of mindfulness
Across the planet
— A web of peace.

Because of you
The Dharma glistens everywhere
Like dewdrops
On spring grass.

Because of you
We gather
And learn to find our bigger body —
Sangha body.

Because of you
Now when I cry
There are warm arms to hold me.
They are in my heart
And every place I look.

Because you have touched us
You live in us
And we in you
Through space and time.

We are immense.
The universe is our heart.

To Water Seeds of Joy

A new chant by Thich Nhat Hanh

My mother, my father,
They are in me,
And when I look
I see myself in them.

The Buddha, the patriarchs
Are in me,
And when I look
I see myself in them.

I am a continuation
Of my mother, my father, and my ancestors.
It is my aspiration to preserve
And continue to nourish
Seeds of goodness, skill, and happiness
Which I have inherited.
It is also my desire to recognize.
Seeds I have inherited of fear and suffering.
And bit by bit to transform them.

I am a continuation
Of Buddha and my spiritual teachers.
It is my deep aspiration
To preserve, nourish, and develop
The seeds of understanding, love, and freedom
Which they have transmitted to me.

I desire to continue
The career of the Buddha and ancestral teachers
And do my best to realize
All the Buddha and ancestral teachers
Expect of me.

In my daily life
I also want to sow
Seeds of love and compassion.
In my own consciousness
And in the heart of other people
I am determined not to water
Seeds of craving, aversion, and violence
In myself and the other.

I know that if I practice
All this in the right way.
After only seven days
I shall already have been able
To change the situation,
Establish communication,
Smile and transform some suffering
And increase my happiness.

Please, Lord Buddha
Be witness to what is in my heart.
With mind and body in perfect unity
I bow my head and prostrate.

Parents of Monastics

A Front-Line Activist in a Venerable Tradition: Thoughts from a Mother of a Monk

Sara Ciborski lives in Great Barrington, Massachusetts. She is an anthropologist and development consultant and now works with a Camphill community in New York State, serving disabled people. She is the mother of Brother Phap Hien.

When my son Michael became a monk in Plum Village some six years ago, my first reaction was somewhat superficial. "This is wonderful," I thought, "because from now on Michael will be in a situation where he will be safe and happy — what more could I want for my child?" I imagined that the only effect it would have on my own life would be to give me an excuse to travel to France.

In fact, what Michael has experienced and achieved goes well beyond mere safety and happiness. The richness and fullness of his life as a monk in the Order of Interbeing is astonishing. He has traveled all over the world, met and often been helpful to thousands of people, learned to navigate comfortably in Vietnamese — both the language and the culture — and immersed himself in the study and practice of an extraordinary world religion.

Far more important than these outer effects, his choice has brought him the incomparable challenge of living in a multicultural monastic community of people who, while single-minded in their practice, are complex as individuals. In embracing this community, Michael has needed to confront and embrace himself, unflinchingly and with love.

As for me, Michael's choice has meant far more than a few trips to France. All the monasteries — Plum Village, Maple Forest Monastery, and Deer Park (though I have not yet been there) — are there for me whenever I need them. I once stayed for two months in Plum Village at a time when I was suffering from acute anxiety and deep despair. I think it was the only place in the world I could have gone then to feel safe. Gently supported by the peace of the brothers, the rhythms of the practice, the simplicity of our daily life together, and the loving attention of my son, I found blessed relief.

Toward the end of this stay, I began to experience the limitations (for me) of Buddhism, and to yearn for my own spiritual path (anthroposophy, which is Christ-centered). But this was another gift to me from Plum Village: the universality and potency of mindfulness practice always seems to renew and enliven other spiritual streams.

Being the mother of a monk has one major drawback: Michael is rarely free to visit home. Our main holiday, Christmas, falls in the middle of Winter Retreat, and monks do not leave their monastery during Winter Retreat. Several times, I have really needed Michael to be home with me or with his sisters. But unless it's an emergency, the Sangha's needs always take precedence.

Notwithstanding this drawback, Michael's vocation has been a blessing to our family and has opened up opportunities for me. One of the supreme occasions in my life was a trip to Vietnam in 2001, which was a direct result of my connection, through Michael, with Buddhism. And part of that trip, the special day that I spent with Michael at Tu Hieu Monastery (Thây's root temple) in Hue ranks as one of my most precious memories. I wouldn't trade that day for a dozen family occasions with Michael at home.

Michael is indeed happy, but I am no longer sure that he is always safe. On September 25, 2001, I went to New York City to hear Thây give a public talk, at Riverside Church, to several thousand grieving people. A small figure standing exposed in the front of that enormous sanctuary, he calmly and courageously put the tragedy of September 11 into its true context. Every day, forty thousand children in the world die from hunger, in large part because too many of us, especially in the West, fail to practice mindful consumption. The right response to September 11, Thây said, is forgiveness. What a deed for the world if America could practice forgiveness and compassion!

Sara and her son, Brother Phap Hien, at Tu Hieu Temple in Hue, Vietnam

These words were, and are, radical in the extreme — they're revolutionary. Given the atmosphere of revenge that prevailed in the aftermath of September 11, I feared for Thầy and the monks and nuns sitting quietly around him, Michael among them.

Who are these monks and nuns, exactly, who accompany Thầy wherever he gives public talks? They are not window dressing. They are a presence, as a group, and each as an individual — an active presence that is both the source and the manifestation of Thầy's meaning. Out of love for the good and deep understanding of the essential oneness of humanity, they offer themselves as a living picture of a viable, joyful alternative. They *are* the revolution. We should not idealize them, for they are also ordinary, fallible men and women. But that's the point: there is no safety for anyone in these violent times. Ordinary people can, do, and must freely choose activism on behalf of mindful consumption, compassion, and forgiveness.

My son is, among other things, a front-line activist in a venerable monastic tradition. Michael has become, and is always becoming, who he was meant to be through the grace of Plum Village. I am grateful for and open to whatever will now unfold.

Walking with My Son

Jonathan Arazy, True Path of Peace, lives with his wife, Michal, in Kiryat Tivon, Israel, where they practice with the Jerusalem Sangha. They are the parents of Brother Phap Minh, True Dharma Brightness, and were the first members of the Israeli Sangha to become members of the Order of Interbeing in December 2001.

I visited Plum Village for the first time with my wife Michal in September 1998, after our son Amir (now Brother Phap Minh) called us from Plum Village to tell us of his decision to become a monk. At that time, we knew nothing about Buddhism, Thich Nhat Hanh, or Plum Village. It was difficult for us to think that our son was leaving us forever, but we decided to be with him when he was making the most important decision of his life. I wanted to meet "the monk who took my child from me. . . ."

When we arrived at Plum Village, we immediately felt the quiet, relaxing atmosphere. At first, I had difficulties getting used to some of the "local rules," such as silence during meals, not walking while talking, and bowing before speaking. Soon I began to enjoy and appreciate these "rules," and I joined some of the meditation sessions. The most wonderful practice I learned was walking meditation. I enjoyed it from the first moment. I even realized that I had practiced walking meditation, without calling it by this name, during some periods in my life. I was deeply moved by our first walking meditation, when my wife and I walked with our son, each holding one of his hands, with half-closed eyes. It was like accompanying a child to his first day of school, like Abraham walking with his son, Yitzhak, to the fire.

Returning home, Michal and I decided to practice meditation and mindful living. Since then, my life has changed a great deal. I am much happier. I focus on developing inner peace and stability, and I have become more open and compassionate towards others. I feel I am growing. Michal and I feel that we did not sacrifice our son. In fact, in spite of the physical distance, our relationship with him has deepened. We are as close to him as ever. We support him on his way and feel he has become our teacher. We enjoy walking with him on his spiritual path.

A Sangha Dad

Al Lingo, True Seal of Virtue, is from Atlanta, Georgia, where he practices with the Breathing Heart Sangha and has started a Mindfulness Practice Center. He is an ordained minister, a practitioner of Psychosynthesis, and leads workshops on unconditional love and forgiveness worldwide. He is the father of Sister Chau Nghiem.

When Phap Co, newly ordained in 1999, said to me as I energetically swept and mopped the dining hall floor in Upper Hamlet, "Go more slowly. Take it easy. We are not working to just make the floor cleaner. This is about meditating as we work. Just take your time and breathe," I experienced being in a place of mindfulness.

When Thây went to North America in September of 1997 and the community at Plum Village held their first retreat without him, I experienced the sturdiness of monastic and lay leadership together and their gentle openness in guiding a Buddhist-Christian dialogue.

When Thây and the larger Sangha transmitted to me the Five Mindfulness Trainings and gave me my Dharma name, Precious Gem of the Heart, I experienced deep relief from suffering and coming home to myself.

When I became aware that I had begun to fall in love with the resonance of the mindfulness bell, I experienced the deep quiet of peacefulness and the intention to offer others this wonderful experience.

When my daughter, Kaira, was ordained as Chau Nghiem at Plum Village in 1999, I experienced the beginning of a personal journey of engagement with a true community of service. I also realized that I was somewhat painfully releasing a child, to whom I was enormously attached.

When I had the opportunity to be in Plum Village for two and a half months during a Winter Retreat, I experienced my ordinary patterns of living stopping, coming to rest deep in myself, calmness that allowed my disguised sorrow to surface, and courage to grow in the direction of inclusiveness.

When, in a Vietnamese New Year's play, the "King of Heaven" and I had a delicious discussion about what a nonsectarian Mindfulness Practice Center might be, apart from Plum Village, I experienced myself drawn toward establishing a Mindfulness Practice Center in Atlanta, Georgia.

When the monks and nuns gather to chant before Thây and the retreatants, I experience in their predominantly Vietnamese presence a profoundly welcoming, untroubled oasis, an invaluable resource, especially for parents and family members.

When I joined the Order of Interbeing at Plum Village, I experienced the strength of the many brothers and sisters across the world with whom I might serve and from whom I find support.

When it dawned upon me that, as the parent of a monastic, I am also a parent to many monastic sons and daughters who are equally beautiful, genuine, and valuable, I began to experience the great value added to my life and that of my entire family by the twenty-year journey of Plum Village and its monasteries in North America.

Al and his daughter, Sister Chau Nghiem,
visiting a Congressional representative in Washington, D.C.

Thây Ananda and his newly-ordained mother, Sister Gia Nghiem, in the Upper Hamlet Buddha Garden

Mother Is Always Alive!

Sister Chân Y Nghiem, True Adornment with Taking Refuge, is from Vietnam and ordained in 1998.

Our garden is full of beautiful flowers
Blooming in the morning sunshine.
Everybody's face looks bright with smiling eyes.
But look!
A young boy sits alone against a plum tree
whitened with fragrant flowers.
I walk slowly to him
And sit down beside him.
Gently I take his hand with my warm heart
And look deeply into his sad eyes.
Are you tired, do you have sadness within your heart, dear child?
Yes, my mother has just passed away and I have lost the blue sky.
  I have fallen on my Knees in despair.
Oh, my dear child!
Look deeply within the palm of your hands
And you will find your mother's love.
She is all around you.
She dwells in pretty white flowers
And in your face blooming with sweet smiles.
You haven't lost your mother,
Haven't lost your blue sky,
Because she has always been
In the depths of mindful breath,
Every moment of your life.

blossoming of community

My Happiness Is Plenty

A Dharma Talk by Sister Chân Không

Sister Chân Không, True Emptiness, is Vietnamese and has lived in France since 1968. She is one of Thây's earliest disciples and his closest assistant. To learn more about her life, see Learning True Love, *her journey of practicing social change in Vietnam and the West. She lives in Plum Village.*

Sister Chân Không

December 6, 2002

The Roots of Plum Village

Plum Village was officially established in October 1982 in two French provinces: the Upper Hamlet, a former farm with twenty-three wooded acres in the village of Thénac in Dordogne Province; and the Lower Hamlet, with fifty acres of hilly farmland in the village of Loubes-Bernac, in Lot and Garonne Province. Just as with a tree, in order to see Plum Village deeply, we need to look at its roots.

I believe the roots of Plum Village lay in the hearts of all the young people who yearn to lessen life's suffering. When we have that yearning, we open our hearts and we do all kinds of things to answer this calling. We work day and night. We give of ourselves with all our strength and heart until one day we become so tired and, just like a car with a flat tire, we feel the need to *stop* and to *look deeply,* to ask ourselves who we are and where our work is leading us.

At the age of twenty-six, I was doing so many things. At that time, war was raging in our country. Countless bombs were ravaging the distant countryside. While newspapers were reporting the number of battles, casualties, and dead soldiers, we were safe in Saigon amidst music cafes, trendy restaurants, gambling houses, dancing halls, cinemas, and theaters. I saw myself living a superficial life in a beautiful house with fashionable clothes and a big salary, while other Vietnamese people were suffering the pain of war. I often told myself that something seemed incorrect, unjust. I had to do something.

The Call for Peace

In 1964, Thây proposed three plans of action to the Executive Council of the Unified Buddhist Church of Vietnam (UBCVN). These plans, if realized, could help our people escape the current situation. The first task was to help poor, hard-working farmers. We wanted to recruit educated and talented young people to be trained at our proposed School of Youth for Social Service (SYSS) to come to the countryside to aid the farmers. The second task was to establish a university with programs that emphasized inclusiveness and nourished many qualities of Vietnamese culture. If the educated youth could learn the best aspect of Buddhism — inclusiveness — then these future national leaders would never consider their own ideology and religion supreme. They would not suppress others for their religion or beliefs, they would know how to listen to others and never harm those who thought differently. The third task was to immediately and officially wage peace in the name of a big and highly respected institution like the UBC. This was 1964, before the United States military entered Vietnam. We were hoping the Unified Buddhist Church of Vietnam would promptly call for an end to the war so that the entry of the United States army could be avoided. Alas, the high officials in the Executive Council did not support any of Thây's proposals except the agreement, in principle, that a Buddhist university be established.

In early 1964, Thây founded a Buddhist university, which came to be called Van Hanh University. At the same time, he began to pilot "Villages of Compassion," preparing the ground for the School of Youth for Social Service. At this time, 90 percent of our supporters came from the younger monastics and lay students in various universities of Vietnam, with a few coming from the senior monks. Higher officials in the Executive Council of the Unified Buddhist Church all felt that Thây was too idealistic. There were many difficult but also very wonderful moments during these times.[1] At the same time that Thây was working to set up Van Hanh University, meeting and planning with intellectuals in the capital, he led young people to the countryside, working alongside farmers to build schools for their children and improve their lives without waiting for outside assistance.

In 1965, when the United States military was preparing to enter Vietnam, Thây, as chief editor of the weekly *Hai Trieu Am (Sound of the Rising Tide),* the voice of the Unified Buddhist Church, called on the North and the South to find an immediate solution to end the war. The Church Council was not pleased at all, and they terminated the weekly. We young people felt the gut-wrenching pain of seeing the publication shut down by our elders. Buddhist high school and university students held forum after forum, also asking for an end to the war.

The Dream of a Practice Center

Before we had a practice center, Thây's students, including myself, made the decision to have one day of mindfulness per week, which meant that no matter how busy we were, we would have this one day of quiet practice to settle our minds (we did not know the term "mindfulness" then). On that day, no one was to do anything but rest, read the teachings, recite the precepts, and have Dharma discussions. I remember being so busy all week; I spent only a little time teaching to make a living, and much time soliciting assistance in public service work, making phone calls, attending meetings, and connecting with other students to publish underground books and magazines telling the painful truths about the war.[2] But on the day designated for practice, I was determined not to do anything. I had to practice stopping! The moment I hopped on the moped to return to the temple, my mind would begin to become still again. Entering into the practice room at the temple, everything came back to the breath only. My mind was not allowed to race to Binh Long or Quang Tri, villages where we had service projects. I stayed in mindfulness while cleaning the room or boiling water for a bath. After dwelling peacefully like that for about three hours, I began to feel quite well again. Afterwards, I would do walking meditation in the village, looking for bamboo twigs, leaves, and wildflowers to make a bouquet to offer to the Buddha.

Thây had drafted a series of Bodhisattva Precepts — based on the most profound teachings in the sutras — into the Fourteen Mindfulness Trainings of the Order of Interbeing in order to help us practice in a deeper way as lay practitioners. Everybody gathered in the main hall to recite the Fourteen Mindfulness Trainings, then to discuss how the trainings had been applied in the work of the past week. Then we returned to our rooms to read and study the sutras. But I also "cheated" — discussing work with Thây Thanh Van, or taking advantage of moments of quiet-mindedness to meditate on projects for the next week.

After the two successful pilot Villages of Compassion at Cau Kinh and Thao Dien, Thây officially established SYSS in June 1965. At that time, the SYSS was a part of Van Hanh University and did

The first six members of the Order of Interbeing. Sister Chân Không is second from left.

not yet have any facilities of its own. This was a difficult time for us. We had to use rooms from temples and universities in different locations in Saigon. The situation was so inconvenient that Thây decided to transfer everything to a new location so that we could build classrooms and dormitories together.

After over a month of urgent work, we were able to build a house with a thatched roof and wooden walls, divided into seven small rooms. Each Order of Interbeing member occupied one room, and the seventh one was for visitors. Even with such a facility, the dream of a practice center remained. Many of the students who came to be trained did not have the same desire for practice. That was why we had the idea of a separate practice center so that we could quiet our minds.

At that time, on the road between Da Lat and Bao Loc, there was forestland that was very cheap. So I thought it might be possible to cultivate a parcel of land where we could grow fruit trees to support ourselves. Also we could divide the land into different sections: this section for monastics, that one for single laymen, the other section for single laywomen, and another area for families. We wished for a practice center like this, but it was only a dream, and we did not know if it could be realized.

In the spring of 1966, Thây received an invitation from Cornell University in New York to participate in a forum on the policy of the United States government towards Vietnam. Professor George Kahin, head of Cornell's Department of International Politics, was a member of the Advisory Committee to the United States government. He wanted to hear the real experiences of the Vietnamese people, and invited Thây to be on a committee representing the voice of peace. When we bid Thây farewell at the airport, we thought he would be away for only three weeks; little did we know that, once abroad, Thây would be exiled to this day — thirty-six years! When he arrived in the West, Thây realized that not only did Western governments misunderstand the issues concerning Vietnam, but popular opinion also reflected a wrong understanding of the Vietnamese people and their aspirations. Thây decided to stay a few more months to help people better understand the situation in Vietnam. Because he spoke truthfully, the Vietnamese government accused him of being communist, while the communists attacked him repeatedly on Radio Hanoi and Radio Beijing for being pro-American.

Meanwhile, back in Vietnam, there were many difficulties at the SYSS. I remember on the first day of the second year, the school building had not been finished, Thây was still overseas calling for peace, and we had no funds left. When we had campaigned for the formation of the SYSS, a few thousand families had donated money to provide food for the three hundred students. But because we needed to complete the school building so urgently, we used that food money to pay the construction workers. When the students began the second year, there was no money left for food. But our days of quiet practice made our minds more clear, and we came up with the idea that each Tiep Hien member would solicit donations from a few well-to-do families that they knew. If we could get ten donors each to give a one-hundred-kilogram bag of rice, we would definitely be able to feed the three hundred students for at least the first month until we could figure things out. In three days, seventeen bags of rice and several trucks of slightly wilted vegetables from the Cau Ong Lanh Market were donated to us to feed the three hundred students. In the morning, we would eat plain rice with boiled vegetables and soy sauce, and in the evening, soy sauce with boiled vegetables and plain rice, yet we found much joy in our work. But after less than six months of this joyful service, the first hand grenades were thrown.

People are Not Our Enemies

The first time that masked men tossed grenades with the intent to kill SYSS students, three young men were seriously injured. One of them, Le Van Vinh, was paralyzed for life due to a head injury. A net deflected the grenades tossed into Thây's room after he had left for the United States. The government said the communists wanted to assassinate us, while pro-communists were adamant that it was the CIA. Each side wanted us to protest against the other side. We kept silent and simply went to the hospital to tend to the injured.

A few weeks later, some of us noticed that every time we had activities with the children in the villages there were unfamiliar people passing back and forth who seemed angry with us. One evening, there was a joyous get-together where SYSS youth gathered to sing folk and love songs. Most of the songs were either Thây's poems or were inspired by his teachings and put to music. One of the songs stated: *"Our enemy is not people, for with whom will we live if we've killed one other? Our enemy's name is dishonesty, its name is ignorance, its name is resentment, its name is vengefulness, its name is jealousy, so our enemy does not lie outside of us, it's here inside each of us."*

While we were singing, a dozen grenades were thrown into the group. People ran in all directions. Two friends were killed, Tran Thi Lien and Nguyen Thi Vui, and sixteen injured.

On the funeral day for Lien and Vui the executive board of SYSS designated me to write a speech for Thây Thanh Van to read. I wrote:

> We dare not be angry at you in spite of the fact that you've just killed our friends because we know you've had a very wrong

> perception of us, and based on that wrong perception, you've killed people who are completely different from your perception of them. You've killed innocent people. We hope that the deaths of our friends will make you understand that our only aims are to lessen the suffering of hard-working farmers in the poor countryside, to help children to have a place to study, and to provide sick people a place to receive medicine for common illnesses.

While trying our best to declare this, I still felt anger towards the people who had just assassinated my friends, but we simply had to try not to blame or accuse. We had to practice loving kindness and compassion. Otherwise, where would things lead?

However, not more than two months following such loving speech, in the early hours of July 5, 1966, armed men took five members of the SYSS to the river where they shot and killed four of them: Tho, Hy, Lanh, and Tuan. Thanks to Ha Van Dinh, the only survivor, we know that before the shooting, the men asked if their intended victims were SYSS members. Upon hearing our friends say "yes," they said, "We are sorry, but we have to kill you," before proceeding with the shooting.

Writing a second speech in response to this tragic event was very difficult. I had to do walking meditation every night, and on the fourth night I remembered the sentence Ha Van Dinh heard before the shooting: "We are sorry, but we have to kill you." That sentence enabled me to write the following:

> We know that before killing our friends, you told them that you were sorry but you were *obligated* to kill them. This means that after the first killings and our statement at the funeral, you have found compassion for us, but in the present war atmosphere, if you had refused to carry out your order, you could have been imprisoned or killed. Therefore, we thank you, and we know that the next time you receive the order to kill us, you will definitely find ways to help us.

Indeed, there was no more killing after that.

Two years earlier, at the beginning of 1964, when Thây presented the SYSS idea for the first time to the officials of the Executive Committee of the Unified Buddhist Church, the majority of the members commented that his vision was too utopian. But, after seeing that the leaders of the SYSS continued to act resolutely according to the Buddha's teachings even after the murders of their friends, using loving kindness and compassion in the face of anger and vengefulness, the people on the Board of the Unified Buddhist Church began to develop compassion and respect for us. Senior monks such as the Venerables Tri Quang, Thien Hoa, Tri Thu, and Thien Minh all became very supportive of our efforts.

We received love and support from all directions, and from then on, our movement quickly grew strong. Most moving of all were the parents of our murdered friends, for example, Hy's father, who came to Saigon from Quang Nam. When he arrived, I was worried, not knowing what to say to him in front of Hy's remains. To my surprise, he just cried profusely, lamenting that his only son was now already dead and asking what other son could he find to continue the social work! In 1975, the movement had nearly ten thousand members. The very war victims whom we had helped became effective volunteers in our programs.

Plum Village Beginnings

I joined Thây in Paris in 1968 and worked with the Buddhist Peace Delegation until the war ended in 1975. Because the number of people asking to meet Thây to learn the practice of mindfulness kept increasing, Thây decided to teach the practice four weeks per year, mid-July to mid-August, at Phuong Van Am (Sweet Potato Village) near the town of Troyes in Aube Province. It was only large enough for fifteen people, using the meditation hall and the kitchen for lodging. Thây had a separate stone cottage of his own, but four permanent residents already took up one room in it. Sweet Potato could receive only twenty guests each week. After one group moved out there was room for the next.

In 1982 we looked for a larger facility in southeastern France, but it was too windy there. Thây inquired about the west of France where it was a little less sunny but not as windy. We found a piece of land in Thénac on a graveled hillside among beautiful woods. There were three stone buildings originally used to raise cows, pigs, and chickens. We named it the Upper Hamlet.

Because the soil contained so many stones, it was hardly possible for Le Nguyen Thieu and his family to cultivate the land and be self-sufficient as farmers there. (Anh Thieu had been Thây's student in Vietnam, and when Thây learned Thieu's family had escaped to France, he invited them to come and settle there.) Thây asked me to look for a second piece of land. We found it only four kilometers from the Upper Hamlet: twenty-one acres with four stone buildings used originally to raise sheep, dry tobacco, and store hay and wine, plus a three-room building large enough for one family. This became the Lower Hamlet where Thieu's family lived and farmed.

After Thieu's family came to Plum Village, workers began to renovate all the animal stables at each hamlet. Because Thieu's French was still weak and no one else in the family could speak the language, I took care of everything from A to Z. I purchased the tractor and translated the manual. I also translated and transcribed an entire automobile driving manual onto two cassette tapes so that Thieu's brother Dung could learn to drive. I took the children to and from school, went through their lessons with them, took each person to the doctor, drove them on errands, contacted the tax office, prepared social security documents, purchased a greenhouse for growing Vietnamese vegetables, searched for the seeds, placed orders for the best type of plum trees, and hired people to plant them.

Although I was working very hard, I felt a lot of joy because I had learned from Thây to simply dwell peacefully in the work and to find joy in it. I did not distinguish between myself and those for whom I was working. I saw that Thieu was me, his wife and brother were also me, and so, too, were their children. Considering others as myself, I did not distinguish whose work it was to do. The more work I did, the more joy I felt. It was strange that one could do so many joyful things within the limit of the twenty-four-hour day. When we were working hard campaigning for peace, I had not yet learned to take such joyful refuge in my work!

Sister Chân Không with a friend in the Lower Hamlet before she became a nun

The First Retreats at Plum Village

One hundred and seven people attended the first retreat at Plum Village. I planned everything very carefully: 110 wooden planks to be used as beds, 110 mattresses, 110 sleeping bags doubled as blankets, very big pots and pans, and gas ranges for cooking. But I had forgotten about setting up restrooms! There was only one restroom for the entire Lower Hamlet, one for both showering and using the toilets! It was the same at the Upper Hamlet. Seeing the situation, the male retreatants took up shovels and dug two "combat" latrines at the Upper Hamlet and another two at the Lower Hamlet.

Despite simple facilities, practitioners still came to retreats. Plum Hill Building — the building with the twenty rooms in Lower Hamlet — looked very pitiful during that period. With no walls and a tin roof, it had been used for drying tobacco stalks. We hired workers to erect walls and convert it into a twenty-room building. Because the cost of plastering the walls was as high as the cost of building them, we left the walls bare. We poured a cement floor rather than paving it with tiles. Despite this, people kept coming to attend the retreats, and many were transformed by the practice. People valued Thây's teachings and invited him to teach in England, Holland, Italy, Switzerland, Canada, and the United States. The number of people learning about Plum Village kept increasing.

In the first years, Thây could handle the arduous schedule of giving Dharma talks in the morning, then teaching walking meditation, mindful eating, and Tea Meditation, and then offering individual interviews in the afternoon. As the number of retreatants grew too large, he had to drop the interviews. However, because Thây's teachings dealt with real life and resolved real suffering, many people still wanted to see him privately. Because Thây's health did not allow this, I helped by listening to their problems. On less busy occasions, I presented them to Thây. After listening to a certain situation, Thây would tell me what advice to offer. But after a time, Thây told me to do this work myself because he was tired. From that point on, I accepted this responsibility and was able to help. I only reported to Thây on the most difficult cases, and he would meet these people separately.

Thây envisioned Plum Village becoming a practice center for everyone. But only Thieu had the desire to practice, while his wife and the other refugees were not yet comfortable with it. The first practitioner who asked to stay permanently at Plum Village was an American named Carole Melkonian. She lived in the Upper Hamlet. Then came Sister Annabel Laity, who had been in India practicing under a Tibetan lama for several years. Thây invited Sister Annabel to Plum Village to help the young refugees learn more French and to organize the practice for Westerners. Later on Eveline from Holland, then Duc and Doan, then Huyen Chau Tinh Thuy (now Sister Quy Nghiem) all came as practitioners. A practice center was finally established.

The Finances of Plum Village

In the first year, we asked practitioners who came to Plum Village to pay whatever they could — for meals and other expenses — without specifying an amount. Vietnamese practitioners, aware of the tradition, contributed well. Westerners only contributed the amount if asked, so the first year there were practically no contributions from them. Some gave only five or ten dollars. But once they were aware of the specified fee, they would find work in advance and save up to

Sister Chân Không guiding Total Relaxation in Lower Hamlet

pay Plum Village the amount corresponding to their length of stay. The second summer, I decided that each practitioner should pay 600 francs (about 125 Euros) per week because—although one cannot put a price on the Buddha's teachings—food, fuel, utilities, and taxes were so costly that Plum Village could not handle the expenses on its own. Now and then, we came across Western practitioners who were so poor because of difficult circumstances that, instead of asking them to pay, we offered them money.

After twenty years, the retreat fee is now about 250 Euros per person per week. As a matter of fact, the cost for food is not very much. The more serious expenses are for taxes, gasoline, and the maintenance of the living quarters, as well as traveling expenses of Sangha members. Cooking, transportation for practitioners, laundry, housecleaning, and ground maintenance are all handled in mindfulness and joy by the brothers and sisters, which saves on labor costs. The time spent on work is also the time for practice. Therefore, after we have paid our expenses, the leftover money is used for construction work, and any excess is sent to help hungry children in Vietnam or to assist Vietnamese writers and artists whose talents have been badly neglected by the government. Expenses for Plum Village residents are kept to a minimum because we recognize that we are a conduit between the affluent Western world and poorer countries.

Two Kinds of Hunger

One day while doing walking meditation with the Sangha, Thây stopped and pointed to a practitioner. This young woman was walking with uneven steps. Her face showed so much suffering. Thây said, "Look there, my children, that young woman is indeed a hungry ghost. She walks, but her feet don't seem to touch the ground." The next day, Thây explained that hungry ghosts are creatures with very small throats and very large bellies. Hungry ghosts need to fill their stomachs, but the food cannot go down their throats. They can never be full. We have to treat a hungry ghost with real peace, real mindfulness, and real love; our wholesome energy will be the magic mantra capable of helping them transform their pain.

The woman's parents hated each other and treated each other horribly. Her father raped her when he was drunk, so she lost any trust in her parents. Because her parents were trusted members of the church, she also lost faith in the church. At school, teachers did not act according to the things they taught, so she lost confidence in school. A person who has lost faith like that will not know how to bring happiness to her family and community.

I realized then that the suffering caused by hunger might not be as great as the suffering of a hungry ghost. There are people with large bank accounts who want to commit suicide. They live with wealth and fame, but are full of unhappiness, shame, and confusion. Through the teaching of the hungry ghost, I saw the wider importance of the Buddha's teaching that can truly satisfy the hunger of those desperately in need of love and understanding. I no longer saw the difference between sharing the teachings of the Buddha and sharing material sustenance with the needy.

No More Waiting

When I first came in contact with Buddhism around 1958, I wanted to join a monastic order. As with everything else that I did, I wanted to commit myself fully. Strangely enough, when I asked to join the monastic ranks under a venerable monk in Vietnam, he commended me for my capability but discouraged me from becoming a nun. He said he could not deny my bodhicitta but my enthusiasm might not be sufficiently deep, and without a good environment for practice, one day I might leave monastic life and end up disliking Buddhism. At the time, the various temples could not understand the aspirations of the young people in my generation. Another venerable monk also refused to admit me. When I made the request to Thây, he said, "Not yet" because the environment was not right. I was not the only one to ask to be ordained by Thây. There were others.

Since the conditions were not sufficient for us to become monastics, we practiced as lay members of the Order of Interbeing. It wasn't until 1988, twenty-two years after I became an unofficial novice, that I officially had my head shaved.

I felt that it was time to officially enter monastic life and was determined to ask for Thây's permission — no more waiting. Thây said that because I had been practicing as a novice since 1966, leaving my family to do Dharma work for the last twenty-two years, I had accumulated enough merit and practice to be worthy of the full ordination (the bhikshuni precepts). Since there were not enough precept masters (the three Dharma teachers and seven witnesses bhikshus need to preside over a full ordination ceremony) at Plum Village, Thây allowed me to travel to India to receive ordination from the Buddha.

That trip had all the right conditions. Thây wanted to ordain Thanh Minh, who had been living in Lower Hamlet since 1987, and me. I would be ordained as a bhikshuni, and Thanh Minh (now Sister Chân Vi Nghiem) would become a novice. Fifty-two people joined Thây on this trip through India, guided by Shantum Seth. At each of the locations significant in the Buddha's life, Thây would give a Dharma talk and we would practice there for several days. We learned to walk as the Buddha walked, eat as the Buddha ate, and sit as the Buddha sat.

As the day of ordination drew near, Annabel also wanted to be ordained, but dared not ask Thây. She looked very sad. We did not invite her to join us because we did not want to impose on her, and we thought that maybe as a Westerner she didn't want to ordain. But seeing her unusual demeanor, I asked her, "Annabel, would you like to be ordained with us?"

"Yes," she answered with a lot of joy, "but I am afraid Thây will not allow it. Would you please make the request on my behalf?"

Thây wished to grant her ordination, but because she had been practicing under a Tibetan teacher for six years in India, he did not want to pressure her. Once she was permitted to ordain, Annabel (now Sister Chân Duc) looked very beautiful.

Working with the Culture Gap

In the early years at Plum Village, we had serious lay practitioners, but there were difficulties regarding food among the Eastern and Western cultures. Westerners who had to eat Vietnamese food three times a day were quite distressed. They only liked Asian food once in a while. It is the same with Vietnamese. It's all right to eat Western food once in a while, but if we had to eat potatoes for lunch and spaghetti for dinner all the time, it would be very difficult. For this reason, Thây divided the Sangha into two hamlets. Western residents, male and female, stayed at the Upper Hamlet, and Vietnamese Sangha members, monastic and lay, went to the Lower Hamlet. However, this arrangement led to unwholesome things that we did not uncover until three or four years later. Although the Western residents all received the Five Mindfulness Trainings, some did not seriously practice the Third Mindfulness Training concerning mindful sexual relations. We later learned their behavior had brought about much suffering. When we found this out, Thây rearranged it so the Upper Hamlet was only for monks and laymen; the Lower Hamlet for nuns and laywomen.

Couples Choose the Monastic Path

This arrangement led to the story of Michael and Fern. They arrived as a lay couple, asking to stay together. Learning that they were not married, we invited Michael to stay at the Upper Hamlet, and Fern to go to the Lower Hamlet. Fern's stay with the sisters watered her childhood wish to become a nun, which brought her much happiness. She begged Michael to become a monastic with her, but he was not ready. A year later, Michael had a powerful dream and made

Sister Chân Không, Sister Chân Duc, and Sister Chân Vi just after their ordination in India in 1988

Sister Chân Không shaving the head of Sister Ha Nghiem (Fern) at Vulture Peak, India, in 1997

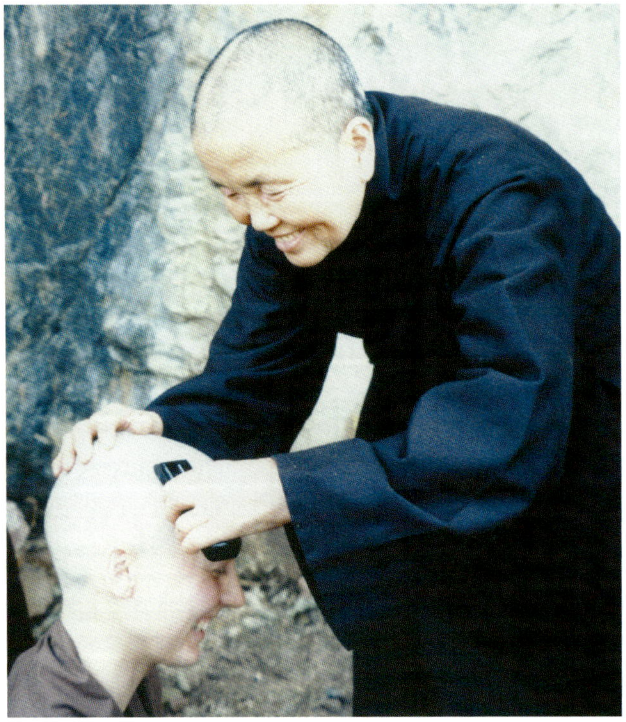

the decision to become a monk. Fern was very happy. They both asked to be ordained and they became Brother Phap Hien and Sister Ha Nghiem. Their love continued because it had gone beyond physical attachment towards spiritual depth. Occasionally, there would be younger Western sisters and brothers who encountered difficulties in their practice. In these situations, Sister Ha Nghiem and Brother Phap Hien would find ways to help. The two have become dear comrades in the path of service.

A second couple, John and Kristin, attended a twenty-one-day retreat with Thây and felt inspired to become monastics, becoming Brother Phap Ngo and Sister Thuong Nghiem. Then Hoang and Tinh Thuy, who had married in Plum Village and lived there together for eight years, became Brother Phap Lu and Sister Quy Nghiem. They felt that only by becoming monastics could they cut the subtle attachments that still bound them, and they decided to ordain together.

Starting the New Hamlet

The brothers and sisters at Plum Village were happy, and their transformation was clearly visible. Then, in 1996, there was an unfortunate accident at Furiani Stadium in southern France. The poorly constructed stadium collapsed, killing several people. After the incident, there was an order for the entire country to form a Committee for Public Safety. One day, the assistant head of our local district, after inspecting the Nectar of Compassion Meditation Hall and the Plum Hill Building, ordered the immediate closure of the Lower Hamlet. That was the most difficult time for the Village. It was March, and there would be eight hundred retreatants coming in July. It would be impossible to complete the reconstruction in time to conform to established standards.[3]

Thây instructed me to go find a hotel with a restaurant that could receive the retreatants. We looked at a dozen properties, but could afford none. But during our search we spotted a real estate office that had been closed down. Thây urged me to inquire anyway. I told the retired agent what we were looking for. He said, "Oh, I know of this place which was a center financed by the government to liven up this rural area, but they went bankrupt and the property has been put on auction."

The next day, he took us to see the place — the present New Hamlet — which had twenty-one guest rooms with restrooms, baths, and a regulation kitchen. I liked what I saw very much, but I thought to myself that the price was certain to be five million francs because this place was much better than any we had seen. When he said the price was one million, I was overjoyed.

The New Hamlet is in the town of Dieulivol, in the province of Gironde. Dieulivol is from the words *Dieu,* which means "God," and *livol* (from *le veut*), meaning "wish." I tell myself, "It is truly God's wish for us to come here." We have brought this village numerous young people whose ways are gentle and light, whose appearance is fresh and joyful.

Thanks to the difficulties with the other hamlets, we came to acquire New Hamlet. After its purchase, I introduced myself to the head of the village, and then at Christmas, wrote a letter to all the people of Dieulivol thanking the land ancestors of the area for their protection and hospitality. I found the names of the original owners of the house at New Hamlet. On November 1, as is customary on that day, descendants remember and honor their ancestors by bringing flowers to the graves of their parents and grandparents. So on November 1, I brought flowers to their graves. The sisters at New Hamlet also wrote a wonderful letter to the deceased original owners of the house and placed it with flowers in front of their graves. The descendants of this family, very much moved by the sisters' letter, wrote lovely responses, expressing their deep empathy for us. We also brought flowers and thank-you letters to abandoned graves. This moved the people, and they appreciated us. Seeing their reaction, I advised the sisters at Lower Hamlet and the brothers at Upper Hamlet to do likewise.

The brothers at Upper Hamlet were full of goodwill. A brother thought that to offer flowers without incense would be amiss. So, following Vietnamese tradition, they offered both flowers and incense with love and respect to each of the graves at the village of Thénac. Alas, this angered the local people, who thought we had used some kind of talisman against their ancestors. They brought the matter to the village head. The senior brother had to remove all the incense, and I had to apologize a lot. That was such a lesson in the danger of loving without knowing others' culture. Every year since then, we hold an "Open House Day" for local people to come visit, view the lotus blossoms, and enjoy traditional Vietnamese delicacies. It helps nourish understanding and harmony between us and our neighbors.

Touching My Happiness

The editors asked me how I envision the future of Plum Village, and what my greatest happiness has been in the last twenty years. Because I always try to practice dwelling peacefully in the present moment and finding the happiness available there, my happiness has been plenty. When Sister Chân Duc decided to become a monastic with me, it was a most happy moment for me. When I see that the number of practitioners who come to visit keeps increasing, I am most happy. Every time a person finds her way to Plum Village to practice and is thereby able to transform her suffering, or when I

The New Hamlet (drawing by Chân Khiem Cung, Australia)

see that a hungry ghost is no longer hungry, I feel very happy, thanking the wondrous Dharma for making these things happen. The beautiful songs composed by Tinh Thuy and Eveline Buemkes have brought me much happiness; I feel like singing them all the time. When someone wishes to join the monastic Sangha at Plum Village and is allowed to do so, I am most happy. Every time I have a chance to do walking meditation with the Sangha, making loving steps on the soil of Upper Hamlet, Lower Hamlet, and New Hamlet, smiling to every flower and every blade of grass, I feel most happy. Whenever I take a meal with monastic and lay Sangha members, I am also most happy. Every time a young child comes to Plum Village and practices diligently, making such profound observations that they sound as if they came from a young Buddha, I feel most happy.

And I know that Plum Village will definitely hold a more beautiful future, even better than now, when I am still helping to take care of it. My younger brothers and sisters will certainly do better than I. They have had the opportunity to learn from Thây when the fruit of his mindfulness is fully ripe. Having been nurtured with such flowers of wisdom while still young, there is no doubt that they will make Plum Village even more beautiful. If my younger sisters and brothers and I always practice with diligence, always turn towards the most beautiful and wholesome path available to us in the most serious and intelligent way we can practice, then the future of Plum Village can only be more and more wonderful in every aspect. Should Thây now become absent or pass away, he would still be present in all the brothers and sisters, in each and every one of us.

I remember that for the first time, at the 1997 Santa Barbara retreat, thirty brothers and sisters traveled along with Thây. (On earlier retreats, he would only bring along a couple of attendants.) The large contingent of brothers and sisters was possible thanks to two generous benefactors who donated thirty plane tickets. The presence of the monastic Sangha gave the 1,200 retreatants many opportunities to return to the present moment by observing the mindfulness practice of the monks and nuns. While coming from the dormitory, some retreatants would see a monastic brother walking in mindfulness on their right. While talking unmindfully or lost in thoughts, others would find a monastic sister walking in calmness and peace on their left. While eating inattentively, some retreatants would suddenly see a brother in front of them taking food with deep deliberation and concentration. These sights served as bells of mindfulness, bringing them back to the present moment. The monastics practiced mindfulness diligently and their Dharma work was very successful. After the retreat, many people declared that in the future, even if Thây were not there, they would still attend retreats like this, provided that there were thirty brothers and sisters from Plum Village to lead them.

The Linden Tree in Upper Hamlet

Therefore, in the future, although Thây may no longer be at Plum Village in his physical form, he will have been reborn in each of his disciples. Thây has prepared our monastic Sangha with great care, telling us day after day, time after time, that we must practice loving one another and that our happiness must not depend on any expectations we impose on each other. Thây has advised us not to be distressed about this sister not meeting certain standards in doing her work, or that brother appearing to progress so slowly in the practice. Although a person might not show much achievement, he or she might have other less tangible qualities, such as the skill to bring harmony to the community or to freshen up the atmosphere among his sisters and brothers. Everyone has his or her special qualities to be discovered. The results of the tasks themselves are not so important. What is important is the ability to love those who are difficult to love and to accept one another.

Thây has offered an image I like very much, that of a beautiful tree branch in autumn, a branch that is vibrant with many different colors. Taking a closer look at it, we might see that this leaf on the left has holes, that leaf on the right is torn, and this other leaf has insect marks on it. But together, the foliage is still beautiful because whole leaves cover the torn ones, the insect-eaten leaves are surrounded by other leaves, and so the whole branch is a symphony of brilliant colors. It is the same with the Sangha. We learn to accept that we may be stronger in some areas and weaker in others, that a sister might be worse than we are in one respect, but better in another. If we supplement and round out one another, and if we accept, love, live in harmony, and support one another, then as time goes on, Plum Village can only grow stronger and develop more vibrantly with the contribution of so many different qualities and strengths.

Love Blossoms in the Wonderful Dharma

Sister Chân Chi Nghiem

Wildflowers carpet Plum Village.
Doves call out from cloudless sky.
The plums blossom at the edge of the forest.
Nature is deepened with colors of
Love for humankind
That has always been in me.
Many times this love was shut off.
There were times it ignited,
Only to become extinguished suddenly.
Not having met enough favorable conditions,
I drowned again and again
In the world of illusions.
Today, the light from the Path and
The wonderful Dharma bring me back
To a life of quietude and joy, where
I may leave behind all enchantments,
Ignorance, greed, anger, and afflictions.

Dear friends! Together with all species,
Let us harmonize in the endless epic song.
In our soft breaths,
Let us listen to the Buddha's whispers:
Look deeply at life forms.
Bring love into places full of hatred.
Cut through ignorance and afflictions.
Come back,
To the boundless land of tranquility.

— April 2002

Family Practice

Be Like a Flower: Thich Nhat Hanh Answers Questions from Children

Question: *Why do you shave off your hair?*
Thây: Many children have asked this. The answer I usually give is that we want to save shampoo! But there are other answers as well. The Buddha said to the monks and nuns that every morning when you wake up you have to touch your head and remember that you are a monk or a nun, not a person who lives in the world. Remembering that you are a monk or a nun, you will know you shouldn't run after fame or profit, but that you should try to cultivate more compassion and understanding every day. That is one of the reasons we shave our heads — to remember we are monks and nuns.

Another reason to shave one's head is that it is a symbolic act: to show our determination not to do as we did before. We really want to begin anew. We want to live a spiritual life. Shaving one's head is a kind of language saying, "I want to pursue the spiritual path of the Buddha." We also want to tell people we are already monks or nuns, and that they should not try to run after us to take us as their husband or their wife. It is an indirect message: I am already a monk; please don't try to seduce me. I am already a nun; please don't try to seduce me. Please leave me alone, so I can follow the path of the Buddha.

Question: *Thây, mosquitoes keep biting me, and I want them to stop it. Can I kill just a little bit every day?*

Thây: How many do you want to kill?

Child: *About one a day.*

Thây: Do you think that's enough?

Child: *Yeah.*

Thây: When I was a little boy I also had that question. Later on, I learned that a mosquito needs food in order to live. A mosquito is always trying to get food. It is like us. When we are hungry we also look for something to eat; that's very natural. I think there are ways we can protect ourselves from being bitten. In Vietnam everyone has a mosquito net to sleep under at night. If they don't use a mosquito net they have to kill mosquitoes the whole night. Not only a few — after you kill one another will come. So killing mosquitoes is not a solution. I think there are a few mosquito nets in Plum Village. Ask and the brothers may let you borrow one so you can spare the life of little mosquitoes.

From time to time, some of the brothers and sisters and I allow mosquitoes to get a bite. When a mosquito lands on us we just breathe in and out and allow the mosquito to get some food. We don't do it very often, but sometimes we want to practice to nourish our compassion and understanding. Sometimes when Thầy sees a mosquito landing, he produces a kind of storm so the mosquito will fly away. We do it without any anger. We just prevent the mosquito from biting.

Question: *Why do we have to die one day?*

Thầy: Imagine what would happen if there was only birth and no death. One day there would hardly be any place to stand on Earth. To die means to leave the place for our children. Our children are our new manifestation. The son is the continuation of the father. The father looking at the son has the feeling he will not die because his son is there to continue him. Looking like that you see you are not dying, you are continuing in your son. And your son is not dying because he is continued in his grandson, and so on. Buddhist meditation helps us look deeply to see there is no real dying, only continuation in different forms.

Look at the cloud in the sky. The cloud may be afraid of dying, but there is a time when the cloud has to be transformed into the rain. But that is not really dying. That is changing form. The cloud changes into rain and the cloud continues in the rain. If you look deeply into the rain you can see the cloud. The cloud can continue in the form of snow, in the form of rain, in the form of a river, or in the form of ice. One day the cloud can become ice cream. If the cloud does not die, how can we have ice cream to eat?

Thầy is not afraid of dying because Thầy sees himself in his disciples — in you. You have come to learn with Thầy, and there is a lot of Thầy within you. Thầy is giving himself to you. If you have received some understanding, some compassion, and some awakening from Thầy, then Thầy is continued in you. Later on if someone wants to look for Thầy they just come to you and they will see Thầy. Thầy is not only here *[pointing to himself]*, Thầy is also here *[pointing to the children]*. This is what I like best about Buddhist meditation. Buddhist meditation can help us transcend death.

You know also that death is important for birth. In our body there are many cells that die every minute to leave space for new cells to be born. Birth and death take place in every minute in our body. If there is no death it is impossible for us to continue in our body. That is why birth and death are linked to each other. Birth gives rise to death and death gives rise to birth. If we cry every time one of our cells dies we will not have enough tears left. If every time one of our cells dies we organize a funeral, then we will spend all our days organizing funerals. We have to see that birth and death take place every moment in us. That is why the role of death is very important.

That is the first answer. But the second answer is better. Looking deeply you don't see birth and death, you see that there is continuation.

Question: *Dear Thầy, how many hours of meditation do you practice daily, and of that, how many hours are of sitting meditation and how many hours are of walking meditation?*

Thầy: Every time I sit it is sitting meditation, whether in lotus position, or half-lotus position, or chrysanthemum position, or any other kind of position. I am not a good mathematician, so I don't count very well. Any time I sit down my practice is sitting meditation. I want to sit quietly and peacefully. During the Dharma talk, although I have to speak, that is also sitting meditation. I sit with stability, with peace. You don't only count the time sitting in the meditation hall; you count the time sitting everywhere. Sitting on the grass, sitting on the hill — any sitting is sitting meditation.

A young practitioner offers incense

Any time you move your feet and touch the ground, anytime you go from one place to another, you can practice walking meditation. In Plum Village it is recommended that we do that. We do not do it just for one hour a day, but all day long. Every time you walk it should be walking meditation because it brings you more happiness, more peace than walking in forgetfulness. Also, we do not talk while we walk because we have to invest ourselves completely in the walking. You give 100 percent of yourself in every step so that you can produce the energy of stability and peace. If you talk, you cannot focus wholly on your walking. Monks and nuns are especially encouraged to walk like that. If you need to listen to someone you stop and listen with one hundred percent of yourself.

The practice in Plum Village is not limited to certain periods in the day. You try to practice the whole day. Whether you are cooking or washing, you follow your breath. If you do things mindfully, that is already meditation. In Plum Village we practice continuous

Teaching children meditation in Plum Village

meditation, and we want to do everything in a relaxed way. Driving a car, talking on the telephone, washing our dishes — we want to do everything peacefully, enjoying the time. We consider each thing as important as sitting meditation.

Question: *Dear Thây, what should we do when other children make fun of us?*

Thây: There are many ways to practice. If you are a good practitioner, then you can go back to your mindful breathing and smile to the person who is making fun of you. That is the most beautiful response. You don't get angry; you just look at him and smile. It shows him you are not affected by his attempt to make you angry. Although you don't say anything, your message is very clear: *I have peace in me. I am not going to get angry. You cannot provoke me to be angry.* This is also a teaching for him or for her. You can do that only if you practice in advance. At home, if someone says something or does something that is irritating, you go back to your breath. Breathing in, smiling. Breathing out, calming. You just look at him and say silently, "Why are you doing that?" You don't say it out loud. You just look and smile, and there is compassion in you. You see that the other person is not happy and that is why he tries to express his violence and irritation. Because you know that people who are happy don't do that. They don't make other people unhappy.

I hope all children who come to Plum Village will practice this teaching. Every time there is irritation in you, don't say anything. Don't do anything. Just go back to yourself and practice mindful breathing. Breathing in, I feel calm. Breathing out, I am not going to get angry. Keep smiling like a flower, and you will disarm everyone. They will not provoke you anymore. They will learn from you.

Be a flower. When you provoke a flower, when you call a flower mean names, what will the flower do? The flower will continue to smile to you. Be a flower. When someone comes and tries to make fun of you or provoke you, just practice: Breathing in, I am fresh as a flower. Breathing out, I am solid as a mountain. Thây has transmitted to you the flower and the mountain. Right? You have the flower and the mountain in yourself. Make good use of the flower and the mountain in you, and you will not be affected by what other people say or do to you. If you begin to practice at your age you will become a great practitioner in the future, and you will be able to help so many people, including your children and your grandchildren.

Question: *What came first, the chicken or the egg?*

Thây: Did the chicken come first or the egg come first? This is a very interesting question. But because you are a student of meditation, you have to be careful not to answer it so quickly. You see, you have to look very deeply in order to see the answer. Look at the lemon tree. You only see the branches and the leaves. You do not see any flowers or any lemons at all. But that is when you do not practice meditation. If you look deeply, if you are a good meditator, when you look at the lemon tree, even if the lemon blossoms and the lemons are not there, you can already see the blossoms and the lemons. They have not manifested because they need a few more conditions, like time, like rain, like heat. So you cannot say that the lemon is not there. The lemon is there but hidden. The lemon tree and the lemon branch, the lemon leaves, the lemon blossoms, and the lemons — they are all there together at the same time. You cannot say which is there first. The time of manifestation is different, but they are always there, you see? When you look into this flower, you see only flower, but the garbage is already there. If you leave the flower without any water, in five or six days, or maybe just one day, the flower will become a piece of garbage. So the garbage is in there, waiting to manifest. It's not true to say the garbage is not yet there. It is inside. It needs only one or two conditions in order to manifest.

So the Buddhist answer to the question is that the egg is there in the chicken, and the chicken is there in the egg. No after. No before.

Question: *I have two questions. What do I need to do if I have a nightmare and I am afraid to sleep again? The second one is sometimes I have problems falling asleep.*

Thây: I have a few suggestions. Maybe my answer is not complete, but I have a few suggestions. When you wake up after a nightmare, don't go back to sleep right away. You may like to sit up and do massage. Or you may like to stand up and do massage and mindful movement in order to help the blood in you to circulate better before you go to sleep again. Or you can go and drink a glass of hot water. But my advice is not to go back to sleep right away after a nightmare, because a nightmare has something to do with the blood circulation.

The second suggestion is that you should be careful watching television because many of the things we see on television might help to create nightmares. We have to select carefully the television programs that we watch. And we shouldn't listen to stories that can help to create a nightmare inside of us. Children like to listen to ghost stories and things like that. They love it. But it may not be very good to watch the kinds of films and listen to the kinds of stories that can help create the nightmares.

The third suggestion is to learn to do total relaxation, after school, before going to sleep, at any time of the day that you have an occasion. Lie down and follow your breath and practice breathing with the song "Breathing In, Breathing Out," and allow your body to relax like this. That is the practice of love directed to your body and your consciousness as well.

Children in sunflowers, Summer Retreat 2002

Breathing In, Breathing Out

Breathing In, Breathing Out

Breathing In, Breathing Out
I Am Blooming as a Flower
I am Fresh as the Dew
I Am Solid as a Mountain,
I Am Firm as the Earth
I Am Free

Breathing In, Breathing Out
Breathing In, Breathing Out
I Am Water Reflecting
What Is Real, What Is True
And I Feel There Is Space
Deep Inside of Me
I Am Free, I Am Free, I Am Free

Another suggestion is that we should think about how to organize our daily life in such a way that adults can be more relaxed in their way of speaking and their way of acting. That helps tremendously because if a child is surrounded by a peaceful atmosphere, a loving atmosphere, and protected from the elements of violence and fear in television, books, stories, and conversation, the situation will improve very quickly. And the quality of your sleep will get better.

Question: *Hi. What period of time in your life did you enjoy the most?*

Thây: The first three years of my monkhood were very wonderful. I had a wonderful teacher, and I had wonderful fellow monks; and my intention, my desire to practice and to become a good monk in order to help many people, was very strong. So even if I had to

Brothers Phap Vi, Phap Ngo, and teenagers practicing cloud meditation

wake up very early in the morning to study, to practice chanting and sitting and working, every minute was joy. It was very nourishing. They say that if you're happy as a novice monk in your first three years, then you'll be happy for all your life as a monk. And it has been true.

There were difficult times, because when I grew up there was war — the war with the French, the Japanese, the Americans. There was a lot of killing and destruction, and we tried to practice not to lose our hope. And we monks and nuns, we organized teams of workers in order to rescue the wounded people, to bury the dead people, to help protect the orphans whose parents were killed in the war. We did a lot of humanitarian work like that as an expression of compassion.

When the war ended, we were able to rebuild our temples and our villages. It was easier to practice like that because during the war we could not stay in the temple only. We had to go out there to the villages in order to help the people. We set up refugee centers, and we rebuilt villages that had been destroyed. And we tried to meditate, not only in the meditation hall, but during the time we worked and helped the people. We tried to have our moments of happiness and peace even during the war because we knew that without that, we could not survive; we could not go very far.

We learned a lot from that painful situation. And now, if my happiness has become great, it is partly due to the suffering we had to undergo during the difficult times. So as practitioners, we should not be too afraid of suffering because suffering can help us grow and can help us cultivate our compassion and understanding. So I accept every moment of my monkhood because every one of them has been very helpful.

Question: *What do you do on your lazy day?*[4]

Thây: Good question. I would like to ask you, what do you do on your lazy day?

Child: *I sleep.*

Thây: Ah, that is a good thing to do. A lazy day is the most delicious day of the week. That does not mean we don't practice, but we practice on our own. There is no bell; there is no schedule; and everyone is free to do what he or she wants to do, including sleeping or reading. But the lazy day is a very sacred day. That is why we should try to respect the atmosphere of peace in the temple for others to enjoy also. That is why we are very quiet. If we want, we can lie in our hammock. We can practice walking meditation or sitting meditation on our own. Or we can organize a picnic or an outing. But we enjoy them in mindfulness because it is only in mindfulness that we can enjoy deeply whatever we want to do on that day. The meaning of the lazy day is that we try to be as lazy as possible. And it's not so easy to be lazy because you are used to always doing something. People have that habit. If they don't do something, they cannot stand it. We call that "workaholism."

Workaholism is an addiction to work. Not doing anything, just trying to enjoy yourself, enjoying whatever is there, is a very deep practice because there is in you a kind of energy that pushes you to do this or that. You cannot sit still or lie still and enjoy yourself, enjoy the beautiful sky. We have to practice in order to transform that kind of habit energy that is always pushing us to do something, to say something. And if we are capable of doing that, our minutes, our seconds, our hours in the lazy day will be rewarding. You can reduce your stress very much just by learning how to be lazy. Sometimes on lazy day, we want to do the things we have no chance to do on other days, like writing a poem, listening to a tape, just making a cup of tea and holding the cup of tea while looking at the forest and the sky, or inviting a friend to just sit with us silently and enjoy each other's company and enjoy what is there — the blue sky or the white cloud or the beautiful forest. And every lazy day has different things to do — not exactly to do, but to be. So the best thing to do is to be.

Question: *How old are you?*

Thây: Well, how old are you first?

Child: *I am six, almost seven.*

Thây: Listen, I am going to give you a good answer. I am the continuation of the Buddha, so I am 2,600 years old.

Child: *Oh!*

Thây: The answer is not finished! I am also the continuation of my father, so I am 110 years young. I know that you are my continuation; and I feel that I am in you, so at the same time I am six years old also. That is true, because I have been reborn in you. You will carry me into the future. So I am quite young. I am six years old. I am in her too *[Thây gestures to another child]*. She has me within her. So I am also ten years old. If you look around you see me a little bit everywhere. I have different ages. Okay?

Plum Village: A Place for Children

Michele Hill lives in Hawaii and has been a member of the Diamond Sangha and Kahawai collective since 1979.

This summer I traveled halfway around the world, from Hawaii to France, to participate in the simple life of Plum Village. Like others before me, I traveled far only to meet myself. Away from the busyness of everyday life, I realized how much I miss by rushing ahead of myself. I settled into the rhythm of Plum Village, slowing down my walking, eating, and talking, and I noticed others experiencing the same feelings. My bowing and smiling increased as the days passed. I experienced a joyful feeling of connection to everything around me — people, animals, flowers, stars, and myself.

Perhaps most impressive was the role of children at Plum Village. The kind of Zen that many of us have practiced over the last decade or so in the West has essentially excluded children. In the Diamond Sangha — my practice community at home — we have scheduled eight or so week-long *sesshins* each year. Rarely, if ever, have we had visitors with children come to an entire training period, and those who may have come for a brief visit have had to rely on their own resources to deal with the issue of childcare, often sharing with other parents.

As more of our Sangha members had children, the separation between a lay, family life and our essentially monastic practice increased dramatically. This has been felt not only by parents, but also by the community as a whole. In some cases, the participation of the oldest Zen students among us has been lost. When I left for Plum Village this summer, this remained unresolved.

At Plum Village I found children are not only present, they are the center of the community. They participate in everything, and people pay attention to them naturally. At several group discussions, Thây raised the issue of including children in practice.

At Plum Village I sat with children for the first time, and I enjoyed it very much. There were smiling faces next to me, looking up at me, a wonderful connection. One day, two Vietnamese children and I had been teaching each other songs. When the bell rang for meditation we went together to the meditation hall. I filed in behind a five-year-old. The experience touched the child in me.

Thây said that if you cannot explain what you are doing to your children, maybe it isn't real. Children must be included and understand what you are doing if it is to be real Buddhism. He feels that children can understand the most profound Buddhist ideas, which at the core are very simple and straightforward. "You are me and I am you," "to understand is to love," "when a finger is hurt the whole hand suffers," are examples of these deep, yet down-to-earth ideas.

Thây said, "We have to find a practice that is pleasant for children. It is very important, for if we can't include the children, it is a defect. When children are included, practice will be pleasant for the parents as well." These words made a deep impression on me. How often had I heard my friends express feelings of being torn between being with their children and going to the zendo? Working parents whose jobs take them away from home so much are reluctant to leave their children again in the evenings or on weekends. I have noticed that while a few families in our Sangha have tried, most have abandoned the effort. It seems to me that creating a practice that can include children will solve a multitude of problems and enrich the experience for all of us. "Practice is impossible without the support of children. Without this, it is an escape from family and society," Thây said.

At Plum Village, there are many excellent ideas about how to include children in practice as well as how to explain practice to them in a way they can understand. I once heard Thây tell how he explained meditation to a child using the analogy of cloudy apple juice. When the juice sat for a while it became clear, then the child wanted to drink it. Thây told the child, "If you sit quietly in meditation, you become clear like the apple juice."

Chi Phuong explained walking meditation to a Swiss child who was having a difficult time slowing down. She asked him if he liked to be hit hard and roughly or touched gently and lovingly. When he answered the latter, she said that the Earth, too, likes this. So when we walk on the Earth we walk as though our feet are touching the Earth gently and lovingly.

Children have a natural love of ceremonies, rituals, songs, and games. Friends with small children have told me it is often the child who remembers to hold hands before dinner, who recognizes the beauty of a small ritual like bowing before entering the meditation hall. At Plum Village, children are given regular responsibilities, like inviting bells, leading Tea Meditation, and participating in ceremonies.

Twice a week while I was there, children's performances were scheduled. Small groups of children practiced songs and dances during the day. Many people did walking meditation holding hands with a child on either side.

While some Sanghas in the West, including our own, have experimented with many of these same ideas, there was a profound difference at Plum Village. The inclusion of the children was not "tacked on" to anything else. There wasn't "real practice" and "family practice." The ideal of life and practice outside of the meditation hall is a reality. The doors of the meditation hall have been thrown open to the laughter of children and adults; and, as a consequence, our lives were thrown open to practice in a way I did not think possible.

This article was published in the Kahawai Collective Journal *and in* A Joyful Path.

Planting Seeds of Peace: An Interview with Sister Dinh Nghiem by Sister Chau Nghiem

Sister Chân Dinh Nghiem, True Adornment with Concentration, is from Vietnam and grew up in France. She was ordained a Dharma teacher in 1999 and is abbess of the New Hamlet.

Please share your experience with children in Plum Village.

This summer in the New Hamlet, a boy came to me and announced, "Today is my saint's day!" (the day honoring the saint for whom he was named). I wished him a happy saint's day. He smiled and reminded me that last year on his saint's day I gave him an ice cream. I was so touched that he remembered. I got him his favorite: orange flavor. Then I told him that if he came back the following year, I would give him another orange-flavored ice cream.

Sister Anh Nghiem and Sister Dinh Nghiem in Maple Forest Monastery

This encounter reminded me of my own childhood in Vietnam. My best memories of this time are in temples. I really enjoyed playing with the monks, and they always gave me fruit. When I went back to Vietnam with my monastic brothers and sisters, I visited the first temple I went to as a little girl, in Saigon. I'm so grateful because who I am now is thanks to the seeds the monks planted in me. I was so nourished by the temple's peaceful, loving environment. I liked to go to the temple because I always went with my mom. She was very happy with her friends in the kitchen, cooking vegetarian food. I just walked in the garden among the beautiful fruit trees. There was a small pond where my brother and I played with the fish. It was very hot in Vietnam, but the temple was shady so the pond stayed fresh and cool.

The Buddha hall had a high, curved roof where lots of birds flew back and forth, singing all the time. They created very pleasant sounds. After lunch at the temple, my mom, her friends, and I would rest in a corner of the Buddha hall. I listened to my mom and her friends talk and, at the same time, to the singing of the birds. It was so warm and peaceful. I can never forget those times.

In another temple we used to attend, the monks would close the shrine hall during mealtime and all the laypeople would go home. The monks went to eat lunch, but one monk told me to stay in the temple and not go home. He took the whole tray of fruit from the altar and told me to eat it, while waiting for the monks to come back and play. I played chess with them and they told me stories of the Buddha. And every time they took withered lotuses from the altar, they gave me the seeds and we had fun cracking them to hear their funny popping sound.

In the first summer retreats that we had at the New Hamlet, I took care of the French children. Every day I learned so much, and I was deeply nourished by the children. They had lots of energy and it was a tiring job to take care of them. But it was rewarding because they received my love easily and in return they gave me love. The fruits, the consequences, of what I did were immediate. The children told me how happy they were even though we only had a few simple toys for them. They said they were happy because in Plum Village their parents were so gentle, not like at home. They loved being in Plum Village because they saw how their parents transformed.

The children surprised me each day. They would always fidget and move around during the Dharma talk, but when I asked them questions after the talk, they knew everything, they had heard everything. When they return home with their parents, they are always the ones who maintain the practice, who remember it longer than their parents do. They are like blank sheets of paper. When I think back to the things I received in temples as a girl, I see that I remember every little thing. So when I took care of kids in Plum Village, they were a real bell of mindfulness for me. They really helped me to practice. Anything I said, anything I did, they remember for years. I only want to draw beautiful things on those blank sheets of paper.

How did you practice when you encountered difficult situations?

I remember one day the children were too noisy and agitated and I was extremely tired. After just one week, I had lost my voice. They

Children perform a play in the early days

were shouting, jumping, and doing anything they liked. I was so exhausted that suddenly I lay down like a dead person. Then the girls calmed the boys down, saying, "Be quiet, look at Sister Dinh Nghiem. She's so tired because we are too noisy." So they calmed themselves down. I didn't need to use control. Because there was love between us and they saw I was tired, they tried to help me. It was very nice.

It was difficult to take care of the children whose parents had forced them to come to Plum Village. The parents would tell their children, "Oh, we're going to the beach," or something to get them to come. In those cases it was hard, and I had to be very patient. Usually, other kids who were strong and happy with the group slowly embraced those children and pulled them into the group. So I see it is so important to have good "seed children" — those strong in the practice. That is why in the teenager program, we invite the seed teens to come back and give them a full scholarship.

One time there were a few kids who were very violent. They didn't want to follow the group, and did whatever they liked. Before they left Plum Village, I asked them if they had enjoyed the retreat. I was surprised when they said they were happy and wanted to come back. Even difficult children transformed.

As they come back year after year, I see how they grow up. Many of them have received the Two Promises and the Mindfulness Trainings. Last summer, I was really happy because they formed a Sangha during the year and kept in touch. In the Summer Retreat, they came together to welcome the young newcomers and make them comfortable. They were so happy together that even though they were teenagers, they still wanted to be in the children's group!

Through these young people, I see how the practice is taking root in the West. I already see the future of Buddhism in the West. Because I was raised going to temples, even though what I learn from Thây is new, it feels so natural. It feels natural to me to receive the teachings and put them into practice, I don't need to struggle or fight. However, there are some French sisters who really love the teachings and feel this is their path, and they really want to practice, but they struggle so much. When I look at them I see that it is easier for me because the seeds were planted in me at a young age; these seeds are very deep. I see the same thing in the children who come to Plum Village from a young age. Because everything is so natural to them now, when they grow up, mindfulness practice will be very normal, and they will not need to struggle with it. Because they begin learning as children, the practice becomes their life, and they won't get stuck on the intellectual level. If they are at ease with the teachings, I know they will be very creative. They will find ways to make the practice more appropriate to the West, because they understand the essence of the teachings.

What things do they like to do?

They all like to invite the bell and to act. The best way to transmit the teachings to them is to tell stories and have them perform the stories. They all love to do this. They also love the practice of Beginning Anew and Tea Meditation with their parents. It is wonderful to include parents in these activities and practices. Every year these sessions have been successful and very moving.

What is the most important thing to transmit to the children?

Our way of being. They recognize this right away. They are very sensitive; they don't live by their intellect. They live by their feelings, so our presence, calmness, gentleness, and peace is most important. Therefore, we need to really practice to have these things to transmit to them.

Jeffrey, Brother Fabio, and the Mountains at Deer Park

Hung Huu Nguyen, Dharma name Chân Duc Son, or True Mountain of Virtue, lives in San Diego, California. He is a dentist and practices with the Deer Park Sangha and the Joyful Sangha in San Diego. His son, Jeffrey Nguyen, True Goodness of the Heart, is nine.

The day my little boy was introduced to the mountains of Deer Park, he was overwhelmed by their size and fell in love with the place right away. Sometimes, while walking uphill with him, his small body seems to become part of the immense space around us. The brothers and sisters have spoiled Jeffrey very much. Sister Fern (Ha Nghiem) is very close to him, and whenever she used to cook in the large kitchen at Deer Park, he tried to help her however he could. Jeffrey calls Elder Giac Thanh his "Su Ong"(grandfather teacher). Just like other young kids, he loves to be with the monks and nuns. Without being aware of it, he has learned to stop and breathe whenever the clock strikes or the bell is invited, no matter where he is.

Jeffrey has a friend, another young practitioner, who comes along with his parents each week on the Sunday Day of Mindfulness. His name is Sage. Sage and Jeffrey are good buddies. Although they don't always play mindfully, it does help us to see how open their communication is. Just by looking in each other's eyes, they know what the other wants to play. They give and take, open to each other's opinions, without any frustration. They share with each other their treasures —

Sage, Brother Phap Dung, and Jeffrey at Deer Park

a pebble, a leaf, a branch, or a small gummy worm. Their time at the mountain is always well spent, and they fall fast asleep on the way home each week.

One morning, I offered Sage my hand for walking meditation and whispered, "Want to take the shortcut up the hill?" His eyes lit up so brightly that it seemed like the sun had risen a bit higher in the vast sky above. Sage looked at his mom with begging eyes. She smiled and nodded her consent. Hand in hand, Sage and I walked uphill, stopping to listen to the chirping of birds and to look for sagebrush. We found more than one variety — each smelled a bit different. Sage very carefully picked just one leaf of each, placing them in his pocket. We continued to the large, cleared plateau at the top of the hill. I left Sage looking for flowers to give to his parents while I walked toward the unobstructed view at the edge of the plateau. I breathed slowly, taking in the freshness of the morning amidst the lush, mountain vegetation. Hearing Sage's footsteps, I turned to see him carrying the flowers he had gathered. He advised me that his mom likes white ones and his dad likes yellow ones. At that moment, his parents appeared at the turn of the uphill road, and Sage ran to greet them. I saw him offer the flowers first to his mom and then his dad. A smile was born on their faces as they put their hands together, offering back a lotus to a Buddha-to-be.

Earlier last year, Pritam, a practitioner from the East Coast, came to help with the Deer Park project. He spent some time at our home. One evening after dinner, Pritam suggested we take a walk. I carried Jeffrey on my back for a while, but it was hard to carry him uphill while concentrating on breathing. Pritam saw I was running out of breath and offered to carry Jeffrey himself. After a little while, Pritam also grew tired. So he lowered Jeffrey down and asked him if he wanted to learn sign language. Being a young, curious boy, Jeffrey agreed wholeheartedly. Pritam took Jeffrey's hand and gave it three squeezes. He then asked, "Do you know what that means?" Jeffrey shook his head no. Pritam explained, "That means, *I love you.*" Then he instructed Jeffrey to squeeze his hand twice. Again Pritam asked, "Now, do you know what that means?" Again Jeffrey shook his head no. "That means, *how much?*" Pritam gave Jeffrey's small hand a hard squeeze in response. "Now, do you know what this means? It means, *this much!!!*" Delighted to find a new game, Jeffrey beamed up at Pritam. During the rest of the stroll, we walked peacefully, with Jeffrey and Pritam hand in hand, taking turns squeezing each other.

Pritam, on his way back home to Vermont, forgot to take a book Jeffrey had given him. It was *Red Fish, Blue Fish* by Dr. Seuss. I asked Jeffrey why he had given Pritam the book he most cherishes. He responded, "Because he is my best friend."

One day, Jeffrey asked me, "Daddy, when does Brother Fabio come back from Vietnam?" Brother Fabio is Brother Phap Dung's nickname. He was sent with a delegation from Plum Village to share mindfulness practice in different temples throughout Vietnam. Jeffrey's question brought to mind an early morning walking meditation at Deer Park, with Brother Fabio walking ahead of me. From the back, suddenly I recognized Thây. Those steps were the same steps Thây took during walking meditation, and they were the same steps that every retreatant was taking that morning — deliberate steps. As the pungent fragrance of sage hit my face, the intensity of that moment was so great that I let go of all my thoughts and just enjoyed the touching of my feet with the ground. The serenity around us was palpable — we felt it with each movement of our body. I was so thankful to be with Brother Fabio on that day.

Brother Fabio has taken Jeffrey hiking to the highest mountains at Deer Park — and Jeffrey wants to do it again and again. Brother Fabio's unconditional love has deeply touched Jeffrey's heart. Like the other brothers and sisters, Brother Fabio is cultivating the greatest achievement of humankind — the practice of true love. No obstacle can stand in the path of true love. No human heart is impervious to it if even a chance contact occurs. In the Vietnamese culture there is a saying, "Like a full bowl of water," which means to treat

someone with your true love. True love can make people cry, but they are tears of happiness, tears that will embrace our afflictions with forgiveness and lead us to a new beginning together as a community. A friend once asked me what we were planning to do during the weekend at Deer Park. My answer was that just being together in the mindful company of the monks and nuns is plenty enough — we would not go home empty-handed.

Thank you, brothers, and thank you, sisters, for being a refreshing island in the middle of our busy world.

The Two Promises

During every family retreat, children learn about the Two Promises, mindfulness trainings for children. We learn a song about them and talk about how they can help us in our lives. The children have the opportunity to receive the Two Promises in a formal ceremony just before the adults receive the Five Mindfulness Trainings transmission. The children receive a Dharma name and a certificate to remind them of their promises.

I vow to develop understanding in order to live peacefully
with people, animals, plants, and minerals.
I vow to develop my compassion, in order to protect
the lives of people, animals, plants, and minerals.

Before the children receive the Two Promises, they are asked to write about their aspirations and why they want to receive them. Here are some responses:

I want to take the two promises because it will make me more mindful, and the people around me will be happier. I also think they will make me be less nervous when I am meeting new people.

— Joanna Spaeder, Loving Home of the Heart, age twelve

~

I would like to take the promises so I learn how to love others deeply.

— Mary Ann Nason, Precious Stream of the Heart, age eleven

~

1. *I hope the two promises will help me to understand my family's needs better.*
2. *I also hope I can teach myself and other people to feel compassion for other people and myself.*
3. *I would like to take the Two Promises and learn the song better so that I can teach it to kids who are interested in Buddhism, but aren't Buddhist.*

— Siena Dawkins, Healing Joy of the Heart, age eleven

Because I care about nature, animals, and people. I want to live peacefully and to be happy.

— Laetitia Colombo, Joyful Garden of the Heart, age eleven

~

I would like to be more compassion. I would like to understand myself and other people better.

— Djuna Westcott-Lahar, Radiant Smile of the Heart, age ten

~

Because Understanding and Compassion is me.

— Jenna Ballinger, age nine

~

I want to be mindful. — Angelique Carl, age eleven

~

Because they will help me be with people more easily, make my life happier.

— Le Nguyen An, Peaceful Joy of the Heart, age seven

~

To help me remember to be nice to all living things.

— Julia Lamb, Gentle Flower of the Heart, age six

~

I really want to understand and help other things. I want to be a veterinarian to help animals. I want to make sure that there are no more poachers in the world, plant a lot more trees and seeds, and help people who are suffering.

— Maeve Krivchenia, Great Offering of the Heart, age seven

The Two Promises

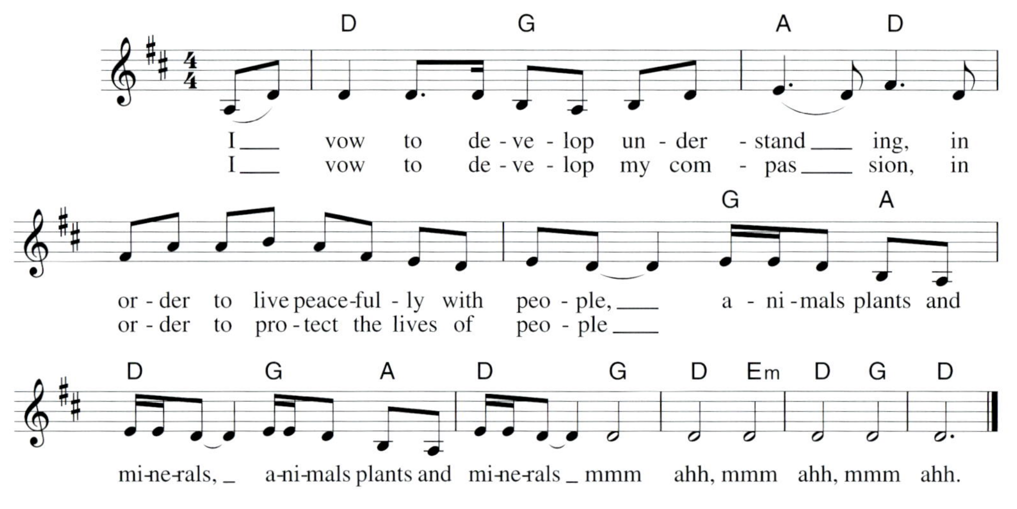

I want to have a memory of Thich Nhat Hanh because he is nice. He is fun with children, and I like singing and praying.

— Max Mondelo, Peaceful Strength of the Heart, age seven

~

I want to climb the path of mindfulness like a monkey. I am flexible; I am deep . . . swimming like a fish.

— Hayden Chichester, Playful Support of the Heart

~

Because I feel I will have a better life if I do it.

— Erin Astin, Amazing Grace of the Heart, age six

I want to receive the Two Promises because it will help me to understand my brother and sister when I water their seeds of anger and seeds of joy and compassion — to live peacefully with them.

— Hylan Kornfeld, Skillful Gardener of the Heart, age twelve

~

I want to receive the Two Promises because if I have understanding then I can be respectful, nice, and helpful, and giving. If I have compassion, then I can love my relatives more, and I can also listen to people better.

— Ryah Bedford, Generous Listening of the Heart, age eleven

~

The Bees

Sister Chân Giac Nghiem, True Adornment with Awakening, is French. She ordained in 1999 and is a mother and grandmother.

If people did not want honey from bees, the bees would not always be so busy! When their hives were full of honey, would they stroll in flying meditation for the sole pleasure of showing the flowers to their friends? Would they fly over calm lakes and fresh streams for the joy of contemplating them? Would they rest, wings spread under the soft sunlight, to let themselves be rocked by the breeze on a blooming flower? Would they meditate together or alone in silence and stillness under the Bodhi sunflower? Would they take days of solo retreat to discover God in them?

Oh! My sweet little friends that fertilize the flowers with your small limbs and your hairy bodies, thank you for this delicious honey. I will live gently under this sky for you!

Touching the Earth for Young People

Touching the Earth is a practice developed by Thây to help us connect with the many different aspects of who we are: our blood and spiritual families; the country we live in; and all beings — animals, plants, and minerals. Sister Thuong Nghiem and Sister Man Nghiem adapted the practice for young people. When the bell is invited, you get down on the ground on your belly with your hands outstretched and contemplate what is being read. For the original text, see *Teachings on Love* by Thich Nhat Hanh.

Sister Chân Thuong Nghiem, True Adornment with Steadiness, is from the United States and grew up in Washington, D.C. She ordained in 1998. Sister Chân Man Nghiem, True Adornment with Swiftness, age sixteen, is Vietnamese and grew up in San Jose, California. She ordained in 1999.

Touching the Earth, I See that I Am a Child of the Earth

(bell, children touch the Earth)

The Earth is like my mom and dad. From the Earth I receive delicious foods to eat, like wheat to make bread, rice, apples, and carrots, and even chocolate from cocoa beans. The Earth gives us material to make our clothes, like cotton and wool from the sheep and wood and stone to make our homes. The Earth takes such good care of me. I feel happy to live on the Earth.

I feel my body lying on the Earth. I feel my arms and my legs and my face touching the ground. I feel that the Earth is solid and can support me. I see the Earth covered with many plants and trees and beautiful flowers, making the air clean and pure. As I breathe in I can feel the fresh, cool air fill my body. I feel calm and relaxed.

I feel happy and safe on the Earth.

(bell, stand up)

Touching the Earth, I Feel Connected to My Mom and Dad

(bell, children touch the Earth)

I am the child of my mom and dad, even though I may not live with both my mom and dad now. I see my mom and I smile to her. I see my dad and I smile to him. I want my mom and dad to be happy. I want them to be safe and free from all worries.

Sometimes, Mom or Dad gets angry at me, and I feel hurt. Sometimes Mom or Dad is so busy she or he does not seem to have time for me, and I feel sad. But other times Mom and Dad take care of me and we can laugh and play together, and we have fun. Mom and Dad have taught me so many things, like how to read, or sing, or do math, or make cookies. I feel thankful to them. I know that my mom and dad were children too, a long time ago, and they felt sad and hurt sometimes, just like me. I know they have had many difficulties in their lives, and I don't feel mad at them.

I think of my mom and my dad, and I feel their love and support, and I feel happy. I know my mom and dad need my freshness and my smiles to make them happy too.

(bell, stand up)

Touching the Earth, I Am Happy to Be Me

(bell, children touch the Earth)

I am a young girl or boy living on the planet Earth. Sometimes I feel small like a tiny bug or a spider happily crawling in the grass. Sometimes I feel big, like a huge, old tree. My branches reach up to touch the clouds, and my roots go way down deep in the Earth drinking from the water under the ground.

Sometimes I am happy like the sunshine, and I make everyone smile. Sometimes I am sad and lonely like a gray cloudy day, and I just want to hide in a tree and cry. But when I cry my tears are like cool rain on a hot afternoon, and afterwards I feel fresh and new. I know whenever I feel sad, or scared, or mad I can go to the Earth and she will always be there for me. The rocks and creatures, the plants and flowers, the sun and the dark starry sky are all there for me. I breathe in the cool, fresh Earth. I breathe out all my fears, my sadness, my anger. I accept myself. I accept myself when I am happy and joyful, and I also accept myself when I have difficulties, when I am angry or sad. I smile to myself, and I see that I am a wonderful flower living on the Earth. I am a part of the Earth, and the Earth is a part of me.

Transforming in the Breathing Room

Hoang Khoi, Chân Dao Hanh, lives in Sydney, Australia, where he practices with the Lotus Bud Sangha. He received the Fourteen Mindfulness Trainings in 1994. He is an Associate Professor of Engineering.

It is difficult to avoid friction in family life. In my family we have gone weeks without directly speaking to each other. However, since we created a room in our house to practice mindful breathing, communication in our family has improved tremendously. When a problem arises, we all gather in the breathing room after dinner. After listening to three sounds of the bell and meditating for about ten minutes — time enough for everyone to calm

Cycle of Life

Lauren Mai Pieczynski, Tam My Hao, is 17 years old. She lives in San Diego and is of Vietnamese and European-American heritage.

I Am Here, I Am Gone, I Am Not Forever:
I am wheat . . .
Glistening gold in the sunlight,
Gray in the moonlight.
I sway gently in the playful breeze
Becoming one with the air and the wind
Along with my fellow friends.
I am rooted firmly in the ground,
Carefree, but very intricate
I am one next to millions
But am I significant?
Without me, everything would be nonexistent —
I am the vital link to people,
animals, plants,
and minerals.
I stretch myself higher
I am one with the elements that give me life
I am gone in the blink of an eye
But I am not sad,
Because I will be back soon.
Please do not grieve for me, I will
embrace the rich soil once again.

I Am Here for You

Sister Chân Dan Nghiem, True Adornment with Making Offerings, is 16. She was born and raised in California and is of Vietnamese heritage. She ordained in 2002.

Support that is pure and goes beyond the
ten directions
Is absolutely inevitable when
Sisters can fully
Trust
Each other.
Reverence with freedom,
Humbleness with NO fear.
Only when we surpass the mental formation
that we are a separate entity can we walk
together hand in hand
On this path of mindfulness with faith and the
ability to
Dwell in the wonderful present moment . . .

and that is when you can say to your sister,
"I am here for you" and really mean it
with all your heart.

down and treasure the presence of all family members — one person starts sharing his or her thoughts. After the sharing, three sounds of the bell are invited, and everyone stands up and practices hugging meditation without a further word from anyone else.

The practice has helped me realize that time alone cannot cure my mental wounds. Forgetting about or ignoring problems does not mean they will disappear. My mental wounds can only be healed when I am committed to looking deeply. I see that the key to success is my willingness to practice letting go, opening my heart to receive and understand the other person's words. I have come to understand that re-establishing communication is the only way to ease the pain in my relationships.

One day I was feeling quite low. I was very happy to hear my son say, "After dinner, I would like the family to gather in the meditation room. I wish to share something." That happened a couple of days after I shared with him my unhappiness about his way of speaking. Sitting down and deeply listening to my son talk, I loved and respected him more.

Gradually, we realized as a family that we could practice breathing outside of the breathing room, particularly during our daily conversations. Since then, the meditation room is not only reserved for re-establishing communication when it breaks down, but it is also a place for the Sangha to gather on weekends, listening to Thây's Dharma talks and sharing our experiences of mindfulness practice.

Joyfully harvesting apples.
From left to right: Sisters Man Nghiem, Mat Nghiem, Annie (now Nho Nghiem) and Christine (now Dan Nghiem)

Practicing as a Couple

Brendan Sillifant, True Virtue of Loving Kindness, is from New Zealand. He has lived and practiced in Plum Village for nearly eight years with his wife Fei-fei.

Blending My Two Loves

When I first came to Plum Village it was my love of mindfulness practice that brought me here; I had never had the thought to ordain. But after a time that wish grew in me, although that wish in me was still quite innocent — even naive. My teacher was a monk, and I wanted to be like him. So I made the determination to return to New Zealand, spend some precious time with my family, and then return to Plum Village to ordain. During this time I grew quite close to a young woman. The blossoming of this relationship created a lot of confusion in me. It seemed like a conflict — to ordain or to marry. I wanted both. I wanted to be with the young woman I was growing to love, and I also wanted to practice wholeheartedly. I spent many months trying to make a decision between these two alternatives, trying to look into my real aspirations and yearnings.

Eventually, I came to see there was no conflict between these two things. I found the most important thing was to see what elements of monastic life were supportive to our practice and to find ways to bring these elements into our life as a couple. I found there was no longer a decision or choice that I needed to make. Instead I tried to blend my two loves and not be caught in my dualistic thinking between monastic life and lay life. I found I could have both a loving marriage and a strong committed practice, and there was no contradiction. I experienced my relationship as a support to my practice, not a hindrance — and my practice also supported my relationship.

Relationship Supports Practice

My wife Fei-fei and I live closely together, and as a result we've grown to know each other quite intimately. This intimate understanding enables us to offer support and guidance to each other, helping each other not to get caught in negative habit energies. The relationship also provides comfort, soul sustenance, and nurturance, which gives me strength to overcome difficulties in my life and practice. I experience my relationship as a kind of Sangha. It supports me in the same ways as the greater Sangha does, yet very intimately. I feel very fortunate to have a small Sangha within the big Sangha. As practicing partners we help balance each other; if I feel sad or anxious, Fei-fei can help me feel bright or relaxed again and vice versa. When one of us is overcome by wrong perceptions about someone or some situation, the other can provide clarity and fresh ways of looking. When we need to nourish the five-year-old boy or girl within us but are unable to do so, the other can offer that loving embrace. When we need the firm words of a Dharma sister or brother to put us back in the practice, the other can provide those words to set us straight. So we have both our own mindfulness to rely upon and when that is weak, we also have the practice of the other to rely upon.

Practice Supports Relationship

The practice of mindfulness helps Fei-fei and me cultivate a loving relationship. It deepens our ability to speak lovingly, listen deeply, and understand ourselves and each other. It keeps our relationship fresh and helps us avoid acting out of our negative habits. The presence of the Sangha also helps us not to get stuck in our habitual ways of relating with each other because it offers clarity and new ways of approaching difficult situations that are usually dominated by habit energies.

The practice of consciously watering the positive seeds has been a tremendous support to us. Watering these seeds in each other has helped us to be aware of the positive qualities in each other and to express our appreciation and gratitude. Because, over time, the positive seeds are watered more than the negative seeds, our ability to appreciate and acknowledge the wonder and beauty of each other is much stronger, even in the midst of difficulty. So when we have disharmony, our motivation is not to hurt each other, but to heal the relationship and establish harmony again.

From Attached Love to Boundless Love

The practice of nonattachment is one that has enhanced my marriage by lessening unhealthy dependence and allowing our love to be light and joyful. However, I also discovered that dependence can be a wholesome part of my life. We have taken refuge in each other because we want to walk together on our path to wholeness. It just depends on whether our way of taking refuge supports us in becoming whole and complete, or whether we rely on the other to complete us in certain ways and do not grow ourselves.

I've found sometimes our love can be a narrow isolated love and other times it is a broad inclusive love. Sometimes in our relationship, our way of loving can be a way of hiding from the world. And the more deeply we invest in each other, the more deeply we cut ourselves off from others. Yet it's clear that our love, to be deep and fulfilling, cannot be limited to each other only. If we only love each other and are alienated from other people, our love grows in on itself; it doesn't flower. It seems natural for our love to want to express itself in service of something greater; that way it can seek a greater expression and flowering. In this way the relationship becomes a nursery for our love, allowing us to cultivate a mature love that can then extend to many others.

Mindfulness and looking deeply help us to see beyond the appearance of the one we love, so our small love becomes a door to great love. In loving each other we can learn to love many people. Over the years I have been with Fei-fei, I see more and more how deeply she is the continuation of her parents and ancestors — that in marrying and making the vow to love her, I have married and made the vow to love also her parents, siblings, grandparents, society, and indeed all beings. Our relationship is really the coming together of two streams, not just two people. We have different opinions, different values, different needs for space and intimacy. Sometimes this can be so challenging. Yet this is our opportunity to reach down to our common humanity, our common need to be loved and appreciated for who we are. This is where we need to embrace love as a practice and where we cultivate a love that can embrace all beings.

Sacred Sexuality: A Meeting of Hearts

I've found that sexuality is one area in our relationship that can become an obstacle to my practice if I'm not skillful. I experience sensual desire as an obstacle to my peace and also as an obstacle to deep communion because my partner becomes merely an object of my desire. But I've also found that sexuality can be an integral part of my spiritual life and practice. With the practice of mindfulness, sex can be no less than a ritual, a sacred and beautiful act that is performed in deep concentration and joy, a deep expression of love and care for each other.

The practice of maintaining our full presence for each other has helped Fei-fei and me keep that heart connection strong even after many years together. This kind of mindfulness is the tofu and potatoes of our love. It is the daily food of our relationship, and with this steady and loving presence, our relationship stays fresh and vital.

Oneness: From Individual to Couple

Life as a couple has a certain vitality and richness that takes me beyond my individual desires and aspirations. We are two, but we are one; and we have really needed to learn to think, feel, and see as one, or there is conflict. If I continue to follow only my own wants and needs and Fei-fei continues to follow only her own wants and needs, we don't find a deep harmony and unity in our relationship. For our love to give us a deep sustenance for our souls, we have really needed to learn to see that the happiness of the other is our happiness and that our happiness is the happiness of the other. This is not an attitude of sacrifice, because we know that deep down, for the other person to be happy, we also need to be happy. So to nurture ourselves and our own deep peace and joy is to make an offering to the person we love. Thây has said that practicing as a Sangha is like practicing as a couple. That it is a true practice of nonself — to see that we are one body and that we can no longer only seek our own happiness without considering the happiness of the other. As a couple, we become so interconnected that way of thinking no longer functions well. We simply have to learn to think in a new way, a way that really acknowledges our true interconnectedness — our interconnectedness as a couple, as a Sangha, as the world.

A Rose for My Father

Terry Barber, True Heart of the Moon, lived as a permanent resident in Plum Village from 1992–1998 and in Green Mountain Dharma Center from 1998–2001.

Yesterday we celebrated the Rose Ceremony for the first time in Green Mountain Dharma Center, a ceremony to honor mother and father. On the day of the Rose Festival one hundred people

Drawing by Sister Tue Nghiem

came, including about forty children and young people, some of whom helped in the ceremony. The Boston Sangha, our local Vermont Sangha, and people from other parts of Vermont came together for a moving and joyful day. The day is mostly for our mothers, but it led me to think mostly about my father.

Since I was young, my relationship with my parents has been strained; but in the past few years our relationship has changed in a fundamental way, though of course we still have our difficult moments! We treat each other with love and a new openness rather than with distance and defensiveness. Now we relax in each other's company and simply enjoy being together. When I remember the past, this seems like a miracle.

From adolescence on I was resolved not to be like my parents — was proud of "not being like them." Now I laugh to see how alike we are — how all my strengths and weaknesses come from them, my other ancestors, and my society. So it is much easier to forgive my parents and to forgive myself for things I am not so happy about in me. I see how the conditions of their lives made them who and how they were with me. I see how their suffering became my suffering. As my love for my parents grows, I find it easier to accept myself. As I come to understand and accept myself, it becomes easier to love and accept them. A small insight in one area brings a bit of clarity in another, and slowly understanding grows and love flows more easily.

I always had more contact with my mother and her family, so it has been easier to see ways I am like her. It was only later I discovered my father, his family, and my father in me. His family was poor, and his parents and older sister and brothers died when he was very young. The younger children were separated, and he lived with relatives and worked for his keep. When I was growing up he was silent, rather critical, and rarely home. He seemed not to love us, but maybe he didn't know how to show his love. I always knew how hard he worked, but I'm struck now by how heroic his efforts were to do his best to provide for his family, to serve his clients who were mostly very poor, and to give his children two parents even though his marriage was not so happy.

Now we seem able to be our better selves with each other, not so easily falling into old ways of relating; and all the love and goodness in my father is being revealed to me. I appreciate his quietness now while we are together; it gives him, me, and everyone a lot of space and peace. In our more loving relationship, childhood and family suffering seem to be carried more lightly.

When I was growing up, I felt so alone in the way I saw the world, so it's strange to discover that my father has always shared many of my dreams and values, and my wonder at life. All along there was someone in my life who could have understood me if conditions had been different. Sometimes when I'm feeling isolated in a group of people, I walk or eat with my five-year-old father. It always makes me feel like a big sister, and he explores and experiences the world without the anxiety he must have felt in his childhood. It's comforting for me and for him, and I feel connected with him and with his parents, brothers, and sister whom I was never able to know.

Since living in Plum Village and Green Mountain, I feel closer than ever to my family, even though they are thousands of miles away. I am no longer running away from them. The deep connection is very real. We are always somehow together and part of each other.

Punk Palace in the Moonlight

Ian Prattis, True Body of Understanding, teaches anthropology at Carleton University in Ottawa, Canada, where he practices with the Pine Gate Sangha.

My eighteen-year-old son, Alexander, was studying at the Glasgow School of Art. From our transatlantic calls, I knew he was in trouble with drugs. I arranged to visit him. At the airport I scarcely recognized him in his multicolored hairstyle. He met me with a warm hug and a big smile.

At his apartment, I knew something was dreadfully amiss. There were no books or art materials. The large apartment was occupied by a shifting population of punks, drug users, and dealers. Alexander left for a while; I sat in his squalid room wondering about him. Several hours later, he returned, badly beaten up in a drug deal gone wrong. He confessed that his requests for money to complete summer courses were false; he needed the money because he was deep in Glasgow's drug world. I listened quietly, calmly washed his damaged face, and learned that he could easily have been killed that night.

We walked to nearby Kelvingrove Park where I introduced him to walking meditation, encouraging him to trust the Earth to absorb his pain and distress on each out-breath. As he calmed, I suggested perhaps the beating was a wake-up call. I offered him two options: £500 cash to enter drug dealing in a bigger way, or spending the next several weeks living mindfully with me. He refused the money, so I will never know how much bluff I used.

Alexander and I read most of *The Miracle of Mindfulness* together and did some of the exercises. Together we practiced sitting and walking meditation, enjoying silent meals, and conscious breathing. I taught him to coordinate body movement with breath, and also to defend himself with martial arts. We discovered that we enjoyed one another's company and humor.

The residents of "Punk Palace," as I named the place, gathered each evening to listen to heavy metal music, do drugs, and talk. Committed not to take drugs while I was there, Alexander smoked cigarettes. I listened quietly to these young people pour out their lives. For this short time, they became my family. No other parent ever visited them, let alone lived with them.

One night several punks asked me to teach them walking meditation. I agreed — if they remained drug-free for two days. Two evenings later, my punk friends boosted me into a tree and told me to crawl along a branch that hung over a private park. They bounced over the fifteen-foot-high railings and caught me as I dropped. After we picked ourselves up and stopped laughing, I introduced them to walking meditation. Slowly and mindfully for over two hours, we walked barefoot in the grass.

The next evening the punks spoke of their awareness of my presence in Punk Palace. Drugs were used less; my new friends turned their music down. No drug deals went down while I was there, and the kitchen even got a cursory clean! I thanked them and quietly said I was also aware of them, of every acid hit and cocaine use, of every moment of their despair and anger. Silence followed. Two people began crying. I softly thanked them all for their kindness and consideration and said I was there for them. I then left them among themselves. These young people knew everything interconnects. They were simply lost.

Alexander and I worked on practical matters for which we prepared with meditation. We met with college tutors who had not seen him for six months, his college counselor, and his bank manager. I enrolled him in a martial arts academy run by a kickboxing champion who treated his students as family and began and ended sessions with meditation.

The final step was to talk to the drug dealers. We met in Alexander's room. They were the most hardened young people I have ever met. I cleared Alexander's outstanding debts, and quietly and firmly told them he was out of drugs. The tension could be cut with a knife. I breathed slowly in and out, extending love and compassion to them. After a time, they too relaxed. They asked about my martial arts background, which Alexander had no doubt exaggerated. It was our only common ground apart from Alexander. I wove a web of stories and showed them some drills, mentioning how many martial arts experts end up in healing and meditative practices. The more I talked quietly and directly to them, the more violence left the room. When they left, I knew they would leave Alexander alone, but their energy disturbed me.

It would be ideal to say the whole situation did not get to me, but it did. After one all-night party, I got really angry over Alexander's wasted opportunities and irresponsibility. I did walking meditation, unsuccessfully trying to calm down. At 6:00 a.m., I packed my bags, found Alex, and asked him to walk me to the bus stop — I was leaving. His face showed fear that I was walking out of his life.

We walked silently. Alexander insisted on carrying my bags. They were much too heavy, but I let him. Then I stopped, told him to put the bags down, and hugged him. I told him I love him. We both cried. I told him why I had been so angry and invited him to join me at the airport hotel for a few days to continue our mindfulness training. Relief flooded his face.

Our mindfulness training continued at the hotel with emphasis on life skills — budgeting finances, handling peer pressure, completing college assignments, etc. We meditated and continued breath work with martial arts training. Once again we drew closer. When I left, Alexander saw me off and the real test began for us both: Alexander has to choose how he wants to walk through life, and I have to allow him the freedom to choose.

Reprinted from the Mindfulness Bell, *Issue 22, Fall 1998.*

Helping My Father Die

Jacqueline Roy lives in Angoulême, France.

My father was a longtime chemical engineer in a lead mine in Morocco. He returned to France for his retirement, sick with cancer. The last time he called me, I felt that he was dying. My husband Serge and I got on the road right away because we wanted to see him alive one last time. It was a 450-kilometer trip, and when we arrived, my father was already in a coma. The whole family was suffering. What made the members of the family afraid was to see him dying. My father's body was agitated by convulsions and uncontrollable movements. Serge and I took refuge in our deep breathing and mindfulness.

Right away, I put my hand on my father, caressing him while talking about Morocco, the sun, the blue sky, the great swimming places, and diving beneath the ocean. He relaxed immediately. We were at his bedside for four days and four nights. Hour by hour our internal peace grew and began to affect other members of the family. In us there was the "heart of the pure sky," a Japanese expression that means serenity and mindfulness. What allowed us to hold ourselves together was our habit of practicing and the presence of our teachers in us. Their energy of mindfulness helped us become solid enough to go through this experience. The longer we were there, the more the peace of God rooted itself in the room and in all those present.

When my father took his last breath, a bird came and sat on a branch in front of the window. He sang a cry of joy and the bell of the village rang seven times. My mother came into the room at the moment of the song of the bird, and she listened to the bird, the bell, and said, "Thank you, my God, Jean is among the happy."

Father's Steps

Sergio Zaccone, Gentle Path of the Heart, is Italian. He practices with a Sangha in Genoa, Italy.

My father's steps
Leave prints no more.
He is now the sun's smile
The wind's freedom

Thousands of moons and stars
Are less bright
Than his last glance at this life

Without using your mind,
Look!
The tears and the smile
On the world's most beautiful face.

★ ★ ★

This poem is about a different way to look at my father's death, which occurred when I was only thirteen. After many years and also thanks to Thây's teachings, I am now able to smile to that and I feel lonely no more.

While I was walking from Upper to Lower Hamlet during the 2001 Plum Village Summer Retreat, I composed this song. It was a day or two after I asked Thây about my mother and family situation. My mom committed suicide when I was one year old.

I never knew my mom consciously. Thây's deep insight inspired me. I realized more deeply that my mom was present right within me. I am my mom, and she is me. As Thây said, "It is certain that you are one of your mother's manifestations. You are her manifestation." I was deeply touched with the understanding that I could meet, know, and heal my mother through looking deeply within myself. This song is for her, for me, for all current, past, and future generations.

—Deborah Ball

Walking Meditation for Mom

Deborah Ball, Gentle Presence of the Heart, recently completed her Master of Divinity from the Union Theological Seminary and now lives in Hawaii.

When I walk for my mother
My heart fills with love

When I practice for my mother
The world fills with love

The sunflower is opening to the sun
The sunflower is smiling to the sun

The orange butterfly, unfolds its wings
To the sky.

When I walk for my mother
My heart fills with love
When I walk for my mother,
I am my mother,
And I am love
And,
When I am love
I give love
And, the world has more love.

Wonderfully Together

Love (For All of My Friends)

Thây Giac Thanh, Sound of Awakening, is from Vietnam. Since 1990, he had been the eldest brother in the Plum Village community. He was ordained a Dharma teacher in 1992. In 1997 he became head of practice at the Maple Forest Monastery and in 2000 he moved to Deer Park Monastery where he served as abbot. He passed away in October 2001.

Life, death, peace, and joy
Are going together beautifully
Human relationships nice in so many ways
A moment you come
A moment of love and care
Turning everything into eternal love!

Drawing by Anneke Brinkerink

Sisters Gioi Nghiem, Uy Nghiem, and Phuc Nghiem

Sister Thuan Khanh and Sister Tue Nghiem enjoying a rest in the Lower Hamlet

Trust

Sister Chân Gioi Nghiem, True Adornment with Mindfulness Trainings, is Vietnamese and grew up in Sacramento, California. She was ordained a Dharma teacher in 2001.

A space to grow
Openness is the key

Trust
  A wide road
  A smile
  A pat on the shoulder
  A river flows without a dam

Trust
  You trust me
I trust you
  (and of course I trust myself too)

Let's practice together.

Going Out to Play

Sister Thuan Khanh, Pure Joy, is from Hue, Vietnam and was ordained as a novice there. She came to practice at Plum Village in 2000.

This late afternoon so joyful, my sister and I
Running here and there in the middle of the wild daisy field
Daisies fully blossomed, daisies in a bud
Picking this flower, I offer it to the Buddha
The flower smiled, my sister smiled
Fragrance carried by the wind to all directions
Offering to the ten directions of the Tathagatas
Bringing peace to everyone
Thanks to the wild daisy and the riverbank
Giving me pure joy
Giving me the spontaneity of a simple smile
In the heart of the Earth with the vast sky above
I smile to nourish the bright heaven
So my youth forever joyful, blooming in a flower
Enriching more the color of my robe
On the path flowers bloom, hearts sing.

Arriving at a Spiritual Home

Lorena Monda, True Perfect Way, lives in Placitas, New Mexico with her husband, John, and daughter, Lisa. They practice with their neighbors, the Mindful Heart Sangha. Lorena is a Doctor of Oriental Medicine and psychotherapist, and the author of the book The Practice of Wholeness: Spiritual Transformation in Everyday Life.

Last summer while practicing walking meditation around the lotus pond in the Lower Hamlet, I saw myself forty years from now walking very slowly with a cane on the same path. At that moment, I realized I had found my spiritual home.

I had been coming to Plum Village since 1991. I was drawn to visit after a retreat with Thây in Texas during the Gulf War. After that retreat, I found myself making plans to stay at Plum Village for one month. I came with my seven-year-old daughter Lisa, and we stayed in the Upper Hamlet. My stay was a bit difficult. There were very few monks and nuns, and with people coming and going all the time, things were somewhat chaotic. I certainly did not know then that I had found my spiritual home. But I received the Five Mindfulness Trainings and kept practicing. In 1993, at a retreat with Thây in California, I received the Fourteen Mindfulness Trainings — but even then, I did not call myself a Buddhist.

In 1996, I returned again with my daughter, now twelve, and my husband. The previous spring, a beloved family friend, who was twenty-seven years old, was murdered. I was in so much despair over this; I felt like it was difficult to go on living in a world with such violence. That summer, after much suffering, I came to Plum Village for refuge. We stayed for one month in the brand-new New Hamlet with a small group of wonderful people, lay and monastic. There I found a group of young people from all over the world who reflected many aspects of our friend. I was so comforted in knowing the Sangha as a reflection of my dear friend that when I left Plum Village that summer, I left with hope. Though I still couldn't quite call myself a Buddhist, I knew that my practice was essential to my well-being. And every question I asked Thây, he answered with the word "Sangha."

Lisa and I returned to Plum Village in 1999, when she was fifteen. I had thought that this might be the last summer she would want to come, as she was getting older, and interested in other things. We practiced for three weeks in the Lower Hamlet. Plum Village has grown so much since we had first arrived eight summers before. On this trip, we reconnected with many old friends and made many new ones. The familiarity with the practice, the teachings, and the place made our stay very pleasant. I began to see the value in returning.

To my surprise, last summer, after a very difficult year between us,

Lay friends at the New Hamlet. From left to right: Jane, Sister Linh Nghiem (before she ordained), and Barbara

my daughter, now seventeen, asked to return to Plum Village. This time, I stayed in the Lower Hamlet and she in the New Hamlet with the teen program. My time there was spent practicing letting go of some of my notions about myself as a mother and my daughter as my child. My Dharma discussion group, the Daisy Flower Family, helped me so much. One week, my family was full of young women in their twenties. As I shared my difficult experiences of letting go and letting my daughter be herself and have her own experiences, they shared with me their experiences of doing the same with their mothers. I was so grateful to hear and take in the wisdom of these beautiful young women, and I knew that my own daughter, practicing in the New Hamlet with other young people, would be okay. I was thankful that this place of refuge and beauty exists for us. And one misty morning walking slowly around the pond, whether or not I was a Buddhist, I knew that I was truly home.

A Circle of Friends

Lisa Monda, Genuine Kindness of the Heart, is eighteen and lives in Placitas, New Mexico. She plans to study theatre and psychology at Sarah Lawrence College.

Last summer I spent three weeks at Plum Village. I had been there three times before with my mother, the first time when I was seven years old, but this time, it was my decision to go. I needed to separate myself from things that had happened during the

Lorena and Lisa Monda

previous school year — moving away from home and adjusting to the somewhat chaotic and competitive life at a boarding school for the arts. After these challenges and changes, I needed time for myself to be able to relax and process everything that had happened. Most importantly, I needed time to figure out who and where I was outside of these life-changing events. It is easy to get caught up in the past and future and forget to live life; I want to live as fully as possible.

At the monastery, I stayed with fifteen girls between the ages of thirteen and twenty from all different parts of the world. At first, communication was difficult, so we divided ourselves into groups by language. However, after the first week, we all branched out. We found ways to communicate and made an effort to learn each other's languages. By the end, it was easy to talk to one another, and we became very close.

Those fifteen girls are amazing people, incredibly open and understanding. There was no cattiness or fighting. Even the youngest behaved with a remarkable level of maturity. We were all there to enjoy ourselves, to practice being mindful of ourselves and our environment, and to get as much as possible out of the experience. We were dealing with our own issues, but always had time to help each other. We were open to any lessons the others had to teach us, and we were willing to offer what we knew to help the others learn.

I never would have thought a group of complete strangers, speaking at least four different languages, could become so close in such a short time. It was also amazing to see how much everyone grew in those three weeks, and to see the change in myself. In many ways, it restored my faith in other people to know that there was an environment where people consciously practiced being at peace with themselves and each other. I am grateful to have had that opportunity.

Love is All Around

Brother Chân Phap Vi, True Taste of the Dharma, is from East Germany. He was ordained in 1999.

The aspirations I held as a child to help people diminished somewhat as I became an adult. As I continue on the path, I see that the child within me is finding ways to embody my deep aspirations, to bring them back to life.

One way that helps me do this is being in this Sangha family, participating in daily activities with so many people. I grew up pretty much by myself, so it has been a big challenge to fully participate in the Sangha activities every day and to learn that love is all around me. It takes time to see and recognize love in all its different manifestations, to experience the growth of trust. Many people in society lack this sense of community life. We don't have the experience of doing something together as a family, something creative and inspiring, something that connects us and contributes to the world. When I can touch this, I am not so ruled by what comes from outside. Instead I am nourished by my deep desire to bring peace into the world, so I am able to respond to external situations instead of reacting to them.

A Place of Stories

Shelley Anderson is American and lives in the Netherlands with her partner, Francoise. She works for the International Fellowship of Reconciliation.

Brothers Phap Vi, Phap Co, and Phap Tue at a picnic in Upper Hamlet

A HUGE LINDEN TREE with a swing. Delicious Vietnamese soups and spring rolls. Weeding in the garden to my heart's content. Getting up way too early in the morning for meditation. Watching a ray of sunlight make its way across the wooden floor. Backaches, leg cramps, and surreptitious glances at the clock — when will this sitting be over? What am I doing here? Enjoying the touch of carrots while chopping vegetables. Silently walking under the stars to the meditation hall.

And day after day, feeling the gritty defenses built up during daily life outside melt away. Letting go of mortgage payments and deadlines and watching instead how steam from the cup of hot tea in my hand swirls in the air. Having time to grapple with disturbing questions about how I react to others, about how I live my life. Having time to learn from others. Struggling in different circumstances with similar issues. Learning to enjoy the sensation of my breath.

I left my first retreat at Plum Village both disillusioned and happy. I had been looking for a magic wand that when waved over my head — presto! — would make me instantly and permanently happy. I came away with a name for what I had been craving in my life: mindfulness. And with a way of cultivating that mindfulness: following my breath.

Over half a dozen retreats later, the impressions of Plum Village have multiplied. These impressions involve, most of all, fellow retreatants — the wonderful support and laughter of the gay and lesbian affinity group during one retreat; the moving story of an incest survivor during another. Plum Village is a place of beautiful simplicity, surrounded by trees and ponds full of lotuses. It is a place where monastic discipline is practiced in order to reach freedom. For me, Plum Village is most of all a place of stories. The story of the Vietnamese woman, now living in Australia, and her life as a refugee. The story of the American Vietnam War veteran, and of the ghosts of war that haunt them both.

Plum Village is a place where stories can be told honestly, a place where there is time to listen to stories, stories of both suffering and joy, and to reflect on their meaning. The stories might be 2,600 years old, from the Buddha's life, or from the life of the 16-year-old German student seated on the meditation cushion next to you. In the telling and listening to these stories in mindfulness, there is healing.

Plum Village is a laboratory. Suffering and its twin, joy, can be dissected here. Both can be looked at safely here. Out of this examination comes something that life in my ordinary world of shuffling papers and grocery lists doesn't lend itself to: a sense of connection, a desire to help others, a determination to heal and be healed.

Plum Village is also a laboratory in another sense; it's an experiment in applying Buddhism to the Western world. The nuns' conference that took place in the mid-1990s was one such experiment, where Western nuns from different traditions met to talk about their experiences. One highlight of that meeting was the laughter when one British Theravadan nun wrapped a smaller Vietnamese nun from Plum Village in her yellow robes. The respect accorded religious sisters in Plum Village is often, unfortunately, lacking in traditional Buddhist countries.

This is why people return to Plum Village; it is a happy place. A place where you can learn and practice mindfulness; a place where you can both relax and reflect. Most importantly, it's a place where

Lorrie, Sandra, and Wibke enjoying fall in the Lower Hamlet

a person can learn to cultivate happiness within herself. The seeds of practice cultivated during retreats allow you to carry a piece of Plum Village with you, wherever you go.

Like a Child Again

Jean-Marc is French and lives in Paris.

Spring '97, Paris.
"A Zen book, why not?"

I want a book that is not difficult, that doesn't give me a headache, if not I won't finish it. Ah! This one looks easy to read, simple concepts, ordinary words . . . OK! I buy *Touching Peace (La Plénitude de l'Instant).* This book touches me. Maybe it's the right time for it to come into my life; it's full of common sense.

What happened to this old dream I had when I was fifteen, to go to India to follow a teaching? Now I'm over forty-five. I deeply buried this spiritual aspect of myself that was guiding me when I was young. At the end of the book I note the address of Plum Village. Why not visit there when I go for vacation in the south of France? It's right on the way. I have nothing to lose. If I wait to go to India, for sure I'll wait forever!

I tell myself, first you should write, and if the price is over 3,000 francs a week, you know that it smells fishy and you should forget about it.

One week later I receive the registration form. 1,150 francs a week, OK. A new experience to tell my friends about, something to pull their leg. Who could ever imagine me on a spiritual quest? It would be the negation of how I appear to others.

I arrive. It takes two hours to register. God! How slow they are! We are queuing and they take time to say a kind word to each of us. Efficiency, performance — Plum Village is not the place to find these virtues. It makes me smile. Anyway, they don't need to be stressful! I already enjoy this Upper Hamlet. There is some gentleness, a special attention from each of us to others. Some monks join their palms and bow after having given me a simple smile. The slightest sound of a bell makes everyone stop, breathe, and go back to his own rhythm. I will surely find something wrong. It sounds too much like, "Everyone is so nice and happy." Eh! The bells of the nearby church are ringing and nobody stops! "Why," I ask with a blaming tone, "are they not as worthy as your bells?" "You are right!" they reply. "We didn't pay attention." All the guests look very normal. They don't have this kind of crazy, baba-cool, or New-Age look. Many of them are young.

Finally, a French brother arrives to lead our group after the meal. We get to know each other. People come from different countries, different backgrounds, and all levels of society, but we have the same needs. Before making the decision to stay for a week I ask, "What is the official stance of the village on homosexuality?" One of the monks, Thây Doji, answers me, "When two people really love each other, it doesn't matter if they are two men, two women, or a man and a woman. Where there is love this question is not needed." No discrimination, that's clear. There is nothing vague about the answer. Now I can settle down and leave my usual mistrust.

The following day, I say to myself when I wake up, I still haven't seen Thây, or the behavior of the monks and nuns toward him. How is he? What game does he play? Is he as clear as what he wrote in this book I just read? The answer comes soon after and comforts me. No, there is no court around him; he doesn't sit on a throne wearing special clothes. No need for external signs; he is there, truly present, and from him emanates a serene gentleness, a joy to be alive. It's obvious; all my resistance falls. Finally, I can let go and feel at ease, confident, becoming a child again.

Several years have passed. It's the beginning of the Winter Retreat of 2001–2002. I'm here again, where I feel at home, at ease, happy. What if I were to stay several months, just to see . . . .

"That's too much; it's not reasonable. No, I forbid myself. It doesn't make sense. What would your beloved ones think of this? You are very

fragile now, you would come back disturbed." Deep inside of me, though, I feel that it's the best choice. During the years since my first visit we developed a Sangha in Paris and shared our practice, but still it's here in Plum Village that I feel at the center of myself.

Faith is the Most Beautiful Thing

Sister Chân Thieu Nghiem, True Adornment with Lightness/Beauty, was born in Vietnam and grew up in Finland. She was ordained a Dharma teacher in December of 2001.

I received a lot of love and care from my parents and my three younger brothers growing up, but I always felt a lot of fear and insecurity. I had to take care of myself and protect myself. When I entered into Sangha life less than five years ago, Thây often taught us that we have to surrender to the Sangha. Just hearing that sentence made me uncomfortable. I could not do it wholeheartedly. I would run outside of myself, looking at what was happening around me in the Sangha, trying to change what was going on outside. I had the tendency to make demands on others. I didn't know how to look back and ask myself, "What do I have to offer to the Sangha?" I didn't know how to come back to the island within. Thây told us that the Sangha is like our garden. In the garden there are big trees, standing very solidly and straight, like a redwood tree. There are also dry trees, or very young, weak trees that need a lot of care. We have to be nourished by the strong trees and allow the weak ones to heal. Inside of ourselves it is the same. We have to be nourished by the healthy parts of ourselves and be patient and allow the weaker parts to heal.

One time an elder sister told me that I am like a bomb that slowly explodes. No one dares to come near me, to play with me, and no one listens to me. Another time a different elder sister said, "Sister Thieu Nghiem, you are like a flower. You are a very beautiful and fragrant flower. Everyone admires your beauty, but no one dares to touch you because you are full of thorns."

I am realizing now that these thorns are rooted in my way of thinking and perceiving things. Most of the time my thinking and my perceptions cause a lot of conflict and disharmony in myself. This conflict and disharmony manifests in my words and actions, which causes others to suffer also. But when I take refuge in my practice, coming back to my breath, I have the chance to look at my thinking and perceptions. The breathing gives me more space and time. I am not so caught in my thoughts and perceptions. I am less likely to act from wrong perceptions and more likely to act from a compassionate and clear view.

In the Sangha we have an agreement not to borrow something without asking permission first. One time a sister borrowed something from me without asking, which made me unhappy. Recently, the same thing happened to me again, and I felt a lot of love and gratitude to my younger sister. I was grateful to her because she trusted me and didn't hesitate to borrow my table. She did it because she wanted to serve the Sangha. The same situation was repeated, but now, because of mindfulness, my way of thinking and perceiving had changed. That helps my capacity of loving to grow and my gratitude to increase.

A sister once asked me, "What do you see as beautiful?" I answered right away, "Faith is the most beautiful thing." By faith, I mean trust between people, the ability to come to each other and share deep things, to share from our hearts. But the faith I speak of is also faith in the Dharma, the Dharma doors that I touch and experience directly through my practice.

Recently in Lower Hamlet, we had sessions of Shining Light (a collective practice of sharing feedback) for those who would receive the full ordination or lamp transmission. Having a chance to take part in these sessions, to share our way of looking and to practice deep listening, I realized that my faith in the practice has grown radically. After each session of sitting together, I practiced looking deeply into my own growth and my sisters' growth. I saw very clearly that in a few Shining Light sessions, my sisters have grown in their way of choosing words, in their tone of voice, in knowing what should and should not be said. They are better able to help the candidate see, understand, and accept the things she needs to accept in order to go forward in her transformation. The growth of my sisters, of my community, gives me a lot of faith.

I also received Shining Light from my sisters. I received a lot of love, acceptance, forgiveness, and inclusiveness. When I received words of praise, I felt joy in my heart. But when I heard words of constructive criticism, many emotions arose in me. There were times when I felt guilty. There were times when I felt gratitude, but there were also times that I felt pity for myself because I felt that I wasn't understood. In all of these situations I always practiced returning to myself, asking, "How have I lived for these things to happen to my sisters? What can I do in order for the communication between sisters to become better? What can I do in order for understanding and love to grow deeper?" When I look into my sisters' perceptions, using them as a light to shine on my own way of perceiving, I can see that the Sangha has become a living energy in me, a catalyst for my transformation.

In the first years of practice, my faith was like the sprinkle of rain. But with time, this sprinkle of rain has become the dew, very sparkly and radiant. Even though there are nights when I have gone

Nourishing sisterhood in the New Hamlet

through storms with big winds, the light in my lamp has never wavered or become less bright. When the wind is stronger, the wick is more solid and the light on the tip gets brighter. My path appears more clearly and I become less fearful.

My Practice is Happiness

From a Dharma talk given July 28, 1999 in Plum Village

Thây Doji, or Brother Chân Dao Tri, True Path of Wisdom, was born in Algeria of French parents. They moved back to France while he was a boy. He received ordination in the Rinzai tradition in Japan where he practiced for nine years before coming to Plum Village in 1992. He became a Dharma teacher in 1994. He has contributed greatly to building the French-speaking Sanghas.

Often, when people talk to a Buddhist monk, they ask, "What is your practice?" Usually I answer, "My practice is happiness," and they are quite surprised. They expect me to say, "Well, I do ten thousand prostrations," or "I walk around the temple all night," or things like this. I just say, "My practice is happiness," and they're very surprised by that.

But we should be careful when we say "happiness." We should not confuse happiness and joy. Those are two different things. If you have met the person you are in love with, and she is beautiful or he is beautiful, every time you see that person, you are so joyful. You meet her in the line waiting for your food, or she is in the meditation hall, and you see that person and you have a lot of joy. But happiness is when you are able to live with that person for twenty or thirty years; then you may discover what happiness is. So joy and happiness are very different. They are not the same thing.

I once met a very old couple in a suburb of Paris. They were in their eighties, and they spent their time taking care of their vegetable garden and flowers. They were very cute, and they got along very well. They were very kind to each other. I told them, "I am very impressed by the way you live because you have been married for more than sixty years and I see a lot of harmony in your relationship." There was a silence after I said that. They looked at each other and then turned to me and said, "It has not been easy." They had realized happiness.

But why does it take so long to find that balance that we call happiness? Because we have to meet and embrace a lot of difficulties and our shortcomings along the way. We have to embrace them one by one, small ones and big ones, to eventually uncover the ground of happiness that is always there, always present. So it takes a lot of patience to reach that balance.

Shining Light

The person in front of us is a mirror, but we tend to ignore that. I realized this very clearly in one of our practices, a collective practice called "Shining Light." Shining Light is about carefully watching the practice, the daily behavior of one brother or one sister, as a group. We gather as a group and we make a list of positive points and less positive points about this person. When I teach this practice in retreats, people become very nervous because who wants to be in the position of being looked at by a group?

Actually, this practice is very beneficial because there are three guidelines we have to respect when we do it. The first one is that when we shine light on someone, we should always start with their positive points. I know that in society we do not usually do this. When we speak about someone else, unfortunately, we are often carried away, and we have a lot of negative things to say about him or her. It just comes out, and it is quite a strong practice to put a break on that energy and to decide to start by saying positive things about this person. And for many of us, it may be very difficult to find positive things about the person because we may have had troubles with him or her and all we can find are the negative points. We have to make a point of looking for positive aspects of that person. It may be a little thing. Maybe this person dresses neatly, or this person speaks very kindly, or he or she walks beautifully. It can be a very little thing, but when we start to list the little things like this, eventually we'll be able to discover more and more important positive things about that person whom we did not like so much at first.

The second guideline is that we have to be willing to change our point of view. We may have an opinion about the person whom we are shining light on, and then find out that thirty other brothers or sisters in the room have a very different opinion about that very point. So that alone allows us to reflect a little bit and to ask, "Is my view correct or not?" So practicing Shining Light, we have to reconsider our point of view, our opinion, of someone. We have to analyze and look at it and say, "Is that really true? If I really think that about this person, and thirty other people who also live with this person think differently, my opinion may be incorrect. So I have to look at this carefully." We have to recognize that our perceptions are very limited sometimes.

The third guideline is we must use compassion. We are not here to put down the person with negative or unskillful behavior. We are here to help the person, so we need to use very compassionate words. Eventually the whole group puts together all the positive and negative qualities and we take a long time to make a very kind, careful letter. Then we give the letter to the person. And it is always a great help to the person when they receive it.

Others are a Mirror

What surprises me a lot in this practice is that very often we will see weak points in the other person that we have ourselves. I am always surprised to see that brothers point out shortcomings in others, which are actually their very own shortcomings. I have realized that we are able to see our own difficulties more easily in other people. The other person is a mirror, and it is very reassuring to find this out because we understand that there are no real separate selves. Through my experience of the practice of Shining Light, I see that our brother, our sister, our spouse, our children, or our colleagues at work may be very much a mirror of ourselves. And once we know that, we are much more at ease with what is going on.

Of course, it not always easy or fun to see the truth. And when we are in a relationship, sometimes we say, "Enough. I want to quit. This is too much, I cannot go on." This is why so many people divorce these days. So many couples separate because it is too difficult to look at their shortcomings in each other. It is almost impossible. Nevertheless, happiness will be born only if we are able to transcend that difficulty and that situation, if we are able to embrace the obstacles like the old couple that I met who are so beautiful, who have walked the path of life together for so long. They have gone through a lot, but they have managed to stay and transform the difficulties, one by one, the big ones and also the small ones. We should not underestimate the small difficulties because the small difficulties piling up will make a big one.

Walking meditation around the Lotus Pond in Lower Hamlet

We may judge someone and think, "That person is so angry. It is so unpleasant to be with that person." But have we looked into ourselves? Have we looked at the angry person inside us? Maybe we feel someone is so dominant, so overpowering, but have we looked at the tendency to dominate, to control in us? Or we feel someone else is so weak and messy, and it is unbearable to live with that person. But have we looked into our own habit of messiness or weakness? We have not done that. So it is very beneficial to remember that the other person is a mirror and first go back to ourselves and ask, "How am I in that area?"

Happiness comes from knowing who we are. That's what we have seen so far. But knowing who we are is not enough. We then have to accept who we are. This is the second important point. Knowing the truth is not enough; it then has to be accepted. And sometimes the truth is very difficult to accept.

Acceptance

Last year, I received a telephone call from Perigeux, a town fifty miles north of here. I could feel right away that the man calling had a lot of difficulties in his life. He was not familiar with the Dharma, but someone very kind just gave him the telephone number of Plum Village. So I listened to him a little bit and then I said, "Please come here to visit on a Monday when we have a lazy day. We have lots of time then, so you can come at any hour and we will talk together." On Monday he arrived. When I saw him, I knew right away that he is the kind of person no one wants to get close to. If you were to meet that kind of person on the street, you would not want to come close to him. First, his face looks very tired, very sad. And he has a wound on his arm, something that's not healed very well. His clothes are not very clean, and his whole person is not very attractive at all. So our tendency would be to go another way if he comes near us because he has so much suffering. You feel that you cannot embrace that suffering, so you move away to avoid meeting him.

When he arrived, I told him to sit down under the linden tree in the Upper Hamlet, and I asked him, "What has happened to you, what is your story?" He told me that seven years ago his wife left him, and he was unable to accept that. He left and went on the road and became a homeless person. He left everything. He had a daughter too, but he left the daughter in the care of another person. He just left and went on the road. During those seven years he met a lot of people on the road, contracted a lot of diseases, was wounded, beaten up, and had many, many difficulties and suffering. He said that now he had a kidney disease that no doctor could really cure. His only contact with human beings was in the hospital. He would go to the hospital twice a week for some kind of treatment. In the hospital, the nurses and doctors were very busy. He was not a person to them. He was Mr. Kidney, Mr. Kidney with a rare disease. They would not receive him as a person. So he had absolutely no contact with humanity. He was really isolated.

This was almost one year ago, so we still had a lot of lotuses in the pond in September. After he spoke, I took him around the pond and we looked at the lotuses. We walked slowly, then I invited him for lunch. On Lazy Day here in Plum Village there is no bell for lunch, no silent meals, so everyone was speaking and was joyful and happy. So we just sat down and had lunch, and that's all we did. He was just there with us. At two o'clock he said, "Now I have to go back, but I want to thank you so much." When he thanked me I swear I never received such a warm thank you from anyone. It was so moving. It was so big. It was such a big, deep sense of gratitude that I felt happy for a week after that. I felt very, very happy after that. I received that gratitude directly, and I reflected on that, asking, "What did I do?" I did not do that much. I just listened to him, and I shared with him our environment, the environment of Plum Village. That's all we did. We shared a meal together. We did not do anything complex, but somehow this man, who was not included anywhere, felt a sense of being included here. He felt that he was a part of a family even though it was just for a few hours. Three hours is enough. He felt that he was a part of something. That seed of being included may develop in him now because he has touched it.

Continuously Clearing the Ground of Our Minds

I tell you that story because it's about accepting. Happiness comes from knowing ourselves and not fooling ourselves about who we are. It also comes from accepting, and accepting is not so difficult. It's just to be with whatever comes up the way I was with this man. Although when I first saw him I felt repulsion, I stayed with this feeling and eventually he felt included, accepted. It's the same with our own suffering, but it is more difficult because sometimes our small sufferings begin to pile up, bit by bit, day after day. Our suffering accumulates, and then it is big and compact and ready to explode. Then it becomes very difficult to accept our suffering.

Sometimes what piles up is also the energy of loving, the energy of sharing that is in us. Each one of us has this energy of love in us, but we may not express it, we may keep it in. Love is exactly like milk. On a summer day, if you keep a glass of milk outside and don't refrigerate it or drink it, it will become very sour. Our love is the same. If we don't express it, it will become very sour. It will be undrinkable. So we have to look into those little stones in ourselves, and we have to express our love for others.

During the Summer Retreat, Plum Village life is quite a bit busier for permanent residents than usual. We have to receive a lot of people. We have to cook. We have to answer the telephone and manage many different things. And sometimes little problems arise. For example, the telephone rings, and having to go a little too quickly, I bump into somebody, but I cannot stop to apologize. It is too late, and I have many other things to do, and I forget about it. But during walking or sitting meditation, when my mind calms down, that event may come back to me very clearly. That is why I always carry a notebook with me because I may remember that event, but I may forget it the next minute. So I write it down, and I remember that I bumped into that person. And the next time I meet that person, I go to him or to her and I say, "I'm sorry I did that, I was in a hurry." Most of the time, the other person does not even notice, it was not a big deal, just a minor bump. But sometimes that same little action may have triggered someone's big suffering. That is why we have to be very careful about those little stones that come up every day in our daily actions and make sure that everything is cleared. We have to clear out our consciousness all the time. It is very important to do that.

The Lower Hamlet Bell Tower at dawn

We have to do this with the positive things, too, not only the negative. Recently during a Summer Retreat a brother came and greeted me after breakfast, asking, "How are you? How is your health?" And at that moment, I had to translate an announcement for the French-speaking brothers and sisters. So I went to the microphone and I couldn't respond to that brother's question. When I finished translating and turned around, the brother was gone. This is a little situation, and I could have thought, "Well, the brother's gone. It doesn't matter." But I make a point when I meet that brother again to say, "Thank you, I know you are very busy. You have many things to do, but you came to me and asked me how I was." This is an act of love. This is a little thing, but it is an act of love. And if we see it in the setting of the Summer Retreat for someone who has a lot of responsibilities, to have the time to do this is an act of love. So I find him and say, "Thank you. You have done this and it is very good for me." Not only the negative things, but especially the positive things need to be remembered and need to be taken care of.

You can start to do this practice with one person, one person who is easy to connect with. And you will see how the relationship with that person will grow and will become very different, much more rich and happy. From the outside, it will be very visible. And once you have started with that person and both of you are used to doing that and not letting anything, any knot remain in your mind, then you can start with another person, and the other person can start with another person.

This is how the practice of happiness can grow in a group, in a family, in any kind of circumstance where many people are living together. It is quite simple, but we have to start from the beginning. We cannot just say, "Oh, this person is so difficult. I cannot embrace her or him completely because it is too much, it is too heavy." But if we start small, gradually, we will see the whole feeling of the relationship change completely and transform. It is the practice. Happiness is the practice — knowing who we are, accepting who we are, accepting our suffering, our difficulties, clearing the ground of our mind continuously, constantly. It's like when you work in the garden; you see a stone, and you put it to the side. You know the peasants who worked in the fields in the past used to do that. They wouldn't leave the stone there because they knew if they left it, the plants could not grow. So when you find a stone, put it to the side. A small stone, a big stone, stones of any size, just put them to the side. Take care of each one of these stones.

My Conditions for Happiness

I have to know the conditions that make up my happiness. For each one of us, happiness is different. When I asked myself, "What is my own happiness?" I wrote down these things: To be able to get up slowly in the morning; to be able to see the sunrise. For me, the day I see the sunrise, even if I'm very busy, is a good day. Then I need to go to the bathroom in peace, and it may sound vulgar but it is extremely important. All those things we do everyday, brushing our teeth, going to the bathroom, should be done in happiness, should be done with pleasure. It may sound funny, but for some of us it may have taken many years to regain our freedom in these activities. Because we are so much in a hurry and there are so many things to do, we go to the toilet quickly, and if it does not pass through us easily, we take some medicine to make it quicker. That's very sad. It is very important to be able to go to the bathroom in peace, to be able to go to the next activity slowly. When I came to the Dharma talk today, I took ten minutes to arrive. I arrived on time, but I took ten minutes, walking very slowly, because I know that if I arrive in a hurry, you will also feel the hurry because I will transmit it to you, and that is not what I want. Another condition for my happiness is to have a clean room. For me, if my room is clean and my desk is clear, it means my mind is clean, clear, and quiet. I don't have to go very far to see if I'm happy or not. I can see right away in my different activities.

Each one of us should write our own *Discourse on Happiness.* It is very important to have it because then we will have a guide. We can look at our discourse on happiness and ask ourselves if we are living in accord with it today. Then we know if we are happy, because we know the conditions for our happiness. ⌘

Healing

Yacov Granot, True Happiness of the Heart, lives in Jerusalem, Israel.

I had gone to a consultation,
For expert advice.

Only after returning home
Did I realize
That with a swift, compassionate stroke,
While smiling at me,
He had cut off my head
Cleaned it out
And put it back

He said, "Come again if you wish."

But, I have been coming and going so much,
I am in collision with myself.

Look at the green leaves over there.

Written in Plum Village
after a private meeting with a monk.

My Teacher Cacahuète

Kai Romhardt, Shining Lotus Blossom of the Heart, is from Germany. He has been living in Plum Village since July 2001 and participated in the Lay Core Group Retreat in West Hamlet, September 2001.

I want to praise the qualities of one of Plum Village's most loved and effective teachers, one who is able to open Dharma doors that most of us cannot touch or even see. His subtle teachings have already deeply penetrated the Sangha, and his reputation is growing. In his young years, he has already cultivated many of the highest qualities a determined practitioner can achieve.

The name of this treasure is Cacahuète ("peanut" in French, pronounced: Kakawet); he has white hair, three-and-a-half legs, and is a dog. During my long-term stay in Plum Village, he has become one of my most important and beloved teachers. He is living total *freedom.* The story goes that he picked the village on his own, running away from his old home. He didn't take anything with him. Not even his dog kennel or his favorite bone. Totally naked he arrived. Teaching total letting go.

His independence was obvious from the beginning. He would not choose one master but hundreds, even thousands, of friends who collectively take care of him, teaching nonattachment. He would choose as his home not one hamlet but all of them, using all kinds of transportation, teaching non-action and non-decisiveness. His feet get easily confused when he is running too fast, but I believe that he is a great actor, who wants to make others laugh, practicing the art of bringing joy to others.

I have enjoyed many walks and runs with Cacahuète and experienced his fearlessness, greeting every car in the middle of the road, thereby supporting the drivers in learning the art of stopping. He seems to enjoy totally what he is doing in the present moment and is well known for his total relaxation in impossible places and positions, exploring the capacity of his body to stretch, and developing beginner's mind. Cacahuète developed a perfect sense for the direction of the Sangha energy and is sometimes even able to redirect it in a positive way all on his own.

He rarely misses a Mindfulness Day or Dharma talk, showing deep determination and interest in the Dharma. If people carry him out of the meditation hall because they don't like his characteristic smell (which helps them to develop non-discrimination), he gives us a lecture in embracing his anger and in non-reaction. Because of his patience, he usually sneaks back into the meditation hall after a short while, giving the person who took him out the opportunity to practice letting go.

Noble Cacahuète

Everybody I have talked to seems to have had very personal experiences with him. He makes them smile, mostly just by his joyful presence. His techniques of bonding and deep listening are very subtle, and over time he has developed skillful means to approach different forms of suffering in his human friends. He is famous for his compassionate licking of hands or feet. His way of bonding is usually quite discrete (most of the time avoiding direct eye contact).

In my experience, he is always present in the right moment. When I left the village in the middle of the night for a journey to Germany, he would wait at the parking lot, and when I returned, he was the first Dharma brother I saw. When I started to write this article he would lie in front of my room late at night as if he knew what I was doing. In many situations, Cacahuète would mirror my mental formations about Sangha members in an extraordinary way, giving unconditional love to those I had been struggling with. His equanimity can best be observed during walking meditation. His slalom[5] between hundreds of legs is the dance of a bodhisattva, creating brother- and sisterhood in every step and jump.

I don't know when Cacahuète will receive the lamp as a Dharma teacher officially, but he teaches anyway — with or without official recognition, demonstrating the art of signlessness. He needs no brown jacket[6] to be heard; an excellent teacher always finds his students. When guests in Lower Hamlet were asked what brought them the biggest joy during the Summer Retreat, three out of ten would say, "Cacahuète." So he is already a star, but his humbleness saves him from becoming disconnected from the crowd.

Everybody who thinks that Cacahuète is an ordinary dog should look more deeply. Let's learn from him. Observing Cacahuète's practice is a practice of its own. Volunteer to be his attendant for one week, day, hour, or minute. It's a very beneficial practice.

Daily Mindfulness Song

*Rupert and Shawn Tower are from England.
They wrote this song in the 2001 Summer Retreat and performed
it at the Thanksgiving Festival to the delight
of the other Lower Hamlet retreatants.*

(To the tune of "Puttin' on the Ritz")
When you feel blue and all dispersed
What you can do to come back to Earth
Is . . . daily mindfulness

When your mind strays from the now
Or if you feel afraid to lose a cow[7]
Return . . . to mindfulness

Nourish mindfulness each day in every motion
Maintain each breath with joy and calm emotion

So if you feel sad, depressed, or bored
There's always a way to be restored
In . . . daily mindfulness

If today is yesterday
And next week comes into play
Return . . . to mindfulness

Follow your breath with ease and you'll feel super
Soon you'll aspire to be a full-time Buddha

So now you know, keep in the flow
And you will reap what you sow
And enjoy . . . daily mindfulness.

Tastes of Plum Village

Brown Rice Recipe

Brother Chân Phap Lu, True Dharma Companion, met and married Tinh Thuy (now Sister Quy Nghiem) in Plum Village in 1990. They have lived in Plum Village ever since and both ordained together in 1999. Phap Lu is a doctor of medicine and acupuncture.

Rice is a main dish in Plum Village. In Vietnamese cooking, it's the first dish we learn to cook because rice is present in every meal. It's a challenge to cook rice for a hundred people so that each grain is soft and delicious. The dishwashers will appreciate your cooking skill if you avoid burning the rice on the bottom of the pot.

Here is a simple recipe for brown rice from the abbess of Clarity Hamlet, Deer Park, Sister Trung Chinh:

1) Measure 350 ml (or 1½ cups) of raw rice for 6–7 adults. Use two portions of water for each portion of rice. Newly harvested rice needs less water. If you want the rice more firm, use a little less water, but too little water can cause the grains to remain hard.

2) Wash the rice, drain it, then add the water.

3) Cook with or without a lid on high heat until it boils.

4) Reduce heat, cover, and simmer for twenty or thirty minutes more. A larger quantity of rice takes longer. (You can use a metallic heat diffuser if your pot does not have a thick bottom, which will prevent burning.)

5) After thirty minutes, remove the pot from the heat and let sit on a cool surface, covered, for twenty minutes. This will allow the heat to condense to steam and loosen the rice from the bottom of the pot. Don't look into the pot! This will interrupt the cooking. You can keep the rice warm for a couple of hours by keeping it covered. Before serving, aerate your rice with two bamboo sticks. Bon appetit!

The best way to learn is to come to Plum Village and cook rice with the community as I have for the past thirteen years. I first learned to cook rice with my mother when I was six years old by watching her cook on a big fire made with palm leaves. She reduced the fire by removing branches and protected the rice from burning by adding water. When the rice was cooked she removed any excess liquid, which we drank with great enjoyment.

When our family moved to Saigon, my mother learned to cook

Ancestors' Day, Thanksgiving offering, Summer Retreat

Drying brown rice in Vietnam

rice with charcoal and she began to use less water to save energy. She taught me many special Vietnamese dishes that I used to cook for my friends on holidays when I was a student living in France. When I came to Plum Village, I learned from my elder brothers and sisters how to cook rice for a large group of people, one hundred or more.

Since 1988, Thây has encouraged us to write a Plum Village cookbook, but there is always so much joy and love in Plum Village that we keep forgetting to realize our project.

Pho (A Traditional Vietnamese Soup)

Brother Chân Phap Do, True Paramita of the Dharma, is from Vietnam and Germany, where he worked as a chef. He was ordained a Dharma teacher in 2001.

If Vietnam could be contained in a bowl, then this would be it. This wonderful soup is enjoyed everywhere in Vietnam, every day. There are many variations of *pho,* this being the most simple. Once you have mastered this version, feel free to improvise according to your tastes, family requirements, etc.

Our Vietnamese brothers and sisters usually enjoy this soup for breakfast, or at night, for supper. In Plum Village, we often enjoy pho in the evenings; it is very warming and really gives a sense of family togetherness. Please don't be put off by the long list of ingredients. It is very simple to prepare and delicious. The name "pho" originates from the French *pot au feu,* "pot on the fire," as we always serve this soup boiling over the fire.

Ingredients are grouped according to usage. When preparing, please lay the ingredients out on your table according to the groups below.

Group 1
(all vegetables are washed well)

1 head of cabbage
1 celery root
1 whole ginger root
(roast it over an open flame, and then wash and mash with a mallet to release juice)
2 whole leeks (remove the root tip — wash well!!)
2 whole apples
2 tablespoons salt
2 teaspoons vinegar

Group 2
4–5 whole cardamom pods
2 sticks cinnamon
5 star anise pieces
1 teaspoon whole white peppercorns
1 teaspoon coriander seed
10 whole cloves
Lightly roast all ingredients in Group 2 in a dry pan over low heat in order to release the aromas, then tie up in a muslin bag.

Group 3
2 large carrots, peeled and sliced into 2 mm thickness
1 large white daikon radish, peeled and sliced into 2 mm thickness
10 dried Chinese mushrooms, halved (these must be soaked for 2 hours in advance)*
1 bag of dried bean curd stick, broken into 5 cm pieces*
Sliced fresh mushroom and chives/coriander for garnish
1 whole lemon
1 bag of rice noodles, cooked according to the directions on the package.*

**these items are available from Asian grocers*

Method

Place **Group 1** (except the vinegar!) and **Group 2** in two liters of water. Simmer over low heat for 2–2½ hours. Bring to a rolling boil at the end of that time. Add the two spoons of vinegar. Wait until the scum rises to the surface and then skim to ensure the clarity of the stock.

Fry the first five ingredients in **Group 3** together with 2 tablespoons of oil, some vegetable stock powder, and assorted spices according to your taste (for example, five-spice powder, chili, cumin, etc.). Add about 1 ladle of the boiling stock to this mixture and allow it to cook quickly until the vegetables are soft.

Cook the rice noodles and divide into four serving bowls. Divide the spicy cooked vegetable mixture among the four bowls, on top of the noodles. Decorate with chopped coriander/chives if so desired.

Pour the hot stock over the top and serve immediately with wedges of lemon, slices of fresh chili peppers, and soy sauce.

Brother Phap Do and his mother in Upper Hamlet

Boiled Chocolate Cake

Chân Phap Hai, True Dharma Ocean, is Australian and ordained in 1997. His freshly baked bread is greatly appreciated, along with his Southern Hemisphere sense of humor.

The following unusual recipe has been in my family for a couple of generations, and each time I have offered it to the brothers and sisters, it has been received very warmly!

I encourage you to consider using Fair Trade cocoa. The Fair Trade organization ensures that cocoa workers are paid a fair wage and that their working and living conditions on the cocoa plantations are satisfactory.

Also, please use free-range eggs and organic dairy products whenever possible.

Making a cake can be a celebration — a celebration of being together, a recognition of the conditions of happiness that exist within and around us.

When I think of this cake, an image of a round kitchen table comes to my mind. There are family and friends seated around the table. Cake is passed, and each person receives his or her slice and begins to enjoy it. Slowly conversation and laughter begin, and after a time the cake may be forgotten as the group simply begins to enjoy being together. It is in this spirit that I offer this cake to you. May your family, your group of friends, your Sangha have many experiences of the simple joy and nourishment of being together, "seated around a kitchen table."

125 grams (4 oz.) butter/margarine
1½ cups of caster sugar (finely ground sugar)
2 tablespoons Fair Trade cocoa
½ teaspoon bicarbonate of soda
1 cup water
2 free-range eggs (beaten)
1½ cups of self-raising flour

Frosting:
¾ cup of dark chocolate pieces
¼ cup of organic heavy cream

Method

Combine butter, sugar, cocoa, baking soda, and water in a pan. Stir over low heat until butter is melted. Bring to a boil and simmer for five minutes. Remove from heat. Allow to cool to room temperature.

When cool, add egg and sifted flour; mix well until smooth. Pour into a well-greased 18-cm (11-inch) round cake pan. Bake in a moderate oven (about 350F or 180C) for 1 hour. Use 1.5 times the mix for a deeper cake.

Frosting

When cake is cool, fill a small saucepan with water and bring to a simmer. Place chocolate pieces in a bowl. Place the bowl over the top of the saucepan and allow the chocolate to melt gently. Ensure that not even a drop of water splashes into the chocolate, or it will be lumpy!

When the chocolate is melted and smooth, add the cream little by little to incorporate.

Once well-mixed, remove from heat. Allow to cool slightly and pour frosting over the top of cake. It will still be a little liquidy. As it cools to room temperature (or cooler), the frosting will set.

Brothers Phap Hai and Phap Hien making cookies in New Hamlet

Bowing to the Food before Me

James Timberlake, Harmonious Relationship of the Heart, lives in Massachusetts.

bowing to the food before me
once a bud
once a blossom
once the pollen dusted
butterfly's knee
from stem to twig to branch to limb to trunk
to root
to living meat in the seed
the wind, rain and days round it all
bowing to the food before me.

Understanding

Sister Chân Hong Nghiem, True Adornment with Pink Clouds, is from Vietnam and Sydney, Australia. She ordained in 2002.

Having breakfast silently in the morning
A flower in a ceramic bowl
Offering its beauty and fragrance
Enjoying person
Deeply moved flower
Dropping her petal as a souvenir.

Sangha Building

Plum Village Is Everywhere

Jack Lawlor, True Direction, lives in Evanston, Illinois, where he practices with the Lakeside Buddha Sangha. He was ordained a Dharma teacher in 1992. He recently helped to edit Friends on the Path, *published by Parallax Press.*

Suppose someone asked you, "Where is Plum Village? And how do you get there?" One way to respond to these questions is to describe the area east of Bordeaux, and how one might arrive by taking the high-speed train from Paris to Libourne, and then the local train to Sainte Foy La Grande.

Yet there is another, deeper answer. It has been my experience that Plum Village is everywhere. It is a "moveable feast."

I say this because I felt that I had been to Plum Village before I had ever been to France. In 1989 and 1991, my family and I were fortunate enough to enjoy retreats in the United States with Thây and Sister True Emptiness, soon followed by a retreat led by Sister Annabel and Sister Jina. They brought Plum Village with them. How do I know? Because if I was then asked to describe Plum Village, even though I had never physically been there, I could do so based solely on my interaction with its mindfulness practitioners. This is how I would then, and now, describe it:

- It is a place where people breathe freely, deeply, and smile. At Plum Village, smiles radiate like the sun.
- It is a place that can bring out the best in everyone, nourishing our bodhicitta, the aspiration to transform not only individual suffering but to bring relief and joy to everyone. Plum Village is proof that "happiness is not an individual matter."
- It is a place where we can nourish healthy seeds within ourselves that we too often tend to neglect.
- It is a place where we can breathe and smile not only when things go well, but also when something goes wrong, knowing that, a breath or so later, a solution will emerge that is touched by equal parts of wisdom and compassion.
- Not surprisingly, it is a place where people come from all over the world to experience such things for themselves.

Who wouldn't become excited about such a place? When I first learned that it physically existed, I smiled in gratitude but didn't really expect that I would ever manage to go there myself, despite warm and hearty invitations from Sister True Emptiness. My wife, Laurie, and I were both young parents with young children, little free time, and modest finances.

This led me to wonder: If visitors from Plum Village could so effectively radiate and transmit its spirit, its living Dharma, could its practices and way of living be transmitted to those who had never been there, and could they, in turn, transmit it to others?

This is what Laurie and I found ourselves trying to do without ever making a conscious decision about it. Our actions were more instinctive than acts of the intellect — of the heart, not the mind. After a while, it became clear to us that the most effective way to transmit the peace and joy of Plum Village was to create a little Sangha right where we live that could be enjoyed by those who wanted to practice the teachings offered by Thây.

The American movie *Field of Dreams* is about a man who has a vision of building a baseball diamond in his corn field that might unite people and their shared heritage. He is guided by a voice that encourages him, saying, "If you build it, they will come." We found this to be the case with Sangha building. If a small group of people wish to create a Plum Village in their local "Buddha field," people will indeed come.

It proved possible to convene a kind of mini-Plum Village each time we met as a Sangha to practice conscious breathing. Originally,

Sister Jina and Jack Lawlor

about twelve people participated. We called ourselves the Lakeside Buddha Sangha, thanks to our proximity to the banks of Lake Michigan and a wonderful graphic of the Buddha sitting by a lakeside drawn by one of our founding members. Today, ten years later, over ninety practitioners visit us with regularity.

As young parents, Laurie and I were wondering how to transmit the fruit of these teachings to our children, who were still in grammar school at the time of their first retreat with Thây in the United States. Before we met Thây, we had tried a variety of things, everything from Christian Sunday school to special ceremonies for children at a nearby Rinzai/Soto Zen Center. Of course, teaching spirituality to your own children is a little precarious, especially when they are approaching their teens, due to what novelist J.D. Salinger might describe as their well-calibrated "phoniness-detector." Nothing we found elsewhere had been sinking in very deeply until our children met Thây and Sister True Emptiness, whose genuineness served as a mindfulness bell that is resonating within them to this day. It was also an inspiration to attend retreats attended by other children . . . something almost unheard of elsewhere.

In one retreat, the children put on their own skit entitled, "Buddha Meets the Jetsons," which described how the Buddha might be received in an even more high-tech and stressed-out society than ours today. The skit demonstrated how insightful the children were about the stress their parents experienced and why mindfulness practice — if practiced genuinely, and not as a bauble or veneer — could be so helpful.

Perhaps the greatest challenge for our family came in 1993, when my father — a Chicago fireman and heavy smoker for many years — became seriously ill with emphysema. He was in and out of the hospital that year for fifty-seven days and died the day after Thây arrived in Chicago. Thây was coming to speak at the Parliament of the World's Religions and to lead another retreat in Chicago, events my whole family had worked hard on for over twelve months. Laurie's young and vibrant father, a musical theatre director who worked with young people out of love and devotion, was simultaneously diagnosed with lung cancer, although he had not smoked for over thirty years. He died less than two months after my father.

All that year was hospital practice . . . walking meditation through parking lots in all kinds of weather, down long hospital corridors, to visit each of the dying men. We did our best with the children, but regretted not being home together with them on weekday evenings. We drew nourishment from mindfulness practice as a family. My son and I spent hours visiting my father in mindfulness, simply being present, telling stories, and reading the nonverbal responses in his eyes. The joy and ease of Plum Village was there too, in us, being a witness to suffering, yet doing whatever is possible to transform it.

Thây observes that the greatest gift a parent can offer his or her child is his or her own happiness. We need to spread this teaching to parents everywhere because it is so true. Mindfulness practice helped us, as a married couple, transform a lot of suffering and minimize the rest during 1993. And it helped our children, too, although as parents we were often impatient to see results. Now that our children are young adults, the seeds of Plum Village are sprouting. Our volumes of Thây's books circulate among our children and their friends; meditation cushions keep moving mysteriously around the house and wind up going back and forth between our home and their apartments. My daughter, Megan, has visited Plum Village and is keen on the basics of mindfulness practice now that she is teaching high school in Chicago's inner city as part of the Teach for America Program. And my son, John, asks for us to send him boxloads of Thây's books now that he is overseas studying painting and filmmaking.

In 1992, I finally had the opportunity to make the first of three visits to Plum Village, together with Laurie. We were surprised that it seemed so familiar. It was already in us! The transmission offered by Thây and his fellow ambassadors from Plum Village had been effective; it was so genuine. Plum Village was in our family, in our local Sangha, and in our Midwestern regional Sanghas. On that same trip, I was reading the *Avatamsaka Sutra* and learned how all this was possible. In the final chapter, the spiritual seeker Sudhana is searching for enlightenment. He is instructed to visit fifty-three spiritual teachers from all walks of life, reminding us how we can learn something from everyone. At the end of the story, he is admitted to the tower of Maitreya, the Buddha of the Future, and is shown in a kaleidoscopic scene how Maitreya Buddha is everywhere simultaneously, at all times, past and present, teaching people in every country, and every universe. When the Dharma is offered mindfully and genuinely, radiance and light from the inexhaustible lamp travels without obstruction.

Where is Plum Village? Plum Village is everywhere!

The Community of Mindful Living in Germany

Karl Schmied, True Dharma Eye, is German. He became a member of the Order of Interbeing in 1992 and a Dharma teacher in 1994. He is one of the three founding Dharma teachers of the Intersein-Zentrum, a lay residential practice center in Bavaria.

The 17th of October 1989 was a very special day in my life. I met Thây for the first time, and on the evening of the very same day, I was sure that I would join, and walk with, this great spiritual teacher for a long time. I realized right away that even though I had already spent a whole decade on the practice and study of Buddhism, here I would still learn a lot that was new to me.

My first visit to Plum Village took place in early January 1990. I spent only a few days there, during the Winter Retreat, but those days were full of manifold impressions. Most of all the spiritual practice and community life in the two existing hamlets had a deep impact on me. Thây's clear and impressive bearing, and my initial discussions with Sister Chân Không and Sister Jina, touched me deeply, renewing my strong desire to spend many years in close contact with Thây and the brothers and sisters of Plum Village.

Sangha Building in Germany

Not long after returning from France, I founded the Community for Mindful Living, Bavaria (Gemeinschaft für achtsames Leben, Bayern). Today, it is one of the strongest Sanghas in Germany in the lineage of Thây and Plum Village. We practice in five meditation groups located in different regions — coming together once a month to share a Day of Mindfulness. We meditate together and enjoy Dharma discussions and other activities to bring mindfulness to our everyday lives.

The Community celebrates two annual festivals. One, the Vesakh Festival, is held on the full moon in May. It is a public event and takes place in the Nepal Pagoda in Munich's Westpark. We offer ceremonies, public lectures, meditation exercises, books by Thây, information, tea, and a richly decorated Buddha shrine — all of which invite the visitors of the park to stay and join us in celebration.

Before Christmas, the Maitreya Festival is held. A ceremony and talk on Maitreya, the coming Buddha, as well as performances, poetry reading, and storytelling make this a special event each year. It is in these moments that we feel particularly intensely the merit of creating such a community of spiritual friends.

Sharing the Fruits of Practice

Perhaps one of the most profound and enriching practices of the Community of Mindful Living is our work with the foundation of Maitreya-Fonds. Maitreya-Fonds is an organization designed to aid people in Thua Thien and Quang Tri, two of Vietnam's poorest provinces.

Since the inception of Maitreya-Fonds, we have collected — through many small and large contributions — over half a million Euros. These funds are being utilized with the help of nuns, monks, and social workers in numerous projects in central Vietnam. The focus of this work is the construction and maintenance of kindergartens and retirement homes, apprenticeships for young people, financial support for poor students, leper camps, and emergency relief for victims of flood catastrophes. When I visited these sites in Vietnam, I was impressed by the people's tremendous gratitude for

Karl Schmied and Sangha friends before a mindful meal

our willingness to help them and renew our personal contact with them. I was also deeply touched by the tireless commitment of the monks, nuns, and social workers and their selfless aid to the people of their country despite the constant peril that prevails in one of the last communist countries.

Reorienting My Life

For two-and-a-half decades I have been continuously trying to make the Dharma the most important thing in my life. While doing so, I noticed numerous deep changes in my way of thinking and speaking, and in my actions. However, there were many lessons that I had to learn over and over.

At times, I found I was moving in a kind of "three steps forward, two steps backward" pattern. But it was in those moments that I learned two important things. First, I realized that falling down is acceptable, especially when I am willing and strong enough to stand up again, beat off the dust, and continue on. Second, I learned that the pressure of suffering continues to rise over the years, until I am forced to reconsider certain situations. Whenever that happened, I had the choice to leave well-trodden paths and thoroughly change my behavior and habit energies. When I saw this clearly, I chose to reorient my life on the basis of the Five and Fourteen Mindfulness Trainings. The Sangha has helped me greatly in this process. Walking with the Sangha is something I would not like to miss anymore. It is like a clear mirror reflecting my way of communicating and helps me better learn and realize Right Speech and Right Action.

Thây and Karl Schmied in Upper Hamlet

During those years, I lost many old friends because we no longer shared the same interests or did the same things. The old ways I spent my leisure time — in the social arena, or in the field of sports — changed completely. The nourishment I provide for my body mind has also changed. The spirit of Plum Village has inspired all this.

I was also able to make changes in my business activities. One of my greatest accomplishments in the practice was when I convinced my Italian business friends to enjoy at least the first ten minutes of a business meal in silence, to help us be aware of the company around the table and the delicious Mediterranean food. In addition, the trust between my business and clients was improved by my mindfulness practice and clear attitude that the client's welfare and success was important.

Traveling with Thây

During the past twelve years Thây has come to visit Germany often. Every time he comes I have the great joy and big responsibility of driving him all around the country. Traveling with Thây is always motivating and enriching, opening me to new insights and experiences. His presence and continuous mindfulness leave lasting impressions on my practice. I remember one particular situation at the Warsaw airport. We arrived there, very late, after a seminar with our Polish brothers and sisters. Our flight to Prague had been called for the third time already. Our delegation was closely following Thây, who, unimpressed, was taking one step after another towards the desk in the departure lounge. When I said that it was high time to catch the plane, he answered, "Yes, I know," and continued his mindful steps, as before. We did catch the plane to Prague.

Another time, Thây, Sister Chân Không, Thây's attendant, and I were on our way from Salzburg to the Allgaeu. A seven-day retreat with about 350 participants was about to begin and we had left late from Austria. So I pushed down on the gas pedal, driving at about 180 km/h on the highway, when I noticed Thây's gentle hand touching my thigh. "Please Karl, it seems to me you drive very fast now." I slowed down.

As we stopped at the next rest area, Thây went for walking meditation on a little path, enjoying the trees, grass, and warming rays of the sun. And upon returning he offered me a small present. It was a beautiful pine cone. "Karl put this pine cone in a clearly visible spot in your car. Every time you drive faster than 140 km/h it should remind you of Thây and his wish that you mindfully take your foot off the gas pedal." I thanked Thây and placed the pine cone on the dashboard. Even when Thây was not in my car, the messenger of the forest reminded me to watch the speed.

On Thây's next visit to Germany, while traveling together by car, Thây asked me, "Oh, where is my pine cone?" I felt guilty. "Thây," I said, "the cone messenger is still there — a little shriveled, but very present. You see, when I am really in a hurry and driving fast, I put the cone into the unused ashtray. I do not see him, and he cannot see me either!" I opened the ashtray, "Look, here he is." Thây laughed and said, "The car and you are one. When the car goes fast, you are going fast as well." ▣

Amici di Thây Sangha, Florence, Italy

Roberto Del Mastio, Clear Inspiration of the Source, is Italian and has practiced with the Amici di Thây Sangha since 1990. He is now developing an "Organic Mindful Agritourism" in the Tuscan Hills.

I first encountered Buddhism in 1975 while living in Nepal. Upon my return to Florence I read and translated everything I could regarding the Dharma. I became active in getting as many people in touch with the Dharma as possible. My wife and I organized retreats and conferences and founded Sanghas. But in 1988 we decided to step down from our positions as Sangha leaders because we felt there was something missing — we had not yet found our teacher.

Three years of sadness and loneliness followed. Then like a miracle a friend gave me a book by Thich Nhat Hanh, *Peace Is Every Step*. It was love at first sight! The next year Thây came to Italy, and after the first Dharma talk we knew that we had finally met our teacher.

I know now that to find your root teacher is the most precious gift and the greatest joy that life can offer. A newfound force came from inside me and pushed me to once again share the Dharma with as many sentient beings as I could. I began to make a list of the people from Florence that I knew were interested in Buddhism and all the people I had met at an earlier retreat Sister Annabel had led in Italy. I contacted them and asked if they wished to start to develop our mindfulness together. And in 1993, Amici di Thây Sangha was born.

I believe that the moment we decide to practice consistently we make the first step towards building a Sangha. We must feel that we do this for ourselves, not for others, so that when we inform people that on a certain day and hour we will be meditating, we will be there. To be present is fundamental.

In our Sangha nobody pretends to teach others anything, we just listen and breathe because we know that things will happen at the right moment by themselves. We all have ups and downs and we know only a strong Sangha can help us to keep our practice alive. In our Sangha we are all leaves on a tree; none is more important than the other — old practitioner, new practitioner, or future practitioner. We are all doing our best to keep the Dharma tree alive, and we sustain each other with our practice. I try to share my personal experiences and encourage others to do the same. Opening our hearts to others helps everyone. For me a lighthearted, joyful atmosphere is most important. A sad practitioner builds a sad Sangha. For this reason we have red clown noses that we put on when someone feels sad. Wearing this nose and looking at ourselves in the mirror helps a lot!

I believe that the Amici di Thây Sangha is now a cozy place to share positive and less positive experiences of life, a place where we do our best to awaken our mindfulness.

Here are a few messages from our Sangha:

Luciano: When I first came to Amici de Thây Sangha, I did not know what a Sangha was. But later I realized that I would really miss it if were not there anymore. For me the Sangha is a safe place where at the end of a good or bad week you can find someone who will listen. The Sangha gives me strength because I know I am not alone. I am connected on a common path with people who are going through the difficulties of life, but who are trying to overcome them. It does not take much to forget our real nature, but it also does not take much to remember it again. We just need to light the little candle of mindfulness and the Sangha is there to help because just a single person, momentarily enlightened, can bathe others with positive energy.

Judy:
The Sangha has meant very much to me:
A comforting silence.
A place to share.
A warm freedom to be who I am.
A foundation for my practice.
A place to express my heart's joy and a place where
  I can be understood.
An international meeting place for our "differences"
  to be united.

It is my home, where I can take my family and establish
a way of breathing and living mindfully.
Without this group, daily growth would be very difficult.

Patrizia: I have been meeting with the Sangha for almost two years. Although I had already experienced meditation with other groups, when I sat with this Sangha, it felt like the first time. The simplicity of the people; the absence of criticism and the push to get somewhere; the silence of each person getting in touch with her breathing; the happiness of sharing our daily experiences with a group that welcomes you; the deep listening while someone shares his feelings; the emphasis on living our lives in mindfulness — all these have made the Tuesday meeting with my Sangha an appointment I cannot miss. I also love the possibility that anyone who feels inspired can guide the meditation and offer incense, transmitting her peace, energy, and joy to others. I often feel a great positive energy that unites everyone and I discover the importance of the moment that I am living. Finally, I love that we hold each other's hands at the end and breathe together for five or ten minutes, sending love to all the people who are suffering, especially to children.

Giancarlo:
The Sangha is here and now,
A rhythmic and conscious breathing.
A loving attention that melts the knots of the physical body.
A tranquil presence that nourishes my serenity.
A light-filled mirror that helps me to silence the wildness
of my thoughts.
Together in intent,
The many in One,
A bridge, a safe haven, a present, that unites us with Eternity.

Enzo:
The first time I heard Thây say, "the Buddha of the future will be a Sangha," I did not fully understand what he meant. When I first met my Sangha I understood, and a new path of light and love opened for me. Then I saw how much our teacher cares for us. It is in my Sangha that I can, with the help of others, bathe in the real Buddha, Dharma, and Sangha. It is my Sangha that helps me to live my daily life deeply in the present, in harmony, peace, and love.

Sangha Building in a Massachusetts Prison
An Interview with Jim G. by Brother Chân Phap Lai

Jim G., Deep Chance of the Heart, is a member of the Phoenix, Arizona Sangha. He came to Plum Village for the Winter Retreat 2001–2002. He is interested in networking with others to bring the Dharma into prisons. Brother Chân Phap Lai, True Coming of the Dharma, is from Manchester, England. He ordained in 2002.

Jim, can you say something of your background and your life before prison?
I'd been in a twenty-year marriage. My wife and I split up when the kids were in their teens. We have one son and two daughters; they're grown now. I taught martial arts, and before that I was in the Navy from 1958 to 1962. That's when my drinking got heavy, in my twenties, though I started younger. When I was six years old I would drink whiskey to numb the pain of the beatings from my stepfather. I didn't drink or use drugs in prison, not that you couldn't do that stuff, but I'd had enough of that particular realm of suffering. I'm still attending AA. I haven't touched alcohol or drugs for ten years now. I know I can't if I want a meaningful life.

When did your interest in Buddhism begin?
I'd been inside about five years when a fellow inmate asked me to help him set up a Sangha. I knew nothing about Buddhism or meditation but I read about the Four Noble Truths and this got to me: suffering exists — I could go with that — and that there's a way out — try it and see, if a teaching works for you, great, if not then you can leave it. I had some funny ideas at the time. I thought eventually I'd learn to levitate over the walls and then I could escape. When I came across the idea of emptiness, I thought I'd make myself invisible and escape that way. I didn't realize then that I was going to discover compassion for my fellow inmates and for myself or that these teachings would help me escape from the prison in my head, the prison of fear and isolation. I didn't used to like myself, but I do now. At first I was just in it for myself, but that changed over time.

What brought about this change in your heart; how did that develop?
Well, it took time and it started with insects, pigeons, squirrels, and cats. I began to notice their hunger, their suffering, and beauty. Caring about them, being with them, transported me to a different

world. If there was a wasp in the cell or day room I wouldn't let anyone kill it. I'd have it crawl up on my finger and take it to the window. It gave me something to care about, to connect with. We all need that connection to nature — it's a human need. Through this and trying to get something going with the Sangha, I started to like myself, and then I started trying to understand the suffering of others. I started to care about the inmates. I still have a hard time when I think of some of the guards. A lot of resentment and anger comes up about things that were done. I realize I've got to work on this and Plum Village is a good place to start.

Can you tell us the story of how your Sangha was set up?
Before we began we knew it was going to be an uphill struggle, but we had no idea how uphill. But it was in going through that, doing it, that the brotherhood began. We spent months writing to Buddhist organizations before we finally got a response from someone from the Shambhala Center in Colorado. Then a few of us sat in the half-lotus position outside the Director of Programs office to get him to talk to us about receiving a visit from a lay Dharma teacher. Many months later it was cleared and a successful meeting was held in the waiting room of the barber's shop. Eventually a teacher was allowed to come every two weeks.

In the meantime, we were trying to get a room to meet in. The Native American group offered us their room twice a week. So with rolled-up coats for cushions we seated ourselves in this room for the first time. It felt like a true beginning, and we continued to meet like this twice a week. We sat in front of a small picture of the Buddha pointing to Earth in response to Mara's demand, "Who can bear witness to your enlightenment?" In the following months a Spanish friend made an amazing two-foot-high statue from a picture using cardboard and toilet paper as *papier-mâché.* Since we were rationed to one roll a week, we had a hard job getting the paper, having to barter for it with coffee and cookies. We "painted" it with coffee syrup smuggled from the chow hall. Similarly, we aquired some bowls for rice and water offerings and came up with a small table to put them on. We covered a library book with blue paper to represent the Dharma. Our Sangha had a beautiful-looking altar. After three months or so the Department of Corrections took the statue, saying it could be used to hide drugs or weapons. They agreed not to destroy it, but gave it to a Buddhist nun who visited us on occasion. A friend's wife drew us a beautiful picture of the Buddha to replace the statue.

Parallax Press and Wisdom Books kindly sent us damaged books. I must have read four hundred books in the five years before I got out. We were sent many of Thây's books and videos, and I was impressed by the clarity and the simplicity of his teaching. I could really understand it. I don't know if Thây has any idea how much help he's given to people inside. We made other contacts with Buddhist teachers, some of whom came in to visit. I'm so grateful for their time. For us it was golden to have these visits, especially to have something on a regular basis. To be able to have regular visits is crucial.

Brother Phap Lai

You've told me your Sangha friends called you "Mother Hen." What was that about?
They called me "Mother Hen" because I took such good care of the room we had. I wasn't satisfied with the routine cleaning the inmate cleaners gave it. The others didn't mind so much, but I would say, "We have important guests, we're inviting the Buddhas, bodhisattvas, and dieties to be present." I gave up my breakfast so I could clean the room. That way there was no argument — it was clean enough because I had made sure it was. Even some of the guards would take their shoes off before coming in the room.

What advice would you give to people in prison thinking of starting a Sangha?
Go for it. We did it, so you can. If there are a couple of people dedicated to change and ending their suffering like the Buddha taught, it'll happen. By forming a Sangha you create a legacy that money can't buy. You have to be willing to stand up for your rights and be prepared to be punished and ridiculed for this. It took us years going through the courts before we were given the right to be vegetarian. Perhaps I've made it sound tough. Well, it was, but there were good times and everything you go through is worth it. As Thây says, "A lotus cannot grow on marble, it needs the mud." You get a tough time from everyone, but, in the end, you get respect, and you get protection, because it's something genuine and people respond to that.

And going through it you get strong, and with the practice and the different way of thinking that Buddhism gives you, you acquire some calmness. This calmness can help people. One time we heard that one of the prisoners was pretty upset because he had been refused his last chance for parole. We put the word out that he should come and see us. He came to the room and I was there, sitting in front of the shrine. He was desperate and, feeling he had nothing to lose, he had the intention of killing someone. I said,

"Before you do anything you might regret, try to calm yourself down, sit down here with me and breathe with me for a while." He did this and in ten minutes he'd calmed down and began to talk. He expressed his fear: the fact he was going to die in prison, spend the rest of his life behind bars, that he would never get to be with his family, his kids outside. He cried. In the end, he was alright and later on he thanked me.

Another bit of advice is to watch out for ego: "This is my Sangha, I started it," "I did this," "It was my idea." Ultimately it's the petty squabbles, the infighting that can destroy a Sangha, not the pressure from the outside. You've got to keep coming back to the source, the heart. You have to practice being inclusive. Anybody that was genuine and wanted to practice with us, we let in. I didn't think of the man's crime, I thought of the suffering. There was a gay man who wanted to be in the Sangha. There was some argument and we were given a hard time, but we accepted him because the Sangha is about inclusiveness.

What would you like to say to the Department of Corrections (DOC) now?

I'm learning. They're under a lot of pressure and it's not a question of blaming them. The Director of Programs who was reluctant to help us ended up making sure we had what we needed. I think he saw something good, and he did what he could to help — I am grateful to him.

But the system is set up to warehouse men and make money. There are two million people in prison in the United States. Each costs around $40,000 a year to house, and very little of this money is going into rehabilition. This is where the investment is needed to start to reduce the re-offending.

There's a need to recognize human needs like having contact with nature. There should be counseling and educational opportunities available. I was able to complete a degree just before they stopped providing this possibility. There needs to be more openness to the spiritual needs of inmates in general.

Buddhism teaches that ignorance creates suffering. We suffer and we cause others to suffer. There's a lot of ignorance in the whole system. Thây says if people offend against society we may sometimes need to lock them up to protect society, but these people need our help, not punishment. We cannot simply go on equating justice with punishment and think that solves the problem. In fact, the problem is getting worse. A change of attitude, a change of heart, is needed, not just in the DOC but in the judicial system, the state governments, and the general public.

Brothers on the Path: Impressions from the Inter-Religious Monastic Dialogue at Plum Village

Father Benoit Billot is a French Benedictine monk. He lives in Paris, France where he is the spiritual director of La Maison du Tobi, a center for spiritual practice of many traditions. He spent one month practicing in Zen Buddhist monasteries in Japan in 1983.

On the 27th of October 1986, heads of all the religions in the world gathered in Assisi, Italy in order to pray for peace. It was the founding event that gave the impetus to an inter-religious dialogue. The "Groupe de la Baume" is an offshoot of the Inter-Religious Monastic Dialogue that works to establish dialogue between monastics of all traditions. In 2001, the group met at the home of the Buddhist monks and nuns of Plum Village for a special reunion commemorating the 15th anniversary of the encounter in Assisi.

In the early morning, meditation is peaceful. The day breaks slowly, lighting the large, white Buddha statue outside of the hall that seems to contemplate his disciples and friends seated on their cushions. No sound, no women either. They are meditating at this very moment in their hall in Lower Hamlet. After the first sitting, chanting arises, itself very soft, accompanied by brass. Here is the *Hannya Shingyo,*[8] which I recognize quite easily because I recited it quite often in Japan. I allow myself to be carried by the Vietnamese softness, which moves me, but in a different way, as much as the Japanese roughness. Ah, it's so good to be taken and carried by this quiet stream!

For the Catholics the day begins with the Eucharist. While the majority of participants begin with sitting in the big meditation halls, while Muslims are prostrating in their morning prayer, while Hindus are chanting, Christians gather in large numbers in the Transformation Hall in Upper Hamlet. Brother Antoine celebrates Mass.

The words of the Gospel and the communion are at the center of this powerful moment. It is an excellent way for me to say the words, to do the gestures that bring back to my consciousness the vital importance of my divine center.

I begin a silent dialogue with the Christ. Like Krishna, like Buddha, like Muhammed, like all these giants of spiritual life, he surpasses by far the frontiers of the Church. For me, he is above all else

Thây and the Dalai Lama

the Divine Face. I practice in order to welcome him as I welcome all others.

After breakfast in silence, there is the time for speaking. We are driving down to Lower Hamlet. Each religion has one hour, more or less, at its disposal to present itself and to invite everyone to a prayer ritual. Zen or Tibetan Buddhists, Orthodox, Protestant, or Catholic Christians, Sufis or Orthodox Muslims, Hindus, each one will have its own time.

I slip into these words, these gestures, these chants. Christ is my living center, but there is also Islam in me because the words of the Koran resonate deeply with me. There is Buddhism in me because I meditate intensely in the Zen tradition. There is Hinduism in me because my body enters so easily into the awakening of the Vedanta. Yes! I'm rooted in my Catholic garden, but I look beyond the walls and I communicate with the inhabitants of the neighboring gardens. They are not strangers, nor enemies, but "Brothers on the Path."

And when someone, Sunday afternoon, will share about his estrangement from established traditions as well as about his spiritual quest, I will feel in communion with him. And isn't it the same Earth that carries us, the same humanity that we want to inhabit?

At night, sharing groups are meeting, groups of about twenty people. There is a high quality of listening, sharing that I always feel to be true, self-questioning that is not content with too-easy answers, long periods of silence where each one meditates on what has been said. The communion is building itself quietly. Here, following Thây, we would say, "Interbeing." An energy is at work that I would personally call "The Holy Spirit" and that pushes each one to be open and truthful. Tomorrow I will need to do the synthesis of these two days. That's why I'm going from one group to another as a bee that gathers pollen and prepares honey.

In the middle of the day, I speak. I try to gather together into a sheaf all that I have felt, all that I have lived, all that I have heard here. So that each one can leave with his or her wheat, transform it into flour, and be nourished with this good "travelers' bread." I was not expecting such a quality of listening, and I feel carried by this large body formed by so many different individuals, all fully present.

The subject of these two days is "Presence," presence to oneself, presence to the divine, to the universe. I feel the power in the present moment so strongly that I speak longer than I thought I would. But I feel I don't have the right to interrupt what is coming from Elsewhere. And I continue until the end.

After another short meeting in small groups, lunch is "formal," as people say here. Brothers and sisters of the two hamlets worked very discretely for everything to be ready at all times during these two days. Serving trays and pots are on the table, we just have to help ourselves, and we enter the meditation hall solemnly, men on one side, women on the other side. We eat in total silence. At the end, three Plum Village brothers, wearing their most beautiful clothes, come to ask for Thây Doji's blessing: tomorrow they will leave for Germany to lead a retreat. Prostrations, well-wishes, smiles. I appreciate the quality of the ritual, of the gesture, of the face.

At the end of the retreat we hug each other with a lot of emotion. I go to clean the small room where I slept, to pack my bag. Coming to the car, I go through the meadow where a wild soccer game is taking place. Young ones (Benedictines and Buddhists) are having a lot of fun. ▣

Two Springs: Blossoming in the French Retreat

Sister Chân Dao Nghiem, True Adornment with the Path, is from France. She ordained in 1999.

April 1999

The first French-speaking retreat is beginning. Seeing that there are more and more French guests in Plum Village, Thây decided to have this five-day retreat in which French will be the official language for all activities. Many people are new to the practice, but some have been here before and they are happy not to have headphones for translation. As I arrive, a French-speaking sister who ordained to become a nun a few weeks ago recognizes me. The previous times I visited New Hamlet she was always there, and at New Year she was still thinking about whether to become a nun. Now it's done, and it's me who is having the same idea in my mind, wishing to commit myself deeply to the practice offered by Thây.

But for now I need to arrive here in this moment. I leave my luggage in my room and take a walk, visiting my favorite trees. I recognize many faces among the retreatants. We smile to each other. We breathe. We find familiar sights here that make us feel at home. The next day, three hundred people gather to listen to Thây. Afterwards we have walking meditation, and we eat together in the big zendo. We wait for everybody to be seated and for Thây to invite the bell before eating in silence. I am touched by this silent meal and by the collective energy that emanates from it. For the first time in my life the meal is not a time to chat. My awareness of the food seems to be more important than the food itself. I appreciate the delicious, simple, and nutritious food.

Thây's voice is penetrating deeply into me, watering my desire to stay here to give my life and my energy to the practice. The fact that he is using my mother tongue to teach may be a part of this.

The third day he gives us a koan: "Who were you before your parents and grandparents were born?" Tears begin to fall. Beside me a monk is seated. He doesn't look at me. He doesn't talk to me, but I can feel his compassion and his understanding while I am crying. My parents? My grandparents? If I put aside my family's expectations of me, I find a face they don't even imagine, the one of a nun. So I take a famous Zen teaching, "Who are you?" and I turn it into a tool to decide who I want to be.

At the end of this talk my decision is made. During the last two days I will share it with two nuns, asking them for advice and support. The end of this retreat has the taste of change, of saying goodbye to lay life, of taking my first step towards the community life.

April 2002

This is the fourth French-speaking retreat. I ordained two-and-a-half years ago, and I have been present for all French-speaking retreats. This year, it is I who welcome guests. I have the pleasure of recognizing many of them. Among them some were here three years ago. Even if I don't know all the names, I have a strong feeling that it is like a huge family reunion. We are counting who is present and who is absent. We are exchanging news about sisters and friends. I feel a great happiness in seeing the faces of the people blooming when they respond to a welcoming smile.

This year the retreat will be on Buddhist psychology; and, because the topic is vast, it has been extended to eight days instead of five. Many people registered several months ago, and we are reaching our housing limits. While preparing during the days before the retreat, I worried about the cold and the rain that is frequent at this time of the year in France. But the sun is shining, and the weather is so nice that we can eat outside on the grass and enjoy the space around us, making the silence even tastier.

Thây's teachings are touching everyone deeply. My family for this retreat is called "Joyful Butterflies."[9] The Dharma discussion begins with a question on how to love without being caught by the fear of

A local baker delivering fresh bread

seeing your loved ones suffer or die. "Attachment and suffering always go hand in hand," Thây was telling us this morning. Our friends have been listening to him and they are seeing that in their lives there is excessive worry for their children, anguish for an old parent, or a kind of serenity gained after the dying of a beloved one. We don't hear any answers to anyone's difficulties, and no one is waiting for a miraculous solution. But we hear people sharing about the way they integrate the practice into their lives in order to live better, to love better, to understand better. I am amazed by the quality of the questions about personal practice from my family members.

Looking at their transformation, I can see mine. As a former teacher, during the first retreats I attended I wanted to be able to relieve suffering right away with my words. As a young nun, I still feel very limited when people speak of such tremendous suffering. But I accept who I am. I share small things of my nun's life: my anxiety regarding the health of my family members, the difficulty of feeling separated from them, and how I can let the practice transform this unpleasant feeling.

The last day of the retreat I see with surprise that people who've already come many times to Plum Village are receiving the Five Mindfulness Trainings. The day before, Thây transmitted the Fourteen Trainings, and we witnessed Jacques and Jacqueline, who have been living with us for several years, receiving them. Two days in a row, the trainings' transmission ceremonies enable us to watch our family become bigger. I have the feeling that the practice is growing in each one of us. Three years ago we were bearing only tiny flowers; today they are blooming, and we can already see some nice fruits that will continue to grow. And at the same time the plum trees in our hamlet are following the very same rhythm!

Two weeks after the retreat, two of us lead two days of mindfulness in Montpellier. Cicada songs, pine fragrance, and silent meals harmonize well together. Before saying good-bye to the Sangha there, we asked our friends to share with us their dreams, how they would like to invest themselves in the Sangha's life. Several are thinking of living in community and setting up an "eco-village." These people are the ones who admit that deep inside themselves they still carry the desire to change the world. Others wish that they could meet more often in a less formal way, just to take long walks in nature, to sing or even to dance mindfully. All of them are feeling more and more like a group of friends or a large family. I leave with lightness and a lot of trust concerning this Sangha's future.

That evening we receive the results of the first round of votes for the next President of France. A candidate who represents the extreme right has taken second place. The French people are stunned. In the midst of my anxiety and sorrow, I keep the good energy of this last sharing with the Montpellier Sangha. The number of laypeople practicing is increasing and it is an important part of monastic life to support this evolution. My choice to be a nun is the only answer I can give to this vote. It means not only to bring peace into myself, but also to support the practice in society. There are more and more people longing for peace, more and more people developing tools to help people from different cultural and religious backgrounds live harmoniously together.

I can breathe. I can smile.
In spite of anxiety,
In spite of people's anger,
In spite of intolerance,
Next year trees will continue to grow,
Always straighter, always higher, always showing their beauty.

Morning Walk

Sister Chân Gioi Nghiem

Santa Barbara beach
A white dove sails
Effortlessly across the deep blue sky.

With Thây
Nearly a thousand people walk
Each step
Imprinting peace on the sand
Each breath
In, out —
Radiating joy
Across the seashore.
In, out —
The waves dance continuously
Rising and falling.
A flock of birds
Dash across the wet sand.

Nearly a thousand people sit
In, out —
The Earth beholds
The silence.

At the horizon
The sun has risen
The dolphins leap gracefully
Two children —
A boy and a girl,
Eyes sparkling
Showing each other a piece of algae
Laughing, they run
Splashing water beneath their feet.

Nearly two thousand feet
Walk across the sand
In, out —
What remains:
The peace
The joy
And the stability within.

Footprints

Joost Van Rens lives in the Hague, Holland. He practices with the Hague Sangha and works as a family medicine doctor.

Walking in the morning mist
I see wet footprints on the pavement
The sun shines through the clouds
I follow the Sangha.

Walking meditation at the University of California, Santa Barbara Retreat

Village des Pruniers

Lay Practice Centers

The Six Principles of Harmony

The Buddha taught the following six principles to his disciples to help them have happiness in their daily life together. Harmony is the basis of the Sangha body.

1) Sharing a common space such as a forest or home:
A Sangha lives and practices together as a family in the same space.

2) Sharing the essentials of daily life together:
A Sangha shares food, clothes, shelter, medicine, and all other resources with each other.

3) Observing Mindfulness Trainings together:
These include the Five Mindfulness Trainings, the Fourteen Mindfulness Trainings, and the Monastic Mindfulness Trainings

4) Using only words that contribute to harmony, avoiding all words that can cause the community to break.

5) Sharing insights and understanding together:
A member of a Sangha shares his or her insights and understanding with the rest of the Sangha in order to help everyone grow in the practice.

6) Respecting others' viewpoints and not forcing another to follow your own viewpoint: Members of a Sangha are open to learning from each other and do not hold their own view to be the only correct view.

Living the Dharma: Practicing at Plum Village and the Intersein-Zentrum

Karl and Helga Reidl, True Communion and True Loving Kindness, are German and were ordained as Dharma teachers in 1994. They now live at Intersein Center in Bavaria, Germany. For more information contact: Intersein-Zentrum, Haus Maitreya Unterkashof 2 1/3, 94545 Hohenau. Intersein.maitreya@t-online.de

Receiving the Gift

In June of 1992 we attended the three-week retreat in Plum Village and at the end we knew that after twelve years of searching this was the spiritual practice we had been looking for. It was very clear that we needed a Sangha in order to proceed on our path.

Staying on to participate in the Winter Retreat, we got a taste of living in a spiritual community. We settled into rustic living conditions, with barely heated rooms and the always present mud. At the same time, we were touched by the joyous warmth of practicing with our new Vietnamese brothers and sisters in the Dharma, being in the presence of Thây, and listening to his Dharma talks while squeezed into the kitchen. When Thây invited us to move to Plum Village in May of 1993, we agreed.

Our new home was the former kitchen in Persimmon Building, one of the big, old farmhouses in Lower Hamlet that we shared with another couple, Anh Hoang and Tinh Thuy. We thought that we would settle in and devote our time to a contemplative, spiritual

Karl and Helga Reidl on the 2002 China trip with Thây and the sangha.

life. But after a few days of rest Sister Chân Không kindly and firmly gave us our first task. "Someone donated a house — basically a ruin — and I would like you to renovate it and have it ready for the Summer Opening." What a challenge and an opportunity, to practice letting go of our ideas and expectations, to get in touch with reality, to joyfully turn towards what was asked of us! We renovated the ruin in time, which became known as West Hamlet, and from then on we wholeheartedly offered our skills to the community: gardening, landscaping, building, renovating, and organizing. There was almost no piece of soil or building we did not take in our hands, turn, and put back differently. It was our way to make Plum Village our home. With loving support we learned that each work has its own beauty and meaning, provided we let go of our likes and dislikes and our hankering after recognition and praise. Each task is equally important and can be taken care of with joy and gratitude.

Thây and the Sangha gave us permission to be caretakers of West Hamlet during the Summer Openings, Christmas, and New Year. It was in that cozy atmosphere with a small group of eighteen practitioners that our joy was deeply watered and our "parental mind" found its expression. Though we had lived in big, international communities in England and in the United States, it was in Plum Village that we finally fell in love with living in community — a spiritual community, a Sangha. Since then this deep love has not left us.

Throughout the year there were several events when the whole Sangha came together. The most joyous one was the plum-picking, when we all met for weeks in the orchard: pointed straw hats under the burning sun of southwestern France, the soft dropping of plums on the ground, subdued laughter, loving, teasing words, now and then a mindfulness bell, gathering for tea, a song, happily overloading the famous blue van, and the sweet smell of ripe plums everywhere. Living in this Sangha, we learned that everything has its own time. There is a time for receiving and a time for giving, a time for work and a time for celebration. There are times to share our happiness and insights in Tea Meditations, to celebrate the blooming of the wild daffodils and the Plum Blossom Festival, to honor our ancestors, and to give a new meaning to Christmas. To open up to life in all its aspects was, with the support of the Sangha, a great discovery for us.

By living a life of mindfulness, understanding, and compassion, by being with the Sangha, with people who are deeply committed to the path of liberation, and by being kindly and firmly invited into responsibilities, we slowly grew in the Dharma. And above all, we grew through Thây's presence — his gentle Dharma talks and his loving way of guiding us.

We deeply connected to Thây's spiritual tradition. Having heard Thây so often say, "The noblest task of our time is Sangha building," after seven years of living in Plum Village we were ripe to bring what we had learned back to our native land, Germany. With the help of our Dharma brother, Karl began the Intersein Center in January of 1999.

Intersein

> *We need to establish retreat centers, where we can go from time to time to renew ourselves. The features of the landscape, the buildings, even the sound of the bell can be designed to remind us to return to awareness. —Thich Nhat Hanh*

Soft rolling hills, deep valleys, meadows, and large forests, small medieval towns with cobblestone-paved market squares — that is the landscape of the southeast corner of Germany, where "Haus Maitreya" is located, the home of the Intersein-Zentrum. On the fringe of a forest, sheltered by tall spruce and beech trees, the whole setting radiates tranquility. The gatha "I have arrived," in Thây's calligraphy, welcomes the visitor in the entrance hall. Everything in the house radiates simplicity — solid wood furniture, bright linen curtains, Ikebana flower arrangements, and Thây's gathas. The mind naturally calms down, leaving hurry and worries behind.

The residential community there does not need to be large. Ten or fifteen people who emanate freshness and peace, the fruits of living in awareness, are enough. When we are there, they care for us, console us, support us and help us heal our wounds."
— Thich Nhat Hanh

The Sangha is the foundation of the practice center. Five of us began the same schedule as in Plum Village — meditation, silent meals, walking meditation, and Dharma discussions as well as receiving guests, sharing our practice with them, and leading retreats. The focus of our daily life is the Dharma and the practice.

Before starting the center, the former hotel with twenty bedrooms, pub, and restaurant needed to be renovated. One worker from a neighboring village did all the major work while we continued to live in Plum Village. When we moved, we continued the work in the working meditation period, which we call "Doing (things) joyfully." One of the principles of our Sangha is to never, even in difficult or seemingly pressing situations, put the practice aside or skip the scheduled activities. There is a lot to do for a small group of people — running a big center and many retreats, being there for many guests — and there are a lot of fascinating ideas and projects. But we always ask the question before beginning new work, "Is it in accordance with the life we would like to live, does it fit into our schedule, is it really necessary?" Through this emphasis on a constant, uninterrupted practice, gradually the stability and happiness of the small Sangha increased and radiated out. This concentrated yet light atmosphere intrigued people, who noticed how so much work was done with calm and ease. Most people come back again and again, staying for longer periods to be in close contact with the Dharma and the Sangha. Refreshed and with new insights, they return to their families and workplaces, and coming back, they report their experiences, share their successes and difficulties. By this process, they gradually transform their suffering and experience deep changes in their lives. Some have stayed on, and now after three years, there are about ten people living in the community who have been here for more than a year.

Everyone who comes is immediately considered part of the Sangha. A warm, welcoming, family atmosphere is an important part of the practice center. Every morning we gather as a community, connect with each other in a circle, welcome the new day of practicing and living together with a song. Being accepted as they are, and living in an atmosphere of gentleness, harmony, and trust is for many people a deep experience. They are given a chance to let go of their armor and to open up to life and to other people, often for the first time in their life.

Walking Meditation at 5 a.m.

Margit Irgang is a writer, a member of the Order of Interbeing, and founder and facilitator of the Sangha Freiburg, Germany. Her latest book was published in autumn 2001 in Germany.

Last night the cat
printed
a chain in the snow
step by step:
hundred empty
flower molds
brimming over
with moonlight

A Bigger Family: An Interview with Chiara and Siena Dawkins

Chiara, Graceful Tree of the Heart, age nine, and Siena, Healing Joy of the Heart, age eleven, moved with their mom to the Clear View lay residential practice center in Santa Barbara, California in 2001.

How would you explain the practice of mindfulness?

Chiara: The practice is sort of like relaxing, but it's a way to feel the way you're breathing. Like when you pray to God, you are like meditating to the Buddha; you are praying to the Buddha by listening to your breath. It's like listening to our own breath when we hear the bell. We stop because it's the Buddha saying, "Stop and listen to your breath." That's how I share with my friends.

I feel more relaxed when I stop for the bell, but sometimes I can't always stop. Like when we hear the recess bell at school, we have to go into the school. So sometimes I listen to the bell while I'm running. I listen to my breathing a lot, even when there is no bell. I like to listen to my breathing because it helps me to slow down and stuff. And it can also tell you if you're scared and you need to stop.

What part of the practice do you like the most?

Chiara: I like the chanting because it's sort of naming all the people you believe in — all the gods and goddesses. Because it's like talking to the person you want to talk to even though they're far away. It's like praying. Like when we chant to Avalokiteshvara. It's like talking to Jesus or anybody you want to talk to, you could just make a chant to them. So the chanting is really good.

Do you meditate?

Chiara: I try to meditate when I'm not tired. I try to be awake when I meditate. Sometimes it's good just to breathe and not think about all these things. But sometimes I can't sit still, so I think about things — like what I should do for New Year's Eve, and should I say such-and-such to my friend.

When I meditate, I'm always refreshing my breath. I'm meditating every second. When listening to the teacher, I'm still. I'm not moving all over the place. When I do a math problem, I take time off to breathe because my mind is too full, and then I check over my work. You just need to slow some things down. Sometimes people say, "Hurry up, we have to get something done," but it's better to breathe 'cause then you can think more.

Do you think mindfulness makes you smarter?

Chiara: Mindfulness makes you wiser because you have all that time to think things over.

Do you and your sister get along better after learning about the practice?

Chiara: She and I get along better now. But sometimes I just get really angry. I have a high temper — I get angry easily. And that's why I like to breathe and stop that, because I feel so sorry for the people I always yell at. I don't mean to, but I can't help it. If something doesn't go my way, I get mad and *then* I think it over. But now I try to think it over *before* I get mad.

How?

Chiara: I sort of think about why I'm mad because sometimes I have a really bad temper over nothing. So I ask, "Why am I getting mad? This is a silly thing to be upset over." That helps me calm down.

Sometimes I feel I need to scream over nothing. That's not what I want. It's not good for me. My mom tries to help; she laughs and makes me laugh. She says, "Make that face again, I want to see that face!" She helps me out.

What do you most enjoy?

Chiara: Dancing and listening to music.

How do you feel about coming to Deer Park?

Chiara: I feel excited — if I'm close to where the monks are, I get quieter. I feel I'm in one big community. Like I'm at a camp sort of. I like it. I like that we are all sort of the same and different at the same time. A lot of people like the same things. We are all different, unique people, it's really fun to learn each other's names and see how they are. It's fun when you have all your friends together because it's like one big neighborhood.

Are you happier at Clear View?

Chiara: Yeah, because it feels like I have a bigger family. I can control my anger better. Sometimes I don't like to get angry in front of other people, only my family. So the other people at Clear View are helping me, but they don't really know it. I can also have more fun because if my mom can't take me somewhere, someone else might say yes. I forget all about being mad at my mom if I have someone else to play with. And there are more people to understand all the things I'm saying. It's much better for my mom, she's happier and that makes me happier.

~

How would you explain mindfulness practice or meditation?

Siena: In cartoons, people levitate and stuff, but that's not really what meditation is. It's going inside yourself and being with yourself and realizing what your body needs. Or it's different kinds of practices — like praying for someone else, like for them to get well. Like I said, it's not levitation.

What do you do when you are upset or sad?

Siena: I like to just go by myself usually and sit on this rock that's outside our room. Sometimes our cats come out. Playing with them helps me not be so sad because they are always happy. My cat chases rainbows from this hanging crystal. She never catches them because they are just lights on a wall. But she doesn't know that. She can chase them for hours and it makes me happy to watch.

Chiara and Siena at the New Hamlet, Plum Village

Have you helped your friends with the practice?

Siena: Yeah, probably. One thing I notice is that kids get more moody as they get older. One time my friend, Erica, got really mad at my other friend. To help her when she gets mad, sometimes I take a walk with her around the basketball court. We don't say much; we just walk. I don't know what she's thinking about — probably the person she's mad at, but I look down at my feet and think about both her and the other person she's mad at. I send them prayers to help both of them feel better. Sometimes I just leave her alone because it's nice to be by yourself for a while.

She usually feels better after this. She apologizes or she can hang out with all of us. You can tell she's apologizing even if she doesn't say it in words.

What's the best part of the practice?

Siena: I like deep relaxation and guided meditation. At the Sangha in Santa Barbara, when my mom does the children's program, she leads us in a meditation where we look inside our head to see what the room looks like and what would you see outside. Some people say their room is all pink. My room has numbers and letters on the wall — everything I've learned and notes reminding me not to forget things. When they look outside, some people see a beautiful island or a tropical rainforest filled with snakes. It varies a lot. When I was in kindergarten my mom taught us meditation every Friday. We pretended to be rockets and go see what is on the moon.

What was your first impression at a retreat?

Siena: When I first saw the monks and nuns, I was scared because I was little. But then I got used to them because they were really nice to me. The guy who just died (Thầy Giac Thanh), whenever he saw me, he would come over and smile really big and pat my hair. I liked that; it felt good.

Monks and nuns are always smiling; they're really nice. They make retreats fun. Without them, retreats wouldn't be good. We'd just be focusing on one person. The monks and nuns help and they're also really good singers.

How do you feel about Thầy?

Siena: I like Thầy. His face has lots of expressions. I like to watch his face a lot. Sometimes I don't even listen to what he's saying. He has really good Dharma talks, when I listen to them. I like his voice and how he organizes everything — he doesn't jump around in his talk. And I like how he looks at everyone.

When he lit a candle with a match and asked, "Is it one fire or two fires?" I liked that because I don't know and I like to wonder. I like how he makes us involved like that. And I like that he's bilingual because it helps out people a lot.

Even though I'm baptized Catholic, I didn't really practice that. I went to church every Sunday with my dad, but I didn't really listen. Now I feel like I'm in the right place at the right time. And I *practice* Buddhism — I know I'm still Catholic, I can't forget my past, but I don't really *feel* like I am. It doesn't really matter though — I can practice another religion and still be Catholic at the same time.

What do you most like to do?

Siena: I like to make up dances, and I choreograph them with my sister. Sometimes we perform them with friends. I love drums — if I had them I'd play them a lot. But mom won't get them for me. But that's OK — I can play on cups and pots and stuff.

How do you practice with your sister?

Siena: When we fight, we both go to our own beds. She organizes her room while I sit and read. We'll back away from each other and

Sangha members who established the first Mindfulness Practice Center in Vermont

breathe. Or she'll go out and have breakfast. I follow my breathing for three breaths and then do something else or I try to apologize. I think she stays with her breathing, too. At least she notices it, but I don't know for sure because I'm on the other side of the room.

Sometimes my sister is in a bad mood and she says she hates living in the community. But sometimes she says she loves it because we all do things together. When I do my homework, she likes to join evening sitting meditation with everyone in the community. We don't talk about the practice much — we just do it. Every other week we have Beginning Anew with the kids. We like it because we can share what we appreciate. We don't just talk about one person, we share what we appreciate about everyone there. It's fun.

The other adults in Clear View are like grandparents because I only have one grandfather and he's in Argentina. Larry drives us to school sometimes. They help my mom a lot — she has a lot to do. If she has to stay late at work, they help make dinner for us. It's nice when the three of us can be together; weekends are nice.

How about you and Chiara?

Siena: We now share a room so we have to get along more. She helps me out if I'm scared of going upstairs because there might be a rattlesnake — she just goes ahead. Now she gets to eat breakfast. She loves breakfast and before we never ate it. And I love helping to make dinner and we get to do that more. We eat better now — more tofu and stuff that's healthier for you. So my sister is getting healthier, too. It's like a big family.

Clear View

Larry Ward, True Great Sound, grew up in Cleveland, Ohio and has worked as a consultant with many businesses and communities around the world. He co founded Clear View, a lay residential practice center and home of the Still Water Sangha in Santa Barbara. He was ordained a Dharma teacher in 2001.

Come let the songs of birds help you
let go of old stories
and fill your heart
with a new song.
Sitting in the lap
of the great green mountain
Clear View sings with the song of
a thousand birds.
Touched by the moonlight
and graced by the ocean view,
the islands of mindfulness
become clear.
Open the windows and
doors and dwell in the forest
as the Buddha did.
Find a tree, a granite rock
or build a small hut for your practice.
Come listen to the wind
who gives her Dharma talk
every night.
Quiet settles over us
like a blanket of love
as the night sky appears.
Below the lights of the city
flicker with life.
All is well.
Dwell happily in the present moment.
There is no other.

PUBLISHING

PARALLAX PRESS

PARALLAX PRESS is dedicated to publishing books and tapes on socially engaged Buddhism. In late 1985, when Vietnamese Zen Master Thich Nhat Hanh suggested to Arnie Kotler, a longtime student at the San Francisco Zen Center, "Why don't we start a press together?" Arnie happily bought a small Macintosh computer and a transcribing machine and, with his wife, Therese Fitzgerald, and a few friends, began the work of transcribing and editing a thousand pages of Thich Nhat Hanh's talks from his 1985 United States tour. Mayumi Oda offered ten beautiful drawings, Gay Reineck designed the cover, and in March 1987, 5,000 copies of *Being Peace* were printed.

These sold out in three months, and since then, 200,000 copies of *Being Peace* have been printed in English, and the book has been translated into twenty-six other languages. In addition to more than twenty books by Thich Nhat Hanh published since then, Parallax has published books by the Dalai Lama, Joanna Macy, Maha Ghosananda, Robert Aitken, Sulak Sivaraksa, Chân Không, Mitsu Suzuki, Petra Kelly, Allan Hunt Badiner, and other important leaders of socially engaged Buddhism. Since Thich Nhat Hanh's suggestion that "we start a press together," the growth in popularity of his and others' teachings on engaged Buddhism has been remarkable. This much-needed message is being heard by many individuals and communities of practice around the world.

From the Parallax Website: www.parallax.org

PUBLISHING AS PRACTICE

Travis Masch, True Maintenance of Practice, is German and lives in Richmond, California. He is Publisher at Parallax Press.

WRITING TODAY I feel like the luckiest person on Earth because my connection to Thây brought together two major streams in my life — interest in books and publishing, and spiritual practice. I discovered Thây in a book review of *Peace Is Every Step* in the *San Francisco Chronicle.* Intrigued, I signed up for my first retreat. The retreat touched me deeply, and I began practicing right away with a local Sangha. Over the next two years I became more involved in the practice, receiving the Fourteen Mindfulness Trainings and becoming a member of the Parallax Press staff.

In my publishing activities at Parallax Press, my practice is to apply my Dharma training in every moment and with everyone I come into contact with. The Fourteen Mindfulness Trainings have been an incredible tool for transforming the workplace into a vehicle for practice, in terms of their guidance in "right business conduct." I have been able to see past the barriers of "Travis at work," "Travis at home," "Travis on retreat," etc. and have realized that regardless of what I do or where I am, mindfulness is my guide.

When I joined Parallax Press, my intention was to help make it an expression of Thây's teachings not only through the content of what we publish, but also through the appearance of our covers, the care that goes into every step of production, the vendors and freelancers we choose to work with, and the way the staff and volunteers interact and treat each other.

I encourage anyone who is involved with running a small business to experiment with reading the Fourteen Mindfulness Trainings as if they were the company policies. At Parallax they are in fact the foundation of all our policies and procedures, as is expressed in our current mission statement:

"We practice what we publish by emphasizing a work environment that supports mindfulness and is infused with Thich Nhat Hanh's message to work as a Sangha. Guided by a monastic and lay management committee, our staff of paid employees and volunteers has drawn together to form a work family where ethical values find harmonious integration into the needs of a small business, in a relaxed, team-oriented, nonprofit environment. We value working and practicing together and are engaged in an effort to blur the lines between these two activities."

Parallax Press staff in Berkeley

Mindful Publishing at La Boi

Chau Yoder, Chân Tham Tue, is Vietnamese and lives in Walnut Creek, California, with her husband Jim, who is from the United States. Together they help coordinate La Boi Press. She also practices at the Hayward Buddhist Center and the Peaceful Heart Sangha, which she and Jim host weekly in their home.

I began my path of learning and practicing the Dharma thanks to two books — *The Miracle of Mindfulness* and *Being Peace* by Thây Nhat Hanh. What a happy day for me! I found the path of joy and happiness and the way to transform suffering.

On a trip to Plum Village, in November 1999, I felt so lucky to have my husband, Jim, go with me. While we were there Sister Chân Không asked us to help La Boi — an organization that publishes and sells Thây's books, tapes, and CDs in Vietnamese. Jim and I have been participating in La Boi since then, working with about twenty other volunteers as a work-Sangha.

The task of publishing Thây's books fulfills my wish to do more meaningful and mindful work. We took early retirement with this goal in mind, but did not know what we would do next. Mindful people and activities now surround my days. I feel so blessed. Daily I get to meditate, chant sutras, practice tai-chi and yoga; work with La Boi volunteers on editing and formatting books; make CDs of Thây's talks, poems, and music; plan La Boi meetings; and market the books, tapes, and CDs.

While editing and formatting Thây's books, I get to practice and learn his teaching as I work. I have the opportunity to read Thây's books as we publish them, so I can bring new insights and thoughts to our Sangha right away. I also have the joy of being a part of this wonderful effort to share Thây's teachings. I remember when I edited *Tha Mot Be Lau,* Thây's translation and commentaries on *The Tale of Truyen Kieu*. The author is the Shakespeare of Vietnamese literature. I remember suffering a lot while studying *The Tale of Kieu* in high school. The story is written in old Vietnamese and is very difficult to understand. When I read Thây's explanations, everything made sense. I understood the story and its deep teaching in new ways. My heart and mind opened up.

The La Boi team of volunteers meets once a month for a Day of Mindfulness. In the morning we do sitting, walking and guided meditation, recite the Five Mindfulness Trainings, read from one of Thây's books or watch a Dharma talk on video, and then share our experiences of the practice. We have a potluck vegetarian lunch at noon. We eat in mindful silence for the first fifteen minutes. In the afternoon, we either prepare books for shipping or get ready for the upcoming book-selling events, like Thây's retreats, Vietnamese New Year, Vesakh, the Buddha's Birthday, and Mother's Day.

Once in a while all the La Boi volunteers go on a weekend retreat. Last July, we organized a retreat near Santa Rosa, California. We had a wonderful walk along a tree-lined, country road and picked blackberries and wild plums. We also felt appreciative of our mindful steps and the scenery; we could take the time to notice and appreciate the beauty of a wildflower. Tranquility permeated our meditation practice. Our Sangha friendships are so deep and joyful!

Some of Thây's books in different languages
Old Path White Clouds in Russian, Old Path White Clouds in French, Old Path White Clouds in Chinese, Old Path White Clouds in Hindi, Old Path White Clouds in Korean, Lotus in a Sea of Fire in Dutch, The Miracle of Mindfulness, Peace is Every Step in Hebrew, Peace is Every Step in Chinese, Miracle of Mindfulness in Portuguese, The Sun My Heart in Thai

the fruit of transformation

Being the Practice

A Dharma Talk by Sister Annabel

December 9, 2001
Sister Annabel Laity, Chân Duc, or True Virtue, was ordained a nun in 1988 and became a Dharma teacher in 1990. She is abbess of the Green Mountain Dharma Center in Vermont.

Dear MahaSangha, good afternoon. It seems that the object of mind and the subject are not separate. I could think that I am the subject and Plum Village is the object of my mind. But the way I talk about Plum Village and the way I see Plum Village is not really separate from my mind. It is not separate from the collective mind, the mind of others, either. Plum Village is a collective creation.

Oh, What it is to Be Happy

I have always liked to sing. When I arrived in India in 1979 in order to practice with some Tibetan nuns, I immediately found that I was able to sing in a way that I hadn't been able to sing before. Whenever I had an emotion I would sing about it. The Tibetan nuns liked singing very much. Whenever we had a chance to be a little bit lazy and walk in the forest, which wasn't very often, they would always sing. And they would ask me to sing for them in English. I wasn't quite sure what to sing that would be in harmony with the Dharma. So I had to make up my songs as I went along. Whenever I had even a tiny realization in the practice, I would make up a song about it. One song was called, "Oh, What It Is to Be Happy." At that time I didn't know what it was like to feel really happy inside. One day I was coming back to the monastery carrying some wooden planks on my shoulder because we were building the monastery in the forest. I saw one of the monks sitting on the side of the mountain. The monks live on one side of the river and the nuns live on the other side. We were up on the mountain, and down below us in the valley were rice fields. The rice fields looked very beautiful divided by dikes. In the distance there were more mountains with clouds. You could hear the children laughing in the valley, and you could smell the scent of pine trees. You could hear the boy who looks after the cows playing his flute. Everything was perfect — a Pure Land. But somehow in my heart I was not happy. When I saw the

Sister Annabel with a young friend at a holiday celebration in Lower Hamlet

monk sitting there, he looked as if he were completely free, completely happy. Although I didn't know in myself what happiness was, I thought I could experience it through him. So I wrote that song, "Oh, What It Is to Be Happy." I stayed in India altogether for eighteen months. During that time I appreciated so much the beauty of the place where I was staying. But I never felt as if I really got a hold of a practice that would help me to transform.

I wanted very much to be a nun. When I was seven years old I wanted to be a Catholic nun. When I was twenty-one I asked an abbot of a monastery in Normandy if I could be accepted as a Benedictine nun. He said no. When I went to India to be with the Tibetan nuns, I still had the dream of becoming a nun. They also said no. Because I couldn't become a nun, I thought I might not be in the right place, the place where I could really devote myself to the practice and really transform myself. I felt I had so much to transform to really be able to feel the happiness that I witnessed in the monk sitting on the hillside.

One day, while I was still in India, I was feeling very lonely. There had been a drought so I hadn't had a bath for three months. That sounds like a long time. My skin was very black with dirt, and I knew that I didn't smell very nice. And I felt very hungry because we never had enough to eat. In the morning we had a little bit of tea if we were lucky, and if we were luckier we had a little bit of barley flour to put in the tea, but not always. At lunch we had one or two *chapattis,* a kind of Indian bread. And in the evening we had a little bit of rice soup. As we became poorer and poorer, the rice soup became more and more watery. When I woke up in the morning my stomach was always grumbling. It was also cold because we were quite high up in the mountains. I was shivering and hungry. But because of the beauty of the place, and because deep down I wanted to practice so much, I stayed for a year and a half.

One day a monk came along from the main monastery and he had a radio. In the place where we lived we didn't have any electricity or running water. I don't know how he managed to have a radio, but he did; and he could pick up the BBC world news. He understood English, which was very rare. He said to me, "You know in England now there are thousands of women who are sitting around the missile bases to stop atomic weapons from being transported out." There were many American missile bases at that time in England. He said, "This is a wonderful thing to do." When I heard that, I thought maybe that is what I would do.

Finding My True Teacher

So I left India, went back to England, and joined the women. We would sit there day and night to block missiles from leaving the base. We would put ourselves in front of the gate so that the missiles couldn't come out. This is also part of my deep aspiration: I want there to be peace in the world. I don't want there to be any war. So I thought this was a way to express my deep aspiration for peace. But in fact it is not enough to sit at the gate of a missile base. You need to sit at the gate of your own mind in order to be able to be aware of mental formations in your own mind and to transform them. That is a very important part of peace work. Some people were not peaceful in themselves. I asked everyone at the missile bases, "Does anyone know about Buddhist practice. Does anyone do meditation? Do you know anybody who is in the peace movement and also is a Buddhist?" Everyone said, "No," they didn't know anyone. Then one day someone said, "Oh yes, I know someone. He is a Buddhist teacher from Vietnam," and they said Thây's name. Then I remembered that when I was in India, when I was so sure that I wanted to be a nun in the Tibetan tradition, one of my Tibetan teachers said to me, "No, your teacher will come from the Far East, not from Tibet." Other nuns said to me, "You have to meet your real teacher in the country of your birth."

I heard about Thây and I wanted to find out more about him. I wanted to read what he had written, and I wanted to be with people who knew him. I did my best to find a community. There was a Buddhist Peace Fellowship community in Kent, so I joined them. We used to produce the Buddhist Peace Fellowship magazine. We would go on peace demonstrations and join discussions on peace. Whenever we went on demonstrations for peace, we always tried to practice walking meditation because we were in touch with Thây through his writings. But it was not enough to be in touch with Thây through his writings. I wanted to be in touch with Thây's person also. One day a member of the community in Kent asked, "Why don't we invite Thây to come to England and give some teaching?" So we invited Thây at a very cold time of year, in early March, to a very cold and drafty castle in the north of England. It was not the best place for somebody who needs warmth. So I met Thây in England and Thây comes from the Far East. So I had all the right conditions to meet my true teacher.

When I first saw Sister True Emptiness in the airport I felt that she belonged to my blood family. I don't know why, but that is how I felt. When they had to go home on the last day I was a little bit sad because I didn't know when I would see Thây and Sister True Emptiness again. I was in the car with Thây, and I had to get out to go home. As I stepped out of the car, Thây also stepped out and asked if I would like to come to Plum Village for the Summer Opening that year. When I heard that, all my sadness went away. That summer, in 1986, I went to Plum Village.

Another Pure Land

It was very hot that summer. The temperature was between twenty-five and thirty degrees Celsius. The first thing Thây said to me was, "Here is India, India is here." That made me immediately feel at home because the first time I had experienced the Pure Land was in India. Here was another Pure Land for me to experience. The Upper Hamlet was so simple and so beautiful. The Transformation Hall was not yet there. The Still Water Hall wasn't there. Everyone was busy preparing for the Summer Opening. I immediately felt the atmosphere of complete relaxation. I immediately felt that I was at home. Later on that day someone took me down to the Lower Hamlet, which is also very different from what it is like now; there was no Dharma Nectar Hall. I felt even more at home. It is very strange. From the time that I left the place where I was born, I had never felt at home like that. When I looked at the stones the buildings were made of and when I looked out over the hills, I felt completely at home. Actually I was still a very unhappy person, but I was very happy to find my home, my Pure Land. Thây says you don't need to have transformed all of your afflictions to dwell in the Pure Land. I don't know what good fortune I had to be able to be there. Already I had failed to become a Catholic nun; I had failed to become a Tibetan nun. Now I had more good luck, and I don't know why.

We enjoyed the Summer Opening. I spent two weeks in the Upper Hamlet with Thây and two weeks in the Lower Hamlet with Sister True Emptiness. In those days, Sister True Emptiness was the practice leader in the Lower Hamlet, and Thây looked after the Upper Hamlet. We weren't very well organized. We did everything at the last minute. Sister True Emptiness would have an idea to do something and five minutes later we would do it. It was nothing like the Summer Opening now. The Summer Opening was very beautiful because it was a kind of haven for Vietnamese refugees. When they arrived in Europe from the refugee camps, many Vietnamese refugees found themselves in a situation completely unlike what they had known in Vietnam. They found themselves living in a place where they couldn't speak their own language, they ate food which was very strange, probably did menial work whereas they may have had a high degree of education in Vietnam, and so on. Plum Village is a place where there is Vietnamese language, Vietnamese food, and other Vietnamese people.

Sister True Emptiness said it is very important to speak Vietnamese. The refugees have to speak a language that isn't their own all day long, and they really need to reconnect with their roots. That is one of the reasons why I really wanted to speak Vietnamese. I was lucky because everybody spoke Vietnamese, so it wasn't difficult to learn. In those days, the Summer Opening was quite Vietnamese. Now it is a bit more European and North American also. My real Vietnamese teacher was Sister Chân Vi. She was ordained at the same time that Sister True Emptiness and I were ordained in India. She came to Plum Village from the Philippines' refugee camp. In the winter of 1986, Thây and Sister True Emptiness had gone to share the practice in different refugee camps. They had met Sister Chân Vi at that time and asked her to come to Plum Village. When she arrived she felt it was strange to be in a foreign country and especially to stay with someone who was English and only spoke a few words of Vietnamese. At first it was a little bit difficult.

Sister Chân Vi was the first member of my Sangha that I lived with twenty-four hours a day. Sister True Emptiness was also one of the first members of my Sangha, but she didn't live with me twenty-four hours a day. When I lived in India I had already learned about living with people of a different culture. I knew that things that might seem quite natural to me might be offensive to someone from another culture. When we live with people from other cultures we need to practice mindfulness and be aware of our actions of body and speech because we can easily offend someone without meaning to. I remember in India we lived in a little hut. I was a layperson at the time. The hut was on stilts, and under the hut they kept the rice and other things. From time to time a nun would have to go under the hut to bring something out. When I was sitting in the hut it was my duty to leave the hut and stand outside for the nun to be able to go underneath because it would be disrespectful to sit on top of the nun going under the hut. That is not something I learned in England. At first I was very offended if, in the pouring rain, in the middle of the monsoon, I was told I had to leave the hut so they could go underneath and fetch something. But I learned that this is part of politeness, a way of not offending people and keeping people happy; so after awhile I managed to do it without feeling any resistance in my heart. With Sister Chân Vi, I also tried my best to learn about what is considered correct in the Vietnamese culture.

One thing we shared in common was that we both liked gardening. She loved being in the garden. When she had been in Vietnam she had spent time in a temple in the mountains, and she had looked after the garden there. In our little garden we grew quite a few Vietnamese vegetables. Actually, our garden was under plastic because they wouldn't have grown outside. Whenever you went into that garden you could smell the fragrant herbs, just like when you go into the greenhouse here, today. Every morning we would rise early and go straight out into the garden because there were many slugs and they would eat everything up if you were not careful. We would pick up the slugs and take them out into the forest. We pulled up any weeds. After we had looked after the garden a little bit we would go to the meditation hall and practice sitting meditation together. If it were summertime we would go into the Red Candle Hall.

In the winter it was too cold. We didn't have any heat, so we would go to the little room next to the Red Candle Hall. When it rained, the rain would come in because the roof tiles were loose; they weren't attached to each other with cement or anything else. When a supersonic plane went overhead and broke the sound barrier, all the tiles would move. When the tiles moved, they left a gap. So whenever it rained, we had to put out all the buckets to catch the

Sisters Annabel, Chân Không, and Chân Vi in India right before their ordination

rain coming in. In the winter it used to snow more than it does now. The snow would blow in through the tiles. One time we went up into the attic and there was snow quite high, maybe ten centimeters or so. We had to shovel all the snow in the attic, put it into buckets, and carry it down. Fortunately someone very kind saw that we wanted to practice and offered to give a donation to fix the roof so that snow and rain wouldn't come in anymore. That was the first time we had a big donation. Before that we were really quite poor. In the winter we heated the rooms with some wood stoves. But in order to have the wood we had to go out and saw it in the morning. We had a saw with handles on two ends. Sister Chân Vi held one end and I held the other, and we sawed the wood together. She said in Vietnam that she used to do the same. She used to go into the forest, saw the wood, and sell it to help support her family.

I was very happy when Sister Chân Vi came. To be able to live together with just one other person in the Sangha twenty-four hours a day is already wonderful. When you have a sister who also wants to practice with you, you receive a lot of energy in the practice. The energy to practice was not doubled, but it increased ten or a hundred times. She supported me very much. She had often wanted to be a nun when she was in Vietnam, and she really liked the practice. She wanted to practice sitting meditation, reciting the Fourteen Mindfulness Trainings, and chanting the sutras. She chanted very well. She taught me how to chant the sutras. Sister Chân Vi was also a very good cook, and she showed me how to cook Vietnamese food.

Sister True Emptiness also supported me, and Thây was always patient. I don't think I was an easy younger sister to have. I think I have transformed quite a bit since then, but I haven't transformed everything since you can still see some of the weaknesses I had then. Sister True Emptiness was very patient with me and very open. She never showed any kind of discrimination at all. No one had any kind of strong racial discrimination, but sometimes we find it a bit easier to be with people of our own culture. But Sister True Emptiness is just as easy with people of different cultures as she is with people of her own. She used to ask, "Oh, would you like to eat some muesli? Would you like to eat some brown bread?" and things like that.

Ordination in India

In 1988, Thây said that we would go to India. When Thây says we will do something, we always do it. Thây had been thinking about going to India for a while; and it was arranged, and we were able to go. I was very happy because India had always been my spiritual home, and I couldn't think of anything better than to go there with Thây. I didn't know that Sister Chân Không and Sister Chân Vi had asked to be ordained as nuns in India. I didn't know anything about it, and when I found out I thought, Why can't I become a nun, too? I had already tried twice. And in fact I had even asked Thây one time if I could become a nun when I first came to Plum Village, and Thây said, "No, you have to do like Sister True Emptiness and become a lay member of the Order of Interbeing." I was very sad when I thought that maybe I couldn't become a nun with Sister True Emptiness and Sister Chân Vi. I thought, My goodness, if we come back to Plum Village and they are both nuns and I am not, I don't know if I could bear it. Thây said that is not a good reason for becoming a nun. But I don't think that was the only cause. The main cause was my bodhicitta, my deep desire to love and serve. I think that was there somehow. Maybe an additional cause was Sister Chân Không, who intervened on my behalf. Thanks to her, Thây agreed.

We went to India. We went to Bodhgaya. We went to Uruvela, the village where the Buddha had gone after enlightenment, and we had Tea Meditation and tangerines with all the children there. We waded across the Neranjara River. We practiced walking meditation. What I remember the most was the beauty of doing walking meditation in the places where the Buddha had walked.

One day early in the morning, before it was light, we rose and went to the Vulture Peak. The police went with us because there are bandits there. It was the middle of November, so it was not too hot and not too cold. We spent the whole day there. Out of great compassion, especially for me who popped in at the last moment, Thây ordained us as nuns. Sister Chân Không gave me one *ao trang* (robe) of hers. When I was ordained I was very happy because I felt very light. I thought I had cut off everything that had bound me — the past and all the fetters — and they were all gone. The next morning when I woke up and put my hand on my shaved head, I felt very light and very happy. But when I came back to Plum Village, I realized that I hadn't at all cut off all my afflictions and fetters. I still got angry, I still got sad, and I still had a tremendous amount to transform. But I don't think I can ever be shaken in my aspiration, in my determination to realize as fully as I can in this lifetime my own transformation and my desire to help others to transform. I was thirty-nine when I ordained. It was a little bit late. I already had built up many worldly habit energies. Maybe my transformation is not as fast as other people's. It is slow, but it is there. When I received the Dharma Lamp from Thây in 1990, Thây gave me a gatha that said, *"The work of transformation is what reveals the sign of truth."* I think this means that all my life I have to keep transforming and transforming and whenever I do transform it helps me to see the true nature a little bit more.

Every Summer Opening people come and I am always there. The first Summer Opening I missed was my thirteenth summer when I went to Vermont and didn't come back that year. Apart from that summer, I have been to fifteen Summer Openings. Every Summer Opening someone comes up to me and says, "You are much better than last year." Or, "My goodness, you have changed a lot." They still say that. They say, "Two years ago, you were so arrogant and now you have changed a lot." That gives me and others so much confidence in Thây's way of practice.

Practicing in Green Mountain Dharma Center

In 1997 I went to Vermont. When I first had been in Plum Village, Thây sometimes said that maybe one day I would go to Canada to look after the practice center there. I think somehow Thây connects me with that part of North America. In the beginning of November 1997, I heard from Sister True Emptiness that I would go to Vermont because there were some monks and nuns there who were not able to come to France. They had only just been ordained and they needed a big sister over there.

Vermont is extremely beautiful. If you have not been there it is difficult to describe. The snow and the mountains in the winter, the gold and red of the autumn trees, the tremendous shock of green in spring — a very deep, bright green which comes after four or five months of white — the mists of the summer and the clouds in the mountains. The place we live is very beautiful with lakes and a teahouse built in a Japanese style. It was rather different than when I came to Plum Village. When I arrived in Plum Village, I thought it was a five-star hotel because compared to where I had been in India, it was like that. To have a foam mattress and a sleeping bag, to have four bricks and a board to make your bed, to me that was a first-class bed — because in India I had to lie on the floor with the rats and sometimes we had scorpions as well. When I went to the United States, everything was already very comfortable. We didn't have any work to do. In Plum Village, to renovate the buildings, we had to remove the cow manure from the barns in order to transform them into living quarters. But in Vermont everything was already ready to live in. We had a beautiful house with carpet and hot running water, and everything was in place. We were seven sisters and two brothers at the beginning. We lived in a little house, and the two brothers lived in another little house. Because the brothers were so few they used to come and join us everyday for sitting and chanting. When

Walking meditation in India

I arrived, everything was already covered in snow. It was so silent. You don't even hear the birds because it is too cold for them to come out. Every morning the sun rises over the snow and there is a pink glow about everything. It is extremely beautiful.

I began to know the North American people. We think because we know the same language we have everything in common and we understand each other immediately. But in fact there is quite a difference between the North American people and the European people. It took me about three years to feel at home in North America. Before that, I expected North American people to be like Europeans, and they aren't. In the area around our monastery there is a large Jewish population. According to our tradition in Plum Village, I thought we should also celebrate Christmas in Vermont. So we did and with a very Christian bias. But I realized afterwards, to my dismay, that most of the people who came did not have Christian roots, they had Jewish roots. They weren't very happy at all with the way we completely ignored Hanukkah and only celebrated the Christian festival. So after that we had to be more aware, and we had to change.

Sister Annabel in Vermont

The suffering in North America is tremendous. Although materially we have far more than we need, the psychological suffering is huge. I think this was one of the difficult things for me to accept when I was first there. For instance, frequently we would hear news that the son of someone close to the Sangha had committed suicide, or someone else had killed their mother, and terrible stories like that, especially among the young people. There were many people we had to comfort because of tragedies in their families that arose from psychological suffering. In some ways I think that psychological suffering is worse than material suffering. But luckily the Dharma doors that Thây has taught can bring relief. It is my deepest aspiration to go back to the United States to understand better the situation there and to devote my life to helping in any way I can.

Often in the United States the newspapers contact us. We are also asked to give talks on international affairs. I have been asked to give talks on the situation in the Middle East. I have been asked to a write an article on Afghanistan and things like that. So part of being in a practice center in North America is that you really have to be in touch with what is going on. Luckily I don't have to watch the television or read the newspaper to do that. We have friends in the Sangha who are very much in touch with international affairs, and all I have to do is ask them to let me know what is happening. It is much easier to hear from a lay Sangha member than to hear from the television or the newspaper.

In Vermont, usually once a week, we have visits from schoolchildren. I imagine that religion is not officially taught in the schools, but many schools have teachers who are interested in Buddhism. They organize courses on Buddhism, and the students do a field trip to the Green Mountain Dharma Center to learn how a Buddhist community lives. When the children come, we don't teach them theory. We do our best to have them share about their difficulties. Fortunately we've had some young monks and nuns whom the young people from high schools and universities can easily feel close to. The young monks and nuns understand their situation because they themselves have been brought up in the United States, so they can help the young people. Those young American monastics can help the young people more than I can.

Green Mountain Dharma Center is not very big. It will never flourish like Plum Village does. It will always be a little offshoot of Plum Village. Plum Village will always be the root, the place for us to come back to, to be strengthened by our spiritual roots so that we can go off again to Green Mountain Dharma Center and offer something better. But we need to have that offshoot out there because it is like an antenna that is in touch with what is happening, and the antenna can let Plum Village know what the needs are over there.

Questions and Answers from the Audience

Can you share about the practice of being a Dharma teacher and an abbess?

I think as far as being an abbess is concerned I am in the process of arriving, but I wouldn't dare say I have arrived. The same is true of being a Dharma teacher. The other day I looked at one of my little sisters and I remembered something I read in the book *Hermitage Among the Clouds* by Thây. It was the second book that I translated from Vietnamese into English. It is about the princess Huyen Tran, the daughter of the Bamboo Forest Master, who became a nun. In that book she is walking on the mountain with a little novice. He is boasting a little bit about how he will become a high monk and where and how he will give wonderful Dharma talks. He is called Phap Dang. She thinks to herself, Oh dear, this little monk has a long way to go in the practice. And then she stops and thinks again, That's not right. We both have a long way to go, we have to do it together. Sometimes when I look at a little sister, I think, Oh she has a long way to go. But when I look deeply I don't feel that anymore. I don't feel she has a long way to go, I think we both have a long way to go. And maybe that is part of being a Dharma teacher and an abbess. Thây says it takes at least ten years to learn to be an abbess.

It is not difficult to be a teacher. I was trained to be one. I was a teacher for fifteen years before becoming a nun, standing up in front of a class and giving them knowledge to help them pass an exam. But I don't think that is what a Dharma teacher is. As a Dharma teacher you don't teach by your words. You teach by your body, by your being, by what you are. I don't think I do that very well yet. I think my words are ahead of my body, of what I am.

Thây has done his very best for me, as he does for all his disciples. I remember when we were in Vaishali during the trip to India when I was ordained, Thây was talking about the role of women in Buddhism. He was talking about Mahagotami. Someone asked, "Isn't there discrimination against women in Buddhism?" And Thây said, "I will do everything I can to help Chân Duc become a Dharma teacher."

The other day I had a dream. In my dream I saw that Thây had already gone into a different form. He wasn't with us anymore in the form that we are used to seeing him. In my dream I was crying. When I woke I thought, What does that dream mean? I thought, Thây can never die. And I can never cry because Thây has died. The only thing that can die is the practice that Thây has transmitted to me. If I don't practice then Thây is really dead. But for as long as I practice, Thây is really alive. It is quite right to be crying in my dream if my practice has died. I think to be a Dharma teacher is to be the practice that your teacher has transmitted to you.

Sisters Doan Nghiem and Vien Quang

You can't be a Dharma teacher on your own. It is not something you are as an individual. You have the practice transmitted to you by your teacher and you have your Sangha. To be a Dharma teacher you have to be a part of the Sangha body, the finger of the hand. It makes it very easy because the Sangha's eyes are always better than your eyes. Your Sangha can always put you right when you go a little bit askew. Dharma teachers should go in one direction, but if the Dharma teacher starts to go in a direction that opposes the direction of the Sangha, the Sangha comes along and puts you straight again. The same is true with an abbess. If an abbess goes a bit in the wrong direction, the Sangha can help her to correct herself. A good Dharma teacher or a good abbess is not good because of the individual talents of that person, but because of the teacher and the Sangha.

There was a time when you were head of practice in the Upper Hamlet. Please tell us about that.

In 1990, there were new novice monks in the Upper Hamlet, and they didn't have any senior monk there. Thây Giac Thanh had not arrived yet. Thây suggested I go to the Upper Hamlet because I am a good mindfulness inspector.[1] That was probably the only thing that qualified me to go the Upper Hamlet to look after the monks. The novice monks were Thây Nguyen Hai, Thây Vo Ngai, and Thây Phap Dang. We also had some monks from Kim Son Monastery who came for the Winter Retreat. So in the morning I would come out and sit at the bell in the meditation hall. I would look around and nobody would be there. It was completely empty, just me sitting at the bell. I would invite the bell and sit the first sitting on my own, always hoping that someone would come and join me. Then, after the first sitting was finished, there was still nobody there. So I was not feeling very pleased as mindfulness inspector. I would go out and knock on the door of the sleeping novices. There was no answer. They were fast asleep. So I would open the door and turn on the light. It is the kind of thing that I would not dare to do now, but somehow in those days I dared to do it. I think that after a while the monks from the Kim Son Monastery began to call me "the general." They said, "This place is like an army barracks and you are like the sergeant in charge," or something like that. Fortunately Thây Giac Thanh came, so I didn't feel I had to be in charge so much. I did Beginning Anew quite a bit with my brothers when I was a mindfulness inspector.

~

The practice of Beginning Anew began in 1990 on the veranda of Thây's hut in the Upper Hamlet. It was to help two sisters, who were not happy, to speak to each other. It began in the early evening and went on until late at night. Thây instructed us how to listen compassionately without judging, reacting, or interrupting the other person. We probably did not succeed too well that first time because it takes training and practice to listen deeply and speak lovingly. None of us were too strong in the practice of mindfulness yet.

Over time the practice of Beginning Anew brought a tremendous amount of relief because we were able to talk about our difficulties with each other. Before that we didn't really have a way to tell each other about our difficulties. We had some problems with Beginning Anew. When we did it on an individual basis it worked okay. With the brothers I had success with doing Beginning Anew. We would find the right time and we could talk about our difficulties. But I had less success doing Beginning Anew in a big group. We had guests that came. I was unskillful, and as a mindfulness inspector sometimes I was very unskillful. But it wasn't so appropriate when new guests had just arrived to bring out all my own unskillfulness in front of them. So, when we tried this a few times and decided it was not very beneficial, we decided that a Beginning Anew session should only be held among people who had been together for at least a month. This way the people knew each other's good qualities as well as their negative qualities. If, while sitting in a group, someone would stand up and say, "Sister Chân Duc, you know you are very arrogant. You caused me to suffer a lot this week," then the guests who had just arrived would think, "Fancy having someone like that as head of the practice!" And they might lose confidence in you and in the Upper Hamlet. So we decided that was not a good idea, that people who hadn't been practicing with us for more than a month should not come to the Beginning Anew. In those days we were not very good at watering flowers, at appreciating each other's good qualities. We talked more about our difficulties. Later on we realized the importance of Flower-Watering as well.

~

When Thây Giac Thanh came to the Upper Hamlet there was a wall between our rooms, but you could hear everything between the two rooms. Thây Giac Thanh was a very free monk and he wasn't the kind of person that I was at all. He wasn't a mindfulness inspector like I was. He was more like a tea master. Thây Giac Thanh loved to lie in a hammock. He had a hammock in his room and it squeaked tremendously every time he would swing on it. Thây was very free and a tea master, so he didn't sleep very much, and he would swing in his hammock all night. One day I went to Thây and said, "Thây, would you mind not swinging in your hammock at night so that I can go to sleep?" Thây was very kind and he agreed to that. Thây also kept a bottle of urine in his room because he was a bit lazy and did not like to go out of his room at night. He liked very much to have this bottle there because he would look at this bottle of urine and a bottle of drinking water that he also had, and he would see the interbeing nature of the two. He also gave a Dharma talk about that.

When I was in Vermont Thây Giac Thanh was also there, in Maple Forest Monastery. I always felt that Thây Giac Thanh was able to provide what I lacked. I was this mindfulness inspector and Thây Giac Thanh was someone who could always make you laugh. Whenever we had a Tea Meditation, Thây Giac Thanh would be there, and I would be there. I would keep the form of the Tea Meditation mindful and proper, and Thây Giac Thanh would provide all the jokes and the lightness. Thây Giac Thanh would do the poetry, and I would do the singing. Thây Giac Thanh and I shared the work well, and he helped me a lot. I don't know if the Upper Hamlet benefited from me while I was there; but I think it was a relief to the Upper Hamlet when they managed to have their own senior monks and I could return to the Lower Hamlet.

Can you share your most difficult moment and your most wonderful moment at Plum Village?

I can share my most difficult moment, but I cannot share my most wonderful moment because my most wonderful moment happens every day. Every day I have a most wonderful moment, and I can't say which is more wonderful. I will be honest with you about my most difficult moment. I have shared about this once before. I was in the

Lower Hamlet at the time. It was the end of the Summer Opening, so we were all very tired. Being the kind of mindfulness inspector that I am, I thought that it would be good if we could continue to practice even though the Summer Opening had ended. Even though I was tired and I really would have appreciated lazy days, I still insisted on having the wake-up bell in the morning and having sitting and things like that. At that time Thầy already had his hut in the Upper Hamlet. (In the early years, Thầy did not have a hut and he stayed in the old house above the bookshop.) Thầy was in the Upper Hamlet, and I was in the Lower Hamlet. Someone told Thầy, "Do you know in the Lower Hamlet that they have to get up in the morning," and so on. So Thầy said to his attendant, who was a young lay member of the Order of Interbeing at that time because we were only a few monks and nuns, "Oh, Sister Chân Duc doesn't need to worry about doing the practice now, she can let everyone be lazy." Thầy said something like that. So Thầy's attendant came down to the Lower Hamlet and said, "Thầy says you shouldn't make people get up in the morning," etc. This was perfectly normal, nothing to be upset about.

But for me that was my most difficult moment in Plum Village. I don't know why. A combination of things came together. I don't think I have ever felt so angry with Thầy in my whole life. I don't know if I really felt angry with Thầy or whom I felt angry with. So at first I thought I would grin and bear it on my own, and then I thought, No, I have to tell Thầy that I am really angry with him. I suppose what I thought was, In the old days, Thầy used to tell me things himself; he never told his attendant to tell me, and now I feel cut off from Thầy. I thought I would go to the Upper Hamlet. So I went to Thầy's hut, and I saw him sitting with a lot of Vietnamese friends. This didn't do anything to make my anger seed lessen. It made my anger seed grow because somehow I felt completely left out. Then I went into Thầy's hut and I don't remember what I said. That is probably a mental block because I don't dare remember. Anyway, I remember that Thầy said, "Sister Chân Duc is not well. Sister Hieu Nghiem, please give Sister Chân Duc a massage." So after that we went in the other part of the hut and Sister Hieu Nghiem gave me a massage. That was my most difficult moment. After that I felt very bad. I practiced Touching the Earth a lot. I went and apologized to Thầy. If ever now I have a younger sister who is angry with me and does something I think is not very kind, I remember what I was like that time with Thầy. I do not get upset with my younger sister, and I think she is not as bad as I was.

I never wanted to run away from Plum Village because, since I first came to the Lower Hamlet, I felt so at home. The only thing I was afraid of was that sometime I would be asked to leave because I was a bad disciple. But it never occurred to me to run away.

Please tell us about the first time you went out to lead a retreat.

The first time I led a retreat was with Sister Jina in the United States in the spring of 1992. We led a retreat in Texas. In Texas it is very hot, and the men are quite big, and they all wear shorts in the Dharma hall. I sat in the front of the room, and in the first row in front of me the men were all lying back on their elbows with their knees up. They were wearing shorts and they were sitting like that in front of me. I tried to concentrate on giving the Dharma talk, but it was very difficult for me to concentrate. I told Thầy about it afterwards, and he said, "Why didn't you lie down as well?" I think that Thầy wanted to teach me a lesson. What he meant was that when you give a Dharma talk, you are not really separate from the people you are teaching. If you have the idea "I am the teacher and they are the ones being

From left to right: Brother Phap Thong, Brother Phap Lac, and Thầy Giac Thanh

taught," it is not exactly a good Dharma talk. Thây wrote a gatha about this: *"Teaching Dharma in the ultimate dimension, I see people smiling. Those people are really myself. The listening is no different from the speaking."* You feel that there is no separation between you and the people listening and that they are doing the teaching as well as you. You are also learning from them as they are learning from you. When you feel the interbeing like that it is a much better Dharma talk. When I first began to give Dharma talks, I was very much separated from the audience. I had the idea that they should be like this and they should sit like this and they should do like this in order to receive the teaching. When Thây made that remark about me lying down, too, I think that it had a deeper significance than just to be funny.

Plum Village in the Future

If I think about Plum Village in the future, I see many Western monks and nuns. I know that the practice has to be developed. A tree always has to grow, otherwise it is not a tree anymore. In the future there will be many new Dharma doors, or mindfulness practices, adapted to Europe and the United States depending on where we are. It is difficult for me to see now what those Dharma doors will be because they will develop according to the causes, conditions, and the needs. They will definitely have a Western flavor. Vietnam very much needs our Vietnamese monks and nuns, Europe needs our European monks and nuns, and North America needs our North American monks and nuns. Vietnam needs Dharma doors that are suitable for Vietnam, Europe needs European Dharma doors, and North America needs North American Dharma doors. If the tree is to grow, we will have to continue. It is up to our younger sisters and brothers to develop and transmit these new Dharma doors. I don't have enough imagination to see what they will be, but I think they will involve the arts, such as sculpture, painting, music.

Thank you very much.

Stillness Is a Door

Susan Hadler lives in Washington, D.C. where she practices with the Washington Mindfulness Community. She is a psychologist and writer.

Slowing down, waking up.
Standing, breathing.

A heron glides down to the pond
And folds its wings.

Silence is a window.
Stillness is a door.

The heron flaps its wings
And flies.

Growing and Healing in Plum Village

The Joy of Being Alive

Sister Jina, Chân Dieu Nghiem, True Wondrous Adornment, is from Holland and Ireland. She ordained as a novice nun in Japan. She received bhikshuni ordination in Plum Village and became a Dharma teacher in 1992. She is abbess of the Lower Hamlet.

It was during a visit to the United States in 1990 that I came across the first issue of the *Mindfulness Bell* and saw the announcement of the 21-day retreat on the *Satipatthana Sutra* and Buddhist psychology. I did not know anything about either Plum Village or Thây, apart from having read *Being Peace,* but I immediately wrote to register and received a kind note back saying I was very welcome to attend the retreat. Upon returning to Europe I headed for Plum Village, France, and I realized I had not received any directions on how to get there. All I had was a postal address. However, I had lived in France before and, as it happened, used to frequent a yoga center in Eymet, which lies approximately ten kilometers from Plum Village.

I made my way to Eymet by plane, train, and bus. When I arrived there I checked for a phone number in the local post office and found one listed under *Eglise Bouddhique Unifiée de Vietnam* (Unified Buddhist Church of Vietnam). Could that be Plum Village? It was. I told the person answering the phone that I was in Eymet and asked how to get to Plum Village from there. "What are you doing in Eymet?" she asked. "You are supposed to arrive in Ste. Foy La Grande like everybody else. There is nobody to pick you up. All our cars have gone to Ste. Foy." "Oh well, never mind. I enjoy hiking, I'll walk," I reassured her. I had seen on the map that it was a simple straight stretch of road and ten kilometers is not very much for someone who is used to hiking. However, the idea of someone walking from Eymet to Plum Village seemed to be a bit much to her, and she said compassionately, "All right, start walking and as soon as there is a car available I'll send it to meet you."

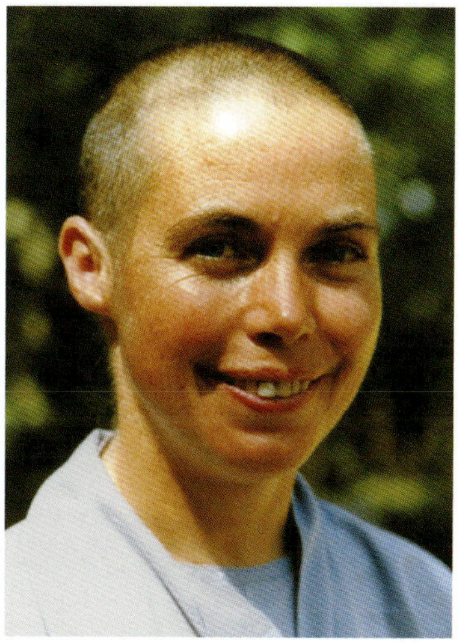
Sister Jina

It was a hot day. I started to walk, carrying my bag on my back. The sun was beating down on my head. Ten kilometers is not a lot, but it had been a long and weary journey and I started to get a migraine headache. Every time I put my foot down, a shudder went through my whole body and a loud "dzong! dzong!" vibrated in my head. Did that hurt! Walking became increasingly difficult and painful. I sat down alongside the road in the shade of a tree for a while and then resumed my walking, this time putting my foot down gently on the Earth with awareness, making the impact lighter. Then, touching the earth more and more gently with every step so as not to cause strong vibrations in my head, I slowed down, my breath slowed down, the pain eased. Thus I walked on, taking gentle step after gentle step. From time to time I stopped in a shady spot to just breathe and look around. After going a few kilometers in this way, a beige Renault arrived. "You must be Jina." It was Mike from the Upper Hamlet. I got into the car and soon we arrived in the Lower Hamlet where I was warmly welcomed by Sister Annabel. After registering, she showed me to my room.

As we were walking down the path to Plum Hill, Sister Annabel said, "I have to follow my breathing while walking." I glanced at her sideways and wondered: What is wrong with her? Does she have a migraine too? The next day Thây gave a Dharma talk about the basic practices of Plum Village, including walking meditation. Every word resonated with me. I surrendered wholeheartedly to the practice and realized that I did not need to wait for a migraine in order to enjoy walking gently in mindfulness on Mother Earth. I felt at ease and at home straightaway in the practice of Plum Village. I stayed on after the 21-day retreat into the Summer Opening and on and on.

After some time I moved into a little octagonal hut in a hazelnut grove. Whenever I walked from my hut to the meditation or dining hall I enjoyed the singing of the birds, the chirping of the insects, and the frolicking of the butterflies over the grass. But one day, when I had walked halfway down the path, all of a sudden I noticed that the birds had stopped singing, the insects had fallen silent, and the butterflies seemed to have gone into hiding somewhere in the grass. What happened? I wondered and stopped. At that moment the birds and insects resumed their concert and the butterflies reappeared.

Standing there it dawned on me that when I left my hut I had just walked, enjoying the gentle touch of my feet on the Earth, arriving in every step, allowing the wonders of the moment to reveal themselves to me. Then I had gotten carried away by some thoughts about an issue we were about to discuss in our Sangha and suddenly, the birds, insects, and butterflies went into hiding until I stopped and brought myself back to the present. That very moment everything else came back too. I breathed, looked around and up to the blue sky, and I stood there and enjoyed the singing of the birds, the insects, the butterflies, the sounds and sights of summer. I felt my heart being filled with joy. The joy of being alive. How true it is that when I am present everything and everyone else is present too. For many years now my favorite gatha to accompany my steps has been, *"I have arrived. I am home,"* turning my walking into walking meditation: the Dharma door through which I entered Plum Village.

I Enjoy Going Back to My Island: Transforming Habit Energies

Excerpt from a Dharma talk given Feb 24, 2002 at Deer Park Monastery

Brother Chân Phap Tri, True Dharma Wisdom/Understanding, is from the U.S. and grew up in Oregon. He was ordained a Dharma teacher in 2001.

My years at Plum Village have been the most difficult years of my life due to my strong and firmly entrenched habit energies. I remember thinking a couple of years ago, When will I ever learn? When will this darkness and attendant suffering, this tangible weight on my shoulders, lift? Without the support of the Sangha, which has given me the space to work through my difficulties with these habit energies, I would never have been able to begin to touch the freedom that I am now beginning to experience.

Thây Phap Tri

There is a song with the words, *"Breathing in, I go back to the island within myself. There are beautiful trees within the island. There are clear streams of water. There are birds, sunshine, and fresh air. Breathing out I feel safe. I enjoy going back to my island."* The way I've been embraced by my brothers has helped me to come back to the island within myself and cultivate a sense of ease that I've never known before. I took refuge in the Sangha so I could learn how to take refuge within myself. I learned how to take refuge in something beautiful, true, and good outside of myself, instead of constantly doing this and doing that, so that I could learn how to touch what is true and good within myself and to cultivate wholesome qualities by selective seed-watering.

A seventeenth century Catholic priest wrote that God can only come and visit us when we aren't there. He was referring to the small self, the self that is always preoccupied with petty concerns, which necessarily excludes others. When I start to disengage from this small self, I have more space for others. This helps me to cultivate big mind, the limitless heart of compassion. Through practice tools like the nine-point *metta* (loving kindness) meditation, the *Anapanasati Sutra (Sutra on the Full Awareness of Breathing),* and the *Satipatthana Sutra (Sutra on the Four Establishments of Mindfulness),* I have come to know what the unwholesome and wholesome mental formations are. I can find the proper antidote for some of what ails me. If I can't recognize an unwholesome mental formation, like restlessness or anxiety, I'm just like the alcoholic who hasn't recognized that he is an alcoholic. Habit energies have often seemed to compel me into actions against my will. So weaning myself from them is work I must do. And when I do it, it is such a relief — a tangible weight lifts from my shoulders.

When I work with my habit energy, I start with basic recognition. For instance, with my habit energy of doing too much, I realized that the question I need to ask myself is not, "Do I have enough time to do this task?" but rather, "Do I have time to do this task mindfully?" If I don't have time to do it mindfully, then I let go of doing it. For a "do-aholic" like myself, this has been quite liberating. Thây teaches that "we need to let go every fifteen minutes." We need to truly let go of any accumulated tension and begin again, fresh and renewed, so we can start the next fifteen minutes with a relaxed body.

The present moment is always available if we are. I'm feeling less and less a stranger to myself. I aspire to become as transparent a vehicle for the teaching as possible, to get myself out of the way, and the path goes on.

Intense Anxiety and Mindfulness

Dorothea Graf is from Zurich, Switzerland.
She spent the 2001–2002 Winter Retreat in Lower Hamlet.

After five years of searching for medicine or some other form of healing, I was about to give up. In all of those five years the doctors hadn't helped me. It was impossible for me to go outside alone. At any moment I could be overwhelmed by an anxiety attack, my body shaking, my mind panic-stricken, preventing me from taking a single step out of the house on my own. The life I had lived before was no longer possible. I was unable to go to work, go out shopping, or undertake any other kind of responsibility.

Conventional Western medicine provided me with some very strong medications, but because of the intense side effects I refused to take them after about two months. When all the different methods and trials I had been subjected to completely failed me, I did not want to carry on. On this particular day I was already considering ways in which to kill myself. Then, I went to the bookshelf and took out a book, *The Miracle of Mindfulness.* It had been there for a long time, alongside many other spiritual books, but I had lost faith in them. It was as if this inner voice, beyond my control, was urging me to go to the bookshelf and take out this particular book. I started to read it, and from that moment on my life has changed "miraculously."

The Miracle of Mindfulness brought mindfulness into my life, and I immediately started to practice while washing the dishes and cleaning the floor. In the beginning, I kept losing myself, but I persistently returned to following my breath as I engaged in my daily activities. The effects of this practice were immediate. As soon as I started, I felt an inner force and strength beginning to build inside of me. This was just what I had needed! My prior experiences with psychotherapy had nearly killed me. The techniques used were only analysis of the sources of my fear. There were not any methods of focusing on building an inner strength that could cope with and embrace my fear in order to transform it.

Anxiety illnesses like mine are widespread and on the rise. There are multitudes of personal stories on the Internet — people sharing the ways in which they have dealt with their sickness. None of them seem to have found a way out. Mindfulness practice was my way out. My psychotherapist has started using the practice of mindfulness in his treatments. Maybe other doctors and psychotherapists will also begin to include it in their methods of treating people with anxiety.

I can go out shopping again. When I begin to experience the incredible fear of a panic attack, I just stand still, follow my breath, and come back to myself. I find this is having a profound impact on my life. I'm here in Plum Village for the fist time, participating in the whole of the Winter Retreat. I'm enjoying it very much, and I feel so safe and happy here. Most important, I can even go outside on my own without any fear.

I want to express my heartfelt gratitude to Thây and also to the Sangha of Plum Village.

Brotherhood is the Foundation

Mikko Mäkitalo, Wonderful Protection of the Heart, is from Finland.

We are all brothers and sisters. This whispering in the trees is a very simple, deep truth. Yet nowadays it takes coming to a place like Plum Village to encounter it. I cannot consider my blood family as my "only" family anymore — the sound of the bell opens me up to an infinite family, which also includes non-human creatures. Recognizing this connection does not resolve all my difficulties, but the open space of infinite family relieves a lot of pain.

Touching and participating in the sense of brotherhood is the most nourishing practice to me in Plum Village. It is the foundation required for anything else to develop. I think that the main transformation that has started to happen with "me" is that I do not feel so disconnected from different kinds of people. Now I find my place in a group with much more ease than before — and I even enjoy it!

The late Thây Giac Thanh is one of the teachers who has helped me go beyond my restricted mind. While I lived with him, he taught me that every face I see is my face, whether a snake's face or beautiful person's face. Thây Giac Thanh was really able to transmit this through his practice. One must recognize everybody's face as one's own — otherwise compassion doesn't have the chance to arise.

At first I felt uncomfortable and disconnected around Thây Giac Thanh. But as things became easier with him, the same process happened simultaneously with the whole community, which I felt was kind of smiling to me. Thây Giac Thanh was the teacher of simplicity — with great ease he pointed out the dangers of living from our intellect and thinking that we "know better."

He also gave me some "rough" Zen teachings. In Plum Village softness is emphasized, but I am very grateful to Thây Giac Thanh for a teaching that has helped me a lot. At one point I was in a depressed state of mind, and he wanted to help me to break through it and see its roots. So when we were in the New Hamlet he invited me to come and listen to the big wind chimes hanging from a tree. He touched the bells very gently with his hand, and as we listened to the soft sound coming from them, he asked, smiling, "Isn't this a very beautiful sound, Mikko?" I nodded and smiled. He lightly touched the bells again and said, "Listen, how beautiful!"

Then as I was standing there, listening and smiling, he suddenly raised his hand and struck the bells with his full force, so that the sound reminded me of hell and chaos. I was terribly shocked, nearly frightened to death. I walked away quickly looking to the ground. In my chaos I was sure this was the end of the world. And worse, I felt as if I was guilty of something. If I had been settled in myself, why would there have been any cause to run away and feel guilty? I could have just stayed calm. But Thây Giac Thanh showed how reactive I was, which was a great teaching. Wherever I am, people will do unexpected, even inconvenient things that I cannot and should not try to control. I may cause some of these actions, but mostly they come from the misunderstandings that different backgrounds, ages, and cultures create. There is no need to be reactive. If someone has a misperception about me and looks at me with cold eyes, rather than trying to defend myself, it may be better to look at him or her in exactly the opposite way, with compassion.

Brotherhood is the foundation. Whatever I am doing, I am connected whether I want to be or not. When I can experience the connection, there is no fear. Then I am nourished and have the ability to be good to my beloved ones. But when distracted, I start to do things that make my beloved ones ugly. As long as brotherhood is the most cherished thing in Plum Village, I wouldn't be worried about the future.

As we continue on this path together, with our eyes bright, our hearts joyful, and our smiles fresh, we can look into each other's eyes with confidence. Don't be frightened. Connection exists always. Grandfather is always there with us. The moon is shining. Be safe.

The Baby Buddha Already Woke Up

Brother Chân Phap Dang, True Lamp of the Dharma, is from Vietnam and lived in California before he came to Plum Village. He was ordained a Dharma teacher in 1996.

I grew up in a very humble family; my father was a fisherman. The education that I received was very simple as we lived in the Nguyen countryside. I lived with the sea, the sand, the sunshine, the rivers, and the sound of the willows. I lost my father when I was four years old. I was too young to know what death meant, but I could feel how much my mother and my family suffered. Growing up in the countryside, I was enveloped with the love and protection of my mother and family, but I was still influenced by the fear and insecurity of the Vietnam War until the day I escaped from my country. From Vietnam I came to the United States.

From the urban American lifestyle that was busy, competitive, noisy, and unsafe, I came to another place that was quiet and peaceful. There I was able to learn the Dharma of compassion, joy, and liberation. Plum Village was my lovely and safe crib. I was able to practice breathing, walking, sitting, and eating meditation. I can still feel the peace and joy of that moment when I first arrived in Plum Village. The rolling hills, forests that turn so many beautiful colors in fall, and the pure air nourished me. My mind and body easily absorbed Thây's compassion, the Buddha's teaching, the loving kindness of my Sangha, and the practice. I started to get in touch with the preciousness of life. That joyful time lasted just a few years, and then I began to face difficulties and suffering.

Thây Nguyen Hai in Upper Hamlet

I was ordained at the same time as my big sister in the Dharma, Bao Nghiem, my big brother in the Dharma, Nguyen Hai, and my younger brother in the Dharma, Vo Ngai. The four of us loved, supported, and embraced one another. Each of us overcame a lot of difficulties and suffering together, so now after many years we understand each other well.

Big brother Nguyen Hai's character is very different from mine. In the first days that I was ordained, I was still very innocent. I just wanted to play, eat, and study. I was very free and didn't worry about the future. I grew up in a big family where my mother always made the decisions and took care of everything for me. Although my mom gave me a good education, I did not learn how to be responsible and take things seriously until the day I came to the monastery. Looking back I see that my older brother was not happy with me. At that time, I didn't know why he was so hard on me; I thought maybe that was his nature. Sometimes I was very angry with him, but we always tried to do Beginning Anew with each other.

In the beginning I thought that my suffering and obstacles came from outside of me, from my big sisters and brothers and other people. But one day in sitting meditation I recognized that my suffering came from my self-centeredness, blaming, and comparing myself with other people. After recognizing this, I suffered less. I came back to myself and looked directly at my mind consciousness, and I no longer ran after people, trying to bite them like an angry dog. Thanks to many years of diligent practice in Thây's tradition, I had enough peace to confront and overcome that difficult period when my mind was spilling out anger, complaints, jealousy, and desire. That time was very hard for me. Sometimes anger, despair, and self-centeredness appeared, and I felt like they were suffocating me. But I still sat there in meditation and breathed. Sometimes I sat overnight. Sometimes I practiced outdoor walking meditation under the moonlight. All I could do was breathe because I knew my mindfulness was still weak and my ego was too strong. I just breathed to bring peace to my mind, and the energy of complaining, of self-centeredness, went away. And slowly, I could restore my peace and stability.

Thây Phap Dang sharing a story with Chinese monks, Bai Lin Temple, 1999

I was also angry at my teacher and felt he did not understand me. I loved my teacher very much, and I wanted him to belong only to me, to pay attention to me, praise me, and recognize only me. When this didn't happen, I suffered a lot. But later I could see that, in reality, my teacher has always loved me. He embraced me so that I could learn his teaching little by little, and so I could practice more deeply. He could clearly see my habit energy, and he didn't hesitate to correct me.

Thây gave me his permission to go back to America to undergo Chinese medical treatment for an illness. During this time, I had the occasion to look into myself, and I began to see more clearly that the source of all my suffering, complaining, despair, and anger was my overgrown self-centeredness and pride. I recognized my faults. I saw Thây's compassion and the support of my Sangha. I realized only my teacher could help me to see the source of my suffering.

When I came back to Plum Village in 1997, I felt lighter and refreshed. I experienced the same kind of peace, joy, humility, and mindfulness I experienced right after I was ordained. Thanks to that experience, I could open my heart to practice again. It was also the first time that I recognized the true face of mindfulness and the other mental formations. Mindfulness means being truly present, it is light, understanding, acceptance, equanimity, and nondiscrimination. I also began to be truly openhearted with my brothers and sisters. I came to my brothers more often to have tea with them; and, thanks to that way of living, the communication between us grew stronger. After awhile we started to open our hearts and share our difficulties with each other, and then we began to understand and love each other even more.

I am learning to take care of and love my younger brothers. I know how to listen, to understand, to encourage, and to remind them about the practice. My daily practice in Maple Forest is to take

A lay friend with a baby Buddha sings in Transformation Hall, Upper Hamlet

care of my younger brothers because we live very far from Thây, and my younger brothers need to be embraced. I am happy that all my younger brothers love me. They like to have tea with me and listen to me talk about my practice. My younger brothers love me because I know how to live in harmony with everyone. I know that I have to be careful because if I'm not mindful I can become proud and force my younger brothers to obey me. Then if I'm not satisfied, I become angry very easily. So communication with my younger brothers helps me to see myself more clearly.

I love my teacher very much, but my love now is very free and at ease. I love my teacher because he loves me, teaches me, and helps me to overcome many difficulties. I see very clearly the energy of my teacher in me, and I no longer feel the need to receive his praise or attention. I now feel the energy of mindfulness in my hands, in my feet, in my eyes, and in my feelings; so I feel I am very close to Thây. I always see Thây beside me.

The energy of mindfulness is present in my hands, and I am aware that I am making tea, inviting my younger brother to join me, and holding the cup of tea and drinking. I am very happy and grateful. Before I had to make an effort to live mindfully, but now I don't need to try. Mindfulness is always present in me. When I pour tea into my cup, I know I'm pouring tea; and when I take food from the table, I know I am taking food. Mindfulness is a source of light. Each mindful breath, each mindful step adds light to that original source of light, making it bigger and bigger, radiating all around and into me. I feel mindfulness in my hands, feet, and eyes, and I know very clearly that I'm walking, brushing my teeth, looking at the blue sky. I am aware of everything I do. The baby Buddha in me has appeared and is awake, and I know how to live, to love, and to understand. My true self appears in the blue sky, and the melodious sound of the wind is singing a happy song. I vow to offer my deep gratitude to everything and everyone.

Three Mindful Breaths

Mary Myers, Wonderful Gratitude of the Heart, lives in Brooklyn, New York, where she practices with the Brooklyn Sangha.

In Plum Village practitioners have a tradition of pausing when they hear a bell. Every time they hear the bell to announce the schedule, or the clock in the dining room that chimes every quarter hour, or the telephone ringing, everyone pauses for three mindful breaths. Whatever they're doing, they just stop in mid-gesture, mid-sentence, mid-thought, and breathe silently for three inhalations and three exhalations, simply paying attention to the breath. It is a profoundly beautiful tradition.

After three mindful breaths, the world would change for me. I would see what was before me with new eyes. Several times it was apparent to me that whatever I had been saying when I stopped to breathe wasn't worth picking up again. Instead, simply being present to the moment was so rich, so joyous, and so vital that I was utterly happy to be there and alive. I felt my heart opening. I found that after three mindful breaths, I looked at the person in front of me with a fresh sense of her presence. I fell in love with some of the women I met, and they too were deeply touched by our meeting. My sense of their presence was so uncluttered that our hearts seemed able to speak to one another. We would look at one another and just smile without saying a word, and I felt the warmth of my love flood through my body.

Three mindful breaths. Such a small part of the trip, this pausing when we heard a bell; yet its effect on me was so powerful. Now I am back in New York, and I am trying to pay attention here, too — to return to the present moment and simply be.

Poems

Marie Favorini lives in Emeryville, California.
She visited Plum Village in 2000 and 2001.

The Lotus Bud

This ache in my heart
Is a flower, lotus bud
Wanting to open

Breathing, I tunnel inside
Through dark passageways
And into the center chamber
A hollow room, tight, constricted
A place of emptiness without the light of completion
I look, breathing,
Breathe, looking more deeply,
Looking, breathe more deeply

My nostrils draw in universe-breaths
All wanting to travel to that hidden place
Where the seedling, I see
I have surrounded it, it is clutched, choked
By thick tangled layers of vines

Tendrils of pain, resistance, darkness, threat
Show me that I have been
Afraid of this seedling's life unfolding,

I have not yet seen what has been hidden:
That its growth is its own protection.
It does not need
My dense web of confusion to shelter it anymore

Suddenly, one breath gets through,
Penetrating into the present moment
And I see, now

It is beginning to open.

The tangled masses are retreating
Creating wondrous space
As the lotus begins its shining
Opening
Outward into the vastness
Inside me
And a half-smile comes to my lips
With each petal's slow blossoming

I am no longer afraid of you, reading this,
I know we inter-are

What can I tell you that
You haven't heard before

I can only remind you
Of what you already know

The lotus is the opened heart
At its center sits your real self
A Buddha, awakened,
True,
Unafraid

Gatha for Calming the Mind

A seed no longer blown by the wind,
I have taken root in the ground of all being.

Poems

Sister Chân Dang Nghiem,
True Adornment with Nondiscrimination,
grew up in Vietnam and Arizona.
She is of Vietnamese and American heritage
and was trained as a medical doctor
before she ordained in 2000.

Are You?

You are the rain soaking my body,
The tear rolling down,
The hands I rub my head with, recalling the old vow,
The feet that bring me back to the present.
No more waiting, no more pursuing a puff of cloud.

Who are you
If not the voice of my teacher calling me home,
If not the early temple bell, resounding my heart's motion.

I sit still in eternity,
So your innumerable hands may embrace and console me,
So your breath may imbue me with the awakening life source.
A smile manifests in the deep night.

— *January 14, 2002, marking my two years in Plum Village*

Reflection on the Commentary on the Middle Way (Madhyamaka-sastra) by Master Nagarjuna.

Embrace

i am here for you, little sister.
The swollen slashes on your wrists and
Forearms are translucent like leaches.
Some resemble fibrous stumps.
They gasp under the strokes of my hands.

i am here for you, little sister.
Breathing in, i feel the heaviness in my chest.
Breathing out, my abdomen is engorged with pain.
Seventeen years old, sister,
What have you gone through?

i had already lost both parents.
i had already endured curses and beatings.
i had been molested.
i had gone to rivers for comforts
In imagined deaths.
i had left Vietnam;
My inheritance was a young brother,
Grandmother's hopes, and a muted child within.

i am here for you, dear one.
The bell for dinner resounds with insistence.
Breathing in, i know i am breathing in.
My cravings suffocate me.
i want to leave this sitting cushion.
i want to go to the dinning hall.
i want to eat.
Breathing out, i know i am breathing out.
i am aware that my mind wants to take refuge in food.
The solace from its flavors will end at the throat,
But the abdominal bloating and self-defeat
Carry on into the night,
As they have over the years, of eating
Pound cakes and sipping beers by the television.
On one Valentine's night, i finished two kilograms
Of cookies alone on my bunk bed.
i would leave a restaurant, only to return
To order a second meal to-go.
i turned to food, when sadness and
Restlessness were overwhelming.

i am here for you, following my breathing.
Twenty minutes into dinner time, and
The cravings have subsided.
My in-breath is quieter,
My out-breath is deeper.
Breathing in, i am aware of my body.
The space in my chest is more open.
Breathing out, i bring peace to my body.
There is lightness in my abdomen.

Breathing in, i feel gladness,
To have sat here for you, whose slashes
Sag like stretch marks on an old woman's belly.
For the muted child,
Who could not hide from the strips.
For the young woman,
Who has assumed the abuser's role.
Breathing out, i feel gratitude,
For the Buddha, my teacher, and sisters.
For this space and time to stop.
For the energy and the strength to stop.
i have stopped for one hour!

Breathing in, i am aware of my mind.
Faith in the Dharma strengthens.
Breathing out, i liberate my mind.
Quietude imbues me.
Breathing in, i contemplate impermanence.

My cravings have subsided,
And your slashes, too, will return to the Earth.
Breathing out, i see that even your suffering,
However familiar and poignant it may be,
i am not to hoard it or to become it.
Breathing in, i see no birth and no death.
You and i are cuts of the same fabric.
Breathing out, i heal you,
Who fractals inside me.

Breathing in, i practice letting go.
Breathing out, i am home.

Purple Flower on the Side Road

Sister Chân Dang Nghiem,

I thought you had gone on a sunny autumn day.
In the dark night, I howled your name,
As the ocean continued to rage menacing waves.
I am small, God
Please protect my loved one.

Where do you go? Can I find you,
Through my piercing cries?
Down the cliff, where my body is in pieces?
Your portrait stares at me quietly.
In despair, there is only I and the cruel loss.

Because there is still I, there is still you, union, and separation.
In me, the breath whispers non-death.
Is it not true, that we have never been strangers?
When our eyes were still shy to look at one other,
    Our minds were already deeply connected.
Now your hands continue to embrace me.
The purple flower on the side road marks a shared smile.

In one instant, you had gone.
In one mindful moment, you are all that is.

Dancing with Her Sorrow: Reflections on the Drawing

Sister Chân Tin Nghiem, True Adornment with Faith, is Korean and grew up in Florida. She ordained in 1998.

As I was sitting in meditation, an image arose very vividly in my consciousness. It was a person in brown, surrounded by light and countless flowers all around. She was graceful and she was dancing with her sorrow. Although she was sad, she could see the flowers around her. I remember the spaciousness that surrounded her and so many colors of flowers. I felt happy and light.

Later I drew the image and it was Sister Dang Nghiem; the curve of her head, hands, and teardrops. And I left it alone until the anniversary of her partner's death rolled around. I remembered the drawing and I was inspired to give it to her in honor of the occasion.

I loved the orange stars. I felt so happy with this color. I did her robe brown. The tear was very simple. What was important to me was that her hands were really open, in a gesture of receiving, because I knew that she was practicing to transform her suffering. I wanted to express that she has the capacity to embrace her sorrow and continue and that I was proud to be her sister. She was stronger than she had been, and I wanted to acknowledge her strength.

When I gave her the picture, I told her, "I can see your practice. You've developed the capacity to embrace more. Before things could drown you because you thought that sorrow was all that was in you. But with mindfulness you are a lot more than your pain." That is the outstretched hand. She's very aware of her sorrow, but now she sees the flowers and light. And that's why she can dance with her sorrow — the wholesome elements transform the unwholesome ones.

Drawing by Sister Tin Nghiem

Being Who I Am

An Interview with Sister Hanh Nghiem by Lorrie Harrison and Sister Chau Nghiem

Sister Chân Hanh Nghiem, True Adornment with Practice or Action, is twenty-three. She is from the United States and grew up in Indiana. She ordained in 2001.

How did you first learn about Plum Village?

I first came in 1999, when I was nineteen — that was the first time I was introduced to the Buddha, and the first time I meditated. I was full of doubts and self-pity. I was going through a depression and my stepdad suggested I go to a practice center.

Is your family Buddhist?

No. My stepdad's teacher is Christian, but our house is built in a more Eastern way. Before this teacher, he had a Hindu teacher. My mom and stepdad meditated, but they never forced it on me or suggested it to us kids; it was just something they did, and it helped them feel better. But unconsciously, it became a part of who I am. What my mom and stepdad were doing watered a seed of what I'm doing today.

So I looked Plum Village up on the Internet; and when I saw it was in France, I immediately wanted to come because I wanted to go to France. I was in what I call a "froggy" state — always jumping around looking for happiness. I need to be rooted. Being in Plum Village has helped me to be confident that taking one step at a time is okay.

My mind changes a lot. For example, the way I grew up, my mom was always cooking something different. In a year, we almost never repeated the same meal more than once or twice. Here the food is more predictable. For example, I know when Sister Khe Nghiem cooks what kind of food there will be. And at every meal, I know there will always be white rice, brown rice, and soup on the table.

That's okay with you?

It's the best thing in the world! One thing to overcome is greed for food. When you don't feel that fulfillment from the food that you're eating, you're in poverty — always searching for something different. I never think about breakfast, because I know what will be on the table. I am one with my breakfast. When the food is simple it brings me so much comfort and happiness. My mind stops. But then it's also okay when there is something different. I'm American, I like variety.

You don't feel bored by the food here?

No, it doesn't cross my mind. People often ask me if I want American food. But I always say, No, I'm happy here. Something I practice right now is getting over the "more is better" idea. For example, putting a big spoonful of chocolate on my bread, as opposed to a small layer. When I take a little less than I think I need, just spread a little chocolate on the bread, it still tastes just as good. And I don't feel sick! If I drink a small glass of tea in mindfulness, my thirst is quenched. I don't need a huge cup. I consume so much more than I need. It's part of my culture. It's very much in my mind. I'm a very honest person, and one reason I decided to ordain is because of my relationship with food.

How did you decide to become a nun?

The second time I came to Plum Village was in 2000 and I was with people who came here to ordain as monastics. At first I felt, no way, I will never do that. The first time I came I didn't get to know any sisters because they are shy and they are really busy in Summer Retreat. The second time was so different. I felt so welcomed. I was really happy because people recognized me. Little things make such a difference. I became more relaxed. When I realized one of my friends was here to ordain, the same idea came to my mind. But it wasn't at all what I had planned for myself. I wanted to build houses with Habitat for Humanity. I wanted to be out in the world and travel a lot. The idea of ordaining kept coming up, but inside I said, "No!" Then, when the feeling of wanting to be a nun just got stronger and stronger, I called my mom and told her I was pretty sure this is what I wanted.

People don't ordain to save the world. Most of our reasons are more self-centered. It's human nature. We are pleasure-seeking people. We ordain to heal ourselves. I wanted to ordain to lose weight. Before I came to Plum Village, I felt impure. I wanted to lose weight, but I was motivated by a desire to look good for other people, to be physically attractive. I thought, That's not why I should lose weight. So I continued to eat unmindfully. I thought, When conditions are right for me to slim down, it will happen. When my mind is pure, I'll lose weight. So I stuck with my habitual way of eating.

I had a habit of not listening to myself, to what I really want, of suppressing my deep desires, and this was connected to my depression. When I saw I was doing that again in relation to my desire to ordain, I said, "No I'm not doing this anymore." I felt committed to that deeper voice in myself so I just stayed.

What about children? How did you decide to give up having children?

I cried when I thought of not having kids. Then I realized we are Thây's spiritual children and eventually we will have our own spiritual children. I feel that as a nun I'm a young mom.

In the world, if people knew who they were, the world would be at peace. How many moms really want to be a mom? My mom didn't want to be a mom. She was a wreck; her marriage was a wreck — that is when she started her spiritual journey. If a mom could allow herself to be a mom, the world would be at peace. As a mom, when you don't realize you're a mom, you get angry at your kids for spilling some milk. You scream at them for something so minor. That's because you don't realize you're a mom.

What's the hardest thing about living in the Sangha?

The Ten Novice Precepts were really painful for me. I didn't grow up with any rules. My mom taught us that rules are made for people who can't think for themselves. I felt that rules were things that people always had to follow. But I saw that all of us break some of them. I had a lot of confusion — why do we have these rules if we all break some of them? It watered a lack of trust in me as an aspirant.[2]

Now I see that the greatest thing about being a nun is having precepts, so I can at least be aware of what I am doing. True love comes from precepts. We don't do them perfectly. But 99 percent of us are wholeheartedly trying to keep the precepts. The point isn't to always keep them. Like when we go into the kitchen to get bread for ourselves, which we aren't supposed to do. It's not that getting bread is bad. The reason we have that precept is because we live in community, and if we don't have rules anarchy results. People become individualistic. At first the precepts choked me — now they really are my freedom.

And what's the best thing about living in the Sangha?

Well, I like to be a kid. My greatest fear was growing up too quickly and not maturing naturally. If this happened I would be a disappointment to kids. Here I can be a kid, but also be a mom — mature and fresh at the same time, not weighed down by responsibilities and worries. There are nuns that are forty, and I feel they are the same as me. Here I can mature; that's a great happiness for me. I feel stable, rooted, secure, unafraid, not lost. Before I felt despair, a lack of confidence. Now I have confidence that I can do the things I want to do. The fruit will ripen. This environment helps us understand that we should do what we enjoy.

To me this is true humility: to be who I am. The more I do what I want, the happier I am. Then I don't worry about what others are doing. If I'm not taking care of myself and loving what I do, I get angry at my sisters when they don't walk mindfully. But then I don't walk mindfully either. When I do it myself, with love, the judging, discriminative thoughts don't arise. Others are just a reflection of ourselves.

Sister Hanh Nghiem before becoming a nun

A Way Out of Suffering

Irene Ouwehand, eighteen, is from Holland. She practiced in the Lower Hamlet during winter 2001–2002.

When I was asked to share something about my growth in Plum Village I felt a little heavy. I connected the word "growth" with becoming older and wiser. And I don't feel I'm becoming older and wiser at all. I don't want to *become* anymore. So I will share some things about my growth that make me feel old and young and wise and happy without having to become anything.

At a very young age, I had to leave my home to live in an environment where I ingested pain, suffering, abuse, and despair twenty-four hours a day. I grew very old. People guessed me to be at least four years older than I was, and all the therapies and counsels were so complicated that I forgot it was possible to live simply in the here and now. I always thought that I would be happy if I became something else, had something else, or lived somewhere else.

When I reached my aim and moved to another country, I found myself still unhappy and so ran on until I became completely lost and tired. Tired of living. For me, life was something you could only enjoy if you became. Even my first intense Buddhist practice had this intention. I grasped knowledge and told myself that I would be happy if I was recognized as an incarnated Buddha. But nobody recognized me, and I didn't recognize myself.

In the Buddhist center where I lived for a while, they had a wonderful bookshop with a lot of Thây's books. Secretly I watched my breath and took mindful steps. These breaths and steps brought me home to Plum Village. Breathing and walking in Plum Village brings me home to the present moment.

To me Plum Village is just like all other places. The sun rises, the rain falls, the birds sing, the wind blows, the trees drop their leaves, the people laugh, the people cry. Maybe the only difference is that lives are lived in awareness of all these outer and inner processes. Aware of each breath and step taken in each moment. This simple mindfulness has been truly miraculous for me.

I find myself healing from the most horrible wounds — despair, depression, destruction, hate — just by breathing, walking, enjoying, and looking deeply. All the books I brought to study are untouched. I see that I don't need knowledge. I need mindfulness and understanding. All the habits of despair, hate, depression, and destruction are still in me and sometimes very overwhelming, but I have found myself more than once going through such a storm without acting out my usual destructive play. This makes me so grateful, so happy, so free.

Thanks to all my suffering, thanks to the very simple practice, I found a way out of suffering — suffering I once thought of as incurable.

Learning to Love Everyone as My Brother and Sister

Sister Chân Hoi Nghiem, True Festive Adornment, came to Plum Village from Vietnam. She ordained as a novice in 1999.

Respected and Dear Su Ong,
The brothers and sisters of the Cherry Tree family had the idea that each one of us would write something to make a small book to give to Su Ong, to commemorate the day we ordained one year ago. During our discussion, many themes were suggested. I was drawn to the topic "Experiences living in a Sangha," even though I haven't yet had much experience living in a Sangha.

I remember when I first came here, I had the tendency to search for things that belonged to me, like my teacher, my mother and father, my brothers and sisters. But I found that there was nothing at all that belonged to me. Everybody was a stranger to me. Even though I saw that the nuns loved me and helped me, I still felt that they were strangers. I felt lonely, lost, and miserable. If anyone did something not to my liking, I would become upset and angry. But then I thought, I left everything behind to come here, far away from my family and close friends in order to find something more beautiful, not to take on more afflictions. When I was at home, I didn't have afflictions like this. I knew that it was necessary for me to practice to liberate myself. I practiced breathing, smiling, and recognizing each affliction within me so that I could transform.

I remember Su Ong often teaches, "We have to love each person in the Sangha as our very own blood brother or sister." When I am doing any kind of work, I do it with all my heart and to the best of my ability, as I did for my family and friends. But what is the quality of my relationships with people? Why do I find this so hard, Su Ong? There were many times that I wanted to ask Su Ong during a question and answer session, but I was reluctant, so I didn't: What can I do so that I can love each person as my blood brother or sister? Pleasant and loveable people are easy enough, but I would also like very much to love the hard-to-love people as my own blood brother or sister. But when they do something not to my liking I become angry. How can I embrace them? After I become angry I know how to practice to transform the anger within me. But after this anger subsides, then another anger arises. Often, I would think to myself, "Never mind that person. Whatever she does, just pay no attention to her. If I concern myself with her, it will just tire me out." However, then I think again, "If I love Su Ong, then I cannot have that kind of attitude." I have to truly love everyone as my blood brother and sister. If I love Su Ong, I have to live in such a way that each teaching of Su Ong enters my being, enters my life. Knowing that love manifests itself through each action, gesture, and word, I began to practice accepting and embracing.

I remember one time a certain person made me angry. On the outside I didn't say anything or react, but in my heart I was very angry. Afterwards, I lay down and cried. I said, "Dear Buddha, dear Su Ong, why am I so selfish? Why is my heart so small? Why is it that I want to love this person as my own blood sister, and yet I can't? This person has only touched me a little, and here I am already upset. Why is this?"

I cried a lot. I cried until I couldn't cry anymore, then I sat down and looked deeply. I thought, "It is easy to love my own brothers and sisters because we share the same blood, and probably our love for one another was present when we were still in the womb; and it was nurtured and nourished over the months and years that we lived together. Why do I force myself to love this person immediately when both of us know absolutely nothing about each other? Also, my blood brothers and sisters love each other but, that doesn't mean that there is no unskillfulness, that we don't get angry with each other. I have to allow myself time and space to receive and embrace this person. I shouldn't force myself to love immediately if my practice is still weak."

When I allowed myself to feel this way, I was able to embrace and accept more. Once someone said things to me that weren't nice and made me angry. I was able to recognize that I was angry right as it began to manifest. I felt happy because I was able to see its true

Left to right: Thây Phap Dung, Sister Man Nghiem, and Sister Hoi Nghiem on a canoe trip down the Dordogne River with the Sangha

face as it was just beginning to manifest. At the same time it just went away. It felt as if it left faster than an arrow. I thought to myself, It's not necessary not to be angry.

I had the opportunity to eat a meal sitting across from this person. I wanted to sit there to closely follow my feelings. I saw that unpleasant feelings sometimes arose within me. Each time this happened, I looked over at a picture of Su Ong, breathed, and smiled. When my heart calmed and I had more happiness, I smiled as I looked at the person opposite me. Whenever the unpleasant feeling arose, I would smile again and gaze at Su Ong's picture. I practiced like that until the meal was over. While I ate, I followed my feelings, thoughts, and perceptions attentively. Because of this, when I relate to this person now, I no longer feel unpleasantness.

There are times when I am upset about something or I'm angry at someone, but I haven't had the time to look deeply and resolve it. In the evening, during sitting meditation, I invite the image of that person to come up, and I look for the good qualities in that person. I embrace them along with those things that aren't to my liking, and vow that I will be able to love this person as I do everyone else.

When someone gives me input, whether she is older or younger than me, I join my palms, bow, and thank her, even though sometimes within me there are some unpleasant perceptions or some reactions. But if I react or show my anger, then the next time the person will not come to me and give me input. If someone gives us input, that means that she loves us, that she has not abandoned us. Therefore, whether it is a pleasant or unpleasant experience for me, I still thank the person. If there is any unpleasant perception that arises within me, I acknowledge and smile to it. If I see that I am at fault I try not to repeat the same mistake again. If I do not yet see that I am at fault, I allow myself some more time to look deeply, and I do not force myself to follow the suggestion immediately. Sometimes these unpleasant suggestions have helped me to see my unskillfulness and faults that on my own I wouldn't be able to see.

When I want to make a suggestion, I look at myself closely to see whether I truly want the other person to be able to transform and whether the words that I am about to speak are coming from love. Or are they from anger or wanting to criticize and find fault with the other person? If they are from anger or from wanting to criticize, then I wait. I can speak only from love. This is one way that I may contribute towards the work of building a Sangha according to my capacity and practice.

There were times when the community had a lot of work to do, and I felt that there was not enough time to study, to read, or to do personal things for myself. I didn't feel too happy. But right at that moment I thought, Oh, I am still lucky because every day I have twenty-four hours to practice and train. Even if I'm very busy, no one can take away even one hour from me. It depends on us whether we practice fully in each moment. Thinking like that, I became more aware of my practice.

I remember the first year that I was teaching, there were times when I was irritated because my students were slow and didn't understand their lessons. Afterwards, my father told me, "Don't ask your students to be good and obedient 100 percent, to learn and understand their lessons perfectly. They only need to be above 60 percent, the bare minimum." I allowed myself to accept this, and I felt happier and freer when I related to my students. My students responded positively as well, learning their lessons more quickly.

Living in a community is like that. We shouldn't ask people to be 100 percent perfect. We should practice to accept people as they are. And when there is an issue that I want to give someone input on, I give input according to the other's ability to receive it, not aiming for perfection. This way, I feel freer and happier living in the community.

When I am assigned to work with someone who works with responsibility and in the way I like to work, I am very happy. And when I am paired with someone who is a bit difficult for me, it is a good opportunity for me to see myself more clearly. If I were always in easy situations, I could easily be deceived and think that my practice is quite strong, when in fact it isn't. These are the things that I have been practicing while living in the Sangha. The Sangha gives me a lot; it helps my faith to deepen each day.

The following is a poem that I like very much. I like it not because the words are good, but because I wrote it during a time of much happiness and freedom. I would like to give it as a gift to Su Ong.

A Half Moon

Alone, I walk meditatively on this small path
Stopping, smiling, I gaze at the half moon.
The moon this evening is so strangely bright
Clearly printing my shadow on this peaceful path!

~

Continuing to walk I invite the moon to follow my steps
But dear moon! Is it because of my invitation that the moon follows?
If there were three persons going in three directions
The moon would still follow all three
Even if there were a thousand people with a thousand directions
The moon would not forsake anyone.
Oh moon, this evening, always, and forever.
I wish to learn your capacity
To walk with everyone.
No hatred, no discrimination, no abandonment

Even towards the person I have hated the most.
Oh, but dear moon, my mind is still so small
How many times have I promised to myself
Only to never realize it.
This contract I sign with you today
Please, moon, remind me to be aware so my vow today
shall be realized.

You are in Me

Erica Shane Hamilton, Fresh Guide of the Heart, lives in Washington, D.C., where she practices with several Sanghas.

Plum Village. To me you are a wondrous manifestation of love, peace, and harmony. You are nourishment for my deepest aspiration to transform my fears into love. You are the Earth and all of the Earth is in you.

I left you over a year ago, but you still manifest in me every day. You manifest in me when I walk mindfully at the U.S. Capitol, delivering "love letters" to Congress about the need to support programs that improve the well-being of children and adolescents. You manifest in me when I eat my lunch mindfully next to a tree in the park across from the White House. When I lean against the tree and I look with wonder at the beautiful leaves and listen to the birds' songs, I know you are smiling with me — that people in the Sangha are listening attentively to bird songs and admiring the beauty of nature many miles away.

You are with me when I suffer from my illness, a disease of the intestines. And when I feel pain I say to myself, "Breathing in, I feel pain. Breathing out, I know this pain is temporary." When I have stayed in the hospital for weeks at a time I have made signs reminding myself to breathe and come back to the present moment — signs I first saw at Plum Village like, "Breathe! You are alive!" Nurses came into my room and told me they felt a sense of peace. I watched birds and butterflies from my window and knew I was still connected to them, that the glass between us was not a real barrier.

I watch my fears during times of sickness. I watch them rise when doctors tell me alarming facts: "If your hemoglobin levels drop lower, you will need a blood transfusion," or "If your colon dilates one centimeter more you will need surgery." The love that cradles my fears has grown from the practice of awareness I began at Plum Village, where I also healed from an episode of my disease. Time and again I have crossed oceans of fear to see my sick body as part of the cosmos.

"In the ultimate I dwell. In the ultimate I dwell. . . ." I love to sing the songs from the *Basket of Plums* songbook, and even when I am alone I hear the chorus of voices from the Sangha in Plum Village and the Sanghas that I belong to in Washington, D.C. The Sangha is so strong that I have gone many times for refuge and known that I would be supported in myriad ways, with love and care.

Every day I wake up and feel grateful for another day in which to love. And when I meditate, Plum Village, you are in the pink rose that I feel blooming in my heart. And I am in the pink roses blooming in your beautiful gardens.

Plum Village Tears, Plum Village Joy

Richard Brady, True Dharma Bridge, lives in Washington, D.C., where he practices with the Washington Mindfulness Community and teaches math at Sidwell Friends School. He was ordained a Dharma teacher in 2001.

I remember the first time I heard of Plum Village. It was in 1989 during my first retreat with Thây at Omega Institute in upstate New York. A woman in our Dharma discussion group told us this was her first experience with meditation. Tears came to her eyes every time she meditated. She said her life was happy and she had no traumas in her past. She wondered if her situation was normal. If this was what meditation was like, she was not sure that she wanted to continue. People who responded told her that her experience was not so unusual. One said, with a bit of humor, that in Plum Village there was a rule against crying for more than five minutes. It was not uncommon, he added, to find Westerners hidden in the bushes sobbing.

In the years since, I have experienced intense emotions, including tears, many times during my visits to Plum Village. Sometimes I've been alone, sometimes with others. One of these times, a Dharma discussion with two other men, will always be with me. During the previous Dharma discussion, "James" shared that ever since coming to Plum Village he felt he had been carrying the weight of the world on his shoulders. He could not account for this feeling. During the question and answer session the next day, James told Thây that his brother and sister-in-law had committed suicide. He asked Thây for advice. Thây responded that each of us has the seed of suicide and the seed of joy. Which of these seeds sprouts depends on which is watered. The seed of suicide had been watered in James and he was at risk. He needed to examine carefully his life choices (his home, his job, his friends) and change any elements that were not watering his seeds of joy.

That evening our Dharma discussion group met again. There were just three of us. Our discussion soon turned to James's sharing of that afternoon. James added that earlier in his life he had had problems with alcohol. He felt that his sister-in-law was the only person who had supported him. It was this sister-in-law who took her own life during a period of depression, leaving her husband and two small children. Two years later the husband, James's brother, took his own life as well. We were listening deeply.

Following James's story, "William" told us about his brother, a doctor. Two years earlier, his brother had developed an aggressive brain tumor. William booked a flight to visit him but was then told by his brother — whose mood had been darkened considerably by his illness — not to come. With his ticket in hand, William decided to ignore his brother's wishes. At the end of his long flight, William was met by a grief-stricken, orphaned nephew. William's brother, pessimistic about the future of the world, had killed his wife and then himself.

Left to right: Richard Brady, Ernestine Enomoto, and Mitchell Ratner in Plum Village

Our group fell into an extended period of silence. Our tears were flowing. We knew that this suffering was not just personal, or even the suffering of our generation. It came from our ancestors as well. It had been denied, hidden behind stern and proper behavior, held at bay by living lives protected from feeling. Now this suffering had burst into the open. For us it was inescapable. The three of us were holding all this suffering, knowing it was on behalf of our ancestors and on behalf of future generations. At Plum Village we had learned to touch both our ancestors and our descendants through the practice of Touching the Earth. Now we were able to experience their suffering as our own.

I then shared the story of my younger brother, Bob, my only sibling. As a teenager, Bob had a series of physical and psychological problems. Eventually Bob's condition caused him to drop out of school. He left our home in Illinois and moved to California where he hoped to regain his health. Bob became attracted to the idea of fasting to cleanse his body of toxins and began a supervised water fast at a health center. After forty-five days the medical staff advised Bob to stop. He did not follow their advice and continued fifteen more days. Two days after completing his fast, he went into a coma that lasted several weeks. Bob came out of the coma with a stiff hip and brain damage that severely impaired his short-term memory and left him subject to seizures. Since then Bob has lived with our parents and in several communities for people with mental disabilities. He refers to his first life, his death, and his second life. This sharing with James and William was the first time I had ever told my brother's story and been able to feel my grief fully.

Through our tears we contacted a truth beyond suffering. We had learned from Thầy to embrace and cradle suffering as we would a crying infant. Whatever liberation we might achieve through our practice, we were sharing it with the next generation, James with his young niece and nephew as well as his own son, William with his son and his grown nephews, I with my daughter. We were in Plum Village, home to many joyful monks and nuns, many of whom were Vietnamese refugees who had experienced tremendous suffering in their lives. Thầy had shown them how to water the seeds of joy as well as how to hold their suffering. In the depth of our connection with them and with each other, we found ourselves touching our own seeds of joy.

Seven years have passed since this experience. The process of opening to suffering has been a slow one for me. It hasn't been easy on my own to touch my suffering or that of others. Sometimes, when I've been able to hold with awareness emotional upheavals in my current relationships, I have opened doors to old pain. Tension in my body has also connected me to old fears and old anger. I learn to be with both old and new suffering in an accepting way, to hold it with the help of my ancestors and descendants. It is no longer just mine. I have begun to feel lighter and happier.

I Embrace You

Carmen Van Haren is from the Netherlands and came to Plum Village in May 2001. She recently released a CD of her songs.

I embrace you
You are my suffering
You're staying deep
Deep within
I say to you
Please come in
My arms
Let me comfort you
Make you warm
Transforming into a flower
You will shine as the sun
You will make me grow
The Buddha tells me so
You're my suffering
I'm glad we meet
I used to put you down
But now I set you free
You're my suffering
I'm glad we meet
I used to put you down
But now I set you free

Morning Exercise

JoAnn Ross Cunningham

We rise with the sun
And every step
Every
Step
From tall concrete pillars where we have slept
To the courtyard below
We awake
Smiling
Rooting ourselves in the base of trees swaying,
reaching into blue sky.
Breeze flutters through leaves, upstretched fingers,
Tousles the grass, lavender flowers, heads of hair
All sprouted within this celestial embrace.
Like this we rise from the planet
Briefly
Before we become the Earth or breeze or bloom again.

— *Amherst Retreat, 2001*

A Lesson in Deep Listening

JoAnn Ross Cunningham

"Brother, would you like to walk with me and visit on the way to the Dharma talk?" I offer, convinced this brown-robed monk is going my way.

He stops, hesitates, looks at me. I sense he will not accept my invitation. "I'm being rejected by a monk," I think.

"It's our practice to stand still when we speak with someone," he explains as he pauses in the heat of the afternoon sun.

I hedge, uncertain whether I should have intruded on his solitary walk. "But I don't want to keep you in the sun longer than necessary — in those dark robes and all."

"It's okay," he assures me. "What do you want to talk about?"

Halted on the street corner there I pose questions about the practice of mindfulness and Right Path as traffic passes by toward myriad destinations.

Past the language of conversation, this moment fully answers me in its stillness, strength, and solidity — a moment of listening intently, purely, simply, fully listening.

Voices of Veterans

Welcome Home: Awakening from The Suffering Caused by War

Written by the Veterans' Sangha and offered by Roberta Wall

"We evoke your name, Avalokiteshvara. We aspire to learn your way of listening in order to help relieve the suffering in the world. You know how to listen in order to understand. We evoke your name in order to practice listening with all our attention and open-heartedness. We will sit and listen without any prejudice. We shall sit and listen without judging or reacting. We will sit and listen in order to understand. We will sit and listen so attentively that we will be able to hear what the other person is saying and also what has been left unsaid. We know that just by listening deeply we already alleviate a great deal of pain and suffering in the other person."

Since 1994 we have begun the Veterans' Circle at Thây's East Coast retreats with this invocation of Avalokiteshvara, the Great Being of Compassion and Deep Listening.

The Veterans' Circle continues to grow into a beautiful Sangha, reuniting every year to participate in Thây's East Coast retreats. We hear Thây's talks, sit and listen to each other, and feel the healing presence of the whole community. We heal through writing, following our breath, opening our hearts, and not turning away from each other, the veterans — now fathers and grandfathers, who finally trust enough to share the pain, shame, and suffering they have carried for thirty years, since being sent to Vietnam as boys to kill. We sit and listen, fully present, to the sons, daughters, and spouses of veterans, and the peace activists who lived the war here at home. We share by telling and writing stories, speaking to each other with loving and compassionate speech, hugging, walking silently together, and offering our full presence and unconditional love. All that is asked is that we "show up" and be as fully present as we are able to be. As the sharing begins, the veterans call out to one another, "Welcome home."

Here are some voices of our Sangha:

Tom (1996): This is my first visit to Omega. I didn't realize that twenty-six years ago today I actually began my living hell. Today I sit in the Omega garden and think how beautiful everything is. There is peacefulness here. I wish my body could be the same. Tears roll down my face and I do not know why. This is my first time trying to deal with Vietnam. No one ever asked about it, including my family. My father died while I was in country [in Vietnam]. They let me go home, then sent me back. I did not want to go.

On October 8, 1968, I stepped on a land mine with my left foot. I should have died. The explosion lifted me into the air, flipped me over, and laid me face down on the ground. I remember it all. I never lost consciousness until they put me under for surgery.

I remember wondering how many guys I took with me. I never found out. Nobody ever told me. I felt isolated and still do to this day. I find it difficult to express or feel any emotion. I feel if my emotions were to let go I would not be able to control them. They are numb. I hear life all around me, but never experience it. Being here with you people has brought on more pain. When will it end? Where do I go from here? My mind is blank now.

Fred (1996): Tom lost a leg in Vietnam, and, like most of us coming to this retreat for the first time, his pain is raw, palpable. We were all deeply moved by his openness and courage. I saw Tom outside the main meditation hall just before the veterans were to share our writings with the general retreat. I asked him if he was going to read.

Being new and shy he shrugged, and said, "I don't know." I told him that telling his story would not only help him heal, it would help us heal, too. This was his chance to do that for a few hundred other people. So Tom read. There were tears everywhere and it was joyous.

The next morning, after the Dharma talk, we did our usual walking meditation down to the beach and started sharing songs and chants. In the middle of one song, I looked over and saw Tom staring at the water, teary-eyed. I went over and embraced him. While hugging as tightly as two people can, he said in my ear, "You've no idea what you've done for me." I replied, "Yes, I do." My friend Jim, who brought me to the '91 retreat, joined our hug. It felt so right. Perfect, pure love. We were so enmeshed in our caring cradle that it seemed like magic (and it was magic!) when we realized we were surrounded by the rest of the retreatants, singing. They sang "Amazing Grace." My soul soared and my heart has never known such warmth.

Tom continued to come to the retreats. A few years later, one brilliantly golden Omega day, he came to the circle without his prosthetic leg. He stood up and proclaimed, "Today, I am free." It was the first day since his release from the Veterans Hospital thirty years ago that he had gone in public without his artificial leg.

Thây at the Vietnam Veterans' Memorial, Washington, D.C.

Thây (Excerpted from *Love in Action*): I, too, am a veteran. I lost many friends — many brothers and sisters — during the Vietnam War, and I experienced much suffering. Grenades were thrown into my room, but were deflected by a curtain. Social service workers under my direction were killed and maimed. We did our best to confront the violence with love, but we had to cry a lot.

I have been practicing to transform my suffering and share my insight with others. I do not feel any more blame. I feel peace and compassion, and that allows me to help other people.

Veterans are the light at the tip of the candle, illuminating the way for the whole nation. If veterans can achieve awareness, transformation, understanding, and peace, they can share with the rest of society the realities of war. And they can teach us how to make peace with ourselves and each other, so we never have to use violence to resolve conflict again. To make the world a peaceful place, to ensure for our children and grandchildren a life worth living, we need transformation.

Fred: I went to Thich Nhat Hanh's Vietnam Veterans' Retreat in June of 1991 at the Omega Institute. It was the most intense week of my life. I never cried so much, or laughed so hard. My name is Fred Louis. I was a U.S. Army infantryman in Vietnam from February 1968 to February 1969.

I didn't know how fortunate I was to be at that first retreat until later. There were only eighty of us with Thây, Sister Chân Không, and a novice monk. We had two Dharma talks a day, and Thây told us stories about his life. I knew there was magic happening, wondrous transformations. So, I've been to every East Coast Veterans' Circle since then, making me the "elder statesman," I guess. Thây told us how and why he invented hugging meditation when he first came to the U.S. in the mid-1960s. Then he demonstrated, and had us practice, encouraging us, in particular, to hug one of the three Vietnamese participants, saying, "If you hug one Vietnamese, you've hugged them all." So I shared a hug with Thich Nhat Hanh! Can you imagine? I've taught hugging meditation to hundreds of people since then.

In 1991, Thây told us that the veterans were "the light at the tip of the candle," that our pain was everyone's pain, and that our experiences positioned us to show the way toward transformation, healing, peace. I didn't really comprehend those notions then. Now, however, I have years of illustrative memories. I remember a woman showing up where the Veterans' Sangha was sitting — she had tears in her eyes and said, "I don't know why I'm here, but I feel I need to sit with you." She was welcomed, of course. I remember that most of the time we were an unpublicized part of the larger retreat. As word spread that there was a Veterans' Circle, a clamoring rose to hear from us.

I remember dozens of people telling me that the veterans' sharing was the most moving, significant part of their retreat. We were surrounded by people thanking us. At almost every retreat, I'd wonder why I kept showing up — but how could I stay away? Each time I'd witness strangers become family within a few hours. The Veterans' Circle becomes home, that place of safety and unconditional love, that place where you can share your deepest pain, knowing it will be cradled, even cherished. I have learned that the vet's pain is indeed everyone's pain — that, in fact, we are all veterans of a very imperfect world.

Many antiwar activists who lived the war at home sat with the veterans and are part of the Sangha.

Roberta (1996): I too am a child of the war, a veteran as a young woman who dropped out of college in 1970 to organize and demonstrate against the war. In my high school years I sat in front of the television in my parents' living room, digesting cold sandwiches and images of screaming Vietnamese children, running, their backs on fire, their thatched huts on fire, the world on fire. All this as I sat in my living room, so alone, scared, and angry. I too turned to violence, embracing the slogan "Bring the war home."

When I came to the Veterans' Circle and listened to Lindsay sing his beautiful song about never going to war to his sons, when I heard Bob talk about never letting his sons play with war toys, I realized

Fred Louis and fellow veteran at a mindfulness retreat.

that I had cut myself off from half of my generation — the generation that went to war. I never knew them as fathers and sons, as folksingers, as nature lovers, spiritual seekers, or teachers. In short, I never knew them as my brothers, as my other half, as my generation weaned on war, those that miraculously turned away from war and turned toward this gentle monk's teaching. Then I knew what happens in war, what happened in me, in my community. The cutting off. You cut yourself off from the Other, first in your thinking and then, if the government has given you a gun, with your gun. And as I listened to Lindsay sing, I felt my heart break open. Tears came and I knew healing only takes place when your heart opens so wide that all the pain is touched, touched by love. And I knew for the first time that I too had been scarred, deeply scarred, by the war. That I had spent my youth in a rage, a rage against government, against war, against what I called "the great hypocrisy of America."

In the Veterans' Circle I shared parts of me, of my story, that I feared would keep me from being loved or accepted. The story of how I visited the Chinese People's Liberation Army near the Vietnamese border in 1973, where soldiers proudly told us that they had fought with the North Vietnamese. I told them that many Americans supported them, celebrating when they shot down American planes and captured American soldiers and held them as criminals.

I did my best to share this story, but I felt fear, I anticipated hatred. I did my best to breathe slowly and deeply, aware of the tightness and constriction in my body, aware of the Sangha. I touched fear that had been in me for twenty years and found that it was the door to understanding the men and women around me. I learned what it means to share these past deeds, to look deeply into myself and my own suffering, to hold my own suffering with compassion. Then I began to understand what Claude had told me. I was not in the veterans' group just to support them, or to bear witness to their suffering, but to look at my own darkest secrets, to shine the light of awareness and compassion on myself and my brothers and sisters, to surround us all with unconditional love and acceptance. I saw that truly there is no " them" or "us." We are all children of the war. We all long for peace. From the Veterans' Sangha I learned what unconditional love looks like and feels like. It is the love that is offered just because it is needed. For no other reason. In 1997, at Omega I was ordained into the Order of Interbeing, with the Veterans' Sangha as my support and witness. My Dharma name is True Insight of Peace.

In 1997 several Vietnamese monks from Plum Village quietly appeared in our circle. A new chapter in healing began. Brother Phap Ung stood at Ron's side as Ron read his story to the whole retreat.

Ron (1997): I'm called Ron. I say that because I've not yet discovered my true name. I do know that without this group my healing would not be possible. As I look in front of me, I see so many faces and so many eyes that I've met over the last few days. Without your presence, our healing would not be possible. I also want you to forgive us vets as we walk around talking and laughing. We have found that we have been silent for so long that once we start to speak, not even this retreat can make us be silent again. I hope you will excuse us. I've asked this young monk to sit with me because he is the age and the appearance of men that many of us left lying in the jungle or rice paddies. And he is the second Vietnamese person that I have touched and not tried to kill.

This is a poem that came from our breakfast walk:

As we walk, my body remembers walking to hunt men like you.
My body feels the rifle and the heat of killing,
And you smile and hand me a flower,
I am very confused, in a dream.

So here I am, years and lifetimes later, sitting in a circle of fellow veterans, doing morning meditation. Using the always watchful eyes of a grunt, I noticed two very young monks walk in and sit in the circle. They were Vietnamese. They were "the Other." I had never seen the Other except in firefights or postures of death. Sure, I had seen Vietnamese people around main base and the airport as I came to and went from the country, but I never sat with them, never watched them breathe and smile.

As we sat, my mind and breath became more agitated, rather than more calm. I had no idea why. After our session ended, without any intention or idea why, I found myself kneeling in front of one of the young monks. He had the same face of the young men I left rotting in the jungle. He had the same body of the young man I had booby-trapped, using his remains to set a trap for more of his mates. He had the same eyes of the young man killed by my ambush one rainy afternoon.

As the monk and I looked into one another's eyes we began to weep. My heart ached with the suffering of all those young boys that my platoon left decaying in the lovely jungle. It ached for their families who never knew what their end was, for all the suffering from their deaths, for the spiritual damage to us from being the cause of those deaths.

We embraced. My heart broke open with the joy of embracing a man who represented all those I had touched only in death. I never felt the warm, beating heart of a live Vietnamese person before, never fully realized the humanness of that whole people. What a gift!

Brother Phap Ung (1997): Sixty years ago in 1942 in Hue, in central Vietnam, there were two ten-year-old boys running around in their family garden. They got water from a well and carried it home for their mom to use for cooking. We can hear their laughter just like we enjoy the laughter and joy of children nowadays. Children are innocent. They are not aware of the conflicts in the hearts of people in the world.

The boys grew up. One was drafted into the army to serve his country. That young man is my father. He is me, and I am him. Though the fact is simple, I keep forgetting it. I am his continuation. What my father went through, I went through also. His joy, his pain, his aspiration are all in my body and my mind, too. Because I forget the fact that my father and I interconnect, I blamed him for his anger, for his frustration, his fear, his nightmares. . . .

When he and my mom had arguments, I usually took the side of my mom. I wanted to protect my mom. I did not understand that my father needed love, protection, patience, and forgiveness, too. My father carried the wounds of war and suffering. He served as an officer in the South Vietnam army. He was put in a concentration camp in North Vietnam for six-and-a-half years after the war ended in 1975. He was not the only one; many thousands of soldiers endured the same fate. In fact, the communists are people, too. They need understanding and love, too. They have been children, too, like all of us.

Since I met Thây and the Sangha of Plum Village, I have had a chance to reconcile with my father, in fact, to reconcile with myself. For many thousands of people from more than twenty-four countries, the practice of mindfulness in the tradition of Plum Village is their daily food. Thây, our respected and loving teacher, together with his monastic and lay disciples, has offered many retreats for Vietnam veterans in America. One time in the Still Sitting Hut in Upper Hamlet, Thây told a group of young Vietnamese adults that we need to organize retreats for American and Vietnamese veterans in Vietnam. I was very moved. My heart was open and soft. I felt tears coming down from my eyes. Looking at my younger Dharma sister, Dinh Nghiem, I saw her tears, too.

My father died of a stroke in March 1997 while living in Holland. That same year I had a chance to join a Veterans' Retreat in Omega. I wanted to understand the suffering of the Vietnamese veterans and that of my father. My younger Dharma brother, Phap Tru, and I got the support of Thây and the Sangha to help facilitate the Veterans' Retreat. Brother Phap Tru's elder brother had served in the South Vietnam army. Both of us were very open and eager to serve the Vietnam veterans.

For Brother Phap Tru and me it was not easy to listen to many of the stories the veterans told. But the practice of sharing their memories was a way to help them release the burdens of their hearts. Many carried their suffering for more than twenty years without a way to transform it. They lived in constant fear, shame, guilt, hate, despair, and suspicion.

In that retreat there was a big room reserved for veterans only. We did almost everything there together. Each day the veterans joined the larger group of retreatants for a Dharma talk from Thây. Thây often encouraged the veterans to touch the present moment in order to nourish themselves and transform the suffering in their hearts. In that group of thirty to forty veterans, there were people who could do that. They reached out to others who needed help. I remember Sister Chân Không came and offered the practice of Total Relaxation and Touching the Earth. Sister Joan Halifax also came and guided us in the practice of dying in every moment in order to let go of the pain. One day Brother Phap Tru and I did prostrations to our ancestral teachers, then did hugging meditation with veterans as a practice of reconciliation. We felt a big love flowing in our hearts.

One day my heart was so open. I could feel the need to share the suffering of my people with the veterans. I shared it. My tears came down. I touched the pain and let it flow. One veteran who suffered a lot from the war saw the pain of the Vietnamese people in me. He came forward and embraced me. We hugged each other.

Reconciliation took place right there with the support of many other veterans. I felt released, but also very fragile. I went to see Thây. He was so compassionate and took me for a long, beautiful walk in the forest. It was fall. The leaves were colorful. I felt nourished and grateful. At one point Thây looked at a branch full of leaves and said to me, "Our Sangha is like this, each leaf in its own position. No leaf is perfect, but together they make the branch and tree beautiful." I went back to the veterans with more energy of compassion.

Later, we all went for walking meditation to the lake nearby. The veteran, Ron, who did hugging meditation with me, took my hand. I knew he wanted to continue the work of reconciliation within. We walked as a Sangha, very mindfully and peacefully. I remember my younger sister Tue Nghiem saw us walking hand-in-hand. She smiled to us with understanding and support. I smiled back to her. I still remember how the wonderful transformation took place. Ron was trembling. The fear was still there: the fear of war, the fear of the Vietnamese people. I knew I had to be solid, that each step I made should be in the present moment, in mindfulness. I squeezed Ron's hand firmly, sending support and compassion to him, reminding him of the present moment. The collective energy of the Sangha was great. I could feel peace in each step. Finally, Brother Ron could relax and enjoy the peace within his heart. It was a wonderful experience. We walked until we arrived at a beautiful lake. We saw young monks and nuns playing there and we joined them. Ron was walking along the edge of the water. I knew it was a ripe time to play. I came near Ron, and I splashed water on him. He was surprised, but smiled and splashed water on me. We were like birds playing happily. The water was fresh. The lake was peaceful. The sky was blue. Everyone was happy, including my people and my father in my heart.

In the circle we bear witness to fathers sharing the pain of war with their children for the first time.

Karl (2001): I never talked to any of my children about coming home from the war. Like most veterans of Vietnam, I didn't want to be noticed. Being noticed usually meant problems. The habit carried forward for three decades.

My four children grew up with questions that, in our family, had no answers. "Mommy, why is Daddy always prowling around the house at three in the morning?" "How come Daddy jumps, cries out, and leaves the room when we wake him up from a nap?" "How come Daddy loses his temper when someone honks the horn at him?" It wasn't until just four years ago that we heard about Post-Traumatic Stress Disorder.

I never talked about the war very much. I would start to tremble and shake. How could I talk "calmly" about the war with my children? I couldn't. So I didn't.

My body trembled every day when I attended the Veterans' Sangha. It didn't hurt me. No one was repulsed or frightened — at least no one indicated they were. By the last day of the retreat I figured I could tremble and shake in front of a whole group, including my daughter. So I wrote two little essays — one about coming home and one about very difficult decisions made by very young people.

As I was reading them aloud, I would occasionally look up and see my daughter. She was crying. I was busy shaking and speaking. I'm pretty good at staying on task when the adrenaline is high, so seeing her didn't stop me. It is only now, in my memory, that I get stopped. I see her looking at me with tears in her eyes, and it makes me sad and happy. I'm sad that she had all those questions unanswered for so many years. I'm sad that she had to live with my reactions — reactions that saved my life in Vietnam, but were destructive to my marriage when I got back home. I am very sad that my daughter has to say she came from a home where her parents no longer live together. But I'm very happy that she heard my story. I felt her compassion and understanding in those tears. There is such relief when the truth is spoken and heard. Receiving compassion and understanding from someone that you love so deeply brings such great happiness.

Our Sangha includes the children and spouses of war veterans.

Amy (1999): The Veterans' Sangha came into my life when I really needed it. I am the daughter of a Vietnam veteran. My father suffered with Post-Traumatic Stress Disorder since I was a little girl. He has difficulty dealing with his memories from the war. About three years ago, he went into a deep depression and was hospitalized for several months. He also separated from my mother. Needless to say, my family was going through a particularly difficult time. My father had given up hope that he could ever heal from his war wounds. While in the hospital, my brother gave my father Thây's book *Being Peace.* My father, who is not an avid reader, not only read the book, but asked for more of Thây's books. The following summer he attended a retreat with Thây at Omega Institute.

The next year, I attended a retreat with my father and brother. The war had always affected my life, but we never talked about it. We suffered because of the war, but barely acknowledged its presence. Because of this denial, my family suffered greatly. After the retreat, my father started to regain his strength and his will to live.

His depression stabilized and he was better able to cope with his past. It was like a miracle! The doctors had tried hospitals and medicine to help Dad, but what helped was Thây. His words and his presence calmed my dad's ruffled spirit. Other veterans were a great source of support and comfort. Like my father, they were fighting a spiritual battle within themselves. My father found men he could relate to and understand.

My family started to talk about issues we never talked about before. My brother and I got to know my father in a more genuine way. We practice together and support one another in our practice. I no longer feel isolated with my problems.

The Veterans' Sangha was, and is, life changing for me. It is a miracle. I always longed for a place where people understood my suffering and accepted aspects of me and my family that I had never discussed with anyone. The members of the Veterans' Sangha are like a warm blanket that I wrap around myself when I am suffering.

When I think about the Sangha, I smile. Just thinking about them causes me to return home and ground myself. We communicate on the Internet and have created a club site to be in daily contact. We send letters and cards. The support these people give me and my family has gotten us through some very rough times. Ironically, after regaining his will to live, my father was diagnosed with leukemia. The love and energy of the Veterans' Sangha will help my father to heal and see the life purpose of this diagnosis. The Sangha helps me see the spiritual explanations for my suffering. It helps me comfort and soothe myself. The Veterans' Sangha feels like family to me.

Welcome Home

Thây (Excerpted from *Love in Action*): When you went to war, you went for the whole nation. The whole nation was responsible for what happened there, not you alone. Your hand was the hand of the whole nation. If you made mistakes, the whole nation made mistakes. If you went to war believing you were doing something important — trying to save a people, fighting evil — it was not your thinking alone; it was the thinking of the whole nation. You were sent there to fight, destroy, kill, and die. You were not the only one responsible. We cannot just shout at you and say, "You did that!" We all did it collectively. . .

When you came home after the war, the American people were cool, neglectful, and unappreciative, and of course you became angry. But your people did not know anything about the war. . . When you see that they were speaking out of ignorance, you will stop being angry at them. You were ignorant too, but now you have learned, and you are liberated from your anger. Now you can offer your compassion. . .

Members of the Veterans' Sangha at a retreat

We who have experienced war directly have a responsibility to share our insight and experience concerning the truth of war. We are the light at the tip of the candle. It is very hot, but it has the power of shining and illuminating.

At the end of the veterans' reading at the 2001 University of Massachusetts Retreat the men stood before us, vulnerable and exposed. There was a silence filled with emotion and tears. Two hundred awed witnesses. A deeply shared silence that gave way to clapping, whistling, singing, cheering, cries of "Welcome home, welcome home." This was the welcome home that communities, families, and antiwar activists had never known how to give; the welcome home the soldiers never received from us. Welcome home.

Contributors:

Tom Mallabar, Renewed Freedom of the Heart, is from Whitesboro, New York. He attends a local Zen sitting group once a week. When he's with the Veterans' Sangha, he feels it is his home away from home.

Fred Louis, Boundless Transformation of the Heart, is a union electrician. He recently moved to New Britain, Connecticut from New York State to live with his soul mate/best friend/love and is still struggling to grow up.

Roberta Wall, True Insight of Peace, is a member of the Order of Interbeing. She recently moved from Brooklyn, New York, to Woodstock, New York, where she is starting a Sangha.

Ron Orem is from Baltimore County, Maryland, where he practices with the Inspiration Community. He most enjoys breathing and gardening and sitting with others as a counselor. He encourages everyone to look very carefully at the roots of war.

Brother Chân Phap Ung, True Dharma Response, is from Vietnam and Holland. He was ordained a Dharma teacher in 1998. He is the son of a Vietnamese veteran.

Karl Marlantes is from Oregon and was a Marine platoon commander in Vietnam in 1968 and 1969. He currently lives on Bainbridge Island, Washington. With the help and love he experienced in Vermont and at the Amherst Retreat from the Veterans' Sangha (and some psychiatric medicine from the Veterans Administration) he is healing from Post-Traumatic Stress Disorder. He is approaching a regular life (but not a normal one) and is grateful for every period of his life. "Without the war, I would not have experienced the healing. Without the suffering, I would not have learned compassion."

Amy Wise, Renewed Transformation of the Heart, lives in Edgewater, Maryland. She is the daughter of a Vietnam veteran.

The Mindfulness Trainings

From Precepts to Mindfulness Trainings

Thich Nhat Hanh's commentary on the Five Precepts *from the Spring 1990* Mindfulness Bell

The Five Precepts are the foundation for practicing with others. They have been practiced for more than 2,500 years. Buddha gave the Five Precepts to the father of a monk named Yasa, when he asked the Buddha what he could do that would allow him to live more like his son. Yasa was the Buddha's sixth disciple, a wealthy young man, ordained just after the Buddha ordained his five ascetic friends. If members of a family or a Sangha observe and recite these precepts regularly, Buddhism becomes a living reality. Once the precepts are received, we have to practice and recite them at least once a month. If we do not practice the precepts, the precepts' body will cease to be a reality and the practice of Buddhism will become impossible. Buddhists of many generations have practiced these precepts in order to maintain happiness and to be of help to others. The Five Precepts are principles for peaceful coexistence between people and also between nations.

No one can impose anything on us. We are free people, and we do only the things we want to do. But we know that there is a kind of illness in our society, and practicing the precepts is a very good medicine that can protect us and our families and safeguard our happiness. Buddhist precepts are not commandments. To word them in a way that does not sound like commandments may be useful for a lot of people, but we have to word them in a clear, strong way. The wording of the Five Precepts may not be perfect, and those of you who practice them might like to think about the words and help all of us express the precepts in a clear way.

The Five Wonderful Precepts

1) Do not kill. Do not let others kill. Find whatever means possible to protect life. Do not live with a vocation that is harmful to humans and nature.

2) Do not steal. Possess nothing that should belong to others. Respect the property of others, but prevent others from enriching themselves from human suffering and the suffering of other species on Earth.

3) Sexual expression should not take place without love and commitment. Be fully aware of the suffering you may cause others as a result of your misconduct. To preserve the happiness of yourself and others, respect the rights and commitments of others.

4) Do not say untruthful things. Do not spread news that you do not know to be certain. Do not criticize or condemn things that you are unsure of. Do not utter words that can cause division and hatred, that can cause discord and cause the family to break. All efforts should be made to reconcile and resolve all conflicts.

5) Do not use alcohol and other intoxicants. Be aware that your fine body has been transmitted to you by several previous generations and your parents. Destroying your body with alcohol and other intoxicants is to betray your ancestors and your parents and also to betray future generations.

Thich Nhat Hanh's Introduction to *For a Future to Be Possible: Commentaries on the Five Mindfulness Trainings*

The translation of the Five Mindfulness Trainings presented in this book is new. It is the result of insights gained from practicing together as a community. A spiritual tradition is like a tree. It needs to be watered in order to bring forth new leaves and branches, so it can continue to be a living reality. We help the tree of Buddhism grow by living deeply the essence of reality, the practice of Mindfulness Trainings, concentration, and insight.

Until recently I have used the term "precepts" instead of "Mindfulness Trainings." But many Western friends told me that the word "precepts" evokes in them a strong feeling of good and evil, that if they "break" the precepts, they feel they have completely failed. Precepts are different from "commandments" and "rules." They are insights born from mindful observation and direct experience of suffering. They are guidelines that help us train ourselves to live in a way that protects us and those around us. As we continue the training, our understanding and practice of the precepts deepen. No one can be perfect when he or she just begins the training, and even during the time of training. Precepts are the most concrete expression of the practice of mindfulness. That is why it is appropriate and helpful to describe them as "Mindfulness Trainings."

The Five Mindfulness Trainings

The First Mindfulness Training: Reverence for Life

Aware of the suffering caused by the destruction of life, I vow to cultivate compassion and learn ways to protect the lives of people, animals, plants, and minerals. I am determined not to kill, not to let others kill, and not to condone any act of killing in the world, in my thinking, or in my way of life.

The Second Mindfulness Training: Generosity

Aware of the suffering caused by exploitation, social injustice, stealing, and oppression, I vow to cultivate loving kindness and learn ways to work for the well-being of people, animals, plants, and minerals. I vow to practice generosity by sharing my time, energy, and material resources with those who are in real need. I am determined not to steal and not to possess anything that should belong to others. I will respect the property of others, but I will prevent others from profiting from human suffering or the suffering of other species on Earth.

The Third Mindfulness Training: Sexual Responsibility

Aware of the suffering caused by sexual misconduct, I vow to cultivate responsibility and learn ways to protect the safety and integrity of individuals, couples, families, and society. I am determined not to engage in sexual relations without love and a long-term commitment. To preserve the happiness of myself and others, I am determined to respect my commitments and the commitments of others. I will do everything in my power to protect children from sexual abuse and to protect couples and families from being broken by sexual misconduct.

The Fourth Mindfulness Training: Deep Listening and Loving Speech

Aware of the suffering caused by unmindful speech and the inability to listen to others, I vow to cultivate loving speech and deep listening in order to bring joy and happiness to others and relieve others of their suffering. Knowing that words can create happiness or suffering, I vow to learn to speak truthfully with words that inspire self-confidence, joy, and hope. I am determined not to spread news that I do not know to be certain and not to criticize or condemn things of which I am not sure. I will refrain from uttering words that can cause division or discord, or that can cause the family or the community to break. I will make all efforts to reconcile and resolve all conflicts, however small.

The Fifth Mindfulness Training: Mindful Consumption

Aware of the suffering caused by unmindful consumption, I vow to cultivate good health, both physical and mental, for myself, my family, and my society by practicing mindful eating, drinking, and consuming. I vow to ingest only items that preserve peace, well-being, and joy in my body, in my consciousness, and in the collective body and consciousness of my family and society. I am determined not to use alcohol or any other intoxicant or to ingest food or other items that contain toxins, such as certain TV programs, magazines, books, films, and conversations. I am aware that to damage my body or my consciousness with these poisons is to betray my ancestors, my parents, my society, and future generations. I will work to transform violence, fear, anger, and confusion in myself and in society by practicing a diet for myself and for society. I understand that a proper diet is crucial for self-transformation and for the transformation of society.

Inclusiveness of the Heart

Razia Aziz, Inclusiveness of the Heart, is of Indian heritage and lives in London, England.

I came to Plum Village for the first time broken by a sudden bereavement — broken and therefore open. And the sweet water of the teachings and the practice filled and bathed this cracked vessel. The second time, I returned with my partner with whom I wanted to share the precious draught. It was then the Muslim holy month of Ramadan. I was aware of bringing with me my heritage and my ancestors, as well as my own commitment to mindfulness practice.

When I resolved to apply for the transmission of the Five Mindfulness Trainings, I knew that I was stepping into the territory of faith. I did not know what I was doing, and yet I knew. Islam and Buddhism do not immediately appear to fit easily together. Although I was not a practicing Muslim, the influence of Islam on me is obvious to all who know me. In my small way I was faced with a big dilemma — prostrating before an image of any being was strictly forbidden in my own upbringing, as the One, Almighty is beyond form and Allah alone is worthy of such devotion. How would the kind sisters respond to my request to waive that part of the ceremony that requires prostration before the statue of the Buddha?

It was not an easy discussion for me or for the sisters. The meditation hall is a temple where the Buddha is revered in a particular time-honored way. Such traditions are the unbroken threads that connect us generation after generation to deep wisdom. Yet there is another wisdom that helps us remain open, alive, stretching beyond what we know of ourselves to include even that which seems in contradiction with us. This wisdom lovingly prevailed — the wisdom of respectful inclusiveness. Together the sisters and I agreed that we could replace the prostration with a respectful bow.

The transmission I was honored to receive at Plum Village was like a door to a new stage of my spiritual journey. The door, so graciously opened by the sisters at the Lower Hamlet, has revealed new horizons and vistas in my limited understanding of the meaning of true practice. Why? Because the courage, respect, and deep insight shown in the collective decision to embrace difference dissolved the notion that difference must mean separation.

I now know it to be part of my practice to meet with people of

Write Your Own Mindfulness Training

Anh Huong Nguyen, Dharma name Chan Y (True Mind), lives in Fairfax, Virginia, where she and her husband, Anh Thu, founded the Mindfulness Practice Center of Fairfax. She was ordained a Dharma teacher in 1992.

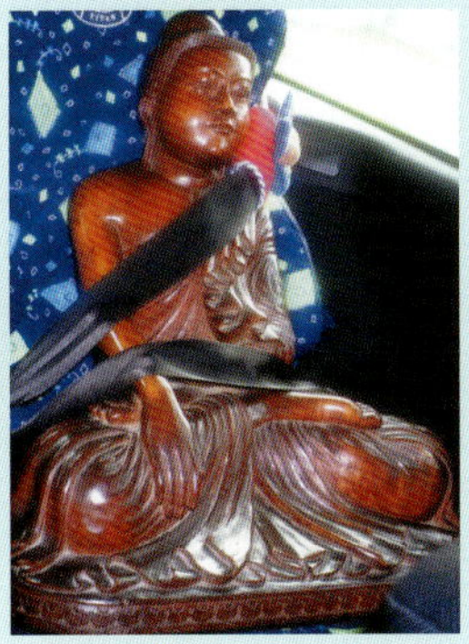

To be diligent and energetic in the practice of mindfulness, we have to be creative and intelligent. In the class "The Path of Happiness" offered at the Mindfulness Practice Center of Fairfax, Virginia, everyone was asked to identify one of their longtime habits and write up their own Mindfulness Trainings for their practice. A training can be written for a particular habit that comes up often in our daily life. Practice wholeheartedly with a mindfulness training you have written for yourself for a day, a week, or a month, and you will be rewarded with the joy, peace, and freedom born from living your own training.

One member of our class was coming from quite a distance in rush hour every Tuesday evening. One of the trainings she wrote for herself was:

"Aware of the escalation of anxieties when I change lanes often, I am determined to stay in one lane as I drive to class. While driving, I am determined to sit relaxingly and maintain my half-smile with my breathing so that I don't have to beat the traffic."

Our habits can be our old friends, not our enemies. They have been transmitted to us from our ancestors and strengthened by our culture and our way of living. Once a habit energy manifests in us, we are advised to return to our half-smile and the anchor of belly breathing. The half-smile brings us back to our deepest desire to be gentle and compassionate to ourselves.

All of our habits and feelings inter-are. The understanding and transformation of one unwholesome habit will naturally permeate the other habits in us. Taking care of one habit is to take care of all related habits. For example, once we can recognize and embrace a habit like expectation, other habits such as judgment, blaming, and anger are taken care of at the same time. To take good care of our habit energies is to take good care of ourselves and our loved ones.

different faiths, or of no faith at all, and promote deeper listening, respect and understanding — both in myself and in others. I am determined to let go of doing things in a particular form, to let go of being "right," and to meet truth with truth, love with love, without the barrier of judgment.

Again and again I return to the Mindfulness Trainings. To me their meaning, like my understanding of my practice, has shifted dimensions. I aim to practice the trainings through my actions where I can, while constantly staying open to learn and study more the spirit of the trainings. It is in this inner dimension that I hope to practice them without rigidity and righteousness, but with ease, gentleness, and spaciousness, not as "thou shalt not," but as "thou art."

Like a newborn babe trying to learn all that is unfamiliar, I try to unlearn getting busy in order to see Allah in all of creation. And for that, there is no better tonic than slowing down, stopping, breathing, and smiling. The Five Mindfulness Trainings remind me that practice is not just in the sitting and contemplating — it is in every living moment.

The Five Mindfulness Trainings: A Practice of Inner and Outer Peace

Bettina Schneider, Tree of True Awakening, is from Berlin, Germany. She has been a permanent resident at Plum Village since 1996.

Growing up in Germany twenty years after the end of World War II, a great question was in my heart and the hearts of many young people: "How could this happen?" And on a personal level, "What is my individual answer to the Holocaust?"

Six years ago, on a mindfulness day with the Berlin Sangha and Claude Thomas, a Vietnam War veteran, we practiced walking meditation in Sachsenhausen, a former concentration camp. It was a cold, rainy day in October. Walking there, setting my feet on the ground where not long ago, the victims and persecutors walked — to touch this Earth now, with pain, respect, and tenderness, at that very moment, I felt deeply, Yes, this is my answer. To walk my life in mindfulness, this is the energy with which I can try to answer the violence and war in the world and in myself.

Nowadays, when I visit Berlin and walk in the streets, in touch with the world of advertisements and the reality of consumerism, poverty, and violence, I see that the Five Mindfulness Trainings are a true and concrete way to bring mindfulness to all areas of my daily life. They offer me a nonviolent, respectful way to relate to myself and to all life around me.

Each Mindfulness Training begins with the words, "Aware of the suffering caused by. . ." This shows immediately what kind of gift the trainings offer: awareness of suffering, war, exploitation, abuse, etc. The trainings help me have the courage to see and let my heart be touched by pain and destruction, so I can wake up from indifference, forgetfulness, and ignorance of myself and others. When I become truly aware of how much I harm myself and others, a wish is naturally born in me to take care of the destruction and violence in myself and to transform it. To have the strength to do so, it is necessary to cultivate qualities like understanding, compassion, loving kindness, and responsibility. Each of the Five Mindfulness Trainings expresses this clearly, ". . .I vow to cultivate. . ." generosity, loving kindness, etc.

As I practice the trainings, my awareness increases — I see my actions, speech, thoughts and intentions on a more and more subtle level. I will never forget the day I realized I don't need a gun to kill someone; I can do it with my eyes. Now I see how I can even do this with my thoughts.

The Lay Core Group meeting in New Hamlet. From left to right: Bettina, Georg, Fei-fei, Shantum, Brendan, and Murray.

The trainings teach me to find a loving, tolerant, peaceful attitude towards myself. I learn to try my best and to accept my imperfection, to accept all of myself. When I can accept all parts of myself, I feel peace is present in me. When my mind and heart are wide enough to accept myself and everything as it is, I experience the Five Mindfulness Trainings as unity, harmony, and even harmony within disharmony. The clearest image of the Five Mindfulness Trainings for me is the sky at night — the immensity of space, the millions of stars in it and every star in its place. Everything is exactly in its place, in perfect harmony, and I have my "right place" in it all.

The practice of the Five Mindfulness Trainings is a practice of love and peace. With them we can learn to be with suffering in a conscious, responsible, loving way, slowly transforming it by the warmth of mindfulness. With the trainings, we can light the flame of understanding and compassion in difficult situations. When we are in touch with this flame, and we think, speak, act from this place, we experience peace in our heart. A peaceful heart beats in harmony with life itself.

The Gift of Non-Fear: Three Moments on the Way to Dwelling in Equanimity

Lyn Fine, True Goodness, is from New York and now lives in Oakland, California. She was ordained a Dharma teacher in 1994.

1: Sunday, September 15, 1996, Plum Village, France. Dharma Talk by Thich Nhat Hanh

We are sitting together in the Meditation Hall at the Lower Hamlet.
Listening, we are aware of our breathing.
We are present together.

In the midst of your Dharma talk, you pause.
Quietly, you strike a match.
You touch the flame to a sheet of paper.
Smoke wafts into the air. Flames appear.
The paper is burning.
Now there is only black charcoal ash.

Gently, between the thumb and two fingers of your right hand,
You pick up the charred remains.
"It's hot," you say softly, calmly.
On your lips, there is a half-smile.
You hold the black charcoal for an instant.
Then, releasing your fingers, you let the burnt remains drop
  into the bell.

In mindfulness I watch, aware of my breathing.

Breathing in, I am aware that ancestors are present
  Jewish ancestors burning in ovens — here, now
  Vietnamese sisters and brothers burning in self-immolation
    to stop the bombs of war — here, now
  wise-woman witches burning at the stake — here, now
  churches of African-American brothers and sisters burning
    in the United States — here, now
  ancient trees burning from human forgetfulness — here, now
Breathing out, I do my best to smile with equanimity and compasion—
  but I cannot — not yet.

Breathing in, I know I am touching seeds of pain and suffering in me
  from the individual and collective storehouse consciousness —
  seeds of terror, seeds of rage, seeds of grief
Breathing out, I am aware that I am unable to smile — nor to cry,
  nor to cry out. I cannot — not yet.
Breathing in, I know I am breathing in
Breathing out, I am aware: conscious breathing is my anchor.

Suddenly, your gentle voice penetrates the clouded-over sky-mind.
"We will put these [charred remains] in the garden,"
  I hear you say.
Tears come, and a half-smile.
Fear has released. The heart opens.

2: Sunday, September 15, 1996, Plum Village. Outdoor Walking Meditation

It is Sunday, September 15, 1996.
It is the second day of the Jewish New Year, 5757.
This year at Plum Village, during a three-week retreat,
 — "The Heart of the Buddha," it is called —
We are observing the highest holy days of the Jewish people,
  in the way that they — or some of them — would observe them.

The seed you planted more than a decade ago has borne fruit.
"To make peace on the planet," you said at a Reverence for Life
Conference in 1982,
"each religious group should observe the most important holiday
of each other religious group
in the way that group would observe the holiday."

For the seed and for the fruit,
And for all the conditions which have allowed the gradual ripening of
the fruit
I am grateful.

Now we are walking together in walking meditation.
Hand in hand, we walk through orchards of plum trees in the Lower
Hamlet.
The trees are bearing fruit — sweet purple plums.
Our steps touch the Earth gently.
We are embraced by sunshine and blue sky.

Breathing in, I know that sunshine and rain, blue sky and Earth have
nourished the fruit
and its gradual ripening
that residents of Plum Village, lay and monastic, have
cared for the trees, harvested the fruit, and turned
it into plum jam
that children in France gave money to plant these trees
so that children in Vietnam could have medical supplies
and food
Breathing out, I am aware that present in us in this moment
are all of our ancestors
and all of our descendants
We are the sunshine.
We are the blue sky.
We are the trees bearing fruit.

Here, now, we walk, hand in hand.
We are walking as a community, a Sangha.
We are walking with each other, we are walking for each other.
I walk for you. I know you are walking for me

"Touching, touching"
"Connecting, connecting, connecting"
With each in-breath, I am walking two steps.
With each out-breath, I am walking three steps.
Step by step I am walking, breathing in, breathing out.
But I am aware that I am not truly present — not yet.

I walk in peace, but the mind goes in a million directions.
The energy of seeds from the individual and collective storehouse
consciousness
remains strong.
The mind remains caught
In a net of burnings

Breathing in, I am aware of regret:
There is sadness in me. I am caught.
Present in me — here, now — are blue sky, white clouds.
But I am not wholehearted. The mind is caught
In the past. The wounds of suffering, still present.
Breathing out, my resolution deepens:
I vow to cultivate mindfulness with determination
I aspire to be fully present to the miracle
of being alive — here, now.
I aspire to open, wholehearted, in joy, to this present moment.

Crossing a narrow plank bridge, we arrive at the pond.
Human beings and trees, we encircle the water.
Together we stand, in the stillness.
Listening.
Waiting.
Breathing in, I am aware: breathing in.
Breathing out, I am aware: breathing out.
We hear the silence.

Hearing, hearing.
Breathing in, aware of birds chirping.
Breathing out, aware of leaves rustling.
Jacqueline begins to play her violin — the ancient Jewish melody
Avinu Malkeinu.
We sing. No boundary.
Touching Jewish ancestors. No boundary.
Touching all ancestors. No boundary.
For some of us, this moment is the first time
To touch our ancestors.

In silence,
We pick up small sticks and stones, take lint from our pockets.
We name the times when we have missed the mark.
We acknowledge that we have sinned, as individuals and
as communities.
By omission and by commission, we have caused suffering.
One by one, and together, we cast our sticks and stones and lint
into the water.

One by one and together as a Sangha we transform consciousness.

Breathing in, I am aware of our multiple origins —
We are from Vietnam, Thailand, Japan, India, Bangladesh,
Israel, Egypt, Russia, Sweden, Finland, Denmark,
Romania, Germany, Italy, Switzerland, France, England, Spain, the Netherlands,
Canada, U.S.A., Indigenous Peoples, New Zealand, Australia
Breathing out, I realize: not two, not one.

Breathing in, I am aware that in our Buddhist retreat center
We are observing *tashlich*, an ancient Jewish custom of renewal.
We are observing *tashlich* as Jews would observe it.
We are observing *tashlich* as Jews around the world are observing it, on this day.
We are observing *tashlich* amidst the trees, around a pond.
We are observing *tashlich* with friends from numerous countries — former enemies.
Breathing out, I know we are returning home, to our true origin and Source.

3: Sunday, September 15, 1996, Plum Village. After Outdoor Walking Meditation

Now the walk is over and *tashlich* too.
We have cast into the water
Our unwholesome states of mind
And those times when we have missed the mark — sinned —
Individually and collectively.
We have deepened our determination
To cultivate wholesome states of mind,
Deep listening, deep looking, and wise action that meets the mark.

A novice monk thanks me for the *tashlich* observance.
He speaks to me from a place of love.
He speaks to me from the depth of his experience.
I hear what he is saying, and I am very happy.
We breathe together.
I speak softly of the burning of the paper,
Of the seeds from the individual and collective storehouse consciousness
which arose in me, and remained so strongly present.
I speak of the black charcoal remains,
Of your suggestion that we would put them in the Plum Village garden —
"We will put these [charred ashes] in the garden," you had said —
I speak of the release in me when I heard you say that.
For a moment, we breathe together in silence.
"The ashes have been put in the Plum Village garden,"
My Dharma brother says with a gentle smile.
And I wonder — is it only by chance that I am speaking to the very monk
Who was given the ashes, who himself scattered them in the garden?

So —
Now it is done.
In nurturing soil of love and remembrance and compassion
In a small hamlet in southern France
Burned ancestors, brothers, and sisters, and children
Rest now. Charred remains renew the Earth.
Burned and burners: not two, not one.

A meditation appears:
Breathing in, I am aware of the seeds of suffering in me
from my [Jewish and other] ancestors —
seeds of terror, seeds of rage, seeds of grief
Breathing out, I vow, for the well-being of all beings, to transform these seeds
with gentle caring

Breathing in, I am aware of the seeds of well-being in me
from my [Jewish and other] ancestors —
seeds of joy, seeds of love, seeds of wisdom
Breathing out, I vow, for the benefit of all beings, to discover and nourish these seeds with tenderness

Breathing in, I touch no birth, no death
Breathing out, I go beyond fear
Breathing in, I touch the Ground of All Being
Breathing out, I know that in this moment I have returned home, to my true self
A smile appears.
The precious gift of non-fear, always offered, has been received.
Thank you, my dear friends, for our observance together.

A Vietnamese-American teenager at a bonfire in Plum Village, Summer Retreat 2001

Ceremony for the Deceased

Dzung Vo, Healing Root of the Source, is Vietnamese and lives in Philadelphia, Pennsylvania.

Seeds planted during and after the war in Vietnam
Have produced fruits of much suffering
Le phong dang, Ceremony for the Dead
Was dedicated to the people who have carried
And still carry that suffering, in Vietnam and in the West
And to transforming that suffering into love and understanding
We meditated on a Vietnamese-American boy
Whose family lived through hell and absorbed hell's anger
Always fought and couldn't listen
He cut his wrists and wanted to die
Seeds of his own anger were nourished
Now a hardened young man
We meditated on doing something for youth like him
Can violence be transformed into laughter?
And we meditated on the boat people who perished at sea
And on the poor around the world who still struggle
Then we carried lotus flowers with candles
To release them into the lake
Singing the name of Quan Am, the Bodhisattva of Great Compassion,
Giving life to peace in the world
Both symbolically and literally
I knew then that the monks and nuns
Had dedicated their lives to practice for us
But also we practice for them
So I sang the name of the bodhisattva
Of deep listening and compassion
With all my presence and heart
I sang to ten thousand bodhisattvas around me and within me
I also knew then
That we must practice with joy, always
In order to manifest joy in the world.

Offering Compassion: Contributing to the Social Work in Vietnam

An Interview with Sister Hy Nghiem by Sister Chan Thuong Nghiem

Sister Chân Hy Nghiem, True Adornment with Joy, grew up in Vietnam and Houston, Texas. She was ordained as a Dharma teacher in 2001.

How did you get involved in the social work in Vietnam?

Even before I was ordained, I really liked to help poor people. Growing up, I learned how to sew. Many people came to me to ask me to sew things for them, and I earned some money that way. I would give it to poor people. One day, my mother wanted to go visit my father, who was in a re-education camp, and she asked me, "My child, do you have some money that I can use to prepare some food for your father?" I said, "Mother, I do not have any money." She did not understand because she saw that many people came to me, and I sewed clothes for them and earned money. She saw that I didn't go to parties, I didn't have many friends, and I just spent my time going to the temple. She trusted me. However, she could not figure out what I did with the money I earned from sewing clothes. Later, she discovered what I did with my money, and she understood, but she did not talk with me about it directly.

One day, I overheard my mother sharing with one of her friends in the neighborhood about this story. She said she asked me for money, and when I didn't give it to her, she felt sad. Then one day she saw that I used all my money to give to poor people, to donate to the temple, or to buy books for the novices in the temple. She felt very happy. Now she had a child who practiced generosity, and she felt I did it for her. When I heard my mother's sharing, I also felt happy. I continued to give my offerings to others.

When I left Vietnam, I gave all my extra money to my friends in the Buddhist Youth Club and asked them to give it to the poor people they met. When I came to America, I bought a commercial sewing machine. I sewed at night, after I came home from school, or before I went to work in the morning. I sewed for a T-shirt company. When I sewed one line, I earned ten cents. That was equal to 1,000 Vietnamese *dong*. When I received the money, I sent it all to Vietnam. One day, I read the newsletter from Plum Village and learned that they had programs for poor people in Vietnam. I did not know how to send money to these programs, so I put a dollar bill in an envelope, covered it very carefully, and sent it to the sisters in Plum Village, asking them to send it to Vietnam. I received a thank you letter from Sister Giai Nghiem from Plum Village. I copied that letter, gave it to my friends at school and at work, and asked them to sponsor the poor children in Vietnam. I also sent money directly to Vietnam.

Thây and Sister Hy Nghiem at the Green Mountain Dharma Center

Once I was ordained as a nun, I had the opportunity to contribute to the social work projects in Vietnam. A number of brothers and sisters worked together. We had a lot of happiness during those times. We would sit together and write letters to the children in Vietnam. We shared the practice of mindfulness with the children.

Most young people spend all their money on entertainment and movies and clothes. What made you want to help people?

Now that I have the opportunity to practice the Buddha's teaching, I think the seed of helping others came from my ancestors. My mother had a store in the marketplace. Every day she supported handicapped people and homeless children. When she saw them, she would buy food for them. When she saw homeless people on the street, she would give them a little money. Even if she didn't have money, she gave them her love, her energy, and her sweetness. After I ordained as a nun, my mother shared a story with me. One day, she saw a homeless man in the market who had a serious illness and was handicapped from the Vietnamese-American War. Before 1975, the government would support him. After 1975, the government changed, and he no longer received any support. He moved around on a cart, because he didn't have any legs. When it rained, the market became very muddy, and moving around close to the ground got him very dirty; the smell was not good. My mother asked one lady in the market to help her boil hot water. After she closed her shop, she came and bathed that man. The man was a little bit shy. She said to him, "Uncle, don't worry. I bathe you like I am your elder sister or your mother, just feel natural."

She shared that story with me, and I was so moved. It watered the seed of loving kindness in me. Before I knew I wanted to help people, but I didn't know why. I just saw poor people and I wanted to help. Hearing that story, I could see clearly that I received the seed of wanting to help others from my parents and ancestors.

Did you also receive inspiration from your father?

When my mother was pregnant with me, my father began studying Buddhism. He received the Five Mindfulness Trainings, and he learned about basic Buddhist teachings. My parents named me Minh Tam, which means "brightness of the heart/mind." People usually think it is my Dharma name, given to me by my spiritual teacher, but that is the name my parents gave me.

My father worked for the South Vietnamese government. In 1975, when the communists took over, he was put in the re-education camp. At one point, he felt that he would die soon. He thought, If I am to die, I wish to die peacefully. He was in a semiconscious state, and he invoked the name of Bodhisattva Avalokiteshvara. When he woke up, he found himself in a puddle of water (guards would pour water on the prisoners to wake them up). After that he was never beaten again. He did not know why the beatings stopped abruptly, but he felt that it was due to his sincere prayers. When he came home from prison he told the whole family that story, and it made a deep impression on me.

My father continues to inspire me a lot. He and my mother practice sitting meditation every day. When I go home, we sit and talk together about the Buddhist teachings. Recently, two of my monastic brothers went to Texas, where my parents live, and they visited my parents. They said, "Your father is wonderful!" They enjoyed drinking tea and sharing together about the practice. When my Dharma brothers told me about their time together with my parents, I felt happy and grateful to my parents because I know they are always supporting me in my daily practice.

What is your relationship with Sister Chân Không regarding the social work in Vietnam? And please describe the social projects in Vietnam.

Sister Chân Không began the social work in Vietnam. When she came to Europe and America, she continued the work and got many people to help her. As the monastic community grew in Plum Village, she wanted to transmit the work to us. She encouraged us to continue the work. The monetary support from Plum Village has helped many places in South, Central, and North Vietnam. We mostly offer help to the remote villages that are hard to reach and to the places that do not have electricity or schools. The parents work in the fields or the towns, and they leave their children at home, so the children don't have adult supervision. We help sponsor daycare schools for children whose parents work. The teacher helps them to wash their faces and hands and gives them soymilk and lunch. They take naps and learn how to breathe mindfully, and how to speak skillfully and kindly.

We also support handicapped and isolated people who do not have any relatives to care for them. And we sponsor students who come from very poor families to pursue a higher education. By helping one person to improve the quality of his or her life, the quality of life of the whole family will improve. When we sponsor the students, we encourage them to become good people. We do not offer Buddhist teachings specifically because we also support students who are from Christian and other religious backgrounds. We just share with them the essential elements of compassion and generosity. We encourage them to help people who are in difficulty. We show them how to deal with anger by calming themselves and being aware of their breathing.

Every time I write a letter to Vietnam or to the sponsors, I show it to Sister Chân Không before I send it. I ask, "Is this letter gentle enough, skillful enough, polite enough?" It is very important to be humble in doing this work. The people in Vietnam receive your money, but they also receive your practice, your loving kindness, and your understanding. It is not just money that we send there. This is how Thây has taught Sister Chân Không to regard the social work in Vietnam. Now she transmits that to all her younger brothers and sisters. If we act like a boss towards the people to whom we send the money, it will create difficulties in them and in us.

Sister Chân Không has a big heart. I am like a little piece of sand. I know my practice and my capacity is very small compared to hers. I take care of some projects, and when I receive news that there's some difficulty with the project, I ask Sister Chân Không how to handle the situation. Sister Chân Không has so much energy. Her daily life is not her own. Her life is for all the people in the world. One day, I asked her, "Sister, why do you have so much energy? I see you do many things. You help the Sangha and the people in Vietnam and people in many places. I want to learn from you." She said, "It is so easy. When you are able to help people relieve their suffering and to recognize their happiness, their happiness is your happiness. My happiness is their happiness. If you do anything to help people to relieve their afflictions, their anger and pain, and you see their daily life is lightened, you also receive their energy of happiness." I have learned this from her. I vowed I would practice like her.

How do you stay in touch with the people in Vietnam and also with the people who contribute to the work?

The Plum Village monks and nuns stay in contact with the social workers in Vietnam over the phone, through letters, and with occasional visits. Every year, lay Dharma teachers connected to Plum Village also go to Vietnam and visit the projects. The social workers send us detailed reports of how the money is spent; and, when they want to start a new project, they also send a detailed proposal. We look at the whole situation and decide whether or not we can support the project. The money we receive comes from many friends, so we are very careful with how it is used. The teachers write us letters about how they teach the children. They share how they respond, using the practice of mindfulness, when children are angry or unskillful in their classrooms. We do not say that the social work programs to which we contribute are the work of the Buddhists. We do it only in the name of wanting to help and support others. When the students and the elderly or handicapped people receive the money, they send thank you letters to us. They share about the days they come to the temple, eat together, and have activities together.

We also have difficulties. Sometimes there may be a gap in communication with the government in Vietnam. The brothers and sisters in Vietnam may also have difficulties with each other because they come from many different backgrounds. The social workers share their difficulties with us. Sometimes their practice is not solid, and suddenly they feel anger. We encourage them to sit together, listen to each other, and practice Beginning Anew. They listen to each other, and when they are able to understand each other, they can continue with the work. This is what Thầy and Sister Chân Không established in Vietnam, known as engaged Buddhism. We practice Buddhism without calling it Buddhism.

When I send thank you letters to the sponsors of the projects in Vietnam, I am aware of the compassion in each person as I write his or her name. I put my whole heart into writing the thank you letter. I try to touch the person's bodhicitta, the mind of love, like that of Bodhisattva Avalokiteshvara who responds to the suffering in the world. I do not meet with the sponsors in person, but I still connect with them. We have many friends who give large amounts of money, and we also have many friends who give a small amount every month, such as five or ten dollars. When I open a letter, regardless of the amount, I practice equanimity. Sometimes we receive a check for ten or twenty dollars, and looking at the address, I see the person lives in

Social workers bring food to the hungry in Vietnam

an apartment. I feel very happy. I look deeply, and I see these people are not rich, but they want to help other people and they share the money they have. When they go shopping or when they go to a restaurant, they are conscious of saving some of their money to share with others. I notice this, and I feel very warm in my heart.

Letter from a Daycare Teacher in Vietnam

Nguyen Thi Thuy Linh, Dharma name Quang Thuu, practices at the Thu Duc Temple near Nha Trang, Vietnam.

Dear Respected Teacher,

Spring has gently passed and the heat of summer has taken its place. This year seemed very long and yet I realize that if I do not practice what I have been taught, I may waste this time. We have finished our school year. When we said good-bye to the children, we could not avoid feeling sad.

We are very happy to have taught the children for almost a year. We are aware that children are the future of the country. Children are impressionable and tend to follow the example of their teachers and parents. Knowing this, we were careful how we talked and acted, especially when we were with the children.

When we had difficulty with a student, when we did not feel

Above: The Luong Mai daycare center, Vietnam

Below: Plum Village social work programs help to feed children at school

well or were unhappy, we did our best not to pour our sadness and suffering onto the students. Children are like buds on a tree. They should receive only happiness. Knowing this does not mean we ignore their misbehavior. There are some children that need a lot of sweetness and others that need a stronger approach. We always tried to understand each child's character and respond to him or her appropriately. We are aware that we have not completely practiced what you have taught us. Yet we have done our best to put the teachings into practice and your teachings will continue to help us in the coming school year and in life in general.

Dear Respected Teacher, I would like to share one example of how I practiced at my school. Young children like new things very much. When they entered the new school building this year, they felt very happy and motivated. The school was cooler and more airy, the walls were new, the ceiling was new — everything was new and clean. They ate and slept very well.

It happened that some children came to school with dirty hands and feet, quickly leaving marks on the brand-new walls. Some children walked in water and then into the new building, making the clean floor dirty. At first, we didn't say anything, felt a little bit unhappy, and cleaned up after the children. But it happened often, and eventually I began to feel very irritated. Sometimes I wanted to yell at the children. But I stayed quiet, followed my breathing, and the irritation disappeared. When I went to clean the mess, I felt light and at ease.

The other teachers and I decided to speak with the children and check for dirty feet. We told the children that although we were tolerant today, we would not tolerate dirty feet and hands tomorrow. The next day, there was progress, but the building was still not completely clean. By the third day, everyone was neat and clean. We were so happy and told the children that we were very pleased with them. I said, "All of you are clean and beautiful. I am very happy." When I looked at the children's faces, I was touched and happy.

Dear Teacher, we are grateful for your teachings. I have had such joy in the practice, but I also know I have limits. Life is not simple. To be a good child in a family is already hard. To become a useful person for society is even harder. But we must not give up. To accomplish a big task, we begin with small tasks. Here is a short poem I learned about this.

Don't look down on small acts of kindness
and think that it is not yet your turn.
As the water drips
the vase will be full and overflowing.

Sincerely,
Quang Thuu

For information on how to support the social work programs in Vietnam, please contact the Committee for Touching and Helping.

Europe: Plum Village, 13 Martineau, 33580 Dieulivol, France

U.S.A.: Green Mountain Dharma Center, Box 182, Hartland Four Corners, VT 05049, U.S.A.

Walking Meditation As Engaged Social Action

Pamèla Overeynder, True Sun of Understanding, lives in Austin, Texas, where she helped to found the Plum Blossom Sangha. She is a massage therapist.

Public walking meditation offers a powerful symbol of the peacefulness inherent in all beings. Plum Blossom Sangha of Austin, in collaboration with the Texas Hill Country Chapter of the Buddhist Peace Fellowship, has taken up the practice of public walking meditation as a form of engaged social action. We walk in public to bear witness to suffering in the world. We also walk as a way to cultivate a dialogue in our community about what it means to be peacemakers.

Walking meditation as a form of engaged practice is a profound and simple way to touch the hearts of participants and observers. A group of silent walkers moving slowly and peacefully in the midst of hurry and confusion offers an island of refuge for everyone. Observers, touched by the visual image of peace, become participants in creating world peace.

The act of walking for the joy of walking, walking as a way to wake up and be fully present to the suffering in the world, contradicts

Peace

Tran Thi Dieu Huong, Janina, age ten, is from Toronto, Canada and of Vietnamese heritage. The niece of Brother Phap Niem, she enjoys reading Su Ong's writings and practices his teachings daily. Her poem is inspired by his book Peace Is Every Step.

If we are peaceful, if we are happy
we can blossom like a flower
and everyone in our family
our entire society
will benefit from our peace
we all have power
to make every step peace
sharing our lives
is the spirit of free
While I breathe in
I smile
While I breathe out
I calm myself
always know
you will forever
have peace

Drawing by
Sister Tue Nghiem

our Western way of life that is increasingly based on speed. Walking — and observing others walking — helps create a gap in conditioned thinking so that we can begin to question who we are and what our "views and positions" are. It nourishes the state of not knowing, from which deep looking, understanding, and compassion can arise.

To date, we have held three public walking meditations at the State Capitol to raise awareness about global issues. The first one, A Walking Meditation for the People of Yugoslavia, was during the Balkan War. We emphasized not taking sides, but rather witnessing the enormous suffering of all parties to the conflict, including troops and civilians on both sides and United Nations peacekeepers. We invited walkers to embrace the Way of Silence, the Way of Compassion, the Way of Not Knowing, the Way of Witnessing, the Way of Interbeing, the Way of Forgiveness.

The second walk, Precious Steps for Peace, was held in collaboration with the Austin Adopt-A-Minefield Campaign to raise awareness about the global land mine crisis — over seventy million unexploded land mines in seventy different countries. Before walking we gathered in a circle and invited everyone to walk in silence, in support of our brothers and sisters around the world, in gratitude, in peace, with all our hearts for those who can't. The walkers included people from many faiths, a woman in a wheelchair, a five-year-old girl, and a pregnant woman.

The third walk, Peace Is Every Step — Cultivating Peace in Times of War, was held in October as the United States was recovering from the terrorist attacks and as we were bombing Afghanistan. The flyer said, "We come together in witness to the immeasurable suffering of all beings caught in the current cycle of war and violence. Peace is created in every moment with every thought, word, and action. We are all peacemakers. Let us begin this moment to practice peace."

The walks were well-attended and we had good press coverage by local television stations. Most of the people who participated in the walks were not Buddhist yet were very moved by the experience of witnessing through walking.

At the last two public walks, we handed out small cards in Thây's calligraphy that said, "The most important thing is to find peace and to share it with others." Several hundred of these cards have been given out to the walkers and to friends and family. Recently a Sangha sister thanked us for the card she received. She had given it to her daughter who later was the victim of road rage. Her daughter was able to remember Thây's words and instead of responding negatively she wished the distressed woman peace.

These ordinary steps for peace may seem small and insignificant individually, yet the symbolic effect of such actions nourishes the seeds of peace in each of us and each small step helps create a culture of peace.

Love Letter to Congress

Carolyn Cleveland, Peaceful Flower of the Heart, practices with the Washington Mindfulness Community, Washington, D.C. She is the Director of Training for the League of Conservation Voters and a Writer in Residence for the D.C. Public Schools. She teaches middle school students to express themselves through poetry.

As a resident of Washington, D.C. and a practitioner of mindfulness I ask myself, How can I support the members of Congress in cultivating their own inner peace and compassion so that it will lead to decisions and actions steeped in deep listening, understanding, compassion, and peace? This concern was in my heart when I visited Plum Village during the Winter Retreat of 2000. When I returned to the United States I found that I was not alone in wanting to explore how mindfulness could be brought into politics. As a result, the Committee on Mindful Politics was born.

The Committee on Mindful Politics is comprised of members of the Washington Mindfulness Community and was inspired by Thich Nhat Hanh's teachings on stopping, looking, and listening deeply. The Committee seeks ways to support policymakers in mindful action — action based on the calmness and lucidity that comes with listening deeply to suffering, whether that suffering is one's own or belongs to other people or other nations. As a committee, we support watering the seeds of love, understanding, and peace within policymakers and encourage others to do the same.

One method that the Committee on Mindful Politics has used to achieve its goals is the writing of "love letters" to Congress. A sample letter was circulated through the Order of Interbeing to Sanghas nationwide, asking Sangha members to send a similar letter of support to their congressional representative. Visits with congressional staff have proven that such letters make a difference. One staffer, while fingering the love letter, said, "This is so good to hear. We need to get more messages like this because we are always hearing the contrary." Politicians and their staff need assistance and they rely upon the constituents they serve to support them. The staffer said that sending a love letter to a congressional representative is important because it tells them that as their constituent you care about the way they conduct business; it tells them that it is important that your representative be mindful in their actions. The following is a sample love letter:

Sample "Love Letter"

Date
The Honorable (full name)
United States House of Representatives
or United States Senate
Washington, D.C. 20515

Dear Representative (last name):
As a constituent of your district I urge you to cultivate peace in response to the acts of terrorism our nation experienced on September 11, 2001. As a citizen of the United States who practices looking deeply before acting, I believe in promoting compassion within ourselves and in the world. I understand that the pressure to respond to this tragedy with an act of war must be overwhelming. Please know that I support you in your endeavors to act from a place of peace and calm. I support you in listening deeply to your compassionate self and your own suffering and in hearing the suffering of our nation and of other peoples and nations.

The Zen Buddhist monk Thich Nhat Hanh is a man who has witnessed thousands of friends killed in the Vietnam War and continues to practice calmness and lucidity. I offer his words as the representation of my message of peace:

"It is only with compassion that we can embrace and disintegrate violence. This is true in relationships between individuals as well as in relationships between nations . . .

By understanding the nature and the causes of the suffering, we will then know the right path to follow.

We are all co-responsible for the making of violence and despair in the world by our way of living, of consuming, and of handling the problems of the world. Understanding why this violence has been created, we know that only those that suffer deeply could act with such violence."

I have the conviction that you as leader of this nation will act with wisdom and courage. I know that as an elected official of our country you possess great understanding. I support you in cultivating peace within yourself, and I am certain that you will ensure peace in the world. I also urge you as a member of Congress to support nonviolent efforts during this time of crisis. Thank you for your leadership. I look forward to hearing from you.

Respectfully,

YOUR NAME

I wrote this poem in 1965 especially for the young people in the School of Youth for Social Service who risked their lives every day during the war, recommending them to prepare to die without hatred. Some had already been killed violently, and I cautioned the others against hating. Our enemy is our anger, hatred, greed, fanaticism, and discrimination against men. If you die because of violence, you must meditate on compassion in order to forgive those who kill you. When you die realizing this state of compassion, you are truly a child of the Awakened One. Even if you are dying in oppression, shame, and violence, if you can smile with forgiveness, you have great power.

Rereading the lines of this poem, I suddenly understood the passage in the Diamond Sutra that speaks about *ksanti* (endurance or tolerance): "Your courage intact, your eyes kind, untroubled (even as no one sees them), out of your smile will bloom a flower. And those who love you will behold you across ten thousand worlds of birth and dying." If you die with compassion in mind, you are a torch lighting our path. Before burning herself, Nhat Chi Mai, one of the earliest Tiep Hien members, read this poem into a tape and left it for her parents.

"Alone again I will go on with bent head" in order to see you, know you, remember you. Your love has become eternal. "On the long, rough road, the sun and the moon will continue to shine."

When there is a mature relationship between people, there is always compassion and forgiveness. In our life, we need others to see and recognize us so that we feel supported. How much more do we need the Buddha to see us! On our path of service, there are moments of pain and loneliness, but when we know that the Buddha sees and knows us, we feel a great surge of energy and a firm determination to carry on.

—from *Call Me by My True Names*

Recommendation

Thich Nhat Hanh

Promise me,
Promise me this day,
Promise me now,
While the sun is overhead exactly at the zenith,
Promise me:

Even as they
Strike you down
With a mountain of hatred and violence;
Even as they step on you and crush you like a worm,
Even as they dismember and disembowel you,
Remember, brother,
Remember:
Man is not our enemy.

The only thing worthy of you is compassion —
Invincible, limitless, unconditional.
Hatred will never let you face
The beast in man.

One day, when you face this beast alone,
With your courage intact, your eyes kind
Untroubled
(even as no one sees them),
Out of your smile
Will bloom a flower.
And those who love you
Will behold you
Across ten thousand worlds of birth and dying.

Alone again,
I will go on with bent head,
Knowing that love has become eternal.
On the long, rough road,
The sun and moon
Will continue to shine.

"Strike Against Terror" is a Misleading Expression

Thich Nhat Hanh

Terror is in the human heart. We must remove this terror from the heart. We must avoid destroying the human heart, both physically and psychologically. The root of terrorism should be identified so that it can be removed. The root of terrorism is misunderstanding, hatred, and violence. This root cannot be located by the military. Bombs and missiles cannot reach it, let alone destroy it. Only with the practice of calming and looking deeply can our insight reveal and identify this root. Only with the practice of deep listening, restoring communication, and compassion can it be transformed and removed.

Darkness cannot be dissipated with more darkness. More darkness will make the darkness thicker. Only light can dissipate darkness. Violence and hatred cannot be removed with violence and hatred. Rather, this will make violence and hatred grow a thousand-fold. Only understanding and compassion can dissolve violence and hatred.

"Strike against terror" is a misleading expression. What we are striking against is not the real cause or the root of terror. The object of our strike is still human life. We are sowing seeds of violence as we strike. Striking in this way we will only bring more hatred and violence into the world. This is exactly what we do not want to do.

Hatred and violence are in the hearts of human beings. A terrorist is a human being with hatred, violence, and misunderstanding in his or her heart. Acting without understanding, acting out of hatred, violence, and fear, we help sow more terror, bringing terror to the homes of others and bringing terror back to our own homes. Whole societies are living constantly in fear, our nerves attacked day and night. This is the greatest casualty from which we may suffer as a result of our wrong thinking and action. Such a state of confusion, fear, and anxiety is extremely dangerous. It can bring about another world war, this time extremely destructive.

We must learn to speak out so that the voice of the Buddha can be heard in this dangerous and pivotal moment of history. Those of us who have the light should display the light and offer it so that the world will not sink into total darkness. Everyone has the seed of awakening and insight within his or her heart. Let us help each other touch these seeds in ourselves so that everyone will have the courage to speak out.

We must ensure that the way we live our daily lives does not create more terrorism in the world. This means we must live with mindful consumption, without discrimination or participating in injustice. We need a collective awakening to stop this course of self-destruction.

— Shanghai, 19 October, 2001

Healing Racism: The Answer is Compassion

From the Question and Answers session with Thich Nhat Hanh at the University of Massachussets Retreat, August 2001.

Question: *As a black man in America, I find myself facing racism and discrimination sometimes on a daily basis — sometimes subtle, sometimes unintentional, sometimes overt — from both individuals and organizations. I have been stopped by the police simply because of the way I look. And I refuse to act in a discriminatory way, to be racist myself, but it is very hard not to hold the anger, the seeds of anger within myself. I'm afraid that this anger will come out in a very dark way, maybe towards people around me that I care about. How do I free myself of this anger? And I must say too that it is very heartening to come here and to be one of very few black people and to feel so much acceptance, that people smile back at me when I smile, which does not happen in my own town all the time. And people don't cross the street when I approach them, and people aren't afraid that I'm going to rape them or that I'm going to hurt them. And that experience is rare. And so I want to know how I can not be angry.*

Thây: There is a lot of discrimination, a lot of ignorance in our society and in everyone — in the white person, in the nonwhite person. Our practice is to transform that tendency to discriminate. I feel that I understand deeply your feeling. We as Vietnamese have been victims of very painful discrimination also. But if you learn to look with the eyes of the Buddha, you can see much deeper. You can see that those who do not understand, who act with discrimination, they suffer also. If they are able to open their hearts and accept and include everyone, their happiness will be much greater. But they don't know how to do it. The answer is compassion. People who are angry suffer; people who discriminate suffer.

The history of civilization is the history of transformation: the transformation of ignorance and discrimination. In the past we discriminated against women a lot. Women did not have the right to vote. Whether black or white, they were discriminated against. So discrimination is not just directed against people of color, but against many others as well. And the history of humankind is the history that is made step by step. We should continue our practice of liberation — liberating ourselves, liberating our society from ignorance, discrimination, hatred, and violence.

Not only do we discriminate against people, we also discriminate against animals, plants, and minerals. We think we can be happy as humans without caring for animals, plants, and minerals. All these beings, forms of life, are being discriminated against very deeply. And ignorance is dictating this kind of attitude. Because if we make animals suffer, we make ourselves suffer. If we make plants suffer, we make ourselves suffer; and if we make minerals — the Earth — suffer, we make ourselves suffer. When we continue to exploit animals, plants, and the Earth — polluting them, destroying them — we are practicing self-destruction, and we don't know it. "Forgive them because they do not know what they are doing." That is the answer.

When we discriminate against other living beings we are drawing suffering to ourselves. We are making ourselves suffer and other people suffer, and yet we do not know it. And if we do know, then we will have compassion: compassion for ourselves and for everyone else also. And only that compassion can liberate us. With that kind of deep understanding, compassion will arise and embrace not only ourselves, but everyone who is still living in darkness, in ignorance, and in discrimination. The amount of darkness and discrimination in our world is still huge, enormous; but if you are a practitioner you should not lose your hope.

The Buddha realized this; he did not lose his hope. He began with his practice. He began to teach others, and his tradition continues. The practice of understanding brings compassion, and understanding and compassion bring about liberation. This is what each of us should do in our daily life. With that conviction we will have a path, and because we have a path we don't have to suffer too much. We are capable of forgiving, of including. And one day other people will see that and they will learn the path of compassion and inclusiveness also.

During the time of the Buddha, he accepted all sorts of people into his Holy Assembly, and he was quite determined to do that. One day he accepted an outcaste person, Sunita, into the Sangha. Sunita was a scavenger (an "untouchable"), and many people, including the king of Koshala, disapproved of the Buddha's decision. But the Buddha was firm and finally convinced the king that an outcaste person has the nature of awakening, the capacity of being compassionate. After only six months of practice, Sunita became a Dharma teacher. And it happens that the king came to the practice center and saw him teaching other monks, many of them belonging to the royal family. He did not know that this Dharma teacher was the former scavenger. So, when he met the Buddha, the Buddha told him the truth. The Buddha also accepted women into his Order, which was a very courageous act at that time. We should be a continuation of the Buddha, even if there are still great obstacles. We should maintain our courage, our patience. Because patience is the mark of true love, of true compassion.

Thank you for asking the question.

Embracing Diversity in the Mindfulness, Diversity, and Social Change Sangha

Charles King, Fearless Compassion of the Heart, grew up in Virginia and is of European-American heritage. He has practiced with the Mindfulness, Diversity, and Social Change Sangha in Oakland, California since 1998.

"Welcome to the Mindfulness, Diversity, and Social Change Sangha. Our Sangha was created during a retreat in the fall of 1997 by people of color and social change activists. Our desire is to create a space where anyone can come together for mutual support and mindfulness practice. Our intention is also to offer people of diverse social identities a safe, welcoming, and participatory Sangha where they can feel at home and in community.

"Our practice is based on the teachings of Thich Nhat Hanh, a Vietnamese monk of international recognition and honor.

"We welcome people of all faiths and practices who wish to explore ways to heal the interconnected forms of injustice and oppression through the practice of mindfulness and to find a place to rest and reexamine their daily lives.

"As a grassroots Sangha we don't have a regular Dharma teacher, so we encourage and actively seek participation by all members in planning and offering Dharma teachings."

This preamble is read at the opening of every weekly meeting at our Sangha, which is nearly five years old. The Sangha was founded with awareness that most convert Buddhist communities in North America reflect the demographics of the dominant culture — their members and leaders are predominantly middle- or upper-class heterosexual people of European ancestry. As we attended retreats, Zen centers, and Sanghas, we have been disappointed that the participants do not reflect the rich diversity of our communities in Northern California and in Oakland, where our Sangha meets.

We believe that aspects of traditional forms of practice and structures of power in Buddhist practice centers and Sanghas often discourage people of diverse backgrounds from feeling welcome and participating fully. Only through conscious examination and awareness of these practices can we recognize elements of the "-isms" (ableism, ageism, classism, homophobia, racism, sexism, etc.) that may be excluding or alienating many people who would otherwise join us on the Dharma path. The founding members of the Mindfulness, Diversity, and Social Change Sangha took up the challenge of creating a Sangha that would be mindful of these "-isms" and aspired to develop practices that would clearly welcome and empower people who have often had the experience of being marginalized and disenfranchised in North American culture. In addition, inspired by the tradition and teachings of Thich Nhat Hanh, they sought to encourage and support socially engaged Buddhism, by providing a community and a refuge for practitioners who are committed to social activism.

"Our practice is based on the teachings of Thich Nhat Hanh and other mindfulness practitioners. We welcome people of all faiths who wish to explore mindfulness practice as a way to help heal the interconnected forms of injustice and oppression, from global threats of militarism and environmental exploitation to everyday, habitual forms of racism, classism, sexism, and other '-isms' which cause such painful separations in our human society."

This statement appears in the handout that introduces new members to the Sangha. It is important to make it clear that members of the Sangha share awareness of the strong habit energy in the dominant culture to create divisions of "us" and "them," divisions that cause suffering and undermine the experience and realization of interbeing. It is important that new members of the Sangha feel that we are open to discourse about these sources of suffering in the world and in our Sangha family.

As a grassroots Sangha, we only have a Dharma teacher available to lead the Sangha about once a month. Over the past couple of years we have been delighted to enjoy the teachings of Lyn Fine, True Goodness. Otherwise, our meetings are facilitated by members of the Sangha. We actively encourage members to participate as facilitators and bell-keepers. A "Guide for Facilitators and Bell Inviters" was written to help newer members to take on this role with less trepidation.

Unfortunately, mindful listening and right speech are not always practiced in groups that gather for the purpose of social activism or for mindfulness practice. Without structures that promote these Dharma practices, the dominant culture's traditional methods of discourse commonly prevail. These methods usually include frequent interruptions and overtalking, domination of time and precedence in speaking by white males, and little space for those who speak slowly, deliberately, quietly, or less aggressively. These factors tend to exclude the voices of people from groups that are disempowered in our society. In our Sangha we use the council circle format so each member of the Sangha is given an opportunity to speak without interruption, while the rest of the Sangha practices deep listening. We believe that adherence to the council circle format for our Dharma discussions allows for safe expression of diverse viewpoints, a principle that is at the heart of the Fourteen Mindfulness Trainings.

"Meditation in Action" sessions provide a particularly useful vehicle for increasing involvement of Sangha members. Many do not feel comfortable taking on a role that they view as ordinarily occupied by a monk, a nun, or an ordained Dharma teacher because they do not see themselves as experts on matters of practice. However, members of our Sangha often do have expertise and passionate interest in some topic of social injustice or social activism. When our members share their knowledge and wisdom, the Sangha benefits in several ways. The Sangha honors the special knowledge, courage, and social change efforts of the presenter. The presenter feels recognized, validated, and empowered. The Sangha learns about a source of suffering in the world and about actions that each individual can take to help reduce that suffering. The Sangha learns to practice deep listening and compassion in the presence of suffering.

Allies

Practicing with our Sangha has taught me many important lessons. I speak from my perspective as a European-American male, from a middle-class background, with an advanced graduate education. I learned that it is not enough for me to be open, accepting, and tolerant in accordance with my liberal values. I learned that I could no longer sit back and expect that People of Color or other oppressed groups would raise the important issues about racism, sexism, or homophobia when such issues needed to be addressed. I realized that if I want to enjoy the benefits of a diverse Sangha, then I also need to do the hard work to assure that these issues of "-isms" get addressed in a way that makes the community safe and welcoming for everyone.

I learned what it means to by an "ally" — someone who takes responsibility for welcoming and supporting people from diverse backgrounds in an environment that may feel unfamiliar and threatening for them. I learned that it did not matter whether I feel qualified, authorized, or sufficiently skilled to fulfill this role. I decided it had to be my responsibility to learn how to be an effective ally, even if I made mistakes, sounded ignorant, or suffered awkward and embarrassing moments in the process. I learned that I had to take this responsibility even when I wished that someone else would do it or doubted that I was the right person for the job. I still struggle with these questions: Should I be facilitating the Sangha tonight? Am I qualified to speak about this topic? Should I be writing this article?

Have We Succeeded?

Not to my satisfaction. We do have a more diverse Sangha than most, even here in Northern California. We have many active gay and lesbian members. There have been Sangha sessions where the majority of practitioners were People of Color. There have been meetings when I looked around and realized that I was the only white male present, causing me to reflect on how this experience of being in the minority is rare for me, but it is the norm for People of Color and gay, lesbian, bisexual or transgendered folk when they attend Buddhist events. I have found that the diversity of our Sangha has enriched my own experience and practice.

As in all Sanghas, members come and go. I have especially strong feelings of disappointment, and sometimes failure, when African-American, Asian, Asian-American, Latino, or young members disappear. I wonder what more we can do. I certainly believe that elements of ableism, ageism, classism, homophobia, racism, sexism, and other prejudices are present and still influencing our Sangha in subtle and detrimental ways. I hope that we will continue to strive to recognize these influences, to name them, and to find ways to heal the harm they have done. I hope we can all learn better ways to be allies. I hope that we can learn from our Dharma brothers and sisters in other Sanghas who share our intention to be continuously open to new practices that honor and promote diversity in our Sangha communities.

Acknowledgments: I would like to acknowledge the founding members of the Mindfulness, Diversity, and Social Change Sangha and subsequent members who have been especially instrumental in developing the format, guidelines, and practices of the Sangha: Rosa Zubizarreta, Lawrence Ellis, Lauri Rose Tanner, Kym Kuzmic, Lee Maddox, Don Marx, Susan Greef, and Olga Grinstead.

Turning towards the Light

Palestinian and Israeli Meetings in Plum Village

by Members of the Palestinian and Israeli Sanghas

Blue Flowers of Peace

Dear Thây,

I am a young Palestinian woman who was part of the Palestinian-Israeli group in Plum Village last week. I lived in paradise for a week. I felt that Plum Village is paradise for two reasons: the location and the atmosphere, and the fact that our enemies were our friends. All the people around me were my family. I could sense the warmth of love radiating from every soul and penetrating my dark heart. The darkness has been living there since my childhood, the darkness that was caused by "our cousins," the cousins that took away my childhood, and are now aiming at my youth. In your paradise, my voice was heard even during the noble silence. My heart was touched and the darkness was replaced by light.

I am back home now. I am ready to accept my enemies as family. I will try to synchronize my breath with their breath. I will let my voice free and I will listen twice as much as I talk.

Thank you for hosting us in your paradise, and exposing us to the Buddha's teachings.

One soul in Palestine has been changed. I am looking towards the light now.

Sincerely,

— A participant from Jerusalem, Palestine, November 2001

~

During the first walking meditation session in Upper Hamlet after the arrival of the Israeli-Palestinian group I found myself walking a few meters behind two Palestinian women. I had not previously met them, and had not had the chance to talk to them before the walk. I was very curious to know them, to find out how they came to join the group and what brought them to Plum Village. I wanted to know what they had experienced during the El-Aktza Intifada and during previous years, how much they and their relatives had suffered. I thought, How will it be possible to contact them, to create communication with them? Will it be possible to do anything together, and how?

When we passed the meditation hall we made a left turn into the open field, where many blue flowers were blooming. In Hebrew the name of these flowers is "Olesh." I do not know the Arabic name. Suddenly I saw that the elder Palestinian woman had also discovered the blue flowers, and was sharing them silently with the younger woman. They both smiled happily. This was a big discovery for me, and I thought, Ahh! The Olesh flowers bloom also in Palestinian fields, and the Palestinian people like them, too. They enjoy the same things as we do. Then I smiled to myself, knowing that there is a way to create communication between the Israeli and the Palestinian people.

— Jonathan Arazy, a participant from Jerusalem, Israel, August 2001

~

In the summer of 2001, fifteen Palestinians and Israelis came together in Plum Village to practice being peace and to learn about the healing power of deep listening and loving speech. Out of the experience, another group emerged that went to Plum Village in November 2001.

The two groups participated in sitting, walking, and working meditation both with the entire Plum Village community, and separately as a group. In meetings with Thây Doji, Sister Jina, and Sister Annabel we learned how to practice deep listening. We tried to

Brother Phap Hoi prepares to invite the bell in Upper Hamlet

listen with compassion to our own suffering and to the suffering of others. We also practiced going back to our bodies through Deep Relaxation, as well as stopping and breathing at the sound of the bell. We shared a session of Beginning Anew in which we had the chance to appreciate each other's positive qualities and express our regrets and difficulties. Sister Chân Không shared with us her experiences during the war in Vietnam, and answered questions. We also shared social activities: singing Arabic and Hebrew songs, playing music and reciting poems, and, before departing, we practiced hugging meditation.

Adjusting to Plum Village was a challenge. The transition from the very tense environment in Israel to the very calm way of life in Plum Village brought up a lot of tension and anxiety. We felt overwhelmed by having to deal with the new way of life in Plum Village and by the group dynamics, which gave rise to stormy emotions in each of us about ourselves and about the conflict. We learned about the depth and complexity of the conflict, and at the same time learned to appreciate every little step that is made toward understanding and peace.

When we first arrived, we wanted to plunge right into the intense issues and get to the core of the conflict. But we were told to focus on the practice, to walk mindfully, to eat mindfully. People in the group were frustrated. "Do they understand?" someone asked. "There is an emergency situation in the Middle East and we only have two weeks here. I know the practice is important but we don't have much time."

When we asked Sister Chân Không and others how to mobilize ourselves, we were told to practice, to deepen our relationship as a Sangha. We wanted to be guided in terms of strategies for social action and all we were told was to walk mindfully and practice. Over and over we were told to slow down. I began to sense that they were giving us a very important key, born out of tremendous depth of wisdom. We were being told that if we were not centered ourselves, if we did not have peace in ourselves, then there was no way we could bring stability and peace to the world around us.

For the first few days we were not to address the conflict. We ate together a few times and then one night we sat until very late in the forest by the Lower Hamlet "watering each other's flowers" in a Beginning Anew circle, where we shared the positive things we saw in each other. It helped nurture a sense of freshness and safety in the group and the next day we began the process of sharing our personal suffering.

Sitting in a circle, the bell was invited and then one person shared their personal suffering, speaking for five to twenty-five minutes. Then the bell was invited again, there was silence, and then someone else shared. No dialogues, no great brainstorming about how to solve the situation. Just simple sharing and listening.

So, in a sense, little happened in our group. But it was very real, maybe more real than what we usually consider to be peacemaking. It taught me that though we may do a lot of peace work that makes great waves in the media and is accompanied by great proclamations of progress, perhaps the work is not very deep or truly transformative. Each one of us here, though involved in such a modest exchange, was transformed.

A lot of pain was expressed in our meetings. The Palestinians spoke about their difficulties as Israeli-Arabs, the discrimination in Israel, and their inferior status in relation to Jews, the Israeli government, and the police. They spoke about not being able to develop their land and the land that had been expropriated and given to Jews. Palestinians talked about time spent in Israeli prisons, about being beaten up, about humiliation and confusion, being jailed in their own towns, the difficulties of educating children for peace in times of war, and about learning to see that the one you think is your enemy is a human being.

The Palestinians who live in the occupied territories talked about the distress that has been going on since the first Intifada (the Palestinian uprising and clashes) in 1987, the humiliating treatment they experience from the Israeli army, the difficult conditions they live under, and their poverty. They shared about the deportation of many of the Palestinians who lived in Arab villages and towns during the 1948 war, and about being scattered around the world, uprooted, unwanted, and homeless. They spoke of hatred for those Jews who took away their home.

The Jewish members shared their difficulties in struggling to protect a state surrounded by enemies, about their great fear of others wanting to destroy them, about difficulties in differentiating between the Palestinian citizens in Israel and the neighboring Arabs who are considered to be enemies, and about life in the shadow of constant fear — fear of terrorist attacks in the streets or on the buses, and the fear of future wars. As a result of this fear, there is a lot of violence and aggressive communication. Jewish members shared that Israeli society is mentally disabled and suffering from disconnection from itself. It also suffers from apathy and a lack of understanding for the other side. They shared that many Israelis want peace and not war, but that they distrust the intentions of the Palestinians.

Jewish members shared about the Holocaust and the genocide of their people in Europe by the Nazis, a trauma that is imprinted on every Jewish soul and which affects their behavior. They also talked about being homeless, in exile, for two thousand years.

What Seems Unchangeable Can Be Changed: Impressions from a Few Members of the Two Groups

"Usually, in the Middle East, we use so much anger to express our suffering, and that is why we cannot speak to or listen to each other. Here we were able to express suffering without anger and to really listen."

~

"It was the first opportunity for me to hear firsthand about the pain and the difficulty of both sides and to know the people in the group closely. For me, the story of the Palestinian refugees was very meaningful and made me reconsider the whole situation and the possible solutions."

~

"Our wounds will be transmitted to the next generations if we do not take care of them."

~

"I felt fear of exposing my inner emotions, fear that I would not be listened to. Here in Plum Village we were offered a way of listening to ourselves, of creating a feeling of space within us, a way to recognize and embrace the demons in us. Being able to do that, we are better able to listen to others."

~

"My experience here has given me a cradle — a place to feel held, warm and safe — so that seeing myself mirrored through others is not so scary. It is beautiful."

~

"The conflict is not about politics. It is about human beings and about their fears."

~

Walking meditation in the Upper Hamlet

Azrael Cohen, an Israeli participant and one of the organizers of the group

"I learned that I can cradle the guilt feelings in me, and the shame, to softly put them to sleep, like a mother with a fragile baby. When the guilt and shame rest like this — calm and safe in my arms — then I can listen with all my heart to painful, shocking things — to the suffering of our Palestinian brothers.

~

"I learned how important practicing compassion is, and accepting the negative sides — the violence, anxiety, and racism — in us Israeli-Jews, so that I can accept with love those elements when I meet them in others.

~

"I learned that all the material I need to make peace is in me, and when I practice, touch it, and am aware of it, I do not suffer anymore."

~

"What seems to be unchangeable can be changed. I was given a chance to see my own inner aggression and to embrace it as part of me, and through that to create a different interaction with others."

Pink Flowers of Insight

At the beginning of the fall, we had a Day of Mindfulness for the Israeli-Palestinian group in a private apartment in the French Hill neighborhood of Jerusalem. In the middle of the day we practiced walking meditation near the cemetery of English soldiers who fell in this area during World War I. On the way back I took a shortcut through the open field, and very soon I discovered many pink flowers blooming. We call them *sitvaniot* in Hebrew; I don't know the Arabic name. These pink flowers were much bigger than the same flowers that grow where I live. I wondered what caused them to reach such a big size? It could not be because of the different climate because in the mountains in the northern part of the country the same flowers are always much smaller. Did the flowers grow this big because of the more fertile soil? Suddenly I made the connection and thought, "Yes, this soil of the Jerusalem mountains is much more fertile because it has absorbed so much blood during all the generations of holy wars."

It is possible for pink flowers to bloom in spite of all that was happening. Will people be as clever as the pink flowers?

— Jonathan Arazy

You Can Use a Knife to Kill or You Can Use a Knife to Chop Vegetables

An Israeli soldier asks about the use of force during a question and answer session with Thich Nhat Hanh on November 29, 2001.

Question: *I am from the Israeli-Palestinian group. I want to ask about force. I was, and still am, in the Israeli army. At times we need to use force to prevent an act that will cause suffering, and that force causes suffering to another person. My question is, can force be used?*

Thây: If you have understanding and compassion in yourself, then what we call force, what we call military force, may help to prevent something, to achieve something. But that shouldn't prevent us from seeing that there are other kinds of force that may be even more powerful. We don't know how to recognize and make use of them so we always have cause to resort to military force. The spiritual force is also very powerful. The spiritual, the social, the educational — they are all forces, and much safer to use. Because we have not been trained to use these forces we only think of using military force.

Suppose there are two people, both of them full of anger, misunderstanding, and hatred. How can these two people talk to each other, even if they are negotiating for peace? That is the main problem: you cannot bring people together to sit around a table and discuss peace if there is no peace inside of them. You have to first help them to calm down and begin to see clearly that we, as well as the other people, suffer. We should have compassion for ourselves as well as for them and their children. This is possible. As human beings we have suffered. And we have the capacity to understand the suffering of other people.

The spiritual and educational dimensions can be very powerful, and we should use them as instruments, as tools for peace. Suppose you live in a quarter where dozens of Palestinians live peacefully with Israelis. You don't have any problems. You share the same environment, you can go shopping in the same place, you can ride on the same bus — you enjoy. You don't see your differences as obstacles, but as enriching. You are an Israeli and she is a Palestinian and you meet each other in the marketplace and you smile to each other. How beautiful, how wonderful. You help her and she helps you.

That image should be seen by other Palestinians and Israelis. If you are a writer you can bring that image to many people outside of your group. If you are a filmmaker, why don't you offer the image of peaceful coexistence to the world? You can televise it to demonstrate that it is possible for Palestinians and Israelis to live peacefully and happily together. That is the work of education. There are a lot of people in the mass media who are ready to help you to bring that image, that message to the world. That is very powerful — more powerful than a bomb, a rocket, or a gun, and that makes people believe that peace is possible. Why don't you invite a few Palestinians and Israelis who have not been in such a safe place, to show them that, "Well, you see, there is no problem living together."

If you have enough energy of understanding and peace inside of you, then this kind of educational work can be very powerful, and you won't have to think of the army and of guns anymore. If the army knows how to practice, it will know how to act in such a way as to not cause harm. The army can rescue people; the army can guarantee peace and order. It is like a knife. You can use a knife to kill or you can use a knife to chop vegetables. It is possible for soldiers to practice nonviolence and understanding. We don't exclude them from our practice, from our Sangha. We don't say, "You are a soldier, you cannot come into our meditation hall." In fact, you need to come into the meditation hall in order to know how to better use the army. So, please don't limit your question to such a limited area. Make your question broad — embrace the whole situation, because everything is linked to everything else.

There are many things we can do today to extend our understanding, compassion, and peace because every bit of it is useful, is gold. When you take a step, if you can enjoy that step, if your step can bring you more stability and freedom, then you are serving the world. It is with that kind of peace and stability that you can serve. If you don't have the qualities of stability, peace, and freedom inside of you, then no matter what you do, you cannot help the world. It is not about "doing" something, it's about "being" peace, "being" hope, "being" solid. Every action will come out of that, because peace, stability, and freedom always seek a way to express themselves in action.

That is the spiritual dimension of our reality. We need that spiritual dimension to rescue us so that we don't think only in terms of military force as a means to solve the problem and uproot terrorism. How can you uproot terrorism with military force? The military doesn't know where terrorism is. They cannot locate terrorism — it is in the heart. The more military force you use, the more terrorists you create, in your own country and in other countries as well.

The basic issue is our practice of peace, our practice of looking deeply. First of all, we need to allow ourselves to calm down. Without tranquility and serenity, our emotions, our anger, and our despair will not go away. And we will not be able to look and see the nature of reality. Calming down, becoming serene is the first step of meditation. The second step is to look deeply, to understand. Out of understanding comes compassion. And from this foundation of understanding and compassion you will be able to see what you can do and what you should refrain from doing. That is spoken in terms of meditation. In that respect, everyone has to practice meditation — the politicians, the military, the businessman. All of us have to practice calming down and looking deeply. You have our support.

Two retreatants practice hugging meditation.

Follow-up Question: *We have to pray and work for a whole lifetime to purify ourselves of anger and to cultivate compassion for those who try* *and succeed in hurting us and causing suffering. There is not a lifetime in Plum Village; there are two weeks. There is a whole lifetime in Israel to meditate. But during that time there are situations in which I see someone who is committing an act of force, and the only way I can stop him is through force, not through education or meditation because those are processes that take a long, long time.*

We do not always have the time to have compassion for that person. At times the act of force that will stop that person from killing, hurting, or wounding so many people is done through anger or hatred and without compassion. But I feel that even though I am still not pure, it is an act that I have to do because I have to protect my people. If a terrorist walks into a restaurant with a bomb on him and I can stop him, the military can stop him, but only by killing him — I don't have time to have compassion. It could be an act of hate and anger to shoot him, but it will stop him from blowing up that restaurant with women and children and people who are my people.

Thây: Of course it is very difficult to not get angry when they are killing your wife, your husband, or your children. It is very difficult to not get angry. That person is acting out of anger, and we are retaliating also out of anger. So there is not much difference between the two of us. That is the first element.

The second element is: why do we have to wait until the situation presents itself to us as an emergency before we act, dealing only with the immediate circumstance? Of course you have to act rapidly in such an emergency situation. But what if we are not in an emergency situation? We can wait for an emergency situation to arise or we can do something in order to prevent such a thing from happening. Our tendency is to not do anything until the worst happens. While we have the time, we do not know how to use that time to practice peace and prevent war. We just allow ourselves to be indulged in forgetfulness and sense pleasures. We do not do the things that have the power to prevent such emergency situations from happening.

The third element is that when things like this happen, it is because there is a deep-seated cause, not only in the present moment but also in the past. This is because that is. Nothing happens like that without a cause. You kill me, I kill you. But the fact that you are killing me and I am killing you back has its roots in the past and will have an effect on the future. Our children will say, "You killed my grandfather, now I have to kill you." That can go on for a long time. When you get angry, when you have so much hatred towards the person who has made you suffer, and you use all kinds of means to destroy him, you are acting out of anger just like he is. And anger is not the only cause. There are also misunderstandings, wrong perceptions about each other, and people who urge us to kill the other side because otherwise we will not be safe. There are many causes.

In the past our fathers and our grandfathers may not have been very mindful and may have said things, may have done things that have sown seeds of war. And their grandfathers also said things and did things, planting seeds of war. And now our generation has a choice. Do we want to do better than our grandfathers or do we want to repeat exactly what they did? That is the legacy we will leave for our children and grandchildren.

Of course in a situation of great emergency you have to do everything you can to prevent killing. And yet, there are ways to do it that will cause less harm. If you have some compassion and understanding, the way you do it can be very different. Bring the dimension of the human heart into it; help the military strategists to have a human heart. It's the least we can do. Do we teach the military to conduct a military operation with a human heart? Is that a reality in the army, in military schools? They teach us how to kill as many people as possible and as quickly as possible, but they do not teach us how to kill someone with compassion.

In one of his past lives, it seems that the Buddha was a passenger on a boat that was overtaken by pirates, and he killed one of them while trying to protect the people on the boat. But that is an earlier life of the Buddha. If the true Buddha were there he may have had other means; he may have had enough wisdom to find a better way so that the life of the pirate could have been spared. Because life after life, the Buddha made progress. You are the afterlife of your grandfather; you must have learned something over the past three generations. If you don't have more compassion and understanding than he did, then you have not properly continued on after your grandfather. Because with compassion and understanding we can do better, we can cause less harm and create more peace.

We cannot expect to achieve 100 percent peace right away — our degree of understanding and love is not yet deep enough. But in every situation, urgent or not, the elements of understanding and compassion can play a role. When a gangster is trying to beat and kill, of course you have to lock him up so he will not cause more harm. But you can lock him up angrily, with a lot of hate, or you can lock him up with compassion and with the idea that we should do something to help him. In that case, prison becomes a place to love and to help. You have to teach the prison guards how to look at the prisoners with compassionate eyes. Teach them how to treat the prisoners with tenderness so they will suffer less in prison, so we can better help them. Do we train them to look at prisoners with eyes of compassion? A prisoner has killed; a prisoner has destroyed. Maybe he was raised in such a way that killing and destruction were natural for him, and so he is a victim of society, of his education. If as a prison guard, you look and see in that way, then you will have compassion, understanding, and you will treat your prisoner with more gentleness. That helps him and that helps you. Help him to become a better person, and help yourself to be happy by helping people in difficulty. That is the principle.

We should not focus only on short-term action. Again, we have to look with the eyes of the Buddha. We must train ourselves to look at things with a broad perspective and not just concentrate on the immediacy of the problem. Our lives are for that, and the lives of our children will be for that because we are a continuation of each other. We build synagogues and mosques in order to have a place to sit down and do that — to look deeply, so that our actions will not only be motivated by desire, greed, or anger. We have a chance to sit in the mosque or synagogue for a long time, and in that time our compassion and understanding should grow. And then out there we will know how to act in a better way, for the cause of peace.

As a soldier you can be compassionate. You can be loving and your gun can be helpful. At times you may not have to use your gun. It is like a knife that is used to cut vegetables. You can be a bodhisattva as a soldier or as a commander-in-chief of the army. The question is whether you have understanding and compassion in your heart. That is the question.

Lower Hamlet lotus pond and plum orchard

A People's Peace Conference

A proposal offered by Thich Nhat Hanh at the end of the Israeli-Palestinian meeting in November 2001

Before you go home I would like to share something that you might like to consider in the near future, a "People's Peace Conference." You could come together as people and organize a peace conference where you can offer your insights, solutions, and proposals. This would be a process of education within the country as well as for the outside world. The participants would act as people and not as governments. And they would come having already cultivated some peace and compassion inside of themselves. This kind of peace conference must be organized in an entirely new and different way. There are two aspects to peace — making peace and being peace. In order to make peace you must also be peace.

We can organize a peace conference where we bring a number of people together to practice breathing, calming, smiling, and embracing our despair and anger. After several days we can begin to sit down, to smile at each other, to share our suffering, and so on. That is the process of practicing peace. We can organize a rehearsal peace conference in Plum Village.

As the peace inside us grows, we will grow, and we can organize a second similar conference. As we make more progress, we can invite people who are more officially representative than we are. We can try it several times in several places, and finally you can hold it in a place where the whole world can see. You can call it a "People's Peace Conference." By that time, supporters of peace all over the world will try their best to draw the attention of the world to the event. And we can invite reporters and the mass media to cover this work.

I think that in this process of practice we cannot expect a miracle. We have to go step by step towards real peace. That is the most realistic way — we should not be too dreamy. We cannot rely on our leaders because they have not been educated in peace; they are not accustomed to making peace, talking peace, or listening deeply. That is why we have to take the situation into our own hands, the hands of the people. This is very much the Plum Village way. We must start from the grassroots.

Mastering Anger

A chant by Thich Nhat Hanh

I bow my head and prostrate
Before the highest charioteer who trains humankind.
Stretch out your arms of compassion
Bring me to the shore of peace and solidity.
For so long confusion has inhabited us
That we have not had the chance to learn
And we have often foolishly
Allowed seeds of anger and violence
To be watered in our deep consciousness.

Whenever seeds of irritation or fury
Arise and operate in my mind
They always cause wounds and sulkiness
In myself and so many others.

Listening to Avalokita's teaching
I begin right now with a deep aspiration:
Whenever anger arises
I shall come back to myself
Take refuge in my mindful breathing and steps
So as to look after and embrace,
Protect and recognize
Painful mental formations in me.

I shall remember to look deeply
To see the true nature and source
Of hatred and anger.
Heeding the Buddha's teachings
I shall know how to guard my mind
I shall not do or say anything
When anger arises in me and
I still have not mastered it.
I shall look deeply to see
The real nature of my pain.

The seed of ignorance
Is the cause of my suffering
And the reason why the seed of
Anger in me has grown so strong.
I recognize that the person who makes me angry
Has so much suffering himself or herself.

seeds of the future

Maple Forest Monastery and Green Mountain Dharma Center

Light of Winter

Thây Giac Thanh, Sound of Awakening, is from Vietnam. He came to Plum Village in 1990 and since then has been the eldest brother in the Plum Village community. He was ordained a Dharma teacher in 1992. In 1997 he became head of practice at the Maple Forest Monastery, and in 2000 he became the Abbot of Deer Park Monastery. He passed away in October 2001.

Facing white snow,
Suddenly,
One-self fading away
The whole universe
Turning into a great lamp.

Above: Thây Vo Ngai playing in Upper Hamlet

Poems by Thây Vo Ngai

Brother Chân Vo Ngai, True No Obstacle, is from Vietnam and Washington State and was ordained a Dharma teacher in 1999.

Gentle Smile

Gracefully I smile
As the pages of the sutras open wide for us to live a life
of understanding and love.
Life is so wonderful that you cannot measure it.
As I awaken from a dream I embrace the sun of my homeland
Even though we are separated.
The happiness of living is still calling from inside of me.
The summer sun is still here shining on the hills
Making the dew and the rain on the tip of the branch disappear.
Become fresh again as the flowers bloom and as the woods
become green,
I come back in order to meet peace and innocence.
I am happy in the life of meditation.
Look there the trees and grass are smiling gently with me.

Coming Home

The hills and mountains are immense
The woods of pine shoot up straight and the stream sings the song of the sky
The path in the woods is wide
The rows of trees offer shade and the snow makes the hills white
Nature begins a festival for me to play
Welcoming the universe, calling me to return home.

—Maple Forest Monastery, November, 2001

We Do It Together

Sister Chân Thuc Nghiem, True Adornment with Ripeness, also called Sister Susan, is from the United States. She received the Dharma Lamp Transmission in 2001. She is a mother and a grandmother.

A tool that Thầy gave us is the ability to find healing in nature, to go sit in the middle of a field and do nothing. In the past two years I have found an apple tree out in front of the Green Mountain Dharma Center in Vermont. I sit under it, near the fence, every morning. I see the same patch of Earth, the same landscape in front of me, and the same trees, in the springtime, in the summer, in the fall, and in the winter. I think I began doing this because one morning I saw a bird watching the sun come up. I felt that that bird was more wholehearted than I was in being with the sunrise. About a month later, I was taken by surprise and I really saw the sun come up. It pierced me straight to my core.

I wanted to watch the sun come up, and after a while I noticed the Earth also. When it was cloudy, rainy, or snowing, I didn't see the sun, but the Earth was very wonderful. I began to feel very close to the Earth. It was so wonderful to go and sit cross-legged on the Earth every morning. I began to appreciate the apple tree in the different seasons, and the chipmunks and the squirrels who would run by me. One time a chipmunk landed on my head. One time a bird landed on my head. I think from this, on a deep level, I began to feel the interbeing of the Earth, and the sky, and the chipmunks, and the raindrops, and I certainly saw them inter-be with my happiness. It was this time I spent under the apple tree that really gave me a smile so easily. It gave me love in my heart very easily. I could see that everything was so connected. The teachings on Buddhist psychology also helped me to see that everything is connected. It is very easy in nature to see that everything is connected. I think that is why I can sit and stare at it for so long, because something in me recognizes that I am looking at everything.

Drawing by Svein Myreng

I could see that my sisters and I are connected very deeply and we affect each other. Perhaps the greatest happiness is knowing that we live in a community. It doesn't matter if sometimes the community has difficulties, or I can't get along with someone, or a million other things that can happen in a community that lives together twenty-four hours a day. The fact that we are living together, that we are trying to make the Sangha work and we are making it work, that we support each other with the same guidelines and we are really there for each other — to me that is one of the most beautiful things on Earth. It makes all the difference when I recognize the fact that we all belong together, that you can't take the father out of the son, you can't take us out of each other, you can't take anything out of us. We all belong together.

On the last morning of our trip to China, after a late night public talk, Thây woke up very early to see some of us off who were leaving for America. He was sitting outside with us. I was sitting at a table with another sister. She turned to Thây and said, "I want to thank you for allowing me to come to China, and I want to apologize for any mistakes I have made." She went on to say, "You know I have many weaknesses, and I am trying to overcome them, and it is difficult." And Thây quietly stopped her and said, "We do it together." To me that was the most incredible thing to say.

All our pain, all our difficulties, all our joy, we do it together. And when we do this we are following the truth of things, and that brings about our greatest happiness. What if all the Sanghas we know had that idea — we do it together, for each other? If in a family something comes up, they can do it together; they work it out together. As a nation, we can all help each other to do it together. So, when some group suffers, we do it together. We think about it. We look deeply into it. And as a world, we do it together. We have many ways of diplomacy and we know we are doing it together for all of us. We know we all belong together as one family and so we are doing this for each other. Since we are one family, we will find the best ways to bring about happiness for all of us.

Sister Thuc Nghiem (far left) and friends in the Upper Hamlet

Beginning Anew

Brother Chân Phap Am, True Dharma Sound, is from the United States and grew up near Chicago. He ordained as a novice in 1999.

I had been practicing at Maple Forest Monastery for several months, and I came to a point in my practice when I could no longer listen with openness to Thây's Dharma talks. I wanted to leave the community. Thây asked me, "What will you do if you are not a monk?" "I will go to another practice center," I replied. "But at another practice center you will have to listen to Dharma talks." "I know, I know," I said, laughing lightly. I could see it was ridiculous. Why leave the community to begin the same thing somewhere else? And yet, something kept me from being completely together, body and mind, with the Sangha.

We had been looking into my situation for months, and it had become especially intense on the previous U.S. teaching tour with Thây and many brothers and sisters. So, right before the last retreat (one for monastics at Kim Son Monastery), I received an ultimatum from Thây — either you are completely here with the Sangha or you must disrobe. I had grown apart from the Sangha too much to continue like this. I had been given a forty-five day suspension from Sangha activities to look into what I really wanted. Inside I felt happy with the new energy the ultimatum gave me.

This question began to underlie everything — what do I really want? Everyone seemed to enjoy being together in the monastic retreat very much, while I was alone. I felt what it was like to be separate from the Sangha, and everything became focused on seeing the situation clearly. There was an overwhelming feeling that I could not waste one second. My old pastimes like reading were out of the question. I just walked and breathed, sat, did relaxation, and wrote.

After a few days like this, a sister told me she saw pride and disrespect in my actions. I felt misunderstood and hurt, and went walking with it. Then, the whole thing broke open. There was no problem anymore. I felt regret for my disrespectful actions, and I felt gratitude and love towards Thây and the Sangha for sticking with me. Everything seemed fresh and new, and I just wanted to rejoice in life, in our brotherhood. The following letter came out of this experience.

September 19, 2001
Kim Son Monastery

Dear Thây, Dear Brothers,
I remember the past months at Maple Forest and the deep brotherhood we shared — the best time of my life. Maple Forest healed me so much, so discreetly. The practice has healed so much, freed up so much — I have failed to realize this and suffered. I looked at doubts too much. I have been easily confused and lost as to what I really want. I just want a simple life, a life of practice, a life where love can flow easily. I want to hold tight to the Sangha and let these doubts and difficulties be dissolved by true living.

I thank you so much, my brothers from Maple Forest — we had a single heart as a true family. It came unnoticed, to me at least. I know I didn't have any clear intention for our hearts to unite like that — how could I? I'd never experienced anything like that before. I feel such strong love and gratitude to you all and to Thây for letting us come together, for living as a collective heart. That's probably the closest I've ever come to myself, to my heart — and it came in the form of all of us! We had a Dharma discussion a few nights ago among some of the brothers from Maple Forest. We were looking into my situation, and I remember coming out feeling that we expressed what was going on in me. I was unable to express it, but in conversation together, it came out.

Well, I love you all so much. It's funny — all the things I thought I was doing as practice were really nothing. The important thing was the love, often hidden beneath the surface, but real nonetheless. Even as I remember the most difficult times last winter, times when pain was all I could see, looking back I can only feel the love. At times it felt like my heart was entirely raw and exposed — the slightest breeze could cut so deep — and even though I wasn't so aware of it at the time, it was the brotherhood that expressed itself in everyday life that kept me hanging on.

I have never felt more at home than I have this past year. When I expressed unhappiness, I guess I just did not see the love that was there clearly enough. It took a strong pull from Thây and the Sangha to call me back to look. It's funny that there was this whole rich world of only love going on underneath; but, because I couldn't see it, I suffered. This is what Thây was talking about last May when he told me formal practice is not the most important thing. The important thing is the love, the brotherhood quietly unfolding, and our real practice is just to be attentive to it. Formal practice is just an expression of our joy at being together and committing ourselves to nourishing this joy day by day.

If possible, I would like to re-enter the monastic community, to be a monk. I know there were many times I was disrespectful without real cause, and there is no reason why the Sangha should accept me back in. What can I say? I want to be a brother again and live within the community's arms, and I have nothing to offer. I can only offer myself.

Brothers in Maple Forest Monastery. Standing from left to right: Brother Phap Co, Thây Phap Dang, Thây Vo Ngai, Brother Phap Hien, and Brother Phap Am. Front row, left to right: Brothers Phap Lac and Phap Tue

What about doubts? Difficulties?

Looking back at the few years I have been in the Sangha, I see that transformation has taken place, and I had very little to do with it! I am much closer to my heart now than I ever could have dreamed of three or four years ago, and it isn't because of some special practice or teaching that unlocked everything. It is because the strong love in the Sangha was playing with my difficulties, underneath everything. The most I could do was get out of the way and surrender to the Sangha.

What about my reactions to the teachings?

They may still come, but let them come, what does it matter? They won't last forever, and someday down the road I will look back and think it funny that I gave something so small so much significance. It would be my greatest joy to have the opportunity to hear the Dharma talks again, and let the work of healing continue.

My brothers, please hear me. I wish to rejoin the path with you all and rededicate my life to this work. I hope that you all can forgive the times I let my difficulties speak for me, instead of speaking about my difficulties respectfully. There were many times I was clouded up and spoke out of frustration. I hope you can see that I did not really want to be like that and that I regret it now.

And Thây, I projected a lot of my frustration onto you — expecting you to give me some "key" to free up the love inside. Thây was trying to help, but I was just not open to receive. I said many unkind things, and I am very sorry. Thây has made it very easy for me to live the life I really want, and I didn't see that. Instead of thanking Thây for his great kindness, I blamed Thây for what I didn't see. Please accept my sincere apology, Thây. This Sangha is the best thing that ever happened to me. I hope it is not too late.

Love,
Chân Phap Am

(Brother Chân Phap Am is still with the community and received full ordination in 2003.)

A Maple Leaf

Brother Chân Phap Tue, True Dharma Wisdom, is from the United States and grew up in Berkeley, California. He was ordained in 1999.

One day, in the second year of my novitiate, I was leading walking meditation on a Day of Mindfulness at Stoneboy Hamlet, Maple Forest Monastery. A few minutes before, we had all listened attentively to a video Dharma talk given by Thây. He spoke of Christianity and the Fall from the Garden, but how Heaven was under our feet, and that returning to the present, we would find Paradise.

It was a gorgeous day. We made our way slowly, reflectively, past the pond and up into the forest path toward the Buddha hall. It is so easy to be mindful when the whole Sangha is walking behind you. I could hear my footsteps alone. I forgot everyone else behind me. It was so silent. The rich, dark soil of the forest floor was blanketed with many-colored leaves. Among them, one particular leaf caught my attention.

It was a maple leaf. I knelt to pick it up. The whole shape was marbled. Swirls of yellow, red, green, and brown ran through the leaf veins like the course of the year. The four seasons were in one leaf; and then I saw the life of ages, infinite and so full of color. I held Earth gently in my palm. I smiled in the silence of my mind and turned around. There stood my elder sisters: Sister Hoa Nghiem, Sister Susan, and Sister Tri Giac, all in a line, motherly in warm, brown robes. They looked surprised to see me turn towards them, for I had abandoned the walking meditation entirely and was walking right toward them.

I felt so supported by the walkers all together behind me. I felt myself a son at that moment, very young and filled with the confidence they may have felt in me, as their child. I walked steadily right towards Sister Susan, who smiled but eyed me warily as I held up the leaf to her. "Beautiful," she said in her reassuring way, as if speaking to a child who shows his mom a new leaf every other second and says, "Look, Mom, look." "Yes, dear, beautiful." She wondered what my smile was about. I held the leaf out for her. Uncertainly, she reached out her hand. "The Fall," I said, and in that moment looked as deeply as I could into her soft, brown eyes. *Nothing falls, nothing falls, nothing ever falls.*

Moving the Refrigerator

Pham Hai Duong, Chân Hien Thuy (True River of Goodness), became a member of the Order of Interbeing in 1994. She is from San Jose, California.

I feel a lot of happiness in myself and with the Sangha for many reasons. Being with the Sangha helps me understand myself better. Engaging in activities with the Sangha gives me the opportunity to see every member in different ways, helping to remove my wrong perceptions, and allowing me to feel closer to and in harmony with everyone.

Drawing by Anneke Brinkerink

Although I have been living with the Sangha, I still have habit energies that are not exactly in harmony with community living. One of these habit energies is to want to eat and drink my own food. Sometimes I feel the desire to eat a dish I have cooked myself and at a time of my choosing. This is what helped me to smile when the Sangha removed the refrigerator from where I was living.

My way of practice when I am eating with the Sangha is to feel gratitude for the person who has cooked. I chew the food until it becomes liquid before I swallow it, and as I chew like that I constantly send my thanks to the cook. This kind of gratitude is also nourishment for me, and it helps to remove any bad feelings I may have with another person in the Sangha. I see the service of the person who has done the cooking. I see the beauty of that person in the service they give, and any annoyance I have because of my perceptions of that person can be uprooted.

One of the things that has made me suffer in my life is that I always want to have the power to arrange things in my own way. When I came to live with the Sangha and practiced eating with the Sangha, it helped me to lessen this habit energy of mine and to find ways to contribute to the greater happiness of those I love. Before, I used to arrange things and correct things as a way of wanting to be in control. As far as eating and drinking are concerned, I also wanted to choose what I should eat and cook it in my own way, flavor it in my own way, and eat it just when I wanted to.

Living with the Sangha, however, I have learned to practice eating with the Sangha, eating what the Sangha eats, eating at the time decided by the Sangha, and eating according to the taste of that day's cook. If the food is bland, I eat bland food, but if it is strongly flavored, I also eat it. If it is tasty, I eat it, but if not, I still eat it. If the food suits me, I eat it, but if it does not suit me, I also eat it. I have practiced not to calculate, not to have expectations, and not to need to know in advance what I am going to eat. As I learned to do this, I realized that I no longer expect others to make me happy or the environment to make me happy. This realization allows me to be much easier on other people. When I practice not longing for my favorite dishes, I am able to enjoy what is actually there.

Drawing by Sister Tue Nghiem

Practicing eating with the Sangha has helped me not to have an individual program and to live with others as a family. When I am not a slave to my individual program, I enjoy a feeling of ease and not being busy as I participate in the activities of the Sangha. I do not have my own plans pushing me on ahead. When I participate in the activities of the Sangha, I have learned to be happy just because of the presence of others; and that presence is the most precious thing. Practicing following the timetable of the Sangha in order not to have individual plans becomes something freeing, and suddenly I have an infinite amount of space in my life. To be present at a meal seems simple. But as far as I am concerned, the moments when we are present for each other are the most important moments of our lives.

I have learned from experience that if we are not present for each other, we don't have a chance to see each other. If we do not see each other, we do not have a chance to understand each other. If we do not understand each other, however good our intentions may be, our love for each other cannot grow. Therefore, participating in the activities of the Sangha is a great opportunity for me to practice letting go of the idea that this is more important than that. It has taught me that my mind changes when I am able to see different aspects of my friends who live with me.

The more I practice, the more I see that the habit energies I have are very deep and subtle. They often bring about conflicts within me. I want to go in one direction, but I take a different path. I deceive myself. I use my surroundings to run away from myself. Nevertheless, I also see the infinite strength, goodness, and wholesomeness of a life based in mindfulness. This happiness comes to me when I practice mindfulness in my daily life with my Sangha, which I love and respect.

Deer Park Monastery

Thây Giac Thanh

Spring Message

Thây Giac Thanh

Laughing, speaking clearly,
Happiness on the lips
News of spring brings forth
Fresh flowers on the branch,
Green grass and warm sunshine,
Blooming flowers and dewdrops,
Open sea and bright moon,
High mountain and plain,
Shining stars and clouds,
All is just one mind.

I bow in respect
To thousands of flowers blooming today.
I bow in respect
To the dry stone on the roadside
Along with the obscuring dust storm
Wandering to the horizon.
And with deep respect
To the dry tears on the bony cheeks
In the immense world
Where deep suffering is
A game of up and down.

Then I bow in gratitude
To the deep blue sky,
The cloud twirling in uncertain destiny,
Freely floating as the days go by.

Gatha for Thây Giac Thanh

Written by Thich Nhat Hanh for Thây Giac Thanh on October 14, 2001, the day before he passed away.

That you are a real gentleman is known by everyone
The work of a true practitioner has been accomplished
When your stupa has just been raised on the hillside
The sound of children's laughter will already be heard.

Taking Root in Deer Park: Letters from the New Monastery

Sister Chân Thoai Nghiem, True Adornment with Auspiciousness, is from Vietnam and northern California. She was ordained a Dharma teacher in 1999 and was one of the first three monastics to settle in Deer Park.

July 2, 2000
My dear friend,
I have spent two nights here. July nights are very calm and quiet. I caught a cold last night, as I didn't expect the weather to change so much. This morning I got up smelling the pure perfume of the forest outside, feeling good. I stood by my windows looking at the majestic mountains, waiting for the first daylight, and feeling the raw energy of the Earth and Heavens. I was sorry for the many lay practitioners who worried that two sisters had to sleep on the wild mountain full of dangers like snake bites, attacks by coyotes or wolves, and unwanted visits by human beings. Who knew that we were quite safe and happy with the calm and quiet mountains?

When we arrived at the Eucalyptus Hamlet, we saw a very different scene from the beauty of the nature all around us. There were empty ammunition shells everywhere, broken windows, walls with bullet holes, and burned grass. The place was desolate. It reminded me of the traces of war like the one we saw in Vietnam. We found out later that this part of Deer Park had been a training area for the local S.W.A.T. team.

We started cleaning the next day. First we cleaned up the largest room in the Eucalyptus Hamlet, readying it for our initial meeting with local friends and lay practitioners. The place was very dusty. I thought no one had been here for more than a decade. I wore a surgical mask, gloves, and a hat during the cleanup, and I was still very dirty at the end of the day. I felt as if I hadn't taken a bath for a month. The hot July sun and hard work made me tired by evening; but I felt delighted. After only one day of care the eucalyptus trees in front of the main hall appeared greener. When I trimmed the dead leaves and broken branches of a pine, I could understand the feelings of the tree, hear its voice, and see it straighten to receive my care.

Now we have been able to move into the first house of the hamlet, small but quite warm. Nobody cared about torn window curtains, worn-out carpets, and the smell of the cleaning chemicals. We appreciated just having a place to live and a shelter from the hot sun. When you come to see us here, I will offer you a hammock with a breeze at noontime. You will hear the birds sing and the leaves murmur from the branches of the trees. You will have to agree with me that happiness is always there with you, easy to touch.

When I finish jogging, I like to climb up a big rock and sit under the shade of a very high oak tree.

Sitting in the grove
Listening to the life around me
A white cloud smiles from the top of a mountain

~

July 7, 2000
My dear friend,
As time goes by we feel more and more attached to this place. A lot of sweat and much joy make me think that we have been here for a long time. Today, someone has offered a vase of sunflowers. At dinner, I sat next to the vase. I felt warm and calm. The sight of those flowers made me miss Plum Village. But when I looked deeply I saw that Plum Village and Thây were in me and there was nothing to

miss. Even though there is a lot of work and it is overwhelming at times, I have a very deep belief that the Buddha, the ancestral teachers, Thây, and the Sangha will take good care of Deer Park. I only have to contribute my part and go through the training. I have nothing to worry about.

~

July 15, 2000

My dear friend,

The response of the laypeople in the area has been very touching. I remember the first meeting at the Eucalyptus Hamlet at the end of last June. Many people expressed their concerns that our objectives were too big. Some felt overwhelmed when they saw how devastated the place was. I shared with everyone Thây's reminder that we should find happiness in our work. Thây was more concerned about our happiness than about the results of our work. My dear friend, do you remember how we felt during the first days of New Hamlet? Just as we overcame our doubt and fear then, with our practice and work, and were able to complete the building of New Hamlet, we will do the same here. This is only a continuation.

Every Saturday and Sunday the first house of Deer Park has been happily invaded by laypeople with plenty of food and best wishes. Everyone helped: some trimmed trees, others swept the houses, and still others painted the houses. An old car and an industrial sewing machine have been donated. "The sewing shop" has started producing cushions for meditation and others for chairs. A man who worked in a sewing shop offered thread, a pharmacist offered surgical masks, and a nurse offered hospital towels and clothes for sweeping very dusty floors. Some donated refrigerators and some even donated personal computers. We have moved into the Oak Area to continue the cleanup. The building we used for the first meeting is being renovated to serve as the main meditation hall. The first house of the village is also to be renovated to receive Thây Giac Thanh and other brothers.

One morning I was meditating on top of the big rock as usual when I heard the leaves murmur and the bushes nearby shake violently. Birds suddenly flew up and away. I became a little nervous. As I ended my meditation and put on my shoes, I heard a loud roar! I retreated quickly to the house, and as I was about to enter it, I heard footsteps moving away slowly on leaves. I thought it might be a mountain lion, but I was not sure because I had never heard a mountain lion before. I thought that if a mountain lion suddenly appeared in my tracks, I would have to seek help from Avalokiteshvara because I do not have the power to persuade the animal to take refuge in the Three Jewels as our ancestral teachers did.

The next day I heard that Brother Phap Dung encountered a mountain lion. He climbed to the top of a mountain to do sitting meditation. When he opened his eyes, he saw a mountain lion sitting on the top of a rock in front of him watching him. Brother Phap Dung slowly put on his shoes, kept track of his breath so he wouldn't tremble, and ran down the mountain. Luckily the mountain lion ran in the other direction.

Sister Trung Chinh had her turn with wild and potentially dangerous animals, too. She ran into a big snake that was searching for food near the public restroom at night. A few days later another snake, quite a long one, hid itself under the rags near the sewing machine looking for a cool place. When Sister Trung Chinh approached the sewing machine, the snake dashed out of the house. In the evening we reminded each other to shake out our sleeping bags (we were sleeping on the floor) in case a snake had gotten into one of them during the day.

~

Late July, 2000

Tonight, looking up toward the sky
Through the pine branches
The moon is magically beautiful
Everyone in the whole hamlet goes to the mountaintop.

Last week, we were invited by Mr. Art, a neighbor, to come visit his ranch. He had won the bid to purchase Deer Park, but he later released it to us. Sitting in the back of a truck, getting shaken up and down and covered by dust, gave me some pleasure. It reminded me of when I lived in Ban-Me-Thuot, in Vietnam, and rode on a jeep around the hills and mountains there.

There are a lot of rabbits here. Once they ate a whole row of vegetables grown by Sister Trung Chinh for Su Ong at the first house we occupied. They ate in a dignified manner: on the first day they ate all the leaves on the first row. The next day they ate the leaves of the next row. After finishing all the leaves, they went back to the first row and started on the stems, continuing their work in the same orderly manner until nothing green was left above the ground. Brother Phap Dung liked it very much. He joked that maybe we should grow more vegetables to raise rabbits. After the rabbits, we ran into coyotes. From time to time a group of them started to howl from one side of the mountain and then another group would howl from the other side. Sister Trung Chinh did not dare to go up to Yen Tu summit alone the next day.[1]

August–September, 2000
My dear friend,
Thây and his Sangha arrived from France. The Day of Mindfulness organized in Deer Park impressed many people. In the Oak Grove area you could feel the Dharma from every direction; the wind seemed to stand still on top of the trees as the nectar of compassion penetrated into all the beings there. Many people cried after the Dharma talk. I sat motionless on top of a rock, wishing you were with me to share this precious moment.

Thây officially named the Eucalyptus Hamlet "Solidity Hamlet" (reserved for monks) and the Oak Hamlet "Clarity Hamlet" (reserved for nuns). Thây's calligraphies were hung everywhere. The name of the Practice Hall is "Trang Dau Non," Moon on the Top of the Mountain. The name of the Main Hall is "Rung Soi," Oak Forest. With these reminders from Thây I had the feeling that Deer Park was only a hamlet of Plum Village.

~

November, 2000
My dear friend,
A number of brothers and sisters from Plum Village are coming to Deer Park to prepare for the winter retreat. The brothers are fixing a house in Solidity Hamlet so they can move in. We are making twelve new beds for Clarity Hamlet. Since we know how to share food, we will have enough; since we know how to squeeze together, we will have enough places to stay warm. One day, when I came up to the carpentry shop of Solidity Hamlet, I saw many sisters taking measurements, cutting wood, nailing things. Not far away, under a pine, Brother Phap Son was sitting gracefully, mending his shirt and watching all of them work. There was a nice feeling of freedom and self-sufficiency.

~

December 24, 2000

Morning
White fog mixes with the great trees
A magical beauty fills the air
Golden sun rays pour down their shining silk
On to the mountains
White clouds
Blue sky.

Dear Thây,
We celebrated Christmas tonight. We did not have you with us; we also did not have our Thây Giac Thanh with us. However, Christmas was celebrated properly. I felt that Thây and Plum Village were among us. During the candlelight procession, I felt I was walking with your steps. When wrapping gifts for older and younger sisters, I saw Sister Chân Không. I saw the experience my younger sisters had gained from Plum Village when they confidently and joyfully prepared for the celebration here. The energy of the Sangha was great and I have faith in the continuation of our efforts by future generations. Since our Sangha is not very big, younger sisters have to mature faster.

We have loved and helped each other during the first days at Deer Park. My sisters and I can see happiness everywhere. I didn't send a gift, Thây, even though I wanted to. But I know the fact we have happiness with each other and can share it with others is the best gift to give you.

From left to right: Sisters Trung Chinh (Abbess), Bich Nghiem, Thoai Nghiem, and Hoi Nghiem

From Here You Can Find Your Way Home: Our First Year at Deer Park Monastery

Brother Chân Phap Dung, True Inclusiveness of the Dharma, was born in Vietnam and grew up in Los Angeles. He ordained in 1998, and became abbott of Deer Park Monastery in 2001.

Our new community has established its foothold on the abused land that is now our responsibility to heal and transform. It is a frontier for our transplanted roots that we long to sink deep into the consciousness and heritage of this place. Long days of committed effort and careful attention to detail have given birth to this outpost community of practice that is bringing calm and harmony to the land and buildings torn by years of neglect, bullet holes, and failed dreams. It is a beautiful undertaking to purify nature's well once again and allow the cool, refreshing waters of peace and mindfulness to flow and restore dignity to all life.

As our first year here went by, we came to understand the Native American wisdom that we belong to the land, not the land to us. We have practiced harmonizing our voices to complement that which marches on here through the ages. Our little Sangha has bandaged the old wounds of the beautiful park with trees and shrubs, replacing the sorrowful shadows of the past. And as is often the case, no one can heal others without being healed themselves. We shared the frustrations, the learning, the laughing, and the calm vision of Thây Giac Thanh, who demonstrated how to touch the land with peace and solidity.

We cannot replicate Plum Village here, just as Plum Village is not Vietnam, but our hearts will always be nourished by the roots of our tradition and fed by the voices of the ancestors. We could not be the same and stay here. It has been a year of us fitting into the mountain's vision, rather than the mountain fitting into the vision of the little brown ants moving about her surface. The lessons of the past are clear; the mountain retains her sanctuary and shares it with those skillful in hearing her needs.

For the land, we brought impermanence; yet impermanence was also brought to us as we entered the fall with one less set of sandals left at the door of the meditation hall. The void left by the passing away of our Abbot, Thây Giac Thanh, opened a window to our center. It touched us in our dreams and in the waking miracles that opened us to a reality much greater than ourselves. Our encounters with the mountain and the mountain lion, with the sky and the ancestors of this land, signaled that the time had arrived to share our lives with the mountain and pay our respects. With a simple ceremony taken from generations before us, the words came, the promise to respect and protect. Through this meeting of the mountain and the honored ancestors in us, we now feel this Earth, and it feels us.

Brothers and sisters enjoy a game of basketball at Deer Park

Thây Is My Teacher

Carl Stahmer, True Realization of Wisdom (Chân Dac Tri), is a poet and peace activist who lives with his wife and son in San Diego, California. They practice together as a family at the Deer Park Monastery and at the Joyful Sangha in San Diego.

The first time that I met my teacher he was called Phap Son. It was early in the year 2001, and I was attending my first Day of Mindfulness at the Deer Park Monastery. He looked nothing like the picture on the back of his book, so I did not know that he was my teacher. But he was very skillful at handling my negative seeds that were surfacing, so I decided that I would make the Days of Mindfulness part of my regular practice.

Over the course of the next few months, I spent much time with my teacher, although I did not realize that I was doing so. He manifested in so many forms — Thây Giac Thanh, Sister Fern, Phap Dung, the trees, the mountain — and I was not skillful enough to recognize him, but he lent me much support and mindfulness as I worked to water my positive seeds through the practice at Deer Park.

As my practice continued, I began to think of the Sangha at Deer Park as my collective teacher; and, as this connection grew gradually stronger, my attachment to Thây himself began to consciously diminish. Because my own thinking was so heavily rooted in an attachment to self, I naturally saw Thây as a "self" that existed separately from the other selves with which I was physically connected in my practice. I knew the Deer Park Sangha, but I did not know Thây — or so I thought.

When I finally found myself face to face with Thây at a retreat in the summer of 2001, I immediately recognized the energy of mindfulness and compassion that had drawn me to the community at Deer Park. His presence was physically, not intellectually, familiar, like returning home after a long journey. I saw clearly in that moment that Thây was the fourfold community at Deer Park and that the community was Thây. I knew that I had, in fact, already met him.

I had heard Thây speak often of himself as a continuation of his ancestors and of his spiritual teachers; but, until the day that I finally met face to face with the particular manifestation that we call Thây, I was unable to fully touch the deep truth of this statement. The reality of interbeing dictates that "continuation" is not an evolutionary progression; it is a present condition. Thây is not himself. He contains multitudes.

I still practice regularly at the Deer Park Monastery, and I have so much love for all of my teachers there. I appreciate each one for the uniqueness of her or his particular manifestation; but, at the same time, I know that when we are truly present to each other we are also present to Thây. He is there in each mindful moment, offering the stability of his practice in support of ours. We truly inter-are. I know this because Thây is my teacher.

Flying

Mark McInerney, Compassionate Understanding of the Heart, lives in Boulevard, California, and practices with the Joyful Sangha in San Diego, California.

Morning birds are skimming
Along the silhouette
Of the great mountain
As we roll
Through the universe.
How can I ever feel
That I'm not flying?

Deer Park

Giovanna Zerbi, True Wonderful Stream, lives near San Diego, and practices at Deer Park, Wat Lao Sangha, and the Still Water Sangha. She entered the Order of Interbeing in 2001.

The wind brushes the palm leaves.
Gentle voices float in the breeze,
Caress my ears,
And dissolve.
The call of a quail, the screech of a hawk,
And the slow steps taken in awareness,
Consecrate this land,
Erasing every trace of violence,
Offering it as a gift to a suffering humankind.

Closing

Continuation

Sister Chân The Nghiem, True Adornment with Vow, was born and raised in Pennsylvania and is of Vietnamese heritage. She ordained in 1999.

Written during a solo retreat, Spring 2002.

Every afternoon, I look out my window,
Out across the road and over the fields.
I follow the movement of the birds,
Shadows of clouds gliding over the land,
The change of late-afternoon sunlight on wooden barns
and stone houses.
Every day is like this, a feeling of movement and change.

Today, my mind wanders as usual—
The horizon, the far-off trees, and then closer
To the farmer's grass yard across the road.

Amidst wide-open sky,
Wandering chickens in the yard,
And windblown grass,
It is here that my mind comes to rest:
A pile of tree branches lying
In a tidy man-made heap.
They are newly cut
And cast aside.

My mind lingers here. Why?
Why do these branches make
Such an impression on me?
I continue to look, and I see:

They are humble and lovely,
These castaways,
The way they lie discarded
At the foot of their mother tree.
Sometime soon, the farmer will
Come to gather up these gems,
Only to throw them away.

They do not seem so extraordinary,
Except that their beauty is speaking to me.
Still young and bare — no leaves, no flowers,
No small offshoots of branches —
They have nothing about them
But their simple presence,
Gentle lines of velvet-purple bark
Brought out
By the greenness
Of grass blades surrounding them.

My gaze lengthens; my heart swells.
Though separated and discarded,
They are still there,
Quietly offering me their beauty.
Something in me responds to this kindness,
And a heartfelt smile emanates.
The thought arises,
Beauty is ever-present.
The farmer doesn't see.
He doesn't really know
What he's cast aside.

Yet. . . would I have noticed these branches
Had they not been lying there on the grass?

What of their source, the mother tree,
Displaying victorious limbs?
Against the wooden backdrop
Of a dark-brown barn,
She stands somehow muted.
A conventional background
Frames a conventional image.

It is the grass
That gives contrast
To the violet branches.
And it is the separation I see
Between mother and child
That engages my heart with my eyes.

Every following morning,
The fallen branches greet me
With their simple beauty,
And I greet them back with a smile.
I see you. I appreciate you.
Every day is like this, unwrapping a hidden present.

Today, a surprise awaits me:
Here and there,
From the pile of branches,
Pink flowers have blossomed.
Open buds perch merrily
Like notes on an uneven score:
No song of the forsaken here.
The branches speak so clearly
Of continuation and of life.

I see this, and I laugh at myself.
The farmer knows nothing about garbage,
And you know nothing
About anything.
What do you really know?

Yes, I don't know anything.
I do not really see.
I can only profit from the presence
Of something deeper that moves me.

For two more days,
I contemplate this wild bouquet,
An offering to anyone who sees it,
A continuation through space and time.
I contemplate more humbly
What is seen and not seen.

Today, the farmer comes with open arms.
He picks up the branches and loads them on his tractor.
They are off to their next destination
To continue their next manifestation
As vestiges of fall
And harbingers of spring.

In New Hamlet,
The sisters will have placed
Branches just like them
In a vase beside the altar.

Hello, my teacher.
Hello, Plum Village.

Calligraphy by Thây

Twenty Years Young

Sister Chân Viet Nghiem, True Adornment with Transcendence, is French and grew up in Paris. She ordained in 2002.

I was born in 1982, the same year Plum Village was born. My twentieth birthday, January 10, 2002, was on a Day of Mindfulness. I received a lot of love from the Sangha that day. I was very moved when Thây wished me a happy birthday before starting the Dharma talk.

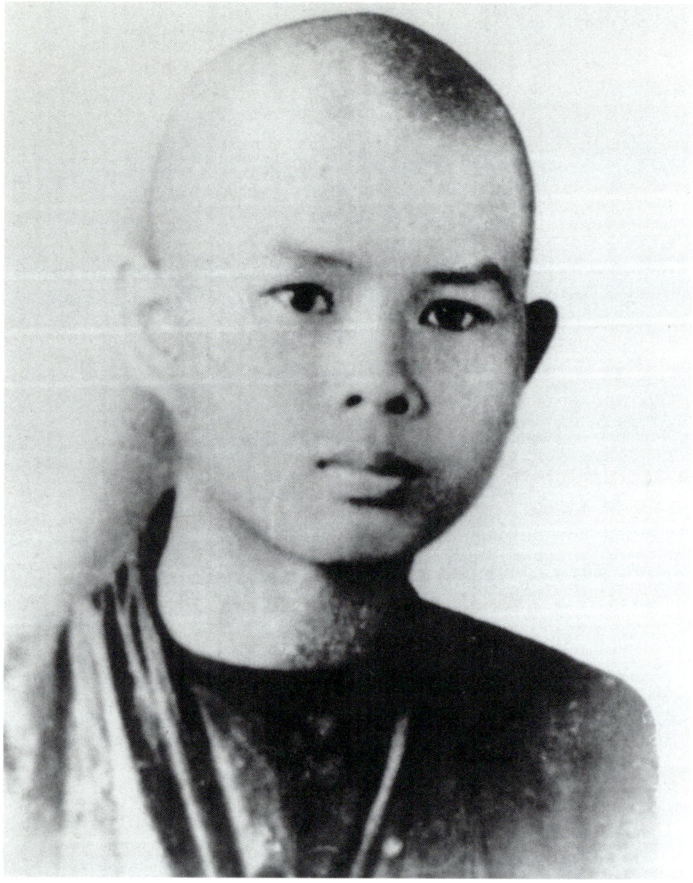

Thây as a sixteen-year-old novice

Later Sister Phuc Nghiem came into my room and gave me a package in a plastic bag. I could see a beautiful yellow-orange color that reminded me of the color of the sun playing with the leaves in autumn. Then I realized that it was my sanghati robe (the monastic robe received at ordination) and that I would be ordained soon. Trying on my monastic robe on my birthday had a deep effect on me. I felt like an angel.

Later on, I shared my birthday cake with my brothers and sisters. I was so happy. My heart was full and my cheeks hurt from smiling, laughing, and singing so much! I turned twenty the same year as Plum Village. But what was the true meaning of this? I am just another manifestation of Plum Village, like so many others. Our monastery has been built up wholeheartedly and with great patience by so many dedicated brothers and sisters in the Sangha.

When I was fifteen, I came to Plum Village for the first time. It was a refuge, a place where I could find the rest and comfort I needed. Then when I turned twenty I ordained in a family of twenty-one monks and nuns, the Sugar Palm Tree family. I had dreamt of having a sister or brother and now I have ten brothers and ten sisters! They are in me and I am in them, and together we bring youth to the monastery because we are the cells of the same body, the Sangha body. I also see future generations in me because by practicing well, I'm more able to open Dharma doors for the ones to come. When I received the precepts I became a link in a long chain that has no beginning and no end.

To turn twenty in Plum Village allowed me to open up and bloom in the Sangha. I feel fresh because I am twenty for all those who came before me and for all those who will come, whoever they are, wherever they are, visible or not visible. I am twenty for my mother, my father, for Thây, for my brothers and sisters, wherever they are today. And I'm also twenty for you!

Newly-ordained teenage novices in the Sugar Palm Tree Family.

The Future Depends on This Moment: Plum Village in Three Hundred Years

Thich Nhat Hanh
Excerpted from a Dharma talk given December 6, 2001, and from a conversation in Still Sitting Hut.

Young novices

The other day I was sitting with Shantum and the 20th anniversary book team in my Still Sitting Hut. I asked Shantum to move close to me, and I invited him to look at the woods down in the valley. It is very beautiful in autumn time, many colors. I asked Shantum, "Look at those beautiful trees. Do you think they will be there three hundred years from now? Is there any chance that three hundred years from now we will still have that piece of lovely woods in the valley?"

That is one question. Because of our tendency to develop, maybe the city will come to us very soon, and then the trees and the woods will disappear one day. Three hundred years is not very long. In fact, it is very short. Shantum said, "Well, one of the ways to assure that the woods will still be there is to buy it and leave a will behind saying that no one can build anything on that piece of land." But will we be there in order to keep those trees in three hundred years? Will we have the same intention then? Will anyone be there in three hundred years from now trying to enforce that kind of will? Maybe at that time, we will be tempted to sell them because land is so expensive and we want to build something. It may become a supermarket. It may still be a woods like it is now. There is a possibility that three hundred years from now, if your descendants come to the Upper Hamlet, visit the Still Sitting Hut, and sit on the platform, they will still see the woods. In three hundred years, the trees will not be the same ones. Many generations of trees will succeed each other, but I'm sure that when autumn comes, the woods will look very much the way it does now because the trees know how to continue their ancestors.

So three hundred years from now, these trees may still be there, not exactly the same, but future generations of the ones there now.

This is a possibility; it is not hopeless. But the question is about us — will we still be here in three hundred years? Who can answer that? Suppose thirty people from Holland want to see my hut and they come here and sit. The name of this hut is "Still or Quiet Sitting Hut," so the most meaningful thing for them to do is sit quietly and feel what I felt three hundred years earlier. But the question is, will the practice center still be here? Who will assure the continuation of the practice center?

The trees will look very much the same in three hundred years. What about us? We are looking at the trees and the trees are looking at us. Who is more impermanent? So the question is, to be or not to be *around?*

The presence of the woods is one thing, but there must be the presence of people, in this case the Zen practitioners. There should be someone sitting there, the one who views, and the one who is viewed. So the second question I asked Shantum and the 20th anniversary book team was whether their children, grandchildren, and their great-grandchildren would be there sitting and enjoying the woods. What can we do to ensure our continuation? How can our children continue us the same way the trees continue the trees? It depends on the steps we're taking now. If we don't know how to take the steps that we're taking now, then there is no hope. There will be no one sitting there in the Still Sitting Hut in order to look at the woods, right? Instead of looking for the beautiful colors of autumn, they may be looking for other things, for things they think are more important, like a diploma, a position in a corporation, or maybe the Pure Land somewhere else.

After I pass away, the brothers say they will keep the Still Sitting Hut as it is. They don't want to build anything. They want to keep the platform the same, so that every time our friends come they can enjoy sitting there and looking at the woods. So they're taking care of the place. But my question is whether they're taking care of people, because if the people are not there then who will take care of the place? And whether or not the people will be there depends on the practice, on whether we know how to take a step in the here and the now. And we have to make sure that our children and their children will do like us, will know how to enjoy their in-breath and out-breath, and their steps. The trees know how to succeed each other. As practitioners, are we doing as well as the trees?

Although the issue of these trees is a small situation, if we can look and understand it deeply we can understand the whole world. The trees have more of a chance of being there in three hundred years than we human beings. We are more intelligent; but maybe, because the trees don't need to make much effort, they will be there a longer time.

There is a Japanese Zen master who said upon dying, "I don't regret leaving anything except the four seasons." He was not truly free. I will not regret leaving the beauty of the four seasons because I have transmitted my eyes to my disciples and they will continue to enjoy nature even after I pass away.

If we can look with our Buddha eyes, we don't have to suffer. We must transmit our Buddha eyes, so that three hundred years from now we and our children will be able to look at this beauty. It depends a lot on us and how we practice.

In India, we were using the Buddha eyes to admire the Gridhakuta Mountain. The first time I sat on Gridhakuta, I used my Buddha eyes. Here the beauty is the same. This place, right here, contains eternity in time and space. Gridhakuta is here, all around us. What can we do for this moment to become eternal? We can make this moment eternal through the transmission of the Buddha eye. If we continue to transmit the eye, there will be hope. This is the story of Plum Village: how to transmit the Buddha eye, not build a big institution and become famous.

In Chinese there is a saying, "Don't reject the goodwill, the beauty of nature, the sunset, the mist on the river at the end of the day, the first ray of sun in the morning." This means, "Be kind to the beauty of nature. If you are forgetful, you are betraying this gift."

So the time we spent together, the book team and me, was not really discussing the book. It was just spending time together in that way, because the book depends on this. Whether or not the book is a good book depends on how Shantum, Sister Chau Nghiem, Brother Phap Ngo and others participate in the being of each moment. We were holding our cups of tea. We were practicing looking deeply at the trees, at ourselves, our children and our grandchildren. We have to share that we are living the future right now, not preparing for it. The future is there in the present moment.

Those of us who have the opportunity to live in or visit Plum Village may not be aware that this is a tremendous opportunity for us to practice for ourselves and our children. We always say that we love our children. We want to secure and assure a good future for our children, and yet are we really preparing a future? In the teachings, we learn that the best way to assure the future is to take care of the present moment. And the present moment is what? It is when you eat, when you turn on the water tap, when you cook your breakfast, when you wash your face, when you take a step, when you sit down. That is the practice of Plum Village.

Sitting meditation is an opportunity to enjoy the time of sitting. We must arrange it in such a way that the sitting time becomes a privilege, because many people don't have that privilege. When Nelson Mandela was in Paris visiting François Mitterand, the press asked him what he wanted to do the most. He said, "To sit down and do nothing." And those of us who live in Plum Village have an opportunity to sit down and do nothing every day, and yet we may not make use of this opportunity. Not only can we sit down and do nothing, but we can also sit down and enjoy our breakfast in mindfulness. We can hold each other's hands and do walking meditation in order to arrive nowhere except in the present moment. We have to cherish these opportunities, and that is the only way to take care of our children, our grandchildren, and future generations.

And the trees know how to do that. They will do their best. If we don't interfere and clear the forest and build a supermarket, they will be able to remain a beautiful forest, a beautiful woods. Shall we be able to do like the trees? The trees know how to take care of the present moment. I am sure they know. We human beings, we are less competent. We run too much to the future. We get lost in the past. So we have to learn. There is much we can learn from the trees. Go to the woods; that is a university where we can learn many things.

Our future, whether it will be in Vietnam or in America or in England, depends entirely on this very moment. So, find what you are looking for in the steps you are taking now.

Still Sitting Hut at dawn

Appendix

A Mindfulness Practice Center: The Gift a Community Gives Itself

Adapted from the Mindfulness Practice Center Guidebook

"I didn't discover the practice of mindfulness until I was fifty. I became a new woman — truly happy for the first time in my life. Not brief, 'excited' happy, but DEEP happy. I'd like to help others reach that happiness in any way I can."
— Mindfulness Practice Center community member

Mindfulness is one of the treasures of human nature. Everyone has a natural capacity to be mindful, which means to be present in the here and now, to be truly present without wanting anything else. It is only because of countless habits of thought and action that we have acquired during our life, as well as inherited from our forebearers, that we find it difficult to be present. By gently bringing ourselves back to the present moment again and again, we can relearn the art of mindfulness that is always available within ourselves. A Mindfulness Practice Center is a place where people come together to relearn the art of mindful living. Mindfulness is an energy and the Mindfulness Practice Center is the greenhouse for that energy, cultivating it to be sent off to many places — individuals, families, hospitals, correctional centers, schools, etc.

In February of 1998, following meetings with community members, the first Mindfulness Practice Center (MPC), called the Mindfulness Practice Center of the Upper Valley, opened its doors in Quechee, Vermont. This center proceeded to create a place where people could gather and practice.

A Mindfulness Practice Center or a Mindfulness Practice Group (MPG) is a completely secular, civil establishment for the practice of mindfulness in a town or a village. At an MPC there are no teachers. Being non-hierarchical, we learn from each other and cultivate our practice as equal partners. An MPC offers outreach programs that enable practitioners from the Center to offer schools, correctional centers, hospices, universities, and hospitals the practice of mindfulness as is appropriate for that particular institution. Our hope is that the establishment of MPGs and MPCs will offer people the opportunity to infuse mindfulness into their daily lives and share it, in turn creating a more mindful society for us all.

The Foundations of the MPC

A Mindfulness Practice Center is a place where the understanding of mindfulness is coupled with the innovations of the democratically run, secular, social institution. Growing interest in mindfulness in the West has created a large audience of Westerners who read about and perhaps practice this way of living individually or in small groups. Some of these are medical based groups or religious based groups. Some are free, some costly, but none have answered the need for something very familiar to Westerners — a community-run gathering place and resource center.

One of the key elements to leading a more mindful life is to practice mindfulness. "Practice" is a word that suggests activity. The activities which produce mindful awareness are practiced in relationships with oneself, loved ones, community, and the world. A practice center offers people a community where like-intentioned friends can develop relationships that deepen their understanding. In this type of community the art of mindful living is explored through shared insights, study, and practice.

The most important characteristics of an MPC are its non-hierarchical organization and democratic stewardship of the center. Everyone has some insight to offer. The MPC creates the proper conditions for insights to blossom and to be shared through the practices of silence, deep listening, and mediation. The unique quality of community practice is the means and end for which MPCs were conceived.

Recognizing that we are not alone, that we are interdependent, that our neighbor's joy is ours, makes it clear that we need to nurture the mindfulness in our collective body and mind. There may not truly be such a thing as self-transformation, for every step we take is a step that carries our neighbor with us. Their strength is ours; their suffering is ours. And ours is theirs. When we come together to practice, we are recognizing this wonderful truth. In order to preserve the integrity of this practice, all MPCs are founded upon and strive to live up to the following principles:

Founding Principles

1) Welcoming to all, regardless of age, race, sex, or spiritual path

2) Consensus-based in its planning and decision-making

3) Non-hierarchical

4) Community-run:
   - ✦ volunteer community members facilitate the programs
   - ✦ meetings of the Board of Directors are open to all members
   - ✦ self-determining — offering whatever each MPC community can comfortably support
   - ✦ nonprofit
   - ✦ independent and free of commercial or private sponsorship which could obligate the center to promote its sponsors
   - ✦ non-religious

The principles on which an MPC is founded support an inclusiveness which best serves to realize its mission:

The MPC Mission Statement

We are dedicated to the creation of a mindful culture fostering loving families, happy individuals, and a healthy planet. We believe that this is both possible and practical. The practice of mindfulness, an innate human ability, has the power to bring about this transformation. We intend to promote mindfulness at all levels of society. These objectives are to be furthered through the establishment of Mindfulness Practice Centers.

For more information on MPCs contact:
Green Mountain Dharma Center
P.O. Box 182
Ayres Lane
Hartland Four Corners, VT 05049
Telephone: (802) 436-1102
Fax: (802) 436-1101
www.plumvillage.org

Notes

Notes to the Preface & Introduction

1. The Buddha taught that there are three Dharma Seals which are the marks of the authentic Dharma: impermanence, nonself, and nirvana. If we don't recognize these three Dharma Seals in a Buddhist teaching then it is not an authentic teaching of the Buddha.

2. *The Mindfulness Bell* is a journal of the art of mindful living in the tradition of Thich Nhat Hanh. To subscribe or order an issue, contact the Community of Mindful Living at Deer Park Monastery, 2499 Melru Lane, Escondido, CA 92026. Email: cmldeerpark@earthlink.net. Website: iamhome.org.

Notes to Section 1

1. The School of Youth for Social Service was established in Vietnam in 1965 by Thich Nhat Hanh. See *Learning True Love* by Sister Chân Không for more details. Thây founded the Order of Interbeing in 1966. See *Interbeing* by Thich Nhat Hanh for more details.

2. See *Teachings on Love* by Thich Nhat Hanh for a description.

3. We practice to see the Sangha as one body and to see ourselves as a cell in the Sangha body. The practice of using our Sangha eyes refers to using the wisdom of the whole Sangha, not only our individual wisdom. Before making a decision or taking action, we consult with the Sangha to arrive at the deepest, collective insight. Shining Light is the practice of sitting together as a community to ask for guidance and insight into our practice. Everyone in the Sangha has a chance to share about the positive qualities and areas that need to be strengthened in the brother or sister who is receiving shining light. The Second Body system is a practice that makes sure everyone is cared for. Everyone has a second body, and we take care of this person when he or she falls sick; we make sure they are at Sangha activities; we are accountable to the community for this person.

4. See the Lay Practice Centers section in Part Two for a description.

5. See Appendix.

6. To learn more about Chi Mai's life, see *Learning True Love* by Sister Chân Không.

7. *Bhikshuni* is Sanskrit for a fully-ordained nun. A *bhikshu* is a fully-ordained monk.

8. The first of the Fourteen Mindfulness Trainings of the Order of Interbeing is about not being attached to any concepts or ideologies, even Buddhist ones.

9. For more information on the Five Mindfulness Trainings, see *For a Future to be Possible.* For more information on the Fourteen Mindfulness Trainings, see *Interbeing* by Thich Nhat Hanh.

10. An ancestor tablet is a large cement or rock tablet that contains a short poem commemorating the qualities of an ancestor. In 2002 all three hamlets of Plum Village held ceremonies in newly-built ancestors' halls to install their hamlet's ancestor's tablet.

11. Amitabha is the Buddha of Light and Sukhavati is the Land of Great Happiness, the Pure Land of Amitabha Buddha.

12. Editors' note: Although this is a letter addressed to Thây, in Vietnam it is not considered respectful to address one's teacher as "you." When writing or speaking to Thây directly, students often refer to him in the third person, as "Thây."

13. *Su Ong* means "Grandfather Teacher" and is used only for well-respected, senior monks. Thich Nhat Hahn is often referred to as Thây or Su Ong.

Notes to Section 2

1. For details, please read *Learning True Love*, Sister Chân Không's book about this historical journey to present-day Plum Village.

2. For example, Thây's book *Don't Forget, Please Don't Hurry to Forget,* his *Vietnam: Lotus in a Sea of Fire*, and books of poems such as *Chap Tay Nguyen Cau Cho Bo Cau Trang Hien* and *Tieng Dap Canh Loai Chim Lon.*

3. The buildings in the Lower Hamlet were finished two years later. The Lower Hamlet now houses nuns and laywomen.

4. Every Monday in Plum Village and its various practice centers is Lazy Day.

5. Slalom is the swerving movement made by downhill skiers as they avoid obstacles.

6. Members of the Order of Interbeing, who have received the Fourteen Mindfulness Trainings, wear brown jackets at Sangha gatherings.

7. "A cow" here refers to a teaching given by the Buddha to his disciples after a very upset farmer passed by the Sangha looking for his lost cows. The Buddha turned to his disciples and said that they were very lucky because they had no cows to lose. Thây often tells this story and asks us to identify what the cows are in our own lives — the things or conditions that we think are essential for our happiness but are actually the biggest hindrance to it. Then the practice is to release these "cows."

8. *The Heart of Perfect Understanding.*

9. During retreats everyone is assigned to a family of 15–20 people to eat meals, work, and have Dharma discussions together.

Notes to Section 3

1. A mindfulness inspector is an older brother or sister responsible for guiding and supporting the practice of the Sangha. They pay attention to attendance at community activities, punctuality, and in general try to encourage everyone in their practice.

2. An aspirant is someone who has formally requested to become a monastic. They live and practice with the monastics.

Notes to Section 4

1. Yen Tu is a small mountain just above Solidity Hamlet.

Parallax Press publishes books and tapes on mindful awareness and social responsibility. All of Thich Nhat Hanh's work is available at our on-line store and in our free catalog. For a copy of the catalog, please contact:

Parallax Press
P.O. Box 7355
Berkeley, CA 94707
www.parallax.org
Tel: 800 863-5290

Monastics and laypeople practice the art of mindful living in the tradition of Thich Nhat Hanh at retreat communities in France and the United States. Individuals, couples, and families are invited to join these communities for a Day of Mindfulness and longer practice periods. For information, please visit www.plumvillage.org or contact:

Plum Village
13 Martineau
33580 Dieulivol
France
info@plumvillage.org

Deer Park Monastery
2499 Melru Lane
Escondio, CA 92026
Tel: 760 291-1003
deerpark@plumvillage.org

Green Mountain Dharma Center
P.O. Box 182
Hartland Four Corners, VT 05049
mfmaster@vermontel.net
Tel: 802 436-1103

For a worldwide directory of Sanghas practicing in the tradition of Thich Nhat Hanh, visit www.iamhome.org.